CARL F. H. HENRY

# gods of this age or... GOD of The Ages?

R. Albert Mohler
General Editor

BROADMAN
& HOLMAN
PUBLISHERS

Nashville, Tennessee

· Unless otherwise stated, all Scripture quotations are from the Holy Bible, *New International Version*. Copyright © 1973, 1978, 1984 by International Bible Society.

Quotations marked NEB are from *The New English Bible*. Copyright © The Delegates of the Oxford University Press and the Syndics of the Cambridge University Press, 1961, 1970. Reprinted by permission.

Quotations marked NASB are from the *New American Standard Bible*. © The Lockman Foundation, 1960, 1962, 1963, 1968, 1971, 1973, 1975, 1977. Used by permission.

Quotations marked NRSVB are from the *New Revised Version of the Bible*. Copyright © 1989 by the Division of Christian Education of the National Council of Churches of Christ in the United States of America. Used by permission. All rights reserved.

Quotations marked NKJV are from the *New King James Version*. Copyright © 1979, 1980, 1982, Thomas Nelson, Inc., Publishers.

Quotations marked RSV are from the *Revised Standard Version of the Bible,* copyrighted 1946, 1952, © 1971, 1973.

Quotations marked KJV are from the *King James Version.*

**Library of Congress Cataloging-in-Publication Data**

Henry, Carl Ferdinand Howard, 1913–
        Gods of this age or god of the ages? / Carl F. H. Henry.
            p. cm.
        ISBN: 0-8054-1548-3
            1. Christianity—20th century.  2. Theology—20th century.
3. Evangelicalism—United States.  4. Paganism—United States.
I. Title.
BR121.2.H37 1992                                                      92-3770
270.8'29—dc20                                                              CIP

_Burns_ '98

# *Contents*

iii

# Foreword

The twentieth century has been—in the main—an era of remarkable theological compromise. Churches and denominations which once stood as the mainline pillars of historic Christianity have fallen to theological abdication and doctrinal atrophy. Many seminaries, colleges, and other centers of Christian learning have long ago forfeited any claim to orthodox Christianity. The chickens hatched in a warm nests of modernity have, it would seem, now come back to roost over a Church in decline and retreat.

But this is only part of the picture. For, in the wake of the dissolution of modernism and neo-orthodoxy, there arose a movement of young Protestant conservatives at mid-century, dedicated to the recovery of Christian truth and the renewal of the Church. Among these young catalysts for recovery, none has exceeded the influence of Carl F. H. Henry.

The evangelicals, as they became known, gave birth to a theological movement which has, among Protestants, been the chief agent of theological recovery and orthodox intellectual vigor. They refused to apologize for serious intellectual engagement, but they also refused to abdicate the high groung of fundamental Christian truth.

For the past half-century, Carl F. H. Henry has combined the stalwart defense of Christian truth and a bold engagement with rival systems of thought. In so doing, Dr. Henry emerged as one of the titans of the evangelical movement. His biography is a narrative history of the evangelical resurgence. He was a member of the founding faculty of Fuller Theological Seminary. He was the founding editor of *Christianity Today,* and under his editorship that journal served as the intellectual flagship for the evangelical movement.

v

But his greatest contribution to the Church has been his voluminous writings, ranging from occasional articles to his massive six-volume work, *God, Revelation and Authority*. In all, he has written over twenty books, providing a library of serious volumes which will stand for years to come as one of the defining marks of modern evangelicalism.

This present volume, drawn from Dr. Henry's essays, lectures, and articles of the last few years, is both a window into the mind of a distinguished and remarkable Christian theologian, and a platform for evangelical advance. The chapters reflect the breadth of Dr. Henry's concerns, ranging from essays on classical themes in theology to warnings of a new dark age.

Dr. Henry's insight into the reality of our situation—perched on the precipice of a new dark age—adds a sense of urgency to each chapter. His intention has been, in C. S. Lewis's words, to "see life steadily and to see it whole." From that vantage point, Dr. Henry warns that our age, stripped of the humanizing and God-honoring protection of the comprehensive Christian world-view, is left to the fate of an inhuman darkness.

In the first volume of *God, Revelation and Authority,* Dr. Henry lamented that "Evangelical theology . . . while preserving the Judeo-Christian verities all too often fails to project engagingly upon present-day perplexities." This verdict does not apply to Dr. Henry's own writings. His forays into theological method and moral theory are never abstract or detached. They pulsate with both passion and insight.

But the essays in this volume are remarkable for their depth of engagement, as well as the breadth of their subject matter. Dr. Henry demonstrates himself the master of both classical and contemporary sources. He engages intellectual rivals on their own turf, and brings to every engagement both Christian conviction and a winsome Christian spirit.

The book which first set Dr. Henry's reputation as a frontline theologian for the evangelical movement was *The Uneasy conscience of Modern Fundamentalism,* published in 1947. In that volume he called for "The Dawn of a New Reformation" which would match clear and uncompromised Christian conviction with confidence in the cultural arenas of a fallen world. Dr. Henry has served as a model for how that reformation may, by God's grace, he begun.

I join with thousands of fellow evangelicals in acknowledging a great debt to Carl F. H. Henry. My debt is quite personal, for it has been my high honor to know Dr. Henry, not only as teacher and mentor, but as friend. He is a true Christian statesman and, by his own eloquent testimony, a fellow sinner saved by grace.

The reformation Dr. Henry saw on a hopeful horizon almost fifty years ago must frame the hopes, prayers, and aspirations of the generaltion of evangelicals who will follow. That is the charge Dr. Henry leaves us at the close of this volume. To that end, we must lay bare the gods of this age, and call men and women to the God of the Ages.

R. Albert Mohler, Jr.
General Editor
President, The Southern Baptist
   Theological Seminary

# *Acknowledgments*

**Chapter 1**, "Christianity and Resurgent Paganism," was first delivered to the Baptist Union of Romania on September 13, 1990, and then to a faculty retreat of Tyndale Seminary, the Netherlands. It was also delivered at the dedication of the Kenneth Kantzer Faculty Center at Trinity Evangelical Divinity School.

**Chapter 2**, "Facing America's Crosswinds," appeared in *The World and I* magazine, Vol. 4, No. 10, July 4, 1989, and is published by permission.

**Chapter 3**, "The Struggle for America's Soul," was the keynote address to the 93rd annual convention of The Christian Civic League of Maine on November 3, 1990.

**Chapter 4**, "Confronting the Challenge of Paganism," was presented to a conference sponsored by the Christian Life Commission of the Southern Baptist Convention, on March 28, 1989, in Kansas City, Missouri.

**Chapter 5**, "The Crisis of Authority," appeared in *The World & I*, Vol. 4, No. 9, August 1989, and is published by permission.

**Chapter 6**, "Knowledge, Power, and Morality: A Congressman's Day-to-Day Concerns," was presented on March 9, 1989, during a symposium sponsored by the Council of Scholars of the Library of Congress to celebrate the bicentennial of the United States Congress.

**Chapter 7**, "Surmounting the Clash of Worlds," was delivered on July 7, 1989, in connection with the dedication of the new campus of Tokyo Christian Institute. The Institute has since become Tokyo Christian University.

**Chapter 8**, "Shall We Flunk the Educators?", was delivered on Reformation Day, 1988, (October 31) at a meeting of concerned Christian leaders in seattle, Washington, sponsored by Covenant College, Lookout Mountain, Georgia.

**Chapter 9**, "The Shrouded Peaks of Learning," was presented on July 5, 1988, during the C. S. Lewis Summer Institute on "The Christian and the Contemporary University," held at Oxford University, England.

**Chapter 10**, "The Renewal of Theological Education," was the address presented at the installation service for Dr. Timothy F. George as dean of the Beeson Divinity School of Samford University, Birmingham, Alabama. It was published in the Spring, 1989, edition of *Vocatio*, and is published by permission.

**Chapter 11**, "Seizing an Evangelical Opportunity," was delivered to the Christian Higher Education Commission meeting during the 48th annual convention of the National Association of Evangelicals, held March 8, 1980, in Phoenix, Arizona.

**Chapter 12**, "Cognitive Bargaining on Evangelical Campuses," was presented on March 2, 1989, during a colloquium sponsored by the Ethics and Public Policy Center in Washington, D.C.

**Chapter 13**, "Besting the Cultural Challenge," was the installation address for Dr. Richard D. Land as executive director of the Christian Life Commission of the Southern Baptist Commission, March 27, 1989, Kansas City, Missouri.

**Chapter 14**, "Evangelical Co-Belligerency: A Next Step?," appeared in *Christianity Today*, Vol. 33, No. 17, November 17, 1989, and is published by permission.

**Chapter 15**, "Will Christianity Outlive Its Critics?," appeared in *Modern Age,* Vol. 33, No. 2, Summer, 1990, as a part of a symposium on "Christianity in Sight of the Third Millennium," and is published by permission.

**Chapter 16**, "Reformed Theology in the Post-Christian Age," was the first of two addresses presented at the First International Christian Culture and Theology Symposium at the Institute of Korean Culture Research in Seoul, Korea, October 12, 1987, on the occasion of the 90th anniversary of Soong Sil University.

**Chapter 17**, "Reformed Theology and the Molding of Culture," was the second address presented to the "International Christian Culture and Theology Symposium" at Seoul, Korea, October 1987.

**Chapter 18**, " The Doing and Undoing of Theology," is based upon comments presented during a dialogue at Yale Divinity School on November 12, 1985. The dialogue engaged Professor Paul Holmer and his volume, *The Grammar of Faith.*

**Chapter 19**, "Narrative Theology:   An Evangelical Appraisal," was presented on November 12, 1985, in a dialogue with Professor Hans Frei, held at Yale Divinity School. The presentation was at the invitation of the Christian Study Center and was published in *Trinity Journal.* It is published with permission.

**Chapter 20**, "Coming Home and Saying Good-bye," is a chapel address given at Wheaton College on April 30, 1990, and published in the June/July, 1990, issue of *Wheaton Alumni* magazine. It is published here by permission.

**Chapter 21**, "Christianity in a Troubled World," was a convocation address presented September 13, 1989, marking the opening of the Orlando campus of Reformed Theological Seminary. An abridged version was published in *RTS Ministry,* Vol. 9, No. 1, Spring, 1990.

**Chapter 22**, "Faith in God and Seven Graces," is a message preached at the annual staff retreat of Prison Fellowship Ministries at Sandy Cove Bible Conference in Maryland, June 11, 1989.

**Chapter 23**, "God, Man, and the Millennium," appeared in *The World & I,* Vol. 5, No. 1, January 1990. It is published by permission.

**Chapter 24**, "Imperatives for the Long Journey," was delivered on July 5, 1989, as part of dedication services for the new campus of Tokyo Christian Institute, now Tokyo Christian University.

# Part I
## The Struggle for
## the Soul of a Nation

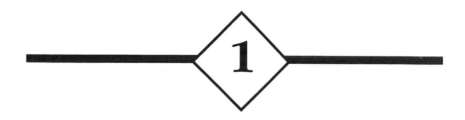

# Christianity and Resurgent Paganism

*The Western world's present defection from the Bible is not the last word. Unfolding judgment is already underway; a death-warrant hangs over modernity, both in the present millennium and in eternity to come. The possibilities of a tide shift are hidden in the ripple of a wave, in the sprouting of a mustard seed, in the faith that moves mountains.*

Whoever opens the Bible will find there a worldview that differs astonishingly from the mass ideas and megavalues of modernity.

The reader of Scripture will discover that the entire universe is the creation of a sovereign personal God, that God's image lifts humanity above all other orders of finite life, that a providential divine purpose governs history and moves nations toward a final judgment, that God came personally in Jesus of Nazareth who conquered death, that the divergent options of eternal damnation or eternal salvation face sinful mankind, and that forgiveness of sins and new spiritual life are even now available to the penitent—these tenets thrust themselves insistently upon every reader who samples sacred Scripture.

These doctrines function not only as beliefs that are perspectival and unique; they reflect first and foremost a concern for truth. They press upon the Hebrews as a chosen people, and upon the mind and conscience of every last human being, truth claims and behavior claims of enduring consequence.

1

This insistence—that the Bible exerts universal truth claims—seems especially odd to our generation. No disciplined observer can minimize the intellectual counter thrust that currently confronts the biblical world and life view. In the Western world naturalism has become biblical theism's major competing conceptuality. The supernatural thought structure is shunned as alien to the academic arena. The Judeo-Christian heritage is attacked as dispensable to the very foundations and highest achievements of Western civilization. Denigrating the reality of God, the antisupernaturalist ideology depicts appeals to divine revelation and authority as regressive, devalues the Bible as a deposit of legend, and rejects life everlasting as myth. Even some theologians dismiss the essential role of truth in religion and deliberately mutilate the historic Christian faith. Agnosticism holds tenure in prestigious divinity schools. Gordon Kaufman, for example, a longtime professor of theology at Harvard Divinity School, projects God as "an unknown X, a mere limited idea with no content."[1]

The secular community welcomes such theological acquiescence in its prejudices. Its avoidance in public discourse of words like *God, sin,* and *soul*—on the ground that intellectuals supposedly no longer comprehend their meaning, or that if they do, they now hear these traditional terms unsympathetically—in effect renders the vocabulary of theology obscene.

The naturalistic worldview is triumphally declared to be alone credible and necessary. Theological and philosophical underpinnings associated with the Christian heritage are eclipsed and skepticism shrouds the validity of Christian convictions. A generation has arisen that deals with Christianity as a grand lie or noble deception. It promotes a religionless modernity. The cultural enterprise is divorced from love for God. Religion is retained only as a matter of personal option and subjective preference. The naturalistic mind elite largely co-opts public education and scientific investigation. The political process views God as a civic irrelevance; democratic majoritarianism displaces divine sovereignty by a profane pluralism. The morally confused print and electronic media trivialize human existence. Many ethical concerns of our era have been held hostage by left-of-center social critics. The widening disavowal of Christian values promotes an agenda that subverts the inherited culture. The result is emergence of unbridled social promiscuity, media approval of divorce and abortion, and growing acceptance of homosexuality and pornography.

In brief, Christianity in the West must now cope with hostile university rationalists and with hostile mass media influences. An illiberal polit-

---

1. Gordon Kaufman, *God the Problem* (Cambridge: Harvard University Press, 1972), 95.

ical mentality welcomes anti-Christian views in the name of free exercise even while it restricts Christian participation on the ground of church-state separation. Social reconstructionists promote government funding of perverse graphics as artistic expression, and free enterprise corporations seek to enhance their stockholders' profits by marketing cinematic films that degrade Jesus Christ.

Dare we raise the possibility that the Third Millennium A.D. will evolve into the millennium of the Antichrist, an end-time conflict between true and counterfeit ecumenism for which apostasy becomes a more terrible and widespread option than anything the church has as yet endured?

It is especially among the white race, and particularly in Europe and in the Anglo-Saxon world, as John Lukacs points out, that this defection from the Judeo-Christian theology and practice has taken place.[2] Meanwhile our century's most spectacular response to Christian evangelism has occurred among Africans and Asians, despite the insistence of radical German critics and their Anglo- American disciples that evidence for the reality of God is no more persuasive than for elves, fairies, and gnomes.

The biblical worldview, which set Hebrew civilization on a course that morally and conceptually transcended the outlooks of the ancient Near East, and which in its Christian turn this worldview raised the West far above its pagan depths, but for contemporary naturalists this view has become the most conspicuous and contemptible example of mythical conceptualities that have had their day. At the end of the second millennium A.D.—so contemporary naturalism insists—the biblical worldview can be accorded truth-status only by showing contempt for legitimate metaphysical and moral realities and by ignoring modern scientific learning.

The unraveling strands of Western civilization are everywhere. Not simply at the future end of history, nor even only at the looming end of this second Christian millennium, but already in the immediate present, modernity is being weighed in the balances. Dismay and distress follow in the wake of the rebellious despiritualization of our once vibrant civilization. Secular hedonism has nurtured the disintegration of the family and the desanctification of human existence. Spiritual dissatisfaction underlies the ready reach for a counterfeit transcendent. The inability to cope publicly with drug use and traffic is painfully apparent. On every hand one sees moral deterioration and ethical upheaval, together with attendant manifestations of melancholy and hopelessness. Amid the

---

2. Ronald H. Nash, "Renewing Christianity's Link to the Past", *Modern Age*, 33 (1990), 176-183.

deteriorating cultural configurations, moral permissiveness has spawned
lives scarred and marred by illegitimate sex and adultery, homosexuality
and pornography.

One clear sign of the times is the retreat of intelligence, the disincli-
nation for disciplined thought, as seen especially in the clouding of the
religious mentality. No objectively ordered structures are acknowledged;
universal meaning is shunned, and a significant common vocabulary
decreases with it. The portrayal of the inherent nature of things is more
and more suspended on human emotions. Man's own will becomes the
only law he tolerates; virtue is whatever makes one feel "good". As epistemological ambiguity plunges the religious realm into a subjectivist
dilemma, many moderns reduce religious doctrines to mere verbaliza-
tions of inner experience. People speak of rights apart from duties. As a
bewildered and bewildering age more and more tilts to current cultural
norms, it denigrates the sanctity of life. Roving bands of alienated youth
rob, beat, rape, and even murder simply for excitement. Western society
manifests a quantum leap of immorality and indecency unprecedented
since the fall of the Roman Empire. We live amid contemporary caesars
who assert brute power; among them are the political successors to the
Red Guards in China and, most recently, Saddam Hussein in Iraq.

Happiness is defined as the gratification of sensual desires: adults and
teenagers become sexually obsessed apes. Society accommodates carnal
appetites that undermine life-giving realities. Malcolm Muggeridge has
observed that as the phallic cult spreads, more people become impotent.

Despite all the secular twaddle about nonreligious modernity, an
immense wave of religiosity continues, nonetheless, to sweep over contemporary life. Endlessly multiplying cultic religions appear, each movement parading its own opinions, while at the same time attesting to
humanity's ineradicable religious nature. Often defective and deficient,
the diverse and proliferating alternatives to Judeo-Christian faith reflect
the spiritual chaos into which society is falling. A Gallup poll reports
that while almost 80 percent of American college students consider religion important, their faith often has little bearing on behavioral attitudes.

Scientifically gifted longer life on earth through age-retarding hor-
mones and organ transplants is now becoming too routine to be media-
dramatic, so Hollywood aggressively probes immortality as the ultimate
horizon. Afterlife films leap over AIDS and senior citizenship, death,
funerals, and grief to concentrate on a world beyond—which often
amounts to nothing more than postmortem out-of-body hankey-pankey.
The movies increasingly banner that death is not final. They tell us that a
spirit world is in store for us—without God, without judgment, without
need of grace, without bodily resurrection, without fear of hell. Take it

from Hollywood and the movie producers, our personal psyche survives the crematory or grave. Feel better about this worldly licentiousness and greed, for a pleasant Karma awaits us in the long future—on the authority of Hollywood script writers who become our generation's Scripture rewriters. Death has lost its sting—Christianity be damned, sin be outmoded, Christ and Easter be eclipsed—for we are secretly eternal quite on our own, thus saith the local theater and video store. An unsatisfied longing for the transcendent survives despite public education's tendency to void faith in a transcendent God. The search for signals of transcendence appears in today's pursuit of gurus and swamis who profess to locate and liberate divinity within ourselves. Scientifically sophisticated learning fails to catechize a youth-generation in the nature of God, so it probes, instead, the reality of Satan and turns to demon cults. Thus the offspring of modernity reflect dissatisfaction with their alienated and provisional existence.

Modernity, therefore, needs to be liberated not only from the shackles of unbelief, but also from its bondage to wrong beliefs. Prominent among these beliefs is the notion that science, as mathematical physicists ideally pursue it, is the only reliable method of knowing. Modern empiricists sponsor an ideological totalism of their own when they confer explanatory crown rights on a theory of truth that cannot decide the final truth of anything. Naturalism, as Ronald Nash says, is "not a decision based on science . . . It is . . . a religious decision,"[3] indeed, an *irreligious* decision. Its presuppositions preclude acknowledging the reality of God, the supernatural, divine Providence, unchanging truth and good, and an afterlife. Its restrictive and reductive assumptions provide no evidence of open-mindedness. They reflect rather a dogmatic closed-mindedness to comprehensive truth. While splitting atoms and chasing quarks in search of an ultimate explanatory principle, naturalism's intellectuals have lost the infinite and omnipresent Deity. Naturalism retains no basis for the discerning of spirits, for distinguishing God from the devil, for differentiating good from evil, truth from error, theology from ideology, or valid idea structures from myth. Whereas even the best pagan minds of ancient Greece argued that human life loses meaning if we cannot distinguish truth from opinion, modern pagans taper truth in order to claim everyone's right to one's own opinion. The only place where the word *truth* seems any longer safe is in the dictionary.

Such aberrations obtrude upon us the foregleams of a new Dark Ages, inhumane and merciless. The world that spoke of a peace dividend as Eastern Europe abandoned its search for a Marxist utopia soon

---

3. Nash, 52.

saw the entire Middle East swept by wild winds of social fury as nations in the Muslim-Israeli theater threaten to bleed each other to death. Are these the signs of the approaching end of all ends? Do we live on the edge of apocalypse? Is it too late for any reclamation and reinvigoration of Western culture? Has the disavowal of the Judeo-Christian legacy so enfeebled the noblest facets of humanity that chemical warfare now replaces nuclear warfare as the way to solve international rivalries?

To those who expected from secular modernity a utopian outcome of history, nothing should be clearer than the highly problematical efficacy of a secular soteriology. Technological science has bestowed convenience and comfort upon a generation that has become neither happier, better nor wiser. Indeed, modernity has so notably closed its mind to the eternal world that it is unsure how to define wisdom, goodness, and happiness. Such a civilization is uncivil; it invites the rubble and ruin that has engulfed all earlier civilizations.

## Hope for a Tidal Shift?

In his book, *After Virtue,* (1981) Alasdair MacIntyre reminds us that the decline of the Roman Empire fostered a time when Christians had to ask themselves whether it was necessary to project new forms of community in order to preserve virtue. In my recent book, *Twilight of a Great Civilization,* I suggest that nightfall for Western civilization may be close at hand.[4] Let me leave no doubt then about my deep conviction. As I see it, the believing church is the West's last and only real bastion against barbarism.

If Christians do not lead the way, people will turn to self-proclaimed gurus from the East, to private revelations, to chemical stimulants, or to other follies of our time; indeed, some of the young even seem to be turning to carbon monoxide.

The right verdict for or against religion and the religions is not a dispensable triviality. It is a matter of cultural self-preservation and of moral salvation. Apart from the new society and its new race of spiritually renewed humans, that is, apart from the regenerate church, the old society is but the rattling skeleton of a social organism once inspired by a powerful faith in God and human responsibility, but now victimized by modernity's contrived alternatives and increasingly set adrift in the wilderness of nihilism.

The church's crucial role in the world is clouded by a twofold miscarriage, namely the apostate Church's mediating reconceptualizations of biblical faith, and the fragmentation and divisions in evangelical Christianity.

---

4. Carl F. H. Henry, *Twilight of a Great Civilization* (Westchester, Il.: Crossway Books, 1988.

In stressing the need for a manifestation of evangelical unity, I need only repeat Jesus' high priestly petition for His disciples to "all be one," even as the persons of the Triune Godhead are one, so "that the world may believe that Thou didst send Me" (John 17:21 NASB). This prayer anticipated no mere sentimental ecumenism that simply rearranges denominational furniture and plays musical chairs with credal commitments. That recent option was less a witness to the world than an accommodation to it. If we evangelicals are to bear world witness as the body of believers whose living head is the crucified and risen and returning Jesus, we shall need on our own part to wrestle, as never before, with the implications of authentic spiritual and moral unity. We must build and network bridges and find ways of reinforcing a mutual witness to a bewildered world. The doctrine of the church has become for us a neglected article of faith that calls for urgent illumination.

The second priority concerns a rectification of concessions to the world in both thought and life. The church can hardly challenge the world's marginalization of the church by ecclesial quasi-conversion to the secular world-life view. Any fusion with the world's appraisal of reality and life will only render the church perpetually vulnerable to every new fad, until at last the church accepts secular society's goal of utopian social reform as her own and has little in common with her Founder's message and mission.

The churches that are languishing are those that deliberately accommodate themselves to the modern mind-set. In all too many circles one could be a humanist, a socialist, and a homosexual and claim to speak as a normative Christian. Even theologians have championed beliefs contravening the central doctrines of Christianity's charter documents. Catholic and Protestant radicals often imply, as Ronald Nash comments, that "Christianity means whatever 'Christians' today happen to believe and practice, be it pantheism, unitarianism, or sodomy." The reduction of apostolic belief to a politico-economic mission fed people on politico- economic theory while they thirsted for personal meaning. Precepts guarding the sanctity of life were neglected. The gospel was accepted only as an ally of liberation theology, which routinely liberated itself from the New Testament, as the so-called "progressive" churches became a way-stop to secularization.

Once again contemporary Christianity needs to grasp the Christian faith's essential connection with supernaturally revealed truth. As Nash remarks, "The church's access to truth is not a consequence of the greater wisdom of the apostles." It flows rather from God's self-revelation and the inscripturation of that revelation in the Bible. There can be no recovery of truly objective authority, of a sense of awe in the presence of statute law, of an unyielding regard for the rights of others, of the family as the basic unit of a stable society, and of the sanctity of human life, apart from supernatural metaphysics that exhibits anew the priority of God the Creator and that focuses on divinely revealed truth and the good. The denial of the absolute validity of Christianity has its basis (not in truth or in logic) but in modern assumptions of comprehensive culture conditioning and historical relativism. Christians need to reclaim philosophy, law, science, literature, music, and art. Only then will the world sense anew that the church is something more than a health spa or sports center or bingo palace. We must rise above notions that religious truth rests only on one's own experience and the impact of a private faith upon its proponents. We must reactivate systematic intellectual formulations.

While I am aware that to dream of a universal Christian culture is now vain, I firmly believe the eschatological end time will embrace it. There is no reason, however, for evangelical Christians presently to withdraw from the world. The secular city may brand this generation "post-Christian," and we may, all too uncritically, borrow this characterization. No generation since the resurrection of the crucified Jesus is post-Christian, however, for He who has conquered death and is the Church's risen Head has, as the writer of Hebrews notes (1:2), turned forward the prophetic time clock into the "last days." Some social observers energetically discuss the church's future prospects in the third millennium A.D. and leap over the decade now underway which may be the most important since the fall of the Roman Empire. We are thrust into this strategic turning time by God's decree and mandate. We have a vast debt to what has gone before, to the resources and energies that have made Christianity the first and only religion with a world presence, and the only faith that continues its unabated concern to reach hidden peoples wherever they may be.

Gratifying signs of hope are appearing. Distant lands that rejected Western colonization have learned to discern the gospel and, despite some relapse into tribalism and superstition, many cling eagerly to Christianity. Despite the long-standing resistance of Buddhism, Hinduism, and Islam, the non-Western world is in some ways more open to the gospel than the West. While the world looks in vain for heroes, Third World churches know that this is a new time for Christian martyrs. The post modernist resurgence of evangelical Christianity in America where more than fifty million affirm a "born-again" relationship; the dramatic proliferation of house churches in China; the reemergence of evangelical theology as a conspicuous academic phenomenon in England and the United States; the spectacular multiplication of Christians in Nigeria, Kenya, and Korea; the opening of Eastern Europe to evangelism through the downfall of the totalitarian Marxist regimes; are all promising landmarks for a hopeful future.

Almost everywhere one finds a network of believers in many vocations including law, philosophy, and science. Not only legislative aides but also some congressmen they serve, and many corporate and business leaders, meet weekly for prayer and discussion of serious theology and study of the Bible and its implications. Countless mustard-seed movements carry on effective local witness and national efforts—sometimes too much given to entrepreneurial triumphalism and heavy investment in public relations and promotion.

Most divinity students going into the pastorate and into missionary activity are enrolled on evangelical seminary campuses. Although Bible-observant professors and students on secular university campuses may still be a marked minority, they have grown in number and influence. Distinguished scholars still read the Gospel of John and, moreover, believe its message; they still seek forgiveness of sins, and readily acknowledge their evangelical identity. To be sure, among avant-garde divinity professors Bible reading is less a devout study of Scripture than a jigsaw dissection of the text into components to be rearranged in harmony with the interpreter's predispositions. It is premature, indeed, to speak of a reconnection of the academy with the great books and with the Book of books, but some campuses do stress the West's intellectual legacy despite the corrosive defection of the humanist knowledge elite.

The vast majority of ordinary citizens still "believe in God," though the concept seldom governs their moral outlook or shapes a significant worldview. Divine grace is still available, and the eschatological finalities remain in place for many even if the doctrines of divine creation and redemption are blurred. The matrix of Christian belief can again become the single most transforming influence in the emerging century. Jesus spoke of a mustard seed when Christianity was the possession only of a handful of followers. If modern technological science demystified the cosmos and history, contemporary Christianity can demythologize humanity of naturalistic dogma. The supernatural has not wilted away: God is no wimp, and we are not left to an unsure reading of the lips of an ambivalent Deity. Science and technology, the media and the cinema, have not displaced the propriety and potency of prayer.

If we obscure the Christian realities, primitive and animistic cults will rise to compensate for them, and if we neglect biblical illumination of the great problems of existence, the links between the theological and intellectual and the material and moral will all be misconceived. The great truths are at stake, and the nature of the Christian mission as well:

fundamental beliefs and governing doctrines like the definition of God, the seat of final authority, the nature of mankind, the identity of Jesus Christ, the ground of salvation, and social issues involving race, gender, class, the church and culture, and the role and limits of political power. We are not simply a tiny band of survivors holding the world of demons at bay. Christ Jesus is the risen and returning Lord, and still possible is a spiritual outburst and genetic transformation of today's prevalent worldview, a tidal shift more spectacular than the fall of the Berlin Wall and the collapse of socialism in Eastern Europe. We need to reaffirm the logos as the true basis of philosophy and philology, to redeploy neglected energies of thought and life, to regain the stride of an apostolic minority that ventured a world mission, and in their same bold spirit to remind our world that the crucified and risen Jesus keeps reiterating the question, "Who do you say I am?" (Mark 8:29).

Our age needs a restoration of true learning and of moral power enlivened by the transcendent supernatural. We do not hold that the infallible authority of the Bible defies the natural sciences and other empirical disciplines, but an immense change is required in the spirit of contemporary civilization. As we near the threshold of the third millennium, we may speak much more of Christianity's strength than of its decay and demise; the gates of hell have not prevailed against Christ's church. Christianity has outlasted many faiths, and its strength is voluntary rather than institutional and organizational. Its global challenge to other belief systems remains compelling. Neither science nor democracy arose independently of Christian influences in the West. Yet the Christian mission is not reducible to scientific and technological advancement or to the victory of democracy. Some have lived in the best societies but have lost the pearl of great price; others have found it who have lived in the most decadent societies. Nor will Christianity be a failure if in the third millennium Christians are outnumbered. Neither Jesus nor Paul taught that believers would be a majority movement, and both warned of impending persecution as the cost of discipleship. But they remind us still that those who accept Christ's proffered place in the kingdom of God are the blessed in both this life and the next.

The Western World's present defection from the Bible is not the last word. Unfolding judgment is already underway; a death-warrant hangs over modernity, both in the present millennium and in eternity to come. The possibilities of a tidal shift are hidden in the ripple of a wave, in the sprouting of a mustard seed, and in the faith that moves mountains.

# Facing America's Crosswinds

*In short I believe that while the drift of history seems careening toward judgment, an intermediate catastrophe is not inevitable or necessary. We stand at a juncture in history where by joining the battle against impending darkness our influence with God's help can make a decisive difference. Twilight is far from high noon, but it is equally far from midnight.*

A great debate is underway among social critics about the state of the nation. Some think America's "glory" days are past, while others think America's best years are yet to come, perhaps in the near future. By and large, political leaders, stock brokers, and other inveterate optimists scorn any suggestion that midnight overhangs the United States. Better relations with nations of the former Soviet bloc and with China; the success of free enterprise alongside the failures of socialist planning, international military cutbacks; our massive work force and the taming of inflation are cited as evidence of an approaching high noon. In the resurgence of evangelical Christianity the new Christian reconstructionists envision not only the restoration of Christian values to the heart of the nation, but also a conforming of American government to Mosaic law.

Other social critics see our country as already in the grip of post-Enlightenment forces, forces bearing Europe and the Anglo-American

West toward an inescapable sunset. They point to the moral decline in contemporary society, the atheistic orientation of humanistic education, tawdry media, and a chaos-generating lack of consensus in ideas and ideals, as well as political confusion spawned by placing pragmatism above principle. Such themes are common among dispensational premillennialists; for them an eschatological doomsday is prophetically anticipated by Israel's return to Palestine and by a revived Roman Empire (perhaps implicit in the emerging European community).

It is midnight, say the pessimists; it is high noon, say the optimists. One group cannot lift the flag off the ground; the other runs it over the tip of the flagpole.

I myself have recently ventured into these crosswinds. My recent book *Twilight of a Great Civilization*[1] places our condition between high noon and midnight; it puts the flag at half staff as a signal of trouble. In that book, my account of "The Fight of the Day" suggests that American culture is sinking toward sunset, that Christian believers are stretching toward sunrise, yet that we are warriors entrusted with a mission to the world. I am, therefore, no mere gloom and doom forecaster. While I do not envision American tomorrow or next week as a millennial utopia, I still see possibilities—slim though they may be—for a renewal of Western culture, but only if conditions for such renewal are met. In her present posture of cultural confusion and moral deterioration I am unsure whether America has the ethical and spiritual survival reserves to withstand creeping civilizational disaster. Today's prevailing spirit no longer perceives in Christ on the cross the uniquely supreme symbol of suffering and sacrifice. He is no longer perceived as the noblest personification and motivation in Western civilization for elevating good and conquering evil.

All is not lost, however, even if Western culture goes the way of countless other cultures. Among us still remains a vigorous and vigilant Christian vanguard to define and implement the ethical stability of the West, just as such a vanguard sustained the moral fortunes of the world when Rome gave way.

In short, I believe that while the drift of history seems careening toward judgment, an intermediate catastrophe is not inevitable or necessary. We stand at a juncture in history where by joining the battle against impending darkness our influence with God's help can make a decisive difference. Twilight is far from high noon, but it is equally far from midnight. Twilight, said Hegel, is when the owl of Minerva flees—that is, when wisdom goes. That eventuality is disconcerting enough.

---

1. Henry, *Twilight of a Great Civilization.*

Thanks to God, the cosmos is not in the clutch of mechanical determinism, of inevitable fluctuations upward or downward. History is not frozen in cyclical models. Nor are the universe and society subject to some involuntary evolution that dooms the present uncontrollably to successive new values, a course that would only demote any and all absolutes to transiency.

To be sure, no one ought to minimize our country's assets. Militarily, it remains the most powerful nation on earth. Technologically, it outranks most of the modern world. Its concern for human rights and for democratic political self-determination is unparalleled anywhere. Its commitment to a free market system has clearly outpaced the economics of world socialism. I am no New Left anticapitalist critic of America and the West who thinks that socialism can do no wrong and that capitalism can do no good. To be sure, capitalism is not the economics of the kingdom of God, but in a society of fallen mankind a competitive market system is what best serves both universal and individual interest by restraining inordinate self-interest.

The United States, more importantly, has a remarkable spiritual and moral heritage derived from Judeo-Christian theism, the religious revelation that lifted the West above paganism. That foundation undergirds the American commitment to limited government, private property as a stewardship, and entrepreneurial energy. Above all else this legacy grounds human rights and duties not in society or in the state, but in God the transcendent Creator of all life.

If we compare and contrast the United States with the more than one hundred and fifty nation-states in the United Nations, it is evident why many inhabitants of other lands envy us and yearn to share in our opportunities. The spiritually oppressed long for our liberties; those living under totalitarian leaders revere our democratic privileges; immigrants come here eagerly from Asia and Eastern Europe and Latin America in search of a better life.

There is another plus—if that is the right word—that we had best not take simply for granted. That plus is the fact that the Lord of history has not yet sounded the last trumpet call for His final judgment of the nations. History does not rule out the possibility of a resurgent Christianity. Its dynamic might even now reverse earthborn thunderclouds of dark paganism to a radiant sunlight and starlight that illumine a nation and culture unsure of its bearings.

For all her greatness America today has lost her sure sense of outcomes and copes with disconcerting liabilities. To academics whose specialty is the economic arena, I leave the sorry implications of our staggering budget deficit, our foreign trade imbalance, and problems of military spending. The Reagan emphasis on family values did not, unfortunately, include the example of balanced budgeting. It is obscene irony that America drifts ever closer to state and national lotteries--which disadvantages those who can least afford gambling--as a mechanism for remedying financial deficits. Although many Americans feel better about themselves, Allan Bloom's appraisal depicts the vanishing role of absolutes in public education and in secular society more incisively than does political campaign rhetoric.[2] The spectacle of rampant abortion, flagrant crime, and the debilitating drug culture are almost ineradicable blots upon our national dignity. Nor dare we forget that many Americans in all parts of our country, in both big cities and small, endure grievous hurts--poor people, homeless people, abused people, emotionally and physically disadvantaged people, to name but a few.

Rejection of our Christian heritage contributes to moral and spiritual apathy which in turn contributes to the decline of secular society and its plunge toward neopaganism. In speaking of twilight, I see no guarantee of a reprieve from the midnight of ultimate cultural collapse apart from a return to God who strives to etch His law upon all mankind. The historian Arnold Toynbee reminds us that every civilization has ended in rubble or ruin. I see no prospect that American society will escape a similar fate--nuclear weapons or not--unless a recovery of spiritual priorities brings ethical renewal.

The encouraging fact is that God-centered people can and, in fact, still do offer to the world a spiritual healing which they themselves are experiencing. Early Christianity was not content to hold a wake for the Roman Empire; it spoke to the world of truth, goodness, freedom, responsibility, honor, and security as a live prospect. The New Testament says more about the regeneration of humanity than it does about the degeneration of culture. Scripture continues to be alive and relevant to the problems of the present, to the religious and moral perils that spell only chaos and catastrophe. Early Christianity faced the realities of spiritual crisis without sentimentality. At stake was not only the worth and eternal destiny of individual human beings but also the nature and direction of society as a whole. Apostolic Christianity linked the providences or tragedies of mankind to humanity's avowal or disavowal of the self-revealing God. It demonstrated how to confront paganism--not ancient paganism alone, nor only the much later paganism of Hitler's Auschwitz, but also our paganism as well, of our civilization whose vision is flawed by scientific naturalism and by rejection of God as irrelevant.

---

2. Allan Bloom, *The Closing of the American Mind* (New York: Simon and Schuster, 1987).

As twilight deepens, the inherited core values of Western civilization become more obscure. The sun sets on *agape* as night enthrones *eros*. God who is Light is obscured by the prince of darkness. The line between good and evil is blurred, melancholy replaces spiritual joy, and freedom capitulates before lawlessness and autonomy. In short, a rootless social disorientation metamorphoses into threatening arbitrary power.

We are faced on many sides today by a dehumanizing loss of humanitarian concern, a trend that inclines secular humanism toward raw naturalism. Such naturalism, in which humanism loses its already tenuous links to social morality, welcomes and shelters a revival of paganism. It has the character of neopaganism, however, in that it rests on a resolute rejection of the revelatory biblical option. It deliberately disavows the Judeo-Christian alternative.

The cause is not yet lost, nor need it be. God's people can still demonstrate and offer a revitalization of conscience and of spiritual awareness. They can still provide scriptural illumination of good and evil, a rational basis for transforming beliefs, a power for redirecting human will and its desires, and an awareness that the self-revealing God of the universe has a moral purpose for history.

We need to enlarge our capacity to reinforce and to lift, and not merely to shock and to rebuke. Ethical expression must go beyond indignation and denunciation. A vigorous Christian minority and its colleagues who purpose to reinforce universal truth and objective good can still give direction to twentieth-century society.

We need to realize that good things are happening in the providence of God. We can see corporate executives, for example, who stand tall in the business world as spiritual beacons and for whom the Bible is not just an antiquarian book but a relevant guide for the present. We need to honor those who in the media are voices for truth and the good, those in academia who acknowledge that apart from supernatural actuality all reality degenerates to but natural processes and energy events, those in the political realm for whom faith in God and moral obedience and a regard for justice determine the destiny of the nation. We need to see the resurgence of evangelical religion for what it is, namely, a protest against politicalization of churches and a rediscovery instead of Judeo-Christian vitalities, of response to the widespread hunger for personal faith and renewed sense of responsibility as light and salt in the world. We need to decide if we will be mere spectators in the struggle for humanity's mind and will, or whether we will exercise leadership in shaping the course and outcome of today's battle of conflicting and competing values.

As never before, universities and colleges have a propitious opportunity to identify, clarify and implement core concerns of the curriculum, and to formulate a structure of convictions immune to the destruction of heady scientism. The identity of ultimate reality, the character of God, the definition of justice, the nature of love, the durability of truth, the stability of absolutes, the role of conscience, the meaning of meaning, and the reality of grace and redemption are all in limbo in our present cultural chaos.

Great books of the past, and not least among them the Bible itself, beckon us anew to wrestle the persistent problems of philosophy, of ethics, and life itself. If biblically oriented Jews and Christians keep silent in a time like ours, we voluntarily impose on ourselves the most devastating censorship of truth known to humanity. When Pilate asked "What is truth?" (John 18:38), he was at least standing face to face with it. As concerned intellectuals we, too, must stir our contemporaries to ask the right questions. More than that, as recipients of the Judeo-Christian heritage we dare not settle for equivocal answers, but must "give the reason for our hope" (1 Pet. 3:15). Equivocation and accommodation will not suffice, for nothing less than the soul of the nation—and of the western world—is at stake.

Equivocation and accommodation will not suffice, for nothing less than the soul of the nation—and of the Western world—is at stake.

# The Struggle For America's Soul

*What stares us in the face today is a conflict over the very nature of our human species, over the legitimacy of religious and moral values, over the reality of God, and the role of human transcendence in the creation and preservation of human rights and duties.*

Social critics now write of our present decade in American history in terms of deepening public rivalry and hostility. Some even speak of *Kultur-Kampf,* or cultural war, and impending civilizational carnage.

A century ago the whole Western world throbbed with utopian expectations. Today we are deeply divided over the nature of truth and of the good. Even after her bicentennial America is confused about her reason for being.

To be sure, inveterate optimists are not in short supply. Emboldened by the myth of evolution, many scientists decree that tomorrow must, of course, be better than today. The secular media think our rejection of traditional values can be only for the good. To professional educators and the humanist knowledge elite, the secular campuses were never more brilliant. Many politicians confidently unfurl and wave the flag despite the staggering national debt, the savings-and-loan scandal, the AIDS crisis, and the breakup of the family.

J. D. Hunter, nonetheless, significantly entitled his recent book *Culture Wars: The Struggle to Define America*.[1] My own *Twilight of a Great Civilization* was followed by Charles Colson's *Against the Night: Living in the New Dark Ages*. The titles speak of a deepening crisis and a culture in decline. Almost a decade ago Alasdair MacIntyre reminded us that with the decline of the Roman Empire, Christians were asking whether to guarantee the survival of virtue they must project alternative forms of community. "The barbarians," warns MacIntyre, "have been governing us for quite some time. . . . Our lack of consciousness of this . . . constitutes part of our predicament."

According to avant-garde barbarians the cultural war is, in fact, already over. The looming progressives, they say, have clearly bested the traditionalists or the *orthodox* or the *conservatives* or whatever you wish to call them. Has not even the "new Christian right" visibly collapsed? Witness the demise of the *Fundamentalist Journal,* the closedown of Moral Majority (which spent $15 million but gained not a single legislative objective), the failure of Pat Robertson's $25 million drive for the Republican presidential nomination, and the neutralizing of pro-life demonstrations by massive pro-choice counterdemonstrations. Recall also the disgrace of high-visibility televangelists who, instead of impressing the nation with their contemporary packaging of the gospel, contaminated evangelical religion with carnality and revived the specter of Elmer Gantry's manipulation and exploitation of religion. Is not the war now won, ask the progressives or revisionists, except perhaps for sporadic rearguard flare-ups and local conflicts over pornography or some headline-making Supreme Court decision that bears on religious values?

Yes, indeed, retort many political conservatives as well, the war is over. The liberals who were soft on communism or socialism have now had their day. Soviet dominion over Eastern Europe has ended—the Soviet Union has itself collapsed. The historical momentum is clearly toward democratic self-determination, free enterprise, and private property. Those who considered socialism the wave of the future—especially liberation theologians who taught that God keeps a socialist eye on the poor—are now exposed as deluded ideologues.

Say what one will about the religious right, it did give evangelicals identity in public life where a Protestant-Catholic-Jewish ecumenical coalition had long largely ignored them. It placed religious values firmly on the public docket for unavoidable discussion. In a day when church

---

1. James Davison Hunter, *Culture Wars: The Struggle to Define America* (New York: Basic Books, 1991).

and state debate focused mainly on nonestablishment and on separation, the religious right elevated free speech and equal access into national issues.

Now conservatives hold that the arena of energetic controversy in America is shifting more from the national party level to that of the local precincts and that this domestic struggle has just begun. While the conservative cause may have faltered nationally, it is being deployed regionally. Established political organizations are already in place, and state and local networks hope to field some five thousand candidates in coming elections. Names in the news may change, and the location of social protests and demonstrations may shift, but the same animating passions persist. The same concerns and causes reappear issue by issue in the arenas of public education, of the mass media, and of law and politics.

Church constituencies reflect this relocation of involvement. Over against long-standing ecumenical centers of political impact in New York and Washington, D.C., new activistic agencies have emerged in Lynchburg, Virginia; Carol Stream, Illinois; and Orlando, Florida. Conservative forces may lack the ecumenical left's many advantages, including well-subsidized ecclesiastical staffs with skilled lobbyists and ready access to church funding. The conservatives, however, have impressive mailing lists and a grass-roots following, even if they need constantly to reawaken this constituency to the new and present dangers posed by "the other side."

Each coalition jockeys eagerly for its own propaganda advantage. Each marshals its language as if for all-out military confrontation. Each imbues revered terms with an argumentative force in truncated discourse that rouses emotional responses. The liberals, it is said, care nothing about the family. They are proabortion with a vengeance; they promote homosexuality as an alternative life-style, defend pornography as art, endorse value- free public education, and so on. Now and then liberals may refer to values, but when it comes to defining and sustaining them, they are notoriously ambiguous.

The conservatives, it is charged, care even less about social issues. They will not tolerate sporadic government funding of pornographic art because, at heart, they promote censorship. They condemn public blasphemy and foul profanity in order to advance a religious establishment. Participants in Operation Rescue are depicted as desperados and terrorists. They are said to betoken that conservatives will stop at nothing to impose their objectives.

What this conflict sacrifices is something that the founding fathers and many early American citizens considered very precious, namely, disciplined moral discourse. They prized reasoned dialogue on the nature and limits of government and open public discussion of religious liberty and the other freedoms. They had occasionally to cope with hotheads on right and left, but they gave their main energies to positive and constructive disputation. Instead of wild political head winds centered mainly in denunciation and confrontation, the early Americans were concerned to clarify the moral justification of competing options.

Today the intellectual context of the political debate is vastly diminished and the conflict over rival social perspectives often reduces to a factious crusade. The political left and the political right share in this costly diminution of ethical disputation. They engage society mainly in what is essentially a propaganda debate. This contraction involves a cultural accommodation that is devastating for both right and left, and even more so for national policy. It reinforces the notion that one's cause is best promoted by dominating the language of controversy so that the opposing side is linguistically disadvantaged. To reduce the support of truth and right to these dimensions is unwittingly to relativize the meaning of the good—and even to ally oneself insensibly with the enemies of civilization. Such a course fails to see that our century as it nears its close is engaged in a colossal feud over moral authority and the nature of sovereignty.

Many political contenders do not discern that competing worldviews are involved. Underway is a tremendous debate over whether God is merely a myth and whether a person is a fragment of divinity or a redeemable rebel or just a clump of cosmic dust. The whole global village is increasingly engulfed by this conflict. Theistic religions send missionaries around the globe; pantheistic religions display their gurus and swamis to the West; technocratic scientism exports secularism to the developing nations and attracts their ablest young minds to prestigious Western universities awash in this-worldly materialism. The mass media umpire this contest with a humanist intellectual-elite bias that disdains traditional values and confuses pluralism and boundless tolerance with progress.

The historical momentum is presently on the side of humanist revisionists who reinforce their cause through education, the media, and the political establishment. These revisionist forces, moreover, view their cause as inevitably victorious. Evolutionary progress fortified by academic, judicial, and media support will predictably carry the day. The extreme views are more emotionally compelling than intellectually reflective. They caricature more moderate positions as no less objectionable than their counterparts. Those who do not acceptably dot every *i* or cross every *t* are deplored as waffling equivocators and fainthearted straddlers.

Periodic government funding of vulgar and lurid art, says one side, will admit of no corrective short of censorship. Protest against sexually perverse TV soap operas must take the form of economic boycott, nothing less. Champions of the "pro-choice" position in the abortion controversy are to be branded in principle as advocates of mass murder. Opposition to abortion must involve barricading the outrageous abortion clinics, legal or not, if one is to be credited with Christian integrity. The effective way to promote humane treatment of animals is to spray paint on women wearing fur coats.

No less defamed as intolerant and undemocratic are the motives of those who skillfully promote orthodox values. Those who oppose new patterns of the family are denigrated as unmodern and regressive. To insist that the National Endowment for the Arts provide aesthetic guidelines to distinguish works of artistic quality from blatant pornography is deplored as essentially a federal funding of Christian orthodoxy.

The two sides square off antithetically in terms of extreme cliches as if no objective considerations and no logical supports remain for the public positions one takes, but only pseudo-arguments. This radicalizing of debate was evident when, for example, educational authorities held that an unofficial Bible study club meeting after high school classes would constitute an establishment of religion, while some clergy held that the prohibition of an officially sponsored agenda of classroom prayer and Bible reading would constitute an atheistic exclusion of God from the public schools. The battle between these two politicized extremes produces little light, but searing heat.

The worse disgrace is that, except for evangelism, funding from religious sources is available mainly for such political diatribe. I do not categorize all religiously funded public-issue programs this way; some are notable exceptions. It is difficult, however, to enlist evangelical investment for reflective think tanks and for serious publications. Someone has said facetiously that more serious moral discussion survives now and then on Oprah Winfrey's talk show than in some churches. That caricature may reflect an antiecclesiastical bias, but from God's people we have a right to expect more disciplined participation in the public arena. Chuck Colson is one of the few emphatic "born againers" today who speaks reflectively to the conscience and mind of America.

We need hundreds like him to focus on the reality and relevance of God as Creator and Judge, on the importance of transmitting our incomparable civilizational heritage, on public truth and decency and justice. For the good of our nation, our neighbors, and our children we dare not settle for cleverly-crafted symbols that ignore the way logic and language are ideally used. Public discourse is now often too lame to cope effectively with the issues. We should model for others the way social debate should be carried on.

That does not mean that *ad hominem* argument is always inappropriate. Effective political debate points out the ridiculous implications, limitations, and consequences of shoddy premises. We must expose the blatant inconsistencies of rival life views. Yet, we are more than protectors of nostalgic memories. We are entrusted carriers in life and in word of the truth and will of a loving and holy God. We need to make a compelling case for the highest options, and not to consider the inherited tradition as self-sustaining. Even the contemporary formulation of issues imposes prepackaged limitations on public concern. We rightly oppose abortion on demand, but has any champion of fetal rights taken up the right of the unborn not to be saddled by a national debt of trillions of dollars as a bequest of their parent generation? Who has opposed our postponing to the oncoming generations the increased taxes that national solvency will require? Is not the debt structure that modern states presently impose on children currently being born staggering enough to raise the question of their involuntary bondage? If they have a right to life, do they not also have a right not to be unconsentingly taxed to death?

We must engage the public square within the rules under which a pluralistic republic functions. Someone has said, rightly, that it is philosophically provocative, politically inflammatory, and theologically unnecessary to press "God wills it" on the public square as the reason for championing proposed legislation. To do so deliberately involves the political arena in a public metaphysical debate over rival religious outlooks, when it is not the prerogative of civil government to arbitrate theological differences. It would be sad indeed if the rightness or wrongness of statute law reduced to a reflex under threat of excommunication of how many Baptists or Catholics or Unitarians or Christian Scientists there are. The Constitutional principles of free exercise and nonestablishment permit public proclamation and evangelism promotive of one's religious beliefs. They also allow believers to exercise their legal preferences without involuntary religious consent.

For all that, we must cope with the fact that the definition of proper beliefs and behavior is undergoing great change in modern society. The moral continuities are raveling. Moral pluralism gains ground in the name of democratic tolerance. Traditional immoralities emerge as new moral alternatives. Confusion multiplies over what is ethically permanent and what is culturally conditioned.

Violence has not yet reached the levels of a pervasively barbarian society; Belfast and Beirut are notably different from Baltimore and Buffalo. Crime has soared to record levels, and Washington, D.C., is now a national murder and drug capital. Fully 83 percent of Americans or their family members now living are likely to be victims of violent crime at some time.

Sex education for minors in public schools is championed as the right to informed choice. Prostitution is approved as one's right of privacy. The time has come when many of the cultural despisers of traditional religion assume a six-month fetus should have no more legal status than a wart.[2] The case for abortion on demand keeps edging toward a case for euthanasia on demand. Is it surprising that some religious leaders warn of an impending return to paganism that accepts pederasty and perhaps even human sacrifice?

The implications for a cohesive society are stupendous. Without obligatory beliefs and behavior no society can long survive. Moral communities, if they are to endure, require boundaries as well as tolerances. Today more than at any time since the birth of the republic, more so than even than during the Civil War, national identity and leadership and purpose are up for grabs. The great American political experiment in democracy will fail if no greater unity remains than a pragmatic accommodation of widening diversity. In the absence of a shared moral vision and mutual values, any democracy will crumble.

Domestic disenchantment with the American political process is growing at the very time when Eastern European nations and mainland China's youth reach for political self-determination and democratic government. Many citizens of lands just now emerging out of communist tyranny are baffled that in national elections almost half of our citizens neglect the voting booth. Such disinterest is not unrelated to the fact that, once elected, presidents and other officeholders frequently abandon their campaign assurances. Political leadership is no longer viewed as a source of hope. The heroes and role models in contemporary American life are less and less found in the ranks of civil government. The feeling grows that America may be losing industrial leadership to Japan, Germany, and an emerging European Common Market. The decline of the American work ethic has contributed to this deterioration, along with other lost or slipping values.

National leaders continue to insist that the present cultural decline is but a momentary condition akin to past historical lapses from which we have recovered. Yet the modern intellectual outlook has few moorings, and many of its cognitive dependencies are adrift. Emotional manipulation of public response circumvents rationally compelling discourse.

---

2. Hunter, *Culture Wars.*

Technological mobilization of conviction through opinion polls is a sensual assault on the public mind rather than an exercise in persuasion. It contributes little to genuine dialogue.

Just as Protestant evangelicalism shaped the colonial outlook in America's early years, so too amid Victorian culture in England Protestant evangelicalism was one of the two most formative national influences. A post-Enlightenment epistemology had a growing impact upon modernity. This soon precipitated in Britain a division of evangelicals into conservatives and into liberals who elevated personal religious experience into a guide to truth.

A great weakness of contemporary conservative evangelicals was to oversimplify public issues, including a readiness to rely on personal image more than on political prudence. Symbols are indeed important in a television age, but it is easy to overrate the influence of a candidate who prays, reads the Bible, and professes to be "born again." Such assurances sometimes fail to cover a multitude of political ineptitudes. They also can encourage image posturing and are readily thought to compensate for skill in public policy matters. Apart from a meritorious agenda, prayer, even in the White House, on Capitol Hill, and in the public schools can resemble harp-playing while the nation deteriorates. A significant worldview involves rationally compelling reasons why one ought to think and live and act in a distinctively Christian way not only in private life but in public affairs also.

Christian engagement in politics is not primarily for the sake of electing Christians to office; it is to model a just nation, to structure public discussion so that truth and right remain central concerns, to applaud godly leaders and to promote a good society. We evangelicals need not remain a silent minority or a silent majority. We sacrifice our claim to a respectful hearing; however, if our motive is simply to identify Christians in national life who, for all their devoutness, may multiply public confusion over what a just society truly demands of us in the political arena.

The evangelical movement, though numerically strong, is publicly much the weaker partner among the cultural contenders. The spectrum of support for traditional or orthodox values is not as efficiently organized or as disciplined in presenting its case in the public realm as are the champions of radical change, or for that matter, the champions of Catholic public philosophy.

Evangelicals may monopolize religious broadcasting with over thirteen hundred religious radio stations, over two hundred religious television stations, and at least three religious networks. Theologically orthodox Jews, Catholics, and conservative Protestants have educational institutions enrolling 18,000 primary and secondary pupils. The Christian

College Coalition embraces evangelical colleges with some 90,000 students. Along with hundreds of religious periodicals, the broadly orthodox wing of American culture has at least seventy publishing houses, including some of the nation's most impressive. Wisely or not, some conservative agencies have ventured the course of civil disobedience, and in doing so reflect a dedication to social militancy not found since the demonstrations against racism of the civil rights era. The conservatives have also gained competent representatives in the legislative, executive, and judicial branches of government. Some of the most devout are evangelicals whose political integrity and astuteness are recognized by their colleagues.

We too seldom ask ourselves, therefore, why the historical momentum, nonetheless, lies with secular humanism in the public schools, the media, and the legislative and judicial arenas, where humanism promotes a steady revision of our cultural heritage. The traditionally orthodox institutions are no match for large circulation newspapers and magazines, for major television and radio networks, or for political processes that currently advance a modification of orthodox values. The great universities are cognitively and ethically committed to notions of evolutionary progress although they do not widely entertain the possibility that their own present academic prejudices might themselves be transcended.

Meanwhile the traditional evangelical centers of power are relocating from the great metropolises to the more remote margins of cultural influence. They, thereby, are largely self-condemned to a role of reaction to formative social forces that others originate and shape. Such frontier resistance can no doubt win occasional skirmishes against blatantly offensive movie or television productions steeped in violence and sexual deviance. This resistance can force a moderation of positions taken by ecumenical bureaucracies now and then, but such relocation hardly promises significant victory in the culture war, because it is too much withdrawn from the main arenas of influence and battle, and, thereby, unwittingly accommodates a swift-changing society.

Not only is consensus vanishing on what is socially good and right, but one faction's virtuous tolerance quickly becomes a rival faction's pernicious relativity. When emotionally based positions taken by the extreme right are not shared by more reflective conservative leaders, the moderate left seeks to detach the cognitive types entirely from the right, thus diluting conservative support. The extreme right, meanwhile, assails the reluctance of moderates to identify with it unreservedly, as a compromising culture accommodation. Worse yet, the traditional cognitive supports of Judeo-Christian morality have lost credibility for a society largely steeped in naturalism. That society, in turn, has itself been unable to adduce persuasive moral alternatives. Unbridled self-interest increasingly supplies the motivation for the secular city's ethical choices. The naturalistic dogmas of the present are inadequate to the cultural strains of tomorrow, or even of today. Far less are they presentable in eternity.

More is lacking than only an agreed public philosophy. Even the awareness seems lost that the American founding fathers bequeathed to us a political and social mechanism for coping with pluralistic differences and cultural conflict. James D. Hunter observes that the most vocal participants in the current social struggle have little interest in seeking a truly pluralistic solution of the kind that founders of the American republic might have approved. Instead, they would annul the legitimacy of each others' participation in the American heritage. To be sure, some radical positions may now and then strain the legitimate limits of democratic tolerance, but the current promotional counter assaults give the impression that one side exclusively preempts the legitimacy of cultural expression and that the other has no cultural validity whatever. Hunter, therefore, pointedly asks whether the founders' ideal any longer remains workable "when pluralism would seem to expand indefinitely and when the traditional sources of moral and legal consensus are either no longer credible or dependable."[3] While Hunter does not consider the nation in danger of imminent collapse, he warns that the growing stresses on democratic practice "could conceivably evolve into a serious threat" if polarization continues and divisions deepen.

Other than dependence on prayer, which is too much neglected, and on spiritual and moral renewal, which is indispensable, a favorable future for the American republic rests on persuasion much more than on confrontation, ultimatum, and imposition. Our grandchildren may well ask us why we failed them and failed history and the nation in this turning time.

What stares us all in the face today is a conflict over the very nature of our human species, over the legitimacy of religious and moral values, over the reality of God, and over the role of divine transcendence in the creation and preservation of human rights and duties. The themes of government, liberty, and order, and the nature of social and political institutions, insistently raise the question of ultimate and contingent authority. The leaders who shaped the American tradition disavowed any religious establishment, but their emphasis on free exercise held wide open the door to voluntary religious commitment. Almost all were convinced that God and a universal moral order imply each other. Their

---

3. James Davison Hunter, "The Challenge of Modern Pluralism," in *Ariticles of Faith, Articles of Peace*.

emphasis on limited government—as against tyranny, aristocracy and monarchy—grew in large part from a recognition of the priority of God—as the Declaration of Independence alerts us—and not from a commitment to unanchored human rights. Some leaders deeply influenced by the Enlightenment, most notably Thomas Jefferson, thought that the fortunes of morality can be separated from religion. Jefferson substituted a remote Seistic God for the self-revealing God of the Judeo-Christian heritage, but the unbridled secularism of the academic world has channeled deism into the mires of naturalism. It has forfeited objective moral values along with transcendent religious values.

We must challenge the false assumptions of our culture and bear our witness in the service of truth and right, without publicly labeling those who disagree with us as bigots. We must also prevent the secular state from devouring the public significance of religion. We must resist the secularization of public education, in respect to both its content and its aims. We must remind the nation that revealed religion has a social dimension which, if stifled, violates free exercise. The social role of the churches in ministry to the poor, in the provision of low-cost housing, in treatment of alcohol and drug addiction, expresses free exercise and is fully compatible with nonestablishment.

Today the convictional vacuum about the nature of the real world is sucking into its skeptical orbit the very foundational principles on which the Republic rests. The post-Enlightenment philosophies through which many academics seek external moorings for human rights are unpersuasive. A Swiss jurist has said boldly that only by sacrificing intellectual integrity can we any longer believe such philosophies.

A decisive culture struggle is underway between three momentous faiths—pseudoscientific naturalism, Asian pantheism, and Judeo-Christian theism, of which Islam is a roaming relative. This clash of worldviews is already deep and wide—indeed, fearfully deep and planetwide—and involves the rivalry of convictional stances now on an accelerating collision course. The most powerful of these is scriptural theism, belief in a supernatural mind and will, in the holy Creator and moral Judge of mankind, and in the Redeemer of the penitent.

We Christians have no intention of forcing upon the nation our treasured Judeo-Christian heritage that so dramatically lifted from paganism both the West and the lands beyond. If, however, secularists complain that in an earlier era of religious cohesion a pan-Protestant ideology shaped American life, we shall remind so-called progressives that in our time of vaunted pluralism we may quite plausibly argue, as Hunter says, "that a secularistic humanism has become the dominant moral ideology of American public culture." We shall, therefore, dispute the efforts of antisupernaturalists to obtrude their theories upon public institutions, even as we shall protest the use of public funds and of public agencies to advance the influx of Asian pantheism, whether ancient expressions of Hinduism and Buddhism or their newer forms of Transcendental Meditation, New Age speculation, and other occultic notions.

We shall indeed defend the legal rights and religious freedom of theists, nontheists, and atheists. Through discreet proclamation we shall also seek to evangelize them in the interest of transcendent truth and the gospel by offering valid reasons for the Christian hope. As adherents of voluntary religion, we shall continue to bear our eager witness in society, extending the confidence of the Republic's founders in the Creator's endowment of all human beings with inalienable rights. We invite all humanity to Christ the Light of the world and earnestly share the Scriptures that speak of Him. Above all, we propose to live in a way that exhibits the life-changing dynamic and the moral power of revealed religion.

We are grateful that today no one should doubt that evangelicals have a distinctive political constituency. We aim to rise above the weaknesses of past evangelical engagement. We purpose to speak not to single issues alone but to a whole range of public issues. We aim, moreover, to speak credibly with a view to consistency in public philosophy. We shall not rely on half-truths but aim to speak and act in a genuinely Christian way. We shall not use this world's methods, and thereby compound the wrongs, by returning evil for evil. We are convinced that the obligations of Christian truth and virtue do not stop at politics' door. In that confidence we hope to engage meritoriously and influentially in the struggle for the soul of America.

We shall work for the preservation of the republic by relating religion both to personal life and to civic responsibility. In the public arena we shall seek to persuade our contemporaries of the superiority of the high moral road and of the costly consequences of ethical relativity. If the humanist knowledge elite evicts us from the public square, let it not be because of Christians' unwillingness to dialogue. Let it be rather because secular ideologists sometimes forget that healthy regard for others' opinions on which the survival of any pluralistic society depends, and thus sometimes forego an earnest curiosity over enduring principles of truth and the good without which no society of any kind can long endure. May we ourselves learn to transcend these same temptations and weaknesses.

At the same time, evangelicals must recognize the true nature of the forces aligned against our participation in the public square. The end of the twentieth century is witnessing far more than the continued course of secularization. We must now address the rise of new and powerful paganisms.

# Confronting the Challenge of Paganism

*Surely the moral outlook is bleak in the secular city. The spiritual condition is depressing. If ever the Christian vanguard inherited an opportune moment for declaring and displaying the vitalities of revealed religion, that opportunity is today and stares us boldly in the face.*

Never has the Christian vanguard had a more propitious opportunity than now to demonstrate the gospel's transforming power and its moral impact on society. Were the apostle Paul in our midst, he would be stunned that Korean Christians now shame the evangelistic apathy prevalent in Europe to which he long ago addressed the gospel. The philosopher Augustine would ask fifty million American evangelicals why we do not apply to the shabby history of our own times his insights in *The City of God and the City of Man*. The Protestant Reformers would ask why we flirt with ailing pluralistic and politicized churches that long for a human magician when they actually need a divine exorcist. Wesley and other evangelists would ask why our congregations forego church discipline and allow a sleazy society to demoralize even the clergy. Does Jesus Christ the Head of the church weep today not only over Jerusalem, but over Rome and Geneva and Washington and Nashville as well? Does a cloud of heavenly witnesses perchance shed tears because we have lost our first love, because the light of the world is flickering, and because our salt has lost its tang?

No longer need the church struggle against grand political visions of a one-world government or other man-made utopias. Religious enthusiasm has waned for a modernist social gospel void of personal regeneration. The forty-year-old ecumenical movement now stirs less excitement than a snow alert in the Dakotas. Secular philosophers are more confused than ever about supernatural reality. Modern civilization boasts more scientists than in all prior generations, but scientists have not produced utopia. We have more psychologists than ever before, yet more people than ever are burdened by anxiety. Most nations have highly compensated political leaders who year after year produce more problems than solutions. We have more financial analysts than ever, yet even leading brokers end up in penitentiaries instead of an easy street, while the poor we have always with us.

The weak-willed humanitarianism of the Anglo-Saxon world is gradually giving way. Stage by stage humanistic culture is deteriorating into callous paganism. An emerging barbarianism is everywhere evident: in sexual revelry that transgresses all the inherited norms of propriety; in the unfeeling abortion of innumerable fetuses; in the dooming of many aged to euthanasia by relatives and friends who justify their performance as an act of supreme love; in terrorists holding innocent people as hostages for political purposes and destroying passenger-laden planes; in bold tabloid profanation of the sacred, and the media's growing carnality.

A deteriorating morality has violated all taboos until the cultural mood considers little if anything irreversibly either right or wrong. The words sex, free and win have become the secular press's leading headline gimmicks. Consumed by monetary and sexual impulses and ego trips, our age measures success mainly in dollars, in secular status, and in sensual satisfactions; money, power, and hedonism have become more important than love and virtue.

Secular history keeps sinking ever downward even while many think it has already bottomed out. Parents have even sold their children for money and drugs. One family sold a baby girl for $5,000 in 1987 and then, allegedly offered its six-week-old son for $3,500 and three ounces of cocaine a year later.

Vulgar brushstrokes more and more scar the portrait of Western civilization. Satanic cults continue to operate in Germany and England as well as in the United States. Spiritualism and the occult attract ever new devotees. What once influenced only society's so-called lunatic fringe now gains a foothold in the oncoming generation. Exotic trends often begin as a teenage protest against merely conventional parental religion and wafer-thin spirituality. Young cultists often come from single-parent homes. Some justify their revolt by citing both their parents' merely nominal religious identity and the aridity of many congregations. Teenagers begin cultic pagan rites by sacrificing pets and drinking urine-tinctured blood, and end them in a lust for satanic power by immolating babies or murdering friends. Some devil worshipers speak of a "church of Satan" and a satanic bible; their "church music" is hard metal or rock whose lyrics salute the prince of evil.

Few developments today so clearly mirror the West's ethical chaos as its woefully inconsistent concern for human life. A generation that once condemned Nazi concentration camp experiments on death-destined Jews now asks whether science should salvage the scarce bodily organs of prisoners on death row, and consider terminally ill AIDS patients also as candidates for research and experimental cures.

Some thirty nations can now produce blood gas and nerve gas; chemical weapons are held by Iran, Libya, and Syria, as well as by several Western countries; some nations are experimenting with lethal weapons based on biological organisms. Americans are alarmed that outside the United States almost three million children die annually of preventable diseases. Meanwhile, inside the United States, Americans readily abort half that number of fetuses annually. Many citizens, in fact, express more indignation over the seventeen million animals used annually in laboratory experiments aiming to save human lives than they do over the deliberate extermination of one and one half million fetuses that mainly attend permissive sexuality. True, sporadic outbursts of humanist compassion have corralled emotional television appeals for famine relief, appeals more spectacular but far less productive and long-lived than those of long-established Christian agencies.

Each year 390,000 American smokers still die preventable deaths from cigarette addiction. Their addiction overpowers the stark warning printed on each cigarette package. Yet our manufacturers export these same lethal cigarettes to foreign nations and do so without the appended warning of danger to multitudes not well informed about the hazards of smoking.

So devoured by greed are some leaders in the financial community that, despite the recent government crackdown on Wall Street insider trading, charges of fraud now have been levied also against commodity market account executives who have rigged trades to profit themselves at the expense of their customers.

The drug habit is a national abomination. Over twenty million Americans use illegal drugs. Americans have given way to the scourge of cocaine, which stretches from ghettos to campuses and on to upper levels of society. Reports now indicate that LSD is making a comeback among students—even those in junior high school.

Alcohol remains America's worst abused drug. Urine samples from infants more and more reflect inherited traces of its use. Alcohol-related traffic accidents, now the leading killer of sixteen to twenty-four year-olds, annually cause 100,000 fatalities. United States beer, wine and liquor companies annually spend $2 billion to attract consumers, especially college students whose major athletic events they strategically sponsor. Long before they reach the legal drinking age, children watch these programs and accompanying commercials. Although the economic cost to national health is estimated as high as $130 billion annually, the liquor industry remains poorly regulated and lightly taxed. Profit on individual drinks often runs as high as 75 percent to 85 percent.

Over and above addiction to drugs and to greed, hypersexuality has become a self-defeating behavior pattern. Society today projects as ideal a self that images money, sexuality, and sophistication. Jesus of Nazareth would not place even last on a list topped by some AIDS- beset entertainment or sports idol. Who today would want to be crucified for concerns of truth, love, justice, and holiness? This manipulation of the ideal has led unwittingly to the brutalization of humans. Some estimates place at 5 percent or 6 percent the number of Americans for whom sex is an uncontrollable appetite. Eyes meet, pulses quicken, and in less time than it takes to watch a soap opera commercial, he and she are upended on a mattress.

The U.S. government currently spends $1.3 billion on AIDS research—more than for heart disease. Over 90 percent of Americans diagnosed in 1984 with AIDS are already dead; half of those so diagnosed in 1987 have also died. Almost one-third of American doctors would prefer not to treat AIDS-infected patients. So intense is concern over AIDS that other sexually transmitted diseases also associated with incurable and fatal conditions continue to take their toll but are downplayed or overlooked.

Even limited statistics concerning sexual immorality in the spiritually backslidden Anglo-American West are highly disconcerting. Almost two in three young women in the United Kingdom acknowledge a loss of virginity before they reach sixteen. In the United States half the girls admit to sexual intercourse by age fifteen. The highest percentage of pregnancies and abortions of any developed nation in the world occurs among American teenagers between fifteen and nineteen years of age. Japan—though only 1 percent Christian—has the lowest rate. In 1984 over 56 percent of American mothers were unmarried teenagers. If this out-of-wedlock trend continues, nearly one-fourth of all American babies born in 1989 will be born out of wedlock to mothers of all ages, races, and income groups. The number of sexually active teenagers in conservative churches is reportedly higher than many churchgoers believe. Many evangelicals would rather not hear the statistics.

So devastating is the nuclear family's breakdown that many sociologists avoid speaking of monogamy as normative. Instead, they speak of a postmarital society of "shack-up" singles and of optional life-styles representing new family patterns. Some 80 percent of unwed fathers do not live with their children. Between 1970 and 1983 the number of unmarried couples living together in the United States rose from 640,000 to four million. Almost half of all couples now applying for marriage licenses have already cohabited; many consider themselves moral on the ground of having lived with but one and the same person. Those seeking marriage often do so for the sake of children born to their cohabitation. For many non-traditionalists intercourse seals a marriage, not a church service nor civil ceremony. Even many clergy, facing their own divorce problems, hold lax attitudes. In a study by a University of Houston law center 40 percent of the clergy surveyed hesitated to label premarital sex as always wrong.

Sociologists predict that by 1993 half of all new marriages will end in divorce. Despite many "guarantees" of bliss—among them contraceptives, safe-sex kits, condoms, sex education, AIDS information, and abortion-on-demand—fewer people now find happiness in marriage. Only one in three women and only one in four men say that they are happily married. Many are unable to find happiness and fulfillment in any relationship—their expectations are so unrealistic that satisfaction is impossible. They dismiss moral and spiritual compatibility and responsibility as irrelevant. Increased spouse abuse and child abuse follow in due course.

Stage and screen have long ago scrapped program standards. Mahogany twin beds, long faded from Hollywood films, are replaced by king-size brass supersizers where heaving bosoms and bared buttocks cavort at will. Some filmmakers deliberately downgrade a G-rating (General Audience) by incorporating enough nudity and expletives to guarantee a more lucrative PG (Parental Guidance) designation. The new NC-17 rating now offers producers the opportunity to release their lurid pornography to a general adult audience.

Well-known in the movie industry is the striking influence of secular Jewish entrepreneurs who once had a Judaic inheritance. A generation ago Carl Laemmle controlled Universal; Adolph Zukor built Paramount; Louis B. Mayer headed MGM; Harry and Jack Warner shaped Warner

Brothers; and Harry Cohn ruled Columbia Pictures. Interestingly enough, what defined the character and atmosphere of most of their productions was not their heritage of the Torah but rather the pseudo-values of secular Gentiles. When those false values were no longer popular, nothing was left to fill the moral vacuum. Unfortunately, evangelical Christians lacked the sense of calling and financial backing to enter this field creatively as writers, editors, and producers; rather, their costly role became one of criticism, censorship and withdrawal.

The present predicament of television is not wholly unrelated to these circumstances. Screen content is occasionally outstanding, yet is often trivial, sometimes coarse, even foul, and now and then contemptible. Loosed from the Judeo-Christian ideals and liberated to the humanist view of humanity and the world, modern cinematography deletes belief in humanity's moral guilt and need of grace, and devalues human worth and meaning. Even the national magazine *Newsweek,* (with no penchant for puritanism), has criticized "Trash TV." Other media complain of its lurid sex, bloodcurdling violence, creeping tabloidism, and programs that mirror sleazy prostitution and degraded Satanism. In the TV world the wages of sin is publicity and a lucrative lecture circuit. Even critics who now and then ask whether the media have lost all conscience are prone to craft features so dripping with sexual overtones that readers need to head for the shower. Networks seem to do whatever they can get by with to spark ratings and to increase dollars; some cable TV and videocassettes have topped all known depravity tests. A few newscasters who try to endow the nightly news with a cognitive dimension must cope with gradual viewer desertion to photogenic rubbish. Even public television offerings minimize the Judeo-Christian outlook and increasingly commend mystical alternatives.

Everything seems to be unraveling in regard to shared values. To be sure, the frequent complaint that schoolrooms produce children who can not tell right from wrong overblames public education. Many classrooms do little, however, to clarify the distinction between good and evil or to reinforce lasting moral imperatives. The considerable drop of Sunday School attendees between age twelve through the college years involves mostly students in public schools and secular universities. Their weekday detachment from God and ethical absolutes can lead in due course to weekend disinterest in them. Whatever else our public schools teach, their sex education classes—presumably to safeguard societal pluralism—do not teach marital fidelity. The American Civil Liberties Union (ACLU) has even opposed classroom teaching that identifies monogamous heterosexual marriage as an American value. Many students enrolled on secular campuses are consequently not only adrift from the spiritual heritage of the West but are in fact profoundly ignorant of it. Meanwhile some coeds consider Easter a three-day bikini frolic in Florida.

In classic Greek thought education was heralded as preparation for moral and intellectual leadership. Day in and day out its mentors would have warned oncoming generations against self-indulgence in material things or in physical gratification as the chief end of life. Unless mortals know what—if anything—they are prepared to die for, they do not know what they live for. If, moreover, we are unsure what we live for, we surely have not really begun to live as human beings at all.

The exceptional learning facilities of many U.S. universities and colleges have given them a world class reputation that attracts many foreigners to become part of a student enclave numbering twelve million. American education boasts no ancient or medieval tradition. Its intellectual roots rise from Jerusalem and Athens, Rome, and Geneva; but contemporary learning finds its cognitive context mainly in modern scientific study of the cosmos and almost solely in an experimental approach to knowledge. Secular education legitimates scientific authority over the verdicts of theology and metaphysical morality. Liberal and humanistic learning espouses cultural relativism. Transient secular values now eclipse the Judeo-Christian imperatives.

As religious pluralism grows, the question of truth in religion diffuses accordingly. Are all religions true (in which case whatever we mean by religious "truth" embraces contradiction), or is Jesus Christ the supreme ground and incarnation of truth to which all religious claims are answerable? Many religionists no longer associate the Bible with fixed and final truth. Their underlying prejudices work against respect for Christianity's conceptual significance. When secular learning retains the Bible in the humanities, it "almost inevitably" subjects the Bible, as Allan Bloom says, "to modern 'scientific' analysis." Comparative religion courses welcome the Bible for its supposed contribution to "the very modern, very scientific study of the structure of 'myths'" and relates that contribution to a universal "need for 'the sacred'."[1] Because the biblical books exhibit a literary structure, critics imply they are "not what they claim to be." Take the Bible "at its word, or Word," remarks Bloom, and one will be "accused of scientific incompetence and lack of sophistication."

This snide demotion of the Bible is a hallmark of current humanistic learning. Not long ago a secular newspaper columnist shared with me his mounting anger over universities once founded on Christian tenets

---

1. Allan Bloom, *The Closing of the American Mind* (New York: Simon and Schuster, 1987), 374.

but now so adrift from their beginnings that in spiritual matters they are little if any better than straightforwardly secular schools. Proud alumni send their teenagers back to *alma mater* for an education costing tens of thousands of hard-earned dollars, and their offspring return with little encouragement to live or think as Christians and instead are often morally diminished. "I'm indignant for two reasons," the journalist volunteered. His son had to tolerate two dorm roommates who on many nights shacked up with women students, and in the classrooms his son gained little worth knowing about the Christian faith. "I'm damned angry," he continued, "and many other alumni are tiring of it and are beginning to say so."

Traditionally the intellectually critical centers of society, the universities, increasingly cope even on campus with rape, robbery, assault, and, on occasion, murder. Four in five of these campus crimes are committed by students. A survey of thirty-two campuses showed that one in six women was a victim of rape or attempted rape. Cheating on exams is rampant, and many students routinely plagiarize in preparing papers.

Surely the moral outlook is bleak in the secular city. The spiritual condition is depressing. From the disconcerting addiction to drugs, alcohol, or sex to the lust for dollars and status and from the slippage in personal morality and public ethics to the loss of compass bearings in academe, we clearly face a massive turning time in cultural history. If ever the Christian vanguard inherited an opportune moment for declaring and displaying the vitalities of revealed religion, that opportunity is today and stares us boldly in the face.

Why, we may ask ourselves, should we care very much about public affairs when 50 percent of our fellow Americans will not even vote, when human rights and political self- determination seem to mean less and less even to those who enjoy them, when parents of children in tax-supported public schools will not even participate in P.T.A. meetings? Why should we care that the tide runs swift against us now when to stand against the forces of evil demands incredible courage and often invites ridicule by townspeople as well as caricature by the media, and when even many Christians laugh at the mass media's spoof of them?

We do care, and we have cogent reasons for doing so. Our mandate to champion righteousness and to carry good news to the masses is a divine mandate. Biblical principles best assure the survival of civilization, the stability of society, and a peaceful future, while redemptive grace alone can remove the guilt and penalty of sin and bestow new life.

Nothing less than complete dedication to our mission will do. We must stand firm against evil and reinforce the right. There must be no slippage in the competence with which we focus our priorities. The tragic aspects of the human situation must not be allowed to overwhelm us. We must honor God's Word and seek to apply it in good conscience. We need to show that in social justice and in the matters of private compassion the capacity of our hearts is larger, the reach of our hearts is longer, the beat of our hearts is firmer, and the love of our hearts is deeper. We need a Spirit-enlivened voluntarism that does not wait for law to put to right all social wrongs, one that displays the new motivations of a new life that grace alone engenders.

We are participants in a continuing relay of faith—a passing of the torch that reaches back to Abraham and Moses and that accelerated on resurrection morning and at Pentecost—a divinely sponsored competition that toppled ancient paganism and blazoned a Christian beacon in every realm of learning. It fostered philosophers like Augustine and Aquinas, engendered Reformers like Luther and Calvin, nurtured evangelists like Wesley and Whitefield, and stimulated statesmen like Shaftesbury and Wilberforce. This relay is one in which we must keep faith with the early Christians. Unlike the New Testament Christians who were "off and running," we still are too much only "at the ready." Long before we hit full stride, we project leadership conferences to determine to whom we shall pass our flickering torch.

There is no need to glamorize unduly the early churches; the New Testament harbors little sentimentality. Redeemed sinners comprised these churches; many lacked missionary zeal; some lapsed from their faith; and some coveted their neighbors' wives and husbands. On balance these fellowships were probably tortured and persecuted less than have been many twentieth century believers.

While in the main, pioneer apostles shouldered the basic missionary mandate, it was vigorous converts who put the long-entrenched pagan spirit on the defensive, not least of all by their cautious sexual code. Christians' espousal of virginity and their condemnation of infanticide separated the religion of redemption by light years from pagan immorality.

To every person snared in the corrupt culture of the day, the Christian movement offered dynamic moral and spiritual rebirth. "The moment of conversion" on which Christianity insisted touched reality and truth more deeply, observes Ramsay MacMullen, than did the many competing and conflicting notions of the divine.[2] The pagan world had neither missionaries nor a Great Commission. Christian believers embraced a hope so convincing and sure that they opted for martyrdom

---

2.  See Ramsay MacMullen, *Pagans and Christians* (New York: Knopf, 1987).

rather than to renounce their faith. To pagan cults obscure about the afterlife, Christianity exhibited no greater miracle than the conviction of willing martyrs who both lived and died by their faith, and who ever stood at the alter ready to exchange this life for eternity with Christ. The hostile pagan powers, as MacMullen says, sought to stamp out Christianity "from the top down . . . taking . . . for granted that only the church's leaders counted."[3] What pagan authorities overlooked is that the martyr-spirit of Stephen represented not primarily the heartbeat of a professional priesthood but the devout devotion of a convinced laity. Our American picture of prosperity theology tends often to view martyrdom—real or symbolic—as sheer folly. To be a Christian leader once meant to share a faith worth both dying with and dying for.

If we profess to be leaders, moreover, we need to preserve the basic building blocks of Christian living. Society's growing separation from the Christian heritage diminishes interest in spirituality. By churchgoers spirituality is viewed mainly as a matter of corralling the flesh. Actually, human nature is not an obstacle to spirituality; rather what we do to and with it, that is the problem. "Put to death . . . immorality, impurity, lust, evil desires, and greed" the apostle Paul commanded (Col. 3:5). A generation that finds martyrdom repulsive will hardly find this exhortation tenable, let alone viable. We are, as the Greek word meaning *mortify* suggests, to become morticians. We are to go into the undertaking business. Although the old life's death may be a lingering one, its final demise is sure. Pastors routinely preside at funeral services for members of their congregations; but they also conduct an even more private funeral, the burial of an old nature that each of us—the clergy included—must daily nail to a cross and crucify. It is not enough for us to deride eight or ten spiritual renegades, including a few televangelists. What about the lordship of Christ in our own daily lives as Christian leaders? "For me to live is Christ," said Paul (Phil. 1:21). If sin and Satan are victorious in our lives, then Christ is hardly "our life." Are we daily becoming more like Jesus? Jesus spent whole nights in prayer; we struggle to spend ten minutes and blame our prayerlessness on the telephone.

If we have trouble finding a half hour for prayer, we have no less trouble finding a half hour for social concerns. All too many evangelicals have invoked separation of church and state to escape involvement in public affairs. Such withdrawal has allowed atheists and non-Christians generally to shape the political arena in a way that sidelines traditional values. In time more and more evangelicals have come to share the

---

3. MacMullen, 129.

emphasis I stated in *The Uneasy Conscience of Modern Fundamentalism* (written in 1947) that Christians must engage aggressively in social concerns. However slowly, the mood is moving beyond one-issue protests to culture-wide concerns that represent a comprehensive spectrum of moral and social issues.

Evangelicals can surely be expected to cast their lot against both pagan assaults on the monogamous family and the ready secular support of abortion. Additionally, we must display joyous nuclear families that manifest life as the treasured gift of a providential God. Christians will surely challenge social vices like pornography and sexual deviance. They need also to personify a community that, while confronting such problems, also extends toward victims a program of compassionate concern and help. Evangelical Christians will predictably deplore a sexually permissive AIDS-prone generation and a pernicious drug culture. But we need also to inspire and motivate a partnership of young people with God that encourages walking daily in virginity and monogamous marriage as elements of a disciplined sex life.

Should not America's evangelical Christians not also want to say and do something about the fortunes and misfortunes of the capital of the United States? Is it not a rebuke to the think tanks, commissions, domestic and federal agencies functioning in the District of Columbia that Washington has now become America's murder capital, where homicides exceed one a day and number seven times the national average? More government spending is clearly not the solution. On balance the District spends more for police protection, more for public education, more for health care, more to develop housing, and much more for public welfare than does any American state or big city. Washington has the nation's worst school dropout rate, the worst infant mortality rate, the worst death rate, the worst poverty statistics, and perhaps the worst government, although its payroll far exceeds the average of all our states and cities.

Long before they become teenagers, children begin to drift into Washington's social service ministries and into the juvenile justice system. In single-parent households the poverty rate is three times that of two-parent families. In 1987, 60 percent of Washington-born babies had unwed mothers, almost one in seven of whom were teenagers. The mortality rate among their low birth weight babies is double that among those of older mothers.

Simply throwing more public money at these problems guarantees nothing but a higher budget deficit. Government social policy seldom remedies family problems and often actually perpetuates family disruptive conditions. President Allan C. Carlson of The Rockford Institute writes that "the assorted crises that mark the history of our domestic policy debates—the poverty crisis, the ageism crisis, the teen pregnancy crisis, the overpopulation crisis, the juvenile delinquency crisis, the eugenics crisis, the child abuse crisis, the youth suicide crisis—have all become, intentionally or unintentionally, vehicles to expand the power of the state at the expense of the autonomy of its old adversary, the family."[4] We need instead to confront government policies that subtly evaporate the relevance of Judeo-Christian ethical imperatives and to embrace marriage, fidelity, and children as components of a moral life.

Despite the cooperative interdenominational engagement of practically all churches in the District of Columbia in evangelistic crusades, the growing specter of drugs, prostitution, robbery, and murder continues to menace the city. Must not evangelicals build on improved race relations to pursue greater cooperation in evangelism, in promotion of work opportunities, and in access to affordable housing?

Important as housing and food are, however, they are not the deepest needs of the lonely psyche. In our large cities traditional black-culture values are swiftly eroding; alcohol and other drugs no doubt contribute to this sorry condition. The problem of the homeless, moreover, is not unrelated to the breakup of the family. We need long-range perspectives; we must match our frustration over the inglorious past and present by dauntless hope for the future and by unflagging witness.

The last thing the world should expect of Christians is that they eagerly champion the *status quo* instead of echoing God's condemnation of personal iniquity and social injustice. Whatever a Christian's position may be on nuclear armament, an authentic Christian must stand fundamentally on the side of peace, even if nations' inventory nuclear missiles like so many toy soldiers. Mankind has suffered so much from past wars and would self-evidently suffer immeasurably from yet another that we must earnestly strive to avoid any further such conflict; among other things we must welcome every balanced and verifiable reduction of military forces and weapons. Christians are also aware that human stewardship includes preserving our planetary space station called Earth; dominion aspects of our creation in God's image do not disregard our duty to preserve natural resources. That does not automatically mean, however, that no legitimacy exists in present history for nuclear armament. What it does mean is that the reasons for nuclear armament must be rationally compelling and not just a concession to saber rattling.

---

4. Allan Carlson, *Family Questions: Reflections on the American Social Crisis* (New Brunswick: Translation Books, 1988), 273.

So, too, compelling considerations are similarly basic to economic concerns. Capitalism is less than ideal economics when it lacks ecological responsibility and sensitivity for consumers, for labor, or for the jobless and the impoverished. In our fragile environment insensitivity to human need encourages indiscreet flirtation with a bureaucratically controlled welfare state. Such possibilities do not automatically legitimate Marxist analysis and socialist economics. Socialist efforts to improve the state of the masses by redistributing wealth displayed little grasp of economics or of the complexity of the human condition; more and more one time champions of socialism now decry it as an abject failure. No Christian ought, however, to confuse the superiority of free enterprise as an economic system with the economics of the kingdom of God.

In social ethics, despite all historical achievements of mankind, the Christian ought not conceal the reality of God's abiding transcendent claims. At the same time Christians ought not distance themselves in reaction to social structures which, if properly respected, would commendably serve human society and culture. The current breakdown of monogamy, for example, offers no basis for espousing alternative family patterns.

Disconcerting social conditions sometimes are so routinely accepted as elements of the environment that we assume their permanence. Despite the modernist social gospel and later humanist professions of concern for human dignity, multitudes of needy fellow Americans earlier this century slipped through the net of humane compassion and concern. One thinks, for example, of homeless people who sleep on public sidewalks and in winter huddle over city steam grates to snatch a bit of warmth.

Far more numerous are the more than half a million Americans who languish behind prison walls and whom we deliberately put out of mind like a plague, despite Jesus' exhortation to be solicitous toward them. Neglect of the imprisoned would still largely be the situation overall in America today but for one providential event. Prison Fellowship sprang from a concern for convicts by Charles Colson, the Watergate offender who, when he found Christ, stimulated widespread compassion for the 600,000 occupants of prisons whose numbers are daily expanding despite a lack of enough cells to contain them. Colson has made the case that a budget-breaking erection of more and more prisons costing billions of dollars is no adequate answer to the problem of crime. Prison Fellowship's ministry of in-prison seminars that builds personal faith, spiritual dedication, and Christian life has in less than a decade spread to thirty-four countries. Justice Fellowship, Prison Fellowship's judicial arm, emphasizes not only punishment for offenders and restitution by offenders but also vindication and compensation for victims, and reconciliation as well as furlough programs for non violent offenders.

Early Christianity did not overlook the needs of any in the overall spectrum of society. It addressed good news to everyone. Europe's first two converts were a businesswoman and a jailer. Christianity is not a message peculiar to the jet-set, not a religion only of middle-class ambitions or of lower-class aspirations. Perhaps our voices are unprophetic because our self-esteem is too great to nurture compassion or to pursue justice for a generation whose deepest need is the transforming touch of Christ together with a heart for God's moral law. Had we suffered in the Gulag with Solzhenitsyn, or languished in an American penitentiary with Colson, our words might be more authentic and our outreach less restricted.

Still another forefront concern is the spiritual life of today's university students and seminarians; they are, after all, tomorrow's leaders in the making. What happens, we may ask, to the two in five college entrants who never complete their campus studies? In the case of myriads who stay the course, we have already noted the stifling effect of secular education upon cognitive commitments and spiritual interests. We must not think that evangelical scholars are necessarily exempt from costly erosion and attrition, even those brought up in our churches and graduated from our schools. Too many gifted young men and women capitulate uncritically in graduate school to novel winds of doctrine. On both divinity school and university campuses I have found on occasion that the deepest hostility to evangelical faith is voiced by supposedly evangelical participants who now seem determined to detach themselves from their spiritual heritage.

Although the late 1980s and the early 1960s are a generation apart, much the same spirit of doubt now as then hangs over Harvard and many other Ivy League campuses. University studies expose students to new worlds of new ideas, but furnish no criteria for identifying truth. Only outside the classroom, if at all, many now belatedly discover that the pall of campus doubt does not destroy the truthfulness of truth.

If colleges launched on Christian principles could be re-invigorated by a compelling spiritual revival, if trustees who share the founding vision were elected to boards of governors, if biblical doctrine were dynamically recovered in its decisive importance for the current crisis of truth and right, if the religious renewal that took place under the presidential leadership of Timothy Dwight at Yale might again in our day overtake professedly evangelical campuses, the faith-affirming institutions could help shape a remarkable new era of greatness. Were evangelical educators presently to fulfill what once-Christian universities like the early Brown, Chicago, Harvard, Columbia, Princeton, Duke, Vanderbilt, Yale, and others long ago promised, they could tap the now-rising flow of alumni discontent over the conceptual plight of non-Christian campuses.

In a time when the common level of life is shamefully debased, Christian theists have an opportunity to uphold the standards of civilization, to replenish spent ethical resources, to provide reserves of spiritual vigor, and to reaffirm the morality that the Bible teaches.

The evangelical witness in America needs a quantum leap forward: in devotion to God and to prayer, in Christian living in the home and in society, in dedication to public justice, in evangelistic energy, and in compassionate outreach. Our problem is not the lack of available power but our lack of resolve.

Our weak batteries can be recharged by a jump cable that reconnects believers to the divine current held in store for us by our supernatural Creator, Preserver, and Redeemer. We rely too much on our own finite power and world energy; we are dazzled by technology more than by theology and morality. To gain God's empowerment for mission we must first acknowledge our vulnerabilities and our spiritual immaturity. Beyond our lifetime, if Christ tarries, others will run the relay and carry the torch. For us, in the rocky terrain of present-day cultural conflict, the time is now, and the race is now.

# The Crisis of Authority

*No single moral authority has been recognized by the American academic elite since the late 1930s. This lack of consensus has gradually gained momentum until serious discussion of ethical dilemmas is now often confused and fragmented. The gradual permeation of society by relativistic naturalistic beliefs has eaten away at a stable cognitive basis for moral convictions.*

The defiant head winds of human autonomy are sweeping over much of contemporary life in a dispute over authority unmatched by earlier generations in scope and intensity. On virtually every front authority now faces scornful challenges, not least of all in the arena of religion.

The rejection of religious authority is specially significant because, as Thomas Molnar remarks, "religious (divine) authority is the prototype of all authority."[1] Not all world religions acknowledge a personal God; but all, nonetheless, claim divine origin and authority.

Conventionally the West has considered the God of the Bible as the ultimate authority over human life and has at the same time viewed Him as the source and guarantor of human freedom.

Today's reigning naturalism, however, rejects both these assumptions. The contemporary humanist Paul Kurtz urged us to "weed out permanently the idea of God."[2] Uncompromisingly hostile to the supernatural,

---

1. Thomas Molnar, *Authority and Its Enemies*, (New Rochelle, NY: Arlington House, Publishers, 1976), 29.
2. Paul Kurtz, *The Fullness of Life* (New York: Horizon Press, 1974), 16.

secular humanism—now often depicted as the "covert metaphysics" of modern liberal learning—disavows a transcendent deity as promotive of an arbitrary or despotic authority, and as an intolerable barrier to human freedom.

## The Fate of the West

Upon the outcome of this conflict over deity, authority and autonomy hinges the future of Western civilization. John Locke (1632-1704) and Friedrich Nietzsche (1844-1900) perceived better than many recent philosophers that a distinctive connection prevails between the reality of God and the nature of Western society. Western culture, Locke emphasized, rests on theistic belief, and atheism threatens its very survival. Nietzsche contended that "God is dead" and that this divine expiration renders inevitable a comprehensive transformation of the whole of Western culture. When Alexander Solzhenitsyn more recently blamed the current disintegration of Western civilization on the fact that "men have forgotten God" he disclosed himself—though a Russian—to be a more discerning critic than many contemporary Anglo-Saxon philosophers.

Rationalism, mysticism, and the Enlightenment all opposed the doctrine of religious authority that derived from Christian orthodoxy. They initially affirmed that, as the structure of reality, the universal law of reason is immanent in humans. Hence, a person was no longer thought of as dependent on a transcendent God and on His objective revelation, or as in need of divine grace. This detachment from the God of the Bible led on to an emphasis on autonomy and then to more radical heteronomy.

Modern liberal thought connects the future of the West not with a preservation of theistic priorities but rather with the genius of technological science. Some social critics, nonetheless, warn that the loss of God shapes a loss of morality as well. They find little comfort in a resurgent amoral scientism. The role of God in western life, they emphasize, has crucial implications for ethics and for philosophy no less than for religion. If God is eclipsed, the inherited conception of authority is affected at every level. A comprehensive redefinition of the nature and content of human duties is unavoidable. The Swiss jurist Peter Saladin warns that the substitution of modern philosophical supports for the earlier theistic supports deprives the conception of human rights of credible foundations: The philosophical bases . . . underlying the idea of human rights—the philosophical systems of the Enlightenment, of liberalism, or utilitarianism—are now crumbling and no longer credible. We can no longer cling to the anthropological optimism on which these systems rest without sacrificing our intellectual and moral honesty.[3]

## The Surge to Autonomy

Along with a rejection of God as the Lord of life, the secular view of autonomy is disclosed in a rejection also of all lesser external authorities. Radical naturalism questions human dependence upon society as well as upon deity and relies on self-assertiveness. Each human is his or her own "lord." Each person's beliefs, ideals, and decisions are ultimately definitive; no outside referent is decisive for individual meaning. As Langdon Gilkey already put it years ago, "Autonomy and coming of age in a secular context . . . mean moving from the tutelage of the external authority of some 'other,' some authority or Lord, to self-direction . . . Whether it be a royal sovereign, an authoritative state, a traditional or sacrosanct law or code, an ecclesiastical magisterium, God, *or a* human savior, any such external, superior authority or Lord over life has seemed to modern secular views of autonomy to represent a relapse into immaturity and a loss of autonomy."[4]

Earlier generations had questioned particular authorities, not infrequently with good reason, in view of rival claims to authority and its frequent abuse or misuse. Hitler's extermination of 6 million Jews, Stalin's murder of 15 million Russians, and Mao's responsibility for the death of 30 million Chinese placed a bold-face question mark over the exercise of totalitarian power. The wild winds of defiance swept chaotically over the several realms of parental, academic, political, and religious authority as the rebellion of the sixties spread into a general questioning of the propriety and legitimacy of authority.

During the past generation the atheistic and humanistic loss of faith in God has accelerated this rebellion and issued in an erosion of confidence in any and all transcendent authority. The eclipse of the sovereign God of the Bible has left a vacuum of authority into which contemporaries readily thrust ideological alternatives and personal preferences.

Radical secular humanism questions not simply the legitimacy of particular authorities. Its exiling of God and relegation of deity to cultural irrelevance accommodates its disputing of all transcendent authority and a hatred for external authority as such. Heinz Zahrnt depicts humanism's destruction of the metaphysical foundations of "science, politics, society,

---

3. "Christianity and Human Rights—A Jurist's Reflections," in Lorenz, ed., *How Christian are Human Rights*, 29.
4. Langdon Gilkey, *Naming the Whirlwind: The Renewal of God-Language* (Indianapolis and New York: The Bobbs-Merrill Company, 1969), 155f.

economics, justice, art and morality" as "the greatest and most extensive process of secularization which has ever taken place in . . . the whole history of religion.[5] Common to contemporary naturalism is a repudiation of all eternal, transcendent, objective, and external authority, and the parallel disavowal of divine absolutes, revealed truths, scriptural imperatives and fixed principles. The rejection of authority *per se*—and especially of religious authority—is now a hallmark of our age. Paul Tillich observed that "when we hear of 'authority' today, we tend to think of it in terms of a tyrant, be it a father, a king, a dictator, or even a teacher."[6]

Creative individuality replaces external authority: every person is lord in respect to history and the cosmos. Whatever patterns we presume to discern in nature and in the course of human events are ultimately human projections not externally present in space-time processes. The entire speculative structure of radical secular humanism rests on the affirmation of comprehensive human autonomy.

The flip-side of this humanistic outlook is a vanishing sense of human dependence not only upon God, or upon God and society, but even upon the universe as an externally given theater of human action. Whatever gods we sponsor or suffer are mere projections from or manifestations of nature in some form or other, and they exist solely by human tolerance. The gods have subjective significance only; they are irrelevant to the cosmos and to the nations. The gods are to be explained by nature and history, not nature and history by transcendent deity.

## Postulating an Internal Authority

With the recent deflation of external authority, atheistic scholars in the West focus instead on internal authority. This contrasts with the reliance of totalitarian powers on the state as the sovereign stipulator of human rights, duties, and morality. Given the erosion of religious tradition and the assault on transcendent sovereignty, they supplement their renunciation of omnipotent authority by reconceptions that provide the self with at least some anchorage amid the shifting social tides and the changing subjective consciousness of authority.

Atheistic existentialism stresses the importance of personal decision for creatively defining one's own selfhood and affirming values on which one would confer historical and cultural standing. Yet the search

---

5. Heinz Zahrnt, *The Question of God: Protestant Theology in the Twentieth Century*, (tr. by R. A. Wilson) (New York: Harcourt Brace & World, 1969), 126ff.
6. *A History of Christian Thought*, ed. by Carl F. Braaten (London:SCM Press Ltd., 1968), 137.

for an authority that will stand the scrutiny of society and that may not die with our parents or change with the culture seems out of reach.

Leonard Krieger thinks we live amid the birth of a "(new) stage in the history of the idea of authority": its arena would be the individual self and the self's internal psychic relations. It would involve the self's assertion of authority "against the repressive power of society."[7] Here external authority seems to be identified only as repressive, and ideal authority seems to be conceived in terms of individual liberty. As Krieger comments, "Even if it is not literally identified with the original idea of authority, the current commitment to a normative psychic hierarchy which should serve to direct the reorganization of society is an indication that the recurrent pattern of a pure, uncoercive authority remains viable."[8]

What the term "normative" here any longer means and with what basis of confidence one can hope to reorganize society by private volition, when all other beleaguered selves share similar prerogatives, is obscure. The notion of inner authority appears instead to gloss an enthronement of autonomy.

## The Edge of the Abyss

In the context of the authority crisis some major shifts have occurred in the recent past in respect to religion and ethics. For one thing, some influential writers now openly acknowledge that Western culture has taken a portentous moral downturn that renders its future highly insecure. Alasdair MacIntyre is not content simply to declare that "the language—and therefore to some large degree the practice—of morality today is in the state of grave disorder."[9] He warns us that, limited though the similarities are between European and North American culture today and "the epoch in which the Roman Empire declined into the Dark Ages," the similarities, nonetheless, dare not be ignored. Indeed, MacIntyre comments, "The new dark ages . . . are already upon us. . . . The barbarians are not waiting beyond the frontiers (but) have already been governing us for quite some time . . . Our lack of consciousness of this . . . constitutes part of our predicament."[10]

Charles Colson indicates that resurgent paganism has already adversely tipped the balance of Western culture. He considers problem-

7. "Authority," in *Dictionary of the History of Ideas*, Philip P. Wiender, ed.-in-chief (New York: Charles Scribner's Sons, 1973), I, 141-162, 161.
8. *Ibid.*, 162.
9. Alagdair MacIntyre, *After Virtue* (Notre Dame: University of Notre Dame Press, 1981), 238.
10. MacIntyre, 245.

atical, moreover, any confident verdict that the Christian church will emerge phoenix-like from the ashes.[11] The possibility that Western culture has already passed redemption's point is no longer a theme preempted by apocalyptic seers. MacIntyre, for example, indicates the Christian propriety of probing for alternatives to the presently crumbling culture:

> A crucial turning point in that earlier history occurred when men and women of good will turned aside from the task of shoring up the Roman *imperium* and ceased to identify the continuation of civility and moral community with the maintenance of that *imperium*. What they set themselves to achieve instead–often not recognizing fully what they were doing–was the construction of new forms of community within which the moral life could be sustained so that both morality and civility might survive the coming ages of barbarism and darkness.[12]

The French social critic Jacques Ellul has for decades warned against the spirit of lawlessness rampant in the West and has stressed that apart from a recovery of the transcendent revelatory basis of law—that is, its ultimately divine source—no pervasive respect for law can any longer be engendered in modern society.[13] While our present twilight is "not yet midnight," we must understand that neopaganism—a paganism born of defection from Christianity—now shapes influential social institutions and seeks to set an agenda for all of Western society. Secular humanism, which has for a generation distinguished itself from naked naturalism, is gradually losing its humanitarianism—that is, its identification with a widely shared social agenda—and is being increasingly threatened and even overwhelmed by raw and rancid naturalism.[14]

We are now living more than a generation beyond any mere acknowledgment that no universal agreement prevails on the nature of moral imperatives, enfeebling as even that is for a stable society. The traditional bastions of authority—family, school, church, and state—are challenged by the younger generation to a degree that the older generation finds not only disconcerting but at times shocking. No single moral authority has been recognized by the American academic elite since the late 1930s. This lack of consensus has gradually gained momentum until serious discussion of ethical dilemmas is now often confused and fragmented. The gradual permeation of society by relativistic naturalistic beliefs has eaten away at a stable cognitive basis for moral convictions.

---

11. Charles Colson, *Against the Night: Living in the New Dark Ages* (Ann Arbor, Mich.: Servant Publications, 1989).
12. MacIntyre, 244.
13. Jacques Ellul, *The Theological Foundation of Law* (Garden City, NY: Doubleday, 1960).
14. *Twilight of a Great Civilization* (Westchester, Ill.: Crossway Books, 1988), 23ff.

In E. M. Adams' words: "The structure of authority is crumbling in our society not so much because of injustice and repression as because of the erosion of its intellectual foundations. The philosophical assumptions on which authority as such, not just the authority of our existing institutions, is founded are being rapidly rejected in our culture. . . ."[15]Adams affirms that "nothing less than civilization itself is at stake" in the elaboration of a compelling alternative to the culturally catastrophic naturalistic erosion of moral authority: . . . The modern naturalistic mind is seriously deranged by false philosophical assumptions about human epistemic power. . . . The only solution is through cultural therapy that exposes and corrects these errors.[16]

## Is Secularization Reversible?

The deterioration of Western culture is highlighting questions over whether the secularization of society is inevitable, desirable, calamitous, or avoidable. Much of this debate, to be sure, turns on differing nuances in the term "secularization", a debate here beyond our purview.

An attack on the prevalent notion that a pervasively secular society is inescapable and even normative comes not only from the side of traditional Catholic and evangelical orthodox scholars, but from that of liberation theologians also. The latter promote liberation from oppression not by traditional Christian regeneration or renewal but by revolutionary social liberation, generously identified with socialism. Among others, the German theologian Jürgen Moltmann, Latin American theologian Gustavo Gutierrez, and American scholar Frederick Herzog have championed political liberation, presumably in the service of biblical representations of Jesus Christ as Liberator.

The tendency of these modern theologians to hold critical views of Scripture deprives them of any consistent epistemological basis for anchoring their representations firmly in Scripture. As Dennis M. Campbell suggests,[17] those who reject Scripture as a uniquely authoritative document cannot confidently appeal to its authority to gain biblical anchorage for their own views. Such use of Scripture is merely arbitrary. Those who deny the Bible as the authoritative Word of God have no right to turn later to claim biblical warrant for their own political or economic agendas. Beyond that, questions arise whether a one-sidedly

---

15. "The Philosophical Grounds of the Present Crisis of Authority," in *Authority: A Philosophical Analysis*, ed. R. Baine Harris (University, Alabama: The University of Alabama press, 1976), 3f.
16. *Ibid.*, 24.
17. Dennis M. Campbell, *Authority and the Renewal of Theology* (Philadelphia: United Church Press, 1976), 94.

societal location of scriptural concerns is justifiable. Even if so, can we legitimately portray the Hebrew exodus from Egypt in terms of political revolution?

The sociologist Peter Berger also disputes the finality of "modern consciousness." Berger concludes that the modern West spurns a religious worldview, but insists that modern consciousness reflects but one era in the long span of history and need not be considered infallible and irreversible.[18]

## Religion and Morality

The modern effort to segregate morality from religion betrays an unfamiliarity with history. It reflects a deplorable misrepresentation whenever it obscures the long dominant role of Judeo-Christian religion in Western culture. James M. Gustafson rightly stresses that

> In the Western religions . . . religion and morality are joined together, intertwined, commingled, indeed in some instances and respects even unified.[19]

In discussing the religious authority-crisis it is therefore not provincial to concentrate especially on the Judeo-Christian heritage as most significant for the West. All world religions today are involved in a clash with modernity, except for Muslim fundamentalism which has yet to pass through the scientific revolution. Even Christianity, sometimes depicted in the Orient as a Western religion, is at root no less Asian than many other living world religions. It has, nonetheless, from the outset claimed to be a universal religion, indeed, *the* universal religion. It is the first religion with a world presence. Biblical theism traces back its beginnings to the very origins of humanity, and it offers a distinctive explanation of the rise of nonbiblical religions.

The assault on biblical theism bears also on all the great living faiths in notable ways. The scientific learning for which prestigious Western universities attract young scholars from around the world tends at the same time to inoculate these young leaders of the future with naturalistic theory. When they return home from America, they take with them the seeds of academic religious doubt. The naturalistic assault on miracle and on the supernatural breeds skepticism, moreover, not only over Christian creedal commitments that Western missionaries and evangelists carry overseas, but stirs waves of doubt also over the indigenous ancient

18. Peter Berger, *The Heretical Imperative: Contemporary Possibilities of Religious Affirmation* (Garden City, NY: Anchor Press, 1979).
19. "Religion and Morality from the Perspective of Theology," *Religion and Morality*, ed. Gene Outka and John F. Reeder, Jr. (Garden City, Anchor, 1973), 129.

cultural traditions abroad. A consequence of Western humanistic learning is that all supernaturalistic authority is looked at critically and skeptically.

To be sure, extensive philosophical differences separate biblical theism and rival religious worldviews. The biblical doctrine of divine authority is part and parcel of a distinctive view of God, of humanity and the world, and of relationships in which they stand—it cannot be grafted onto just any view of divinity. The same may be said, of course, for other world religions. A broad coherence exists between each religious view of the transcendent order and its elaboration of divine morality and authority. The role of rational consistency as a test of truth is therefore ignored at great risk.

Biblical theism insistently holds to personality in the Godhead. It emphasizes just as insistently that God as transcendent Creator is ontologically Other, epistemologically Other, and ethically Other than humans and the cosmos. God is the holy, sovereign Ground of truth and the Source of moral law. He reveals himself intelligibly and objectively. Although humanity in certain respects bears the divine image, it has voluntarily fallen into spiritual rebellion, is confronted by divine revelation and proffered merciful redemption. The God of the Bible personally defines the good and the right. He particularizes His will for all mankind and for the Hebrews as a covenant people. God is transcendently righteous; even the best efforts of a penitent spiritual rebel cannot earn a salvation that God graciously provides in the incarnate redeemer Jesus Christ.

Brahmanism and Buddhism dwarf this dramatic contrast of a transcendent creator-God with the nature of people and the world. The Brahma and the Buddha are comprehensive totalities of which creaturely life is a finite partial appearance. At stake are divergent views of being, revelation, origins, redemption, and not least of all, of authority. If God is perceived as *more* than we are, and not as *Other*, the gulf narrows between God and His creatures both as created and as fallen. The one view is quasi-pantheistic; it accommodates no severe view of sin and judgment. The other is theistic; it holds created selves eternally responsible for their deeds in this life and accommodates neither a transmigration or reincarnation of souls nor an eclipse of the soul by Nirvana. The Christian religion and the nonbiblical religions are therefore engaged in a doctrinal standoff that involves each side in a reciprocal invitation to conversion.

## The Quest for Commonality

The rise a century ago of the *Religionsgeschichte* School moderated religious differences on the assumption of pervasive divine immanence in all reality and history. It held that all religions are doctrinal elaborations of a commonly shared essence. The notion that a worthy God must under any and all circumstances be identically related to all human beings seemed compatible with modernity's rising democratic spirit.

For all its temporary appeal, however, the price of this interreligious bartering was intolerably high. It downgraded the importance of the particular religions to which the masses of mankind devoted themselves and concentrated instead on a speculative "religion in general" that was more or less an evolutionary abstraction. Beyond that, it glossed the question of objective truth in religion. As C.S. Lewis commented, it seemed to level to one and the same category the Christian view that God is present in a special way in Jesus, the Nazi view that God is present in a special way in the German race, and the Hindu view that God is specially present "in the thigh-bone of a dead English Tomme."[20] Inevitably it vacated the authority that adherents rested on special religious grounds rather than solely on universal considerations.

Particular religions continue to mediate authority through their respective traditions and institutions—synagogue, church, mosque, temple, and so on. Even within mainline religious traditions—Jewish, Christian (Catholic and Protestant), Muslim, and others—there are divergent episcopal authorities and priesthoods, rival doctrines, and competing seminaries. American Catholicism is at odds with papal authority in respect to contraception and priestly celibacy. American Protestantism, in the aftermath of a call for ecumenical union, is divided into larger bodies and into even more diverse groups than it was earlier in this century.

Meanwhile antisupernaturalistic metaphysicians tend more and more to proclaim the public irrelevance of religion and of religious authority. Some spokesmen even encourage the abolition of religion, and welcome a deployment of all authority from God to humanity; they think religious authority survives at the expense of scientific enlightenment.

## Religion's Elusive 'Essence'

In the aftermath of modernity's intellectual achievement that focuses on religion in general rather than on particular religions, an ironic embarrassment has overtaken the academic arena. Scholars know what

---

20. C. S. Lewis, "Religion Without Dogma," in *God in the Dock: Essays on Theology and Ethics* (Grand Rapids: Eerdmans, 1970), 140.

comprises particular religions (even though revisionary critics often imaginatively reconceptualize them), but they are increasingly baffled by the question of what *religion* is. Every attempt to isolate a so-called "essence" of religion soon runs into trouble.

Is religion's essence "belief in God"? Then what of Confucianism, or some schools of Buddhism, or modern religious humanism, or atheistic communism—all of which some call religions? Is its essence social protest? Mystical religions tend to be socially passive. Is it liturgy? Some religions consider this an escape from the real world. Is the essence of religion an indispensable religious experience (for example, the new birth)? Some religions emphasize not inner experience but sacramental grace. Still others insist that correct doctrine is the essence of religion. For some people, Satanism is a religion, including the ritual murder of human victims. Peyote Indians locate the heart of their religion in a ritual that involves drug indulgence. To make matters worse, *Webster's Unabridged Dictionary* lists among proper uses of the term religion the popular saying "Cleanliness was her religion."

Religion, it seems, can be almost anything and everything. We know what particular religions are—that is, we can give examples—but we seem to be unsure what religion is—that is, to come up with a serviceable definition of "religion-in-general."

For good reason! Religion-in-general exists in the mind of speculative theorists devoted to certain views of intensive divine immanence or of evolutionary development. Does it exist externally in human life and experience? Anthropologists have happened upon particular and, indeed, sometimes very peculiar religions, but none has as yet located "religion-in-general."

## Religion and Truth-Claims

So we cannot after all escape the question of particular religions and their truth claims. That may be disturbing news to a generation that assumed that all religions are "living on borrowed time" and that no generation can any longer afford to "fall back" on God as an answer for the authority-crisis because science has presumably "demystified" reality. It is bad news especially for those frontier writers on religion and authority whose stance encouraged William Robert Miller to apply to his survey the title *Goodbye, Jehovah*.[21]

At the beginning of our century adversaries of Christianity—or of supernaturalism in any form—seriously wrestled the questions of the

---

21. William Robert Miller, *Goodbye, Jehovah. A Survey of New Directions in Christianity* (New York: Walker and Company, 1969).

truth or untruth of Christian creedal commitments and of Christianity's claim to religious finality. Logical positivism took a different path: That God exists is untrue and meaningless, it held, because the premise is empirically unverifiable. Radical secularism went still further, holding that objective truth and philosophical finality are fictions. No ethical imperatives are eternal and unrevisable, no theological affirmations escape culture conditionedness. Any and all presumption of transcendent divine authority, of unrevisable truths and changeless moral commandments, is dismissed as pretentious and unpalatable.

Humanists played a shell game with the notion of religious truth, by concentrating on religion in general. Religion, they said, lies if it presumes to tell us how reality is objectively constituted; but it is functionally "true" if it delivers us from internal tension and discord and provides an integrated perspective for a meaningful life. Even some theological modernists, who abandoned the miraculous and clung to a fragmented supernaturalism, took this tack.

"Religious truth is utterly crucial; it is the paramount and inescapable issue, before which all other religious matters, however mighty, must bow." So wrote Wilfred Cantwell Smith.[22] Curiously he then proceeded to deny that Christianity is a system of true statements about reality, affirming that while it can become "true" as an inner personal quality, even such internal experiential "truth" might vary from time to time.

Today we have come full circle. It is crystal clear that deities whose being depends upon human craftsmanship or internal decision can only extend the authority crisis. Nor will a mere resuscitation of the notion of divinity assure a significant view of divine authority. The moral counsel and consolation that ancients derived from the polytheistic gods—none of which was all-knowing or all powerful—was, as E. D. Watt emphasizes, not in the nature of *command*.[23] "A creator . . . of all that exists" offers by contrast the highest reason for executive authority. Against the current tendency to locate authority within the individual, Watt protests that "No one can be an authority to himself, or an authority over himself. The sphere of authority is public, not private, social, not individual."[24]

Hence, when Hobbs held that authority can originate only in the consent of the governed,[25] he dissolved the highest justification for author-

---

22. Wilfred Cantwell Smith, *Questions of Religious Truth* (New York: Charles Scribner's Sons, 1976), 67.
23. E. D. Watt, *Authority* (New York: St. Martin's Press, 1982), 65.
24. *Ibid.*, 105.
25. *Leviathan.*

ity. As Richard T. De George avers, however, "We cannot set limits on God's authority. He does not receive his authority from us"[26]

In the ancient world, Hebrew belief in a sovereign personal Creator, who discloses His word and will intelligibly and who universally judges the nations, lifted Yahweh's covenant people far above the polytheistic civilizations of the past. Obedience to God's moral will distinguished ancient Israel from pagan Hittite, Egyptian, Babylonian, Canaanite, and Philistine cultures. Set off from the civilizations of the age, as Eric Voegelin comments, Israel comprised "a new society," one "that began its existence with a radical leap in being." Israel's history reversed the postulations of social evolution whereby "society is supposed to start with primitive myths and advance gradually." By contrast, Israel began "where a respectable society has difficulties even ending."[27]

The recent modern view that, if He exists, God is answerable to ethical norms approved by an evolved and experience-enlightened humanity has led instead "to the ethical collapse of contemporary civilization and to moral futility."[28]

The whittling down of authoritative divine commandment as a prime feature of biblical ethics resulted in costly speculative attempts to justify Christian ethics on other grounds, most notably compatibility with the moral nature of humans. These efforts to make the scriptural ethic compelling on the basis of philosophical appeals succeeded only in eroding the force of the Judeo-Christian ethic. The dilution of authority into human opinion—however dignified—in terms of intuition, mysticism, empirical evidence, philosophical reasoning, or whatever—is an inevitable consequence of human rebellion against an externally given Word of God.

Not for nothing has G. E. M. Anscombe insisted that obligation statements make sense only in a divine law conception of ethics. He stressed that objective morality is indispensably rooted in the presuppositions of biblical theism.[29] The tradition of divine command morality, long obscured in Western ethical discussion, has received new visibility in Janine Marie Idziak's studies.[30]

---

26. Richard T. DeGeorge, *The Nature and Limits of Authority* (Lawrence, Kansas: University Press of Kansas, 1985), 224.
27. Eric Voegelin, *Israel and Revelation* (Baton Rouge: Louisiana State University Press, 1956), 113, 315f.
28. Carl F. H. Henry, *Christian Countermove in a Decadent Culture* (Portland: Multnomah Press, 1986), 14.
29. G. E. M. Anscombe, "Modern Moral Philosophy," in *Philosophy* 33 (January, 1958), 1-19.
30. Janine Marie Idziak, *Divine Command Morality: Historical and Contemporary Readings* (New York: The Edwin Mellen Press, 1979).

The main source of the conception of religious authority in the Western world has been the Bible. Its consistent emphasis is that all legitimate authority rests on religious authority and that as divine Creator and Preserver and Judge of all, the self-revealing God has ultimate authority.

How to make the will of God compelling so that it is reflected in the shared values of modern society is the great challenge of our age. Revealed religion has character-transforming dynamic to achieve that end, but it is not coercive. Rather, it confronts mankind with an inescapable decision: "Choose you this day whom you will serve" (Josh. 24:15). The alternatives, now as in the past, are laden with destiny. On the one hand lies divine blessing; on the other, divine judgment. People may devastate the earth and other people and even oneself, but a person cannot demolish the Ten Commandments or the God whose nature and will the Decalogue mirrors.

Between the apostolic perspective on life looms a day and night difference. Peter and his coworkers said: "We *must* obey God rather than men" (Acts 5:29, RSV). The apostle Paul put the heart of the matter pointedly and succinctly: "There is no authority except from God" (Rom. 13:1, RSV). In these convictions, as Rex Martin notes, the Christian apostles invested their lives and fortunes: "The martyrdom of Peter and Paul at the hands of the Roman state indicates the clear perception they had of the priority of `authorities' and of the subordination of the authority of the state to the divine will."[31]

The contemporary crisis of authority is not likely to be stabilized or superseded unless a generation arises that is, with the apostles, ready to invest its soul, and not merely its semantics, in the transcendent right and good.

---

31. "Justification of Political Authority", in *Authority: A Philosophical Analysis*, R. Baine Harris, ed., 64.

# Knowledge, Power, and Morality: A Congressman's Day-to-Day Concerns

*Does it make a difference that the Christian is to live in the world as leaven, light, and salt? Will it do to be morally aware under the steeple and to be morally ambiguous under the Capitol dome?*

Between tardy arrivals at Washington National Airport and an often delayed return home a week later, a congressman's daily agenda is swamped by time-consuming concerns. So-called escape to the home district offers little relief; there local constituency problems simply channel into a resumption and expansion of congressional duties in Washington. Grateful that air travel and Amtrak have replaced horseback, legislators shuttle between national and district functions, aware that this routine keeps them at least minimally in touch with family and also builds voter support for Election Day. The constituency that elected him by a wide margin may consider him a potential wizard with political magic, but without a covert trust in divine governance his vocational limits may quickly undo him. The founding fathers, at least, believed in an overarching divine Providence, so no officeholder need imagine that he alone shapes this nation's fortunes and destiny. The New Englander had a point in the comment, "Never trust a politician who can't spell Deity or who wears a size-12 hat."

A newly elected legislator, someone has suggested, should bring along four books: Machiavelli's *The Prince,* Dale Carnegie's *How to Win Friends and Influence People,* Christopher Matthew's *Hardball, How Politics Is Played—Told By One Who Knows the Game,* and a well-worn Bible, the more worn the better.[1] For almost from day one he is involved in jockeying for political position, power, and permanence. Assigned congressional office space may depend on the luck of the draw, but political clout will turn predictably on committee assignments and the bartering of influence. Common sense maxims for political progress are to remember what's important to one's home district, to know one's colleagues on a first-name basis as quickly as possible, and to catalog potential supporters by memorizing their wants and weaknesses. An instinct for power will turn adversaries into allies by projecting mutually advantageous deals and perhaps by resorting to the ruse of seeking their counsel. Politics, after all, is depicted routinely as "the art of compromise"; the core-question is when and how that art becomes ethically concessive. The motivation for turning foes into friends may be chivalrous or corrupt; capital chemistry readily confuses the two.

Every legislator knows that since Election Day he or she has been designated *the honorable.* Although the term is vague and not confined to public officials, and in common parlance is often reduced to *his honor,* it now emerges as a political title of respect and a statement of expectation no less insistent than a wedding band. Already used centuries ago in England as a courtesy title for nobles and applied in Colonial America both to political leaders ("the Honorable Governor Winthrop") and to lawyers ("right honorable counsel"), it now clings to virtually every piece of mail and surfaces in almost every public introduction throughout a congressional career.

The conviction that "public service is honorable" reflects a deference to the Bible as much as it does a distaste for Machiavelli's *Discourses.* From Colonial times to the present a conviction prevails that both the state and its agents are answerable to transcendent Divine judgment and to national conscience. Whether or not an elected official contends that one "cannot legislate morality" or insists that private conduct and public duty are unrelated spheres of action, the American national expectation—despite sporadic cynicism—is that public leaders ought to exemplify morality. This heritage anticipates that an honorable office holder would rather be right and do good than be preoccupied with his own reelection and advantage. It reflects faith that the public order rewards

---

1. See Christopher Matthews, *Hardball, How Politics Is Played—Told By One Who Knows the Game* (New York: Summit Books, 1988).

integrity rather than image alone and presupposes that no cleverly-crafted ten-second television blitz will, at the last moment, successfully impugn a just and upright leader as a charlatan.

Just as *the honorable* emerges from such musings, his press aide intrudes a disconcerting question: The home city daily wants to know where the legislator stands on a foreign trade bill scheduled for an early vote. Since *the honorable* opposes the view prevailing in his home district, he is really unsure which obligation to honor. The aide asks, "Shall we attribute the congressman's dissent to constituency letters from voters who bothered to express themselves?" In short, should *the honorable* cloak his vote in a plausible lie?

"Give me ten minutes to think it through," says *the honorable*, who happens to be a churchgoer, a fact that sometimes complicates his decisions. *To be sure,* he ponders, *the Constitution forbids any religious test for office; an office holder may be an atheist or humanist, though he need not always remain in that condition, and there is reason to think that a Christian can serve well—if not necessarily better.* Yet *the honorable* professes to be a practicing Christian, and he suspects that the standard by which many people rate his performance is somehow more exacting than their expectations from some whose only creed is pragmatism. For, if his profession sticks, the believer identifies himself as an officer of government ordained by God to promote justice and to preserve order and peace. In the sanctuary, moreover, one ought never to mislead. Morality has its deepest quality in the fellowship of the saints, he grants to himself. Truth is a priority in marital and other interpersonal relationships, except perhaps when one assures a flustered hostess that her home cooking is much better than it really is.

*The political realm,,* he muses, *is not "the church" which demands a higher level of trust and requires that one always speak "yea, yea" and "nay, nay." Prudential policy in a pluralistic and democratic society is something quite different from the "coming transcendent kidgdom of God." To be sure, obedience to God remains one's highest allegiance even on Capitol Hill. But how is the truth best served in the political arena?* he asks himself. The politician must not lie in church, yet need he tell the truth—that is, the whole truth—in government? Does being responsible to God in the life to come always oblige one to tell the whole truth? Does "not always telling the whole truth" then mean that one's politics are based on irreligion? Inappropriate as lying is in church, can not even a devout churchman lie with integrity—now and then, at least—on Capitol Hill? Does political responsibility license one under some circumstances to tell an untruth? Must the political order cultivate a decent tolerance of honest lying?

Surely, when aggrieved nations are at war, they are fully justified in censoring information that might assist an aggressor nation; indeed, they would be foolhardy not to enforce censorship. The moral use of knowledge, therefore, does not require one always to tell what one knows; some things need for a time to be kept from public knowledge. The very survival of a democracy may depend at times on a distortion of its military capacity and intentions. Surely a terrorist who renounces established civilizational norms forfeits a right to the unvarnished truth. If a ruthless murderer demands to know whether his intended victim is at home, is deception in the service of life not acceptable? "Indeed he was here an hour ago, but have you checked the hardware store?" In such dire circumstances an honorable person can tell a half-truth. Yet we shall need to distinguish lies in interpersonal or family matters and immoral behavior and illegal acts—for example, lies told to perpetuate oneself in power at all costs—from half-truths that become necessary in a fallen world to prevent greater evils. On the surface—but only on the surface—that may seem to contradict the apostle Paul's rhetorical question, "Shall we do evil that good may come?" (Rom. 6:1, author's translation).

The biblical account of the harlot Rahab is instructive here. Her name appears in the glory gallery of the biblical saints (Heb. 11:31) because she recognized God's universal sovereignty and protected Israelite spies by misleading enemies who would have destroyed them (Josh. 2:1-21;6:22-25), an act of faith that put her own life at risk. Yet one would not want to rely much on the sporadic virtue of a prostitute for a resolution of sticky moral matters. Then, why not? Her occasional virtues may stand taller in the sight of God than the deliberate deceptions of a deviant televangelist.

We seem now to be coping with layers of truth, half-truth and lies, not to mention statistics, which often fall somewhere in between. A half-truth is often more difficult to answer than an outright lie. Yet there are two sides (some would say three) to many political concerns; whoever insists on only one side is at risk. Is it then a matter simply of being circumspect in telling lies? Is the main difference between political half-truth and Machiavellian untruth, *the honorable* asks himself, simply that Machiavelli tells "bigger lies"? Not so, *the honorable* assures himself, for Machiavelli rejects an objective good and right, whereas half-truth at least elevates moral submission over the temptation to tell deliberate nontruth.

Can a democracy long survive if it requires distortion to preserve it? Does not political morality in general require candor? Although the political process may sometimes confusingly narrow the line between truth and half-truth, any representative who disavows moral submission and accommodates deliberate untruth not only imperils democracy but stands personally naked in the twilight of a culture on the edge of chaos. Whoever subsumes all of life under a political instinct and dis-avows a transcendent truth and good places in jeopardy the values on which democracy relies for its existence and survival. He readily accom-modates its deterioration. Say what one will about the moral legitimacy of a frugal invocation of truth in political debate and about the role of pragmatic imperatives in geopolitical strategy and foreign policy: no vir-tuous congressman dare acquire a reputation as the bearer of credible lies. *On Machiavelli's coarse premise that self-interest is the ruler's prime motivation,* he muses, *no moral statesman or sincere churchman could possibly enter public service.* One so fundamentally invested in political relativism will soon allow political immorality to govern one's private and church life also, until religion itself becomes simply another realm to be exploited for political gain.

What then of Watergate? Were its lies admissible as "the way politics is"? *Not so, muses the honorable. Watergate involved the breaking of laws, and no politician is above the law.* The oath of office pledges pres-idents to uphold the law and, despite the division of powers, it grants congressmen no exemption.

If politicians should not lie, do they then need to tell the whole truth? Is not the entire judicial system premised on the principle that the defense, while ignoring what a prosecutor can flatly contradict, will nonetheless defend the client as effectively as possible? No competent defense attorney would begin his argument: "Ladies and gentlemen of the jury, granted that my client has been previously charged five times with robbery and twice with rape and was convicted three times for drug-trafficking." An adversarial system requires only that defense and prosecuting attorneys state their case as persuasively as possible before the bar of reason and justice. The prosecutor is not expected to be a spokesperson for the defendant.

Should we, therefore, consider politics as something less than a truth-telling enterprise? Should not each side be as economical as possible with the truth? Is not a half-truth a lie only if one has a right to expect the truth? Is the same half-truth not a lie when one knows he is hearing an adversarial presentation? Is it up to the opposition to fill in the gaps? *The honorable* must not deliberately misrepresent but, like television commercials promoting other commodities, is he free to imply whatever advances his status and devastates his opponents? Is not there room not only for white lies but for blue- black lies also—and perhaps even for occasional rainbow lies? Does politics require one to develop a capacity for lying honestly? Is not it all right—perhaps not all right, but nonetheless right—to lie in politics if your hearer knows that you are not telling the whole truth?

Suppose a legislator and some of his fellow legislators belong both to Congress and to the church? Surely the "born-againers" would insist that they do; still others, while unsure of time and place of conversion, would profess nonetheless to do so. Does a congressman then owe only half-truth to the congressional club in general, but full-truth to his "twice-born" colleagues? One can usually be sure who is in Congress, but can one really be sure who is in the Kingdom? Can every "twice-born" politician be trusted with the whole truth? A Virginia wit said that "evangelicals can keep a secret as well as the next man, but it takes more of them to do it." In a politically-divided assembly, is the truth due only to those of one's own party? Will even a churchman rise above the sporadic temptation to consider members of the opposing party not merely flawed but deranged? Or is the unmitigated truth due, more narrowly, only to those of one's own ideology? Or is it rather the case that, in Congress, half-truths at least are due to all, and three-quarter truths at best to colleagues who share one's religious and/or political commitments? What then becomes of separation of church and state, or is that commitment also suspended on half-truth? Wouldn't these circumstances encourage a non-Christian to believe that a Christian's political statements are those he can trust least? Shall we then get lying out of the world and into the church where some people might be encouraged to think it belongs?

*Perhaps,* muses *the honorable, the House or Senate chaplain can be helpful on the matter of just when it is right to tell the truth.* Suppose the chaplain leads in fervent prayer for divine guidance when *the honorable* would prefer a less circuitous ruling and time is of the essence? One recalls the woman who asked Dean Acheson to explain a complex political problem. After he patiently did so, she thanked him profusely, and added "I'm still confused but at a much higher level."

Does it make a difference that the Christian is to live in the world as leaven, light, and salt? Will it do to be morally aware under the steeple and to be morally ambiguous under the Capitol Dome? To be sure, neither a Christian, Jew, Mormon, nor a humanist should, in a pluralistic democratic society, conduct political activity in confessional terms. Still, are American Christians in some way to contribute to public political philosophy? Shall we then expect not truth—but at best expect only half-truth—from any person in the public order?

The phone rings, and the congressman's secretary says that the truth-in-government committee is inviting him to serve on its advisory board.

"Tell them I'll get back to them as soon as I can," he says. His press aide appears at the door: the deadline is near for replying to that query about his vote on foreign trade. "Tell them," says *the honorable*, that "our mail is running five to one on my side, but don't tell them that we've had only six letters. By the way, call my wife, and tell her that now more than ever I need her prayers for political integrity."

If the price of a good person's participation in public affairs is a deliberate distortion of truth, that price is too high. We must distinguish the essential person, who as such is inescapably bound to objective truth and morality, and that same person who is active in a contingent political role in adversarial representative government. Both as essential and contingent, a person is to recognize truth as normative; even in public affairs, ethical assumptions and beliefs remain significant in political debate and policymaking, lest democratic debate be assessed in terms of moral cynicism. The theme of adversarial half-truth is not to be confused with the contrast between political amorality and private morality, which is a different concern. If, in the case either of the political person or of the person in his essence, half-truth overwhelms adversarial politics and becomes one's life-style, then the person is corrupted by a relativistic and skeptical outlook that disallows an absolute distinction between good and evil.

As human beings, legislators, like everyone else are comprehensively bound to truth and the good and as such are to be basically honest and straightforward. Public servants will not be respected or inspire trust if they are fundamentally dishonest and become a symbol of deception. In that case they no longer acknowledge truth as normative; untruth has become a predicate of his personal nature. Even when they profess to traffic in adversarial half-truth they becloud the objectivity of truth and the normativity of ethics; affirmations in the arena of adversarial politics become pragmatic declarations lacking moral justification. The morality of half truth is preserved only when it seeks to move toward the whole truth. It is forfeited if one gives the palm of victory to untruth. To be sure, no mere human being knows the whole truth. Political debate, like much else in life, often turns on probabilities. But credibility usually attaches more readily to truth amplified than to truth impoverished.

The American founding fathers knew human beings in their present condition to be inordinately selfish and called for government that restrains evil and resolves conflicts. Plato warned that democracy passes into chaos and despotism, but Winston Churchill once noted that the adversarial system is the best yet devised for deciding truth concerns in the public square. Churchill said that democracy seems a terrible form of government until one contemplates the alternatives. Amid the awesome use and misuse of power it remains the best bulwark of political self-determination. Well may the congressman reassure himself, therefore, that a democratic system of government has more potential for making public the whole truth (or more of it) than does a dictatorial or totalitarian government. Descriptive history indicates that no better way now exists of moving toward the whole truth than an adversarial political system whose lawmakers often deal in three-quarter truths and half-truths.

To be sure, each party or support group stresses the strengths of its projected legislation, and each leaves to opponents an unmasking of weaknesses in the bills proposed. The democratic process promotes revision in the interest of bipartisan enthusiasm and in expectation of presidential consent or veto. Credit for the adoption of significant legislation often turns upon whether its legislative sponsor has achieved a balance of interests. A congressman's reputation for anticipating the legitimate concerns of both sides on nationally critical legislation accrues a reputation for political acumen and statesmanship.

A glimpse of the Capitol dome now and then quickens a surge of patriotism in the heart of even the busiest legislator. Since the ideals affirmed by the nation's charter documents remain politically normative, he fends off the skeptical notion that patriotism is insular and illiberal and that un-Americanism is broad-minded and objective. He esteems a government strategically positioned to reinforce human rights and religious liberty in the face of dictatorial and totalitarian powers.

The daily agenda is staggered by committee meetings, conferences, and consultations; correspondence on which staff members need guidance; breakfast, luncheon, and dinner engagements; work on an upcoming speech for corporate heads, political science students, or a political rally; meeting with lobbyists and greeting local constituents who surface unannounced. More important is being in place for debating and deciding on projected legislation. Having urged voters back home to "get out and vote" undaunted by wind, rain, or snow, an elected congressman's poor voting record on the floor of Congress invites questions about his sincerity.

His local constituency trusts him as its representative to mitigate both national and international anxieties, and home district media eagerly quote him for better or worse on the forefront issues. He must commend moves toward democracy abroad, while renovating democracy at home. He must avoid escalating the arms race, yet not risk leaving America too weak to repel a predatory power. None of this delicate balancing is as important as his own part in preserving the balance of power—executive, judicial, and legislative—that now tends at times to fragment rather than to fortify national policy.

A unified nation is most likely when Congress uses power cooperatively with the president. While that relationship must not vacate the White House's answerability to Congress, it does imply that a dubious use of power by one side is best countered, not by restriction, encroachment, and incursion, but by a recovery of the constitutional ideal. The congressman must be perceived as working with the nationally elected president, even if consistency of action and a good conscience may at times place him at odds with the president and even with his own party, albeit at some political risk.

A congressman may well be distressed that a sensational press portrays the political body, flawed though it no doubt is, as a den of corruption. When a magazine writes of "the dishonorable Congressional Club" and projects a "Hall of Shame," he shudders over an indiscriminate equating of political vocation with unethical conduct or self-seeking. Designated though he may be in large meetings and in correspondence as *the honorable*, in private circles he is more likely to be presented simply as "a politician." The connotation is often that of a self-promoter who, in quest of personal advancement, spears his opponents and rewards his supporters. Some consider him a professional money-changer who deals with special interests, courts corporate lobbies, commands outsized lecture fees, and is eager for a free vacation. His unpublished dress code, they surmise, is to be abreast of fashion and always ready for an unexpected television blip; if he is a congressman, dress like a senator; if a senator, dress like a president-elect, but never overdress lest voters consider him a social gadabout.

All this is no compliment, he ponders, to one who has pursued costly graduate studies in political science or law or whatever and now frequently invests a sixteen-hour-a-day and five-or-six-day work week, and who a year after each election must start thinking about rerunning for office. He is well aware that to argue the matter of morality seems to put one automatically on the defensive. He knows that much criticism of public conduct is doubtless merited, but he bristles at an escalated defamation that elevates a minority of legitimate grievances into general condemnation. Such defamation, he is aware, often depends on serious misunderstandings—that Congress was initially an unflawed political body, that the current scandals are worse than anything in the past, that these illegalities and irregularities render the American political establishment irreformable. The fact is, he reassures himself, the democratic process has repeatedly proved corrective of the worst infractions in both the legislative and executive wings of government.

Amid these ruminations the congressman gets word that a messenger bearing a PAC (Political Action Committee) contribution is visiting his office. Since the corporate donor has a stake in pending legislation, the legislator declines with thanks, so he may vote with an untrammeled conscience; he does not mention that he had already independently decided that the bill deserves his support.

Representative governments must inevitably wrestle constituency interests. PAC donors are by no means always on the wrong side and their stance often merits endorsement. The main concern is that "back door" access will not subvert a legislator's "open door" policy by placing a government office in the special service of powerful friends or consultants whose campaign assistance promises tax havens. Deep questions of public trust are involved. Can a congressman given to possible illegalities serve as a political role model? An adverse image can be devastating if "the honorable" is perceived as involved in financial irregularities or in conflicts of interest.

How a congressman responds to such perceptions or misperceptions of his character tells much about his assessment of truth and morality in government. The self-promotive politician esteems public perception more important than personal reality. An anticognitive and morally rudderless society concerned more with style than with substance and style, in turn, can become a mesmerizing political weapon. The decision a legislator reaches early in his career on the relative roles of image and of reality will leave a lifelong mark. If he is smitten by "imagitis," he soon runs the risk of being manipulated by managers who see the noncerebral temper of current society as an opportunity to be exploited in speeches and television ads, rather than as a condition to be deplored and remedied. If a candidate relies for election mainly upon image makers who know how to conduct a successful campaign, he will not easily escape suspicion that advantageously scheduled press conferences are mere extensions of that same technique.

Office holders who win elections by false advertising are hardly in a position to exert pressures on the media for truth in advertising. Aspirants for office whose aides "leak" politically advantageous falsehoods differ little from Wall Street sharks whose rumors of corporate takeover manipulate the market for personal profit. A well-placed rumor that gains momentary media credence can lower the stock market forty points at the closing hour or lower a candidate's political fortunes almost to nil on election eve.

Conventional wisdom is that when in trouble one should above all else do what is "smart P.R.," then negotiate privately for the most acceptable deal, and then publicly sell that option with semantics and style. That procedure may in fact depict the way "the system" now works "most advantageously." One who follows these rules, of course, need not lack moral probity; indeed, "good public relations" is truly at its "best" when placed in the service of ethical integrity. One's reliance on media to vindicate what is dishonorable invites a sequel that is prone also to vilify whoever or whatever is honorable.

If citizens begin with the assumption that their leaders are untrustworthy, and a political leader exploits a climate in which people will not elect a candidate who tells the truth, an election victory may be hollow and, in fact, another step in the decline of democratic processes. Without a morally sensitive citizenry no culture long retains its cohesion, and without a justifiable trust in national leaders, the ethical fabric of a society soon wears thin.

Once ensconced in office, the political leader readily perceives that his perpetuation in power is necessary to achieve his applauded political goals. The allure of status and recognition and the trappings of power have a seducing effect. Acquiring, expanding, and preserving personal power soon seem important if not indispensable to the future good of the republic. Although one may insulate oneself from external corruption, a seductive self-righteousness or pride of office gradually befogs an inner corruption for which all that matters is the successful fulfillment of one's "mandate." What initially involves "cutting corners" and half-truths readily escalates into breaking the law as the end in view comes to justify any and every means.

Many Americans consider the candidate's oath of office on a Bible something more than merely a symbolic part of an inaugural ritual. For at the very least this act is a reminder that the United States—although committed to church-state separation—is in fact held together more by the shared values of its churches than by those of its universities or by pragmatic political programs and mass media enthusiasm. The doctrine of church-state separation may encourage a secular misconception that public life involves no sins but only misjudgments, but even high school students know the difference between poor judgment and immorality.

The moral influence of political leaders holds added significance in a time of cultural instability. America's inherited ideals include an insistent emphasis on family values. Most Americans attach high importance to a candidate's stance on family concerns, including federal funding of abortion and school prayer. Many, but certainly not all, candidates gloss over the importance of monogamous marriage for social stability, and trivialize marital infidelity and would even seal off such concerns from the question of public competency and the propriety of public scrutiny. How a congressman relates to his family often becomes no less important than how he relates to his home district. If he must neglect his own kin in order to chair a panel on family values, he loses on both counts.

Relationships to church or synagogue still hold more than symbolic value in a nation which at one and the same time applauds church-state separation, ethical integrity, and participation in public worship.

In a nonconfessional state a political "use" of the clergy and the clerical "use" of politicians are both corruptive. No major religious body is exempt from the temptation to accumulate power, and to be sure, religious voting blocs have at times been a large factor in elections. Spokespersons presuming to speak for Christian churches no longer sponsor identical social and moral expectations. Yet more than one legislator has discovered a brusque reminder under his office door that a religious bloc holds in reserve so and so many votes for officeholders who favor or oppose some particular legislation. Should the congressman disdain such acts as jeopardizing the cohesion of the nation? Suppose droves of publicly active churchgoers do indeed reflect American mainstream values more accurately than hierarchies that claim to speak officially for the churches. What is troublesome in such situations is the confrontational rather than consultative and cooperative way of dealing with office holders and the growing disposition of aspiring religious leaders to mediate between the masses and their elected representatives. Just as disturbing is the increasing readiness of church bodies to promote and impose upon a pluralistic society moral principles that many in their local congregations disregard and violate.

In the absence of a comprehensive philosophy, the congressman concedes that a neglect of the cognitive aspects of political activity will simply perpetuate the present confusion. Pragmatists will move from one unsure legislative agenda to another. In what ways and to what extent, therefore, can a believing congressman inform the situation without being perceived either as a religious partisan in public life or as engaged merely in a futile attempt to redirect civil religion? To be sure, civil government is not to adjudicate metaphysical alternatives. Can he nonetheless contribute a grand vision that reflects the recognition of God found in the nation's political charter documents along with the emphasis also on inalienable rights, religious freedom, and a just society? Can he resist a secular reinterpretation of church-state separation that makes God irrelevant to a democracy and that fosters a society for which truth is neither what God thinks, nor need even satisfy the requirements of a valid syllogism, but reduces instead to empirical probability or to a simple ballot-box majority? Can he escape the easiest interpretation of church-state separation that religious doctrines are nothing but eccentric beliefs even if it is the most perilous?

Ought we to ignore T. S. Eliot's reminder: "If you will not have God...you should pay your respects to Hitler or Stalin"? Did not even the pagan Plato warn intellectuals that human thought and action faces no issue more important than the priority of God and the eternal verities? Should not even a sporadic reader of the Book of books quickly learn that abiding truth and right are a nation's sturdiest supports and that "No king is saved by the size of his army" (Ps. 33:16)? However much humanists dread the spectre of theocracy and like all constitutional scholars must insist on church-state separation, the reality or unreality of a transcendent God and of a changeless good and truth remain critically fundamental concerns for the cohesion of society and the permanence of a nation. The Christian ethic nurtures and reinforces restraints of character that keep people from selfishly devouring each other. Churches can impart to society the moral impulse that impels people to transcend inordinate self-interest; a mere pragmatist will be prone to do whatever advantages him.

Does a congressman's duty to the nation include some illumination of the permanent validity of knowledge and morality, or are power and glory his prime concern and glory at whatever price? Not even classic Greek idealists, pre-Christian pagans though they were, would think it strange if legislators, immediately after an inaugural ceremony, met—at least in their homes—to discuss the existence and nature and will of God, although *The Washington Post* might report that Congress as an institution had lost its mental balance. Plato advocated philosopher-kings precisely because of their supposed superior insight into the invisible ontological realities and their refusal to narrow temporal concerns to self-interest. The Graeco- Roman sages, who in various ways contributed to the Western tradition of democracy, shared the verdict that a good politician must come to terms with the eternal world. Christianity insisted on the limits of civil government and grounded human equality and rights in the transcendent will and act of the Creator. For both traditions to isolate national concerns from God invites not only injustice and immorality but also the twilight of any great power.

A devout politician who today threads his way to an early morning prayer meeting on Capitol Hill may be surprised that the attendees may include several colleagues who privately feel a spiritual emptiness, some who seek guidance in applying their faith to legislative specifics, some whose personal word is unstable, and even some who are under ethical scrutiny. He soon discovers that any pretense of political infallibility is unjustifiable. Politics is not, even for a devout theist, an ushering in of the kingdom of God and its unchangeable absolutes. It is a matter of prudential judgments amid the affirmation of transcendent norms and goals in a fallen, adversarial environment. It concerns a directional use of power which, unless harnessed to justice, can voraciously consume whatever it embraces.

The costly consequences of past political misjudgment are ever-present to caution us against repeating former mistakes. There is little encouragement in the fact that ancient Rome, the archetypical law-and-order government, handed over Jesus of Nazareth to be crucified though Pilate could find no fault in Him. Yet past miscalculation provides no justification for political withdrawal. None of us is in a position to resign from the human race because it is flawed.

Merely to park on the sidelines and honk for disengagement is not what democratic government is all about. To opt out of political involvement on the edge of regrets over failed policies merely multiplies past mistakes, yields to others the deployment of power, and deprives the democratic political scene of an important contribution to political philosophy. To be sure, whatever we attain, however desirable, will prove to be less than perfect. For all that some worthy goals can be achieved nonetheless by less than wholly good means.

These philosophical issues doubtless seem remote from the modern legislator's daily work load. Legislative aides thrust upon him reams of legal precedents that bear on proposed legislation; other staffers tabulate constituency reaction. To read the entirety and to fulfill other political duties as well would require a thirty-hour day and a ten-day workweek. Yet to follow an aide's recommendations uncritically is to abdicate personal responsibility. The congressman is a delegated representative, chosen to reflect both his constituency and himself at their best. Congressional competence is not indicated simply by unquestioning acceptance of party commitments or of pragmatic administration maneuvers, whether on the federal deficit, taxes, foreign trade imbalance, Social Security trust funds, or whatever else. Should priority be given to preserving dwindling clean air and water resources, to prodding able welfare recipients to pursue workfare alternatives, to meeting needs of the homeless and to better medical care for the elderly, or to limiting defense budgets while modernizing the arsenal for adequate military strength? How does one mentally coordinate a never-ending agenda of political specifics, not to mention the chaos of committee meetings and floor conferences, without characterizing the whole as a convulsive zoo?

The congressman's first commandment now becomes "Keep your equilibrium, however much this requires a cautious balancing act." In negotiating critical legislative issues he can ill afford to have to apologize too often to his home district for "bad judgment." He will seek a happy convergence of local constituency needs, overall congressional concerns, and special committees on which he serves. In this larger context, excessive pork-barrel politics may unwittingly threaten his own political career.

The awareness mounts that he is one of a team—a very special club, if you will—that stimulates an assembly line where each now well-known participant once gave a faltering maiden speech. Each contributes importantly to a process without which no end product would eventuate. To its credit the process imposes limits on a power struggle that would consume us all, were not our knowledge of its perils placed mutually in the service of a greater good. The outcome is always shaped by a majority who tend along the way to paint the minority as rogues, or vice versa. These braying donkeys and trumpeting elephants that roam the range are nonetheless the representatives who regulate the colorful game preserve called democracy.

Those who disdain the democratic concept of government or who because of its shortcomings are prone to indict its institutions, often forget that the functional equivalents of present moral failings were already present two centuries ago. Then, as now, an allegiance to democratic institutions prevails that offers the nation an incomparable possibility for political self-determination, one that enlists truth and the good to fuse moral direction and political power.

Issues of *truth* and the *good* are what is fundamentally at stake in our present culture-crisis. The process of government—like the business of education—is a profoundly moral affair. The moral character of leaders is thus a critical concern, for that character determines the moral quality which will be called out of a people. Moral direction and political power are thus inseparable. *That* truth must be in the forefront of a congressman's daily concerns; and the concern of the people as well.

# Part II
# Toward an
# Education
# That Matters

# Surmounting
# The Clash of Worlds:
# Evangelical Educators
# And the Fight of Faith

*Diligent students are Christianity's intellectual lifeline to the next generation. To guide, motivate, and invigorate the expanding mind is therefore one of the high privileges of classroom engagement.*

We live amid a collision of world-views and the ominous sound of clashing ideas and ideals. Chaotic thunderclouds of cultures in conflict sweep over the human race. Everything noble about human survival—all that we comprehend by majestic terms like spirit, conscience, duty, love—seems cloudy and uncertain.

Traditionally, colleges and universities have served as society's critical intellectual center. Within that academic framework evangelical Christians must inject and articulate the mind-set and heartbeat of revealed religion.

For our Christian mission I consider three concerns critically important. The *first* is the evangelical integrity of every person engaged in the academic task, namely, administration, trustees, faculty, students and alumni. The *second* is the intellectual competence with which we expound the biblical revelation vis-a-vis its competing alternatives. The *third* is the moral and spiritual life that believers manifest in defining personal holiness and social justice.

## Responsible Leadership

First, a word about responsible leadership. The Christian movement has founded and funded great institutions in the past only to lose many of them to others. We are better founders than preservers of our schools. To break out of that spiral of defecting enterprises, evangelical institutions need a discerning, informed, strongly assertive and courageous leadership. Those who would lead educational institutions must stand unwaveringly for the basic Christian doctrines. They must be devoted to the centrality of Christ incarnate, crucified, risen and returning. They must not falter in their commitment to the governing role of Scripture.

However great their world prestige and financial ability may be, trustees must first and foremost be theologically literate. If the founding vision of a school is to be preserved, the institution's trustees must faithfully share that vision. They must know the objectively given truths or doctrines that revealed religion espouses. They must know what is distinctive about the biblical view of God, humanity, history, nature, and the life to come. They should be able to state these essential beliefs in an articulate way. They should be aware of the enemy's persistent counterthrust. Especially today we see a mentally restrictive scientific method being paraded as the only reliable source of truth. At best it sponsors only a mindless religious mysticism. Christian academic institutions—their administrators and trustees—must uphold the primacy of doctrinal loyalty and must be able to distinguish abiding theological truth from speculative philosophical theory and from subjective existential response.

Any faculty, of course, must be fully learned in the subjects being taught. It must also be skillful in communicating content, stimulating interest, and promoting learning. It needs to formulate and present historic evangelical orthodoxy in an orderly, schematic way. It bears also the even higher intellectual challenge and duty of exhibiting the Christian world-life view on a curriculum wide basis. Faculty must impart to students an awareness of the Christian revelation's doctrinal interrelatedness, systematic coherence, and rational consistency. This tremendous interdisciplinary task is often at risk when faculty members—even if they share a devout personal experience of Christ—have pursued their studies mostly in institutions that have little regard for the Christian revelation. To be sure, an alert evangelical scholar can survive theologically and even grow stronger in faith while enrolled in a nonevangelical institution. It must be recognized, however, that little content will be provided from nonevangelical professors that enforces and deepens evangelical insights and commitments.

The faculty of an evangelical academic institution must also exhibit Christianity's intellectual power vis-a-vis nonbiblical alternatives. It must wrestle in depth against the world's counter-theories. It must encourage nonevangelical academicians to see what Christians consider the disabling cognitive liabilities of secular theory and why they do so.

Diligent students are Christianity's intellectual lifeline to the next generation. To guide, motivate, and invigorate the expanding mind is, therefore, one of the high privileges of classroom engagement. Students tend to reflect the strengths and weaknesses of their teachers. The more disciplined and exemplary the teacher, the sharper the honing of a student mind will be. It is imperative that students win the great Christian convictions for themselves and not merely parrot the views of their mentors. The bright gleam in a learner's eye, the flash of interest in a captivating idea, the sense of looming discovery, the suddenly riveted attention of students, and the shared experience of classroom excitement, make formal study a channel to future leadership. What a tragedy when young minds learn evangelical heritage only in terms of aphorisms and cliches, memorize views whose wealth they do not really comprehend, know little about the best books that expound their heritage, and are not taught to do battle with formidable competing views!

The graduates a school disperses into the larger world are a gauge of its academic strength. Alumni are living commentaries on the Christian world-life view whose implications they must think through and live out in the public arena. If graduates betray an institution's ideals or scorn or neglect them, something is amiss in how their mentors have conveyed the faith-once-for-all-given to the oncoming generation. Strong alumni are among the supreme assets of a Christian academic institution as they invest their vocational gifts in various arenas of human service, and as they mirror both the conceptual claim of the biblical heritage and its spiritual and moral vitalities.

In brief, together the president, trustees, faculty, students, and alumni of a concerned and determined Christian school can become an army of intellectual stimulation and occupation at a time when society lacks cohesion and is searching for ultimate meaning and worth. The evangelical integrity of every person linked to this academic mission is of the highest importance.

## The Christian World-view and Its Rivals

The Christian revelation insists that human beings can know something fixed and final about God, about the human situation, about the possibility of rescue from our present alienation, about God's purposes for nature and history, and about our coming eternal destiny.

Today's dominating world wisdom is highly subjective; it disallows the reality and significance of transcendent divine revelation. Many of us, I am sure, in our own earlier years were open to vague religious speculation or to repeatedly revised philosophical theory. We have long since turned from conjectural commitments to worship the one true and living God who has revealed Himself universally in nature and history and more specifically in Christ and the Bible. We now revel in the biblically revealed God who has disclosed objectively true information about Himself and about His purposes. We fellowship with the crucified and risen Jesus as the Way, the Truth, and the Life. We delight in rewarding relationships with Him that even the frailest human being can experience. Comprehensive exposition of the Christian world-life view is essential. The biblical revelation is a vitally interconnected organic whole. Orderly exhibition of divinely revealed truths and of their implications for nature, history, government, and final destiny will impinge on every discipline of learning.

The Christian outlook cannot be effectively maintained by piecemeal retention of a few selected and respected tenets and the surrender of other important elements. The fact is, the naturalism that now pervades many influential universities of the modern world is far less vacillating in what it believes or disbelieves than are some so-called religious institutions. Naturalism does not selectively dispute only the doctrine of creation, or the human fall, or the singular divinity of Jesus Christ, or His bodily resurrection. Naturalism's mindset and willset is hostile to the entire body of miracle and the supernatural. It disputes the Hebrew-Christian view in its totality.

We must challenge this naturalistic reconceptualization and restatement of existence we must challenge *in toto*. It teaches that empirical scientific method alone gives us reliable information. It categorizes the supernatural as legend and myth. It reduces ultimate reality to impersonal processes and quantum events. It limits knowledge to tentative inferences. It denies the very possibility of ever knowing ultimate and abiding truth.

The Christian world-life view challenges such naturalistic reductionism at every turn. It does so not by defending merely the credibility of one isolated miracle on which current unbelief momentarily focuses its hostility. Far more is at stake, namely, the very definition and delineation of reality and existence. Does the universe comprising humans and nature have its source and support in a supernatural, self-revealed God? Does a moral and spiritual purpose overarch all of finite reality? Does a possibility of redemption exist for fallen humanity? Is there an afterlife in the world to come? Or is naturalism right in asserting that the universe has its ground of being in itself, or that it perchance originated in some primal cosmic accident or explosion, so that the human species in consequence is merely an animated confluence of space-time contingencies?

It bears repeating that in affirming God's intelligible self- disclosure, the Christian view disputes the naturalistic option not simply in respect to isolated issues, but in its entirety. Christianity propounds a view of God, a view of origins, a view of the nature and worth of humanity, a view of sin and divine rescue, a view of Jesus Christ the ever-living Redeemer, and a view of meaningful history and of eternal moral destiny.

We are self-deceived if we allow naturalistic speculation to parade as something modern, when in fact it was repudiated almost twenty-five hundred years ago by the great philosophers of Greece. Pagan though they were, the classic Greek sages recognized that naturalism cannot bring into being or sustain a stable society and, in fact, robs human life of distinctive value and meaning. The Greeks insisted that if time and change control all reality, and if truth and right are subject to ongoing revision, then human civilization becomes impossible; moreover, human life loses fixed meaning and special worth. They found no basis for optimism in ultimate process and change. It remained for modern evolutionists to argue conversely that change means progress and that human history is headed for utopia. In this respect secular philosophy borrowed the biblical doctrine of the coming kingdom of God but cannibalized it. Naturalism's abandonment of unchanging truth and of a fixed good has resulted not in utopia but in a relapse to paganism and barbarianism that increasingly corrupts modern life.

Christianity's control-beliefs acknowledge the eternal, sovereign, rational, and moral God. They stipulate that God has revealed Himself intelligibly and verbally. God created the universe *ex nihilo*, out of nothing, and governs it for moral ends by His transcendence over it and by His presence in it. He fashioned the human race in His image for spiritual fellowship and holy service. Adam's voluntary fall disrupted Edenic harmony and implicated both the cosmos and human posterity in divine judgment. Through the patriarchs and prophets God graciously promised salvation for penitent humanity. That promise God mercifully fulfilled by His covenant relationship with Israel and by the incarnation of the eternal Logos (Word) as the God-man Jesus of Nazareth.

Jesus Christ attested the Triune selfhood of Deity, exemplified ideal spiritual obedience in the flesh, and provided for the sins of mankind a propitiatory atonement to be appropriated by personal faith. Through bodily resurrection and ascension Christ Jesus became living head of a new society of redeemed and regenerate believers over which the Lord now rules through the inspired Scriptures by the Holy Spirit. Christ Jesus mandates the church to preach the gospel to all mankind and in His name to advance the good and to challenge the forces of evil. The church lives in expectation of Christ's return and anticipates the final triumph of righteousness, the doom of evil, the punishment of the impenitent, the full conformity of believers to Christ's holy image, and the comprehensive inauguration of God's kingdom in universal vindication of God's moral purpose in history. The competence with which this biblical revelation is set alongside its competing alternatives is crucially important for our witness in this world.

The collision of thought worlds, the clash of moral claims, and the conflict of principalities and powers were no less intense in New Testament times than today in ours. The apostle Paul was concerned about the Christian use of the mind and about the Christian manner of life, that is, about both right thinking and right living. Christianity is both a doctrine and a way of life; anyone who thinks that a holy life is unimportant defaces Christian doctrine as well. Christianity prizes the unity of spiritual truth and moral dynamic. Our planet is the stage for a cosmic drama whose outcome embraces all realms of being, and which presently involves the angelic hosts, Satan and the world of demons, and all mankind. God's ethical purpose revealed in the Scripture is exhibited in His incarnation in Christ and will finally be vindicated in divine judgment of humanity and the nations.

However important and indispensable world-life view elaboration is, it is not the total objective of Christian education. Knowledge alone cannot solve the problems of ethics. The crowning goal of redemption is the shaping of the Christian mind and will. The Apostle Paul exhorted the Colossians: "Set your minds on things above, not on earthly things" for we are raised with Christ who now is seated at the Father's right hand (Col. 3:1-2). The Apostle urged Christians to "be transformed by the renewing of your mind" (Rom. 12:2) and "be renewed in the spirit of your mind" (Eph. 4:23 KJV). "Let this mind be in you," he exhorted, "which was also in Christ Jesus" (Phil. 2:5 KJV) who set aside the prerogatives of divinity and came as the God-man for our sakes and endured death on a cross so that we unworthy sinners might be redeemed. Christ's mind must therefore take us captive. More and more we are to see all existence and life from His point of view. Indeed, it is the mind of Christ to which all God's people will be finally and fully conformed.

Great empires of the Occident and of the Orient have worshiped power above justice and mercy. They have been betrayed by this lust for power to eventual collapse. This earth is a graveyard for the ruins of once-great civilizations. By contrast, the heartbeat of the Christian revelation is that the Son of God was "pierced for our transgressions" and "crushed for our iniquities" (Isa. 53:5 NIV). At the climax of the Gospels the world crucifies and entombs the best humanity it knows, the One whose final resting place belongs to a different world, and the eternal world, whose God supremely exalts the trusting Servant who bows before Him.

The shaping of a technological mind with its exaltation of computer intelligence has become a hallmark of our generation. In a recent invitation-only meeting of prominent Americans, a Stanford University emeritus professor of humanities commented on modern technological education and morality. What he said might well send a shudder throughout Europe and the United States and Japan. Once again, noted Dr. Gordon Craig, some modern universities are producing technical scholars who lack a sense of ethical responsibility for society and the human race. Be forewarned that the most technologically sophisticated nations, the most scientifically literate, can also through amoral scientism become brutal and savage whenever science replaces theology and ethics as the locus of truth. A nation that will not have God sooner or later will accommodate Adolph Hitler's protégé. We must make the alternatives crystal-clear amid the current clash of ideas and ideals.

## Virtues and Values

Already as a young man, the apostle Paul was exposed to what pagan Graeco-Roman culture enthusiastically applauded as virtuous and praiseworthy. His home city was Tarsus where presumably he attended university. Rabbinical teaching in Jerusalem under Gamaliel subsequently reinforced his Hebrew inheritance. Paul's Christian conversion then deepened the contrasts and reoriented his horizon to the crucified and risen Jesus.

When Paul wrote to the Philippians, he was under house arrest in Rome. From one city in the Roman Empire he addressed fellow Christians in another city in the Roman Empire. A single verse in his letter Philippians 4:8 opens a wide picture window on the virtues or excellencies that Roman society approved. The context strikingly illustrates how the Apostle thrust the Christian revelation across the reigning world-wisdom of his own age.

Paul referred to "whatever is true, whatever is noble, whatever is right, whatever is pure, whatever is lovely, whatever is admirable" (or, "of good report"). He then added, "if there be any virtue and anything praiseworthy, think on these things" (KJV). The only reference in all the apostle's epistles to the Greek term for "virtue" (*arete*) occurs here. In translating the Old Testament the Septuagint largely avoids the term *arete* even as the New Testament, likewise, kept it at a distance. "In the whole of Pauline literature," as the German New Testament scholar Otto Bauernfeind notes, the word "occurs only once and quite incidentally."[1] In truth, Paul mentioned *arete* almost only in passing: "If there be any virtue."

Yet Paul did not wholly ignore the prevalent socio-cultural deference to what is virtuous and praiseworthy. Unlike the Roman world of Gentile culture that assigned preeminence to public virtue and praise, Paul was not dazzled or preoccupied with it. He neither caricatured nor wholly overlooked nonchristian moral sensibilities. Neither did he absolutize those sentiments. Quite in line with his early Letter to the Romans about a moral imperative divinely and ineradicably inscribed upon the hearts even of Gentiles, Paul was somewhat respectful but not unrestrictedly so.

We may note several things. The Bible pays only sparse attention to the constellation of values that the secular Gentile world revered except to critique it. The New Testament as a whole makes only fleeting laudatory references to the moral stance of Gentiles. Paul, in any case, assigned to Gentile conduct no more salvific value than he did to the Hebrew good works that he, like his fellow-Jews, once trusted for salvation. Finally, in contrast to the values that Gentile society esteemed, Paul expounded what in the context of revelatory-redemptive Christianity truly constitutes ideal morality.

Broadly speaking, Philippians 4:8 mirrors the moral qualities commended by the ancient classic world at its best. The apostle listed six approbations that had currency in Graeco-Roman life and culture, that is, in the nonchristian world of his day: things "true", "noble" (honest), "just", "pure", "lovely" and "of good report". Paul neither defined these terms nor affirmed their adequacy. The terms *semnos* (noble; honest) and *prosphilos* (lovely) occur nowhere else in the New Testament, and *euphemos* (praiseworthy) appears only in Corinthians. Words gain their meaning from the logical universe of discourse in which they are used. They carry no inherent metaphysical significance. Sometimes a word is so deeply associated with a particular meaning, and is so culturally weighted, that it becomes a liability even in another context. The New Testament's avoidance of terms in Paul's list is likely due to the special

---

1. *Theological Dictionary of the New Testament*, ed. Gerhard Kittel, I:460.

philosophical orientation they acquired in Roman society. *Eros*, the Greek term for affection, that Plato could apply even to love between the gods, finds no place whatever in Paul's listing. In the nonchristian world "virtue" (*arete*) could mean simply human mastery of one's field; it came also to mean ethical prominence. As a term for moral accomplishment and merit, it was too anthropocentric to reflect what is essential to the biblical revelation human responsibility before a holy God. The Greek ideal of virtue focused on independent human accomplishment; this emphasis on human virtue the New Testament displaces by inquiring how in view of the revelation of God's holy law, a person can confidently stand before God's judgment. The Bible does not distill virtue from fallen human nature and laud it. In Scripture the evils that enslave humankind are not horizontally outweighed or overcome. Rather they require the acknowledgement of sin and Divine redemption and renewal. Graeco-Roman culture gave the prevalent vocabulary overtones of a life view that Christianity disowned.

No less than the term *arete*, the term *epainos* (praise) was predominantly anthropocentric; the cultural emphasis was on public approval and the applause of people in this life. The reference, therefore, commends human achievement and excellence that society in general—not only ancient Greek or Roman, but for that matter modern American or Japanese also—tributes in fellow humans. The New Testament, by contrast, uses the term especially with a view to God's approval.

Paul did not, by any means, imply that Christians should aspire to what the world applauds; yet he would not disapprove of Olympic competition or civic recognition. He allowed the world of Gentile morality to become the object of Christian meditation but on Christianity's own terms. Instead of aspiration for human recognition and for public applause, so evident in Graeco-Roman society, he routinely commended craving that which on the future day of judgment will be approved by God who searches the depths of the human heart. Even on the horizontal human level, the recognition we are most to covet is not the acclaim of society in general but rather the verdict of the Christian community of believers who join in praise of God.

Although the New Testament virtually skips over the emphasis on virtue and praiseworthiness as Graeco-Roman civilization viewed them, Paul indicated that something was to be said for this emphasis, flawed though it was. After stringing together the cultural approbations, Paul added, "if there be" any virtue and "if there be" any praise. The *ei tis* (if there be) needs comment. Paul had earlier (Phil. 2:1-2) used the same construction *ei tis* in connection with indubitable evangelical qualities. Surely he did not intend to speak interchangeably and identically of virtues sponsored by pagan moralists. Yet the pagan virtues call for reflection and meditation.

To meditate on the present cultural ideals is quite an order—no less in Washington or in Tokyo than in Rome, and all the more in a television and mass media society overarched by humanism, pragmatism, and materialism. In every society the Christian community must ponder secular morality and probe its possible relationships to God's general revelation, its fidelity to or its reduction of the desired ideal, and its significance in the light of God's incarnational and inscripturated revelation/ The Christian mind is thus engaged soul to soul in the clash of cultural perspectives and involved actively in the collision of thought worlds and the moral conflict of the ages.

Earlier in the Philippian Letter Paul had referred to the human excellencies the rabbinical Hebrew society of his day commended. He outlined his own superlative personal qualifications: "If anyone else thinks he has reasons to put confidence in the flesh, I have more circumcised on the eighth day, of the people of Israel, of the tribe of Benjamin, a Hebrew of the Hebrews, in regard to the law, a Pharisee; as for zeal, persecuting the church; as for legalistic righteousness which is in the law, faultless" (Phil. 3:4-6, NKJV). Yet all this he brushed aside for another life view, not Roman but Christian, "What things were gain to me, these I have counted loss for Christ . . . I count them as rubbish, that I may gain Christ" (Phil. 3:7-8, NKJV).

If Paul trashed his own works reflecting the Hebrew behavior code, insofar as these might merit divine praise and final acquittal, he was surely not about to assign a higher value to the Gentile behavior code concerned more with the earthly plaudits of people than with divine approval.

Yet Paul did not wholly strip away the importance of the Gentile or of the Hebrew sense of moral obligation. He held the Gentile concepts in mind for thoughtful evaluation. He recognized a relative ethical distinction both in Roman and in Hebrew society between those who do and those who do not devoutly seek to fulfill their obligations.

Although Paul urged meditation on the public moral agenda, at the same time he stood much of the Gentile program of behavior on its head. We have noted that the New Testament entirely ignores some of the indicated Greek perfections and only infrequently uses others in their secular intention. The New Testament also alters the sense of some of the terms; it widens and deepens their context to include the transcendent divine. It transfigures the cultural emphasis in the interest of a larger reality. The biblical mind thus takes on an impressive new dimension. In short, only what *Jesus Christ* considered "noble" and what *He* ennobled by the way He considered it, now becomes decisive.

One term in the chain of Gentile laudations towers compellingly above the rest. The term *dikaios* (just) becomes more than a spacious mirror of contrasting world-views. In the Bible the terms "just" and "justice" hold a special importance in both the Gentile and the Hebrew worlds. God's general revelation seems to be universally reflected into human affairs in the unremitting demand for justice.

Paul did not teach, nor does Scripture, that fallen humanity's predicament in sin has in no way impaired the definition of justice and diluted the content. In view of the *imago Dei* (image of God) and of general revelation, the sentiment of justice as a divine imperative remains vital in and for humankind despite the Fall. All human beings distinguish between justice and injustice as objective categories. Moreover, conscience links to God this moral sentiment in approving justice and in condemning injustice. In unavoidable anticipation conscience hails transgressors before God's judgment throne. The Hebrew prophet Amos condemned even Israel's neighbor nations who lacked special revelation. He held them guilty for transgressing general revelation and for their violations of justice. Despite the fall of humanity the sense of justice survives universally as a property of humanity made in God's image. Sin, moreover, has not totally obliterated either its divine ground in the Deity or the conviction that God will punish unjust acts that even unregenerate conscience condemns in a broken or fractured way. The just people in Greek culture were those who—without any specific reference to God—fulfilled their civic duties and legal expectations. The New Testament retains this relative moral distinction of publicly just or unjust persons, but it calls even the best of such persons to the need of regeneration. The truly just have been justified by faith in the righteous substitute and live in harmony with God's revealed will. However "virtuous," however, "just" they may be, both the Old Testament and New Testament affirm that all humanity is subject to divine judgment. God alone is intrinsically just and the justifier of sinners. The justice of the absolutely righteous Deity is demonstrated by the atoning sacrifice of Christ. The transcendent world thus overhangs Paul's exhortation, "whatever is just . . . if there be any . . . meditate!" The Messiah alone conforms totally to the divine moral norm.

The terms preempted by society for secular approbation Paul coordinates with divine revelation and grace so that their sense is enlarged in the context of the supernatural world. Through this Christian context the concepts cherished by the Roman masses gain profounder significance. If the unregenerate Gentile world gloried in what is "lovely," the New

Testament resounds much more with the *agape* or love of God displayed for sinners. So too, "of good report" gains but little mention outside Philippians, although the prophets and apostles echo a heaven-sanctioned report or good news (Compare. Isa. 53:1, "Who has believed our report?" NKJV) (See also. John 12:38, Rom. 10:16-18).

Paul did not entirely reject the Greek terms and conceptions. He did not, however, uncritically take over the secular sense and implications. He connected the cultural vocabulary with a higher spiritual purpose. Nothing in this adaptation caters to natural law or to natural theology. Neither is there an implicit denial that the light of the Logos is everywhere reflected throughout creation and history, however much sinfully skewed humanity deflects and distorts that light. The virtues that secular society applauds are not considered as either pristine or sufficient in their moral significance, even though in some way they salute moral submission and responsibility. Even at their highest, they provide no authentic basis for human pride in works to escape the judgment of God. They offer little if anything that revealed religion does not present more clearly and profoundly.

Paul's immediate concern was to constructively confront Graeco-Roman idealism. In the West today our concern is to confront radically secular humanism that now is deteriorating swiftly into raw naturalism. In much of the East, the concern will be to interact with Buddhism's shaping influence in religious thought and life and on the fine arts and social institutions, and also Shintoism's role as an indigenous religion and Confucianism's role as an ethical system.

The vocabulary in which Paul located his own mind-set and will-set, as every reader of the New Testament is soon aware, rings with terms like *glory, grace* and *joy,* and with phrases like *the peace of God, the gospel of Christ, and good works.* Scholars have long noted the New Testament's studied preference for the word *agape* in contrast to the cultural *eros* whose selfish connotations obscured the self-giving love of God. When Paul introduced Christian virtues by the phrase *ei tis,* he did not leave matters suspended in midair: "If there be ei tis any encouragement from being united with Christ, any comfort from His love, . . .if any tenderness and compassion . . ., being like-minded having the same *agape,* being one in spirit and purpose" (Phil 2:1-2). There is no ambiguity here about Christian identity and adequacy; Paul pleaded with us to be "like-minded."

Alongside and above worldly glory in self-achievement, whether by the Jewish religionist or the Gentile moralist, Paul set the eternally enduring realities of revealed religion. When Paul went to Athens, the pinnacle of Greek learning, he spoke to the philosophers not of human virtue but of the holy Creator, of Divine regeneration, of future judgment, and of the crucified Christ's resurrection and ours through Him. Central to all else is the righteousness which is ours through faith in Christ. Paul exhorted us at one and the same time to manifest the "same mind" and the same [*agape*] that Christ exemplified and to find enablement through a new and higher catalytic than pagan society knew. He emphasized the Holy Spirit's role in character formation.

This brings us to the climactic point. Paul set the Christian life-view not in the framework of the Roman virtues but rather in the context of revealed religion. As the ground of his eternal salvation, the apostle counted both his civic virtues as a Roman citizen and even his superior credentials as a Jewish Pharisee as unimpressive in God's sight. He linked human destiny not with merit but with grace, and with faith that claims for oneself what grace offers. For a behavioral model he pointed the Philippian believers to the surpassing excellence of the self-emptying Logos, incarnate, crucified, and risen. It is on Jesus that the apostle modeled his own life. Paul could, therefore, offer his own model of Christian living to others as a pattern of a divinely approved morality.

The apostle, therefore, was not interested only in theologizing. God's purpose is not merely our mastery of a theoretical system, but actual redemption from sin. Real Christianity has an indispensable practical side. "Whatever you have learned or received or heard from me, or seen in me—put it into practice. And the God of peace will be with you" (Phil. 4:9). "Join with others in following my example, brothers, and take note of those who live according to the pattern we gave you" (Phil. 3:17).

Let us obey our Risen Lord and safeguard our heritage as a devout and holy Christian community. Let us turn high the bright fires of revealed truth and the moral fervor of evangelical redemption. We are convinced that the risen Lord transcends the clash of worlds. Girded in full armor we need now to stand fast where the intellectual, moral and spiritual battlelines are drawn, to counter contemporary alternatives with the biblical view and to implant and demonstrate in thought and life the superiority of redemptive revelation.

# Shall We Flunk
# the Educators?

*Future generations will look back and ask why, amid a colossal culture-crisis torn by furious thunderclouds of conflicting minds and wills, American evangelicals–fifty million of them– were so intellectually ineffective while the outlook of modernity swayed in the balances. We who live in this greatest world-power in all history seem to be embarrassingly and incredibly silent amid the deeply divided heart and soul of this nation.*

American education is in disarray. Public schools not only face mounting problems, but they also seem to forfeit the very resources they need to cope with those problems. Adrift from God's commandments and divine truth, they have abandoned the Word and will of God. No longer do they acknowledge unchanging ethical imperatives and intellectual finalities; moral absolutes and fixed truths they consider antiquated.

Students are left without objective criteria for deciding the truth of a premise or worth of an idea. Truth and right are declared culture-relative. *Veritas* (truth) has taken flight; campuses have lost their intellectual and moral cohesion, and their residual social conscience is increasingly geared to self-interest. Someone has said that the *universitas* has yielded to the *diversitas*.

Students can no longer automatically expect either truth or godliness from their teachers. Yet the earliest American colleges were founded by

Christians to preserve and promote Christian influences. The first nine colleges to open their doors before the American Revolution were all sponsored by Protestant Christians; all but one were denominational schools. Early American universities not only taught but also upheld moral philosophy and ethical standards. Many campuses had Christian clergy as presidents and academically competent ministers as revered faculty members. Students attended Sunday church services and participated in voluntary university chapel meetings. Sometimes spiritual revivals broke out; classes were accordingly suspended so that the schools could give themselves to prayer.

Today our battle is for the future of civilization. In detaching God from nature and history and conscience and cognition, people have become brutalized. Morally and intellectually adrift from true religion and revealed ethics, multitudes increasingly succumb to paganism. The dangers that now engulf our vagabond culture are so serious that civilization itself is now endangered.

Recently the president of an ecumenically pluralistic seminary told a group of academic administrators that we now live in "a post-Christian age." "There is no hope," he said. "The seminary is a coffin; as president, I am polishing the coffin." He added, "the trustees are pallbearers carrying the coffin, and we are all on the way to the cemetery looking for a hole in which to bury it." One would be less surprised had a disillusioned secular educator voiced those sentiments. Much of modern education has lost not only fixed and final truth and unchanging morality, but it has also lost any basis and reason for hope. Liberal education is slipping into the black hole of paganism.

I grieve over the condition of many of the secular universities, for in this colossal turning time they lack intellectual consensus and flounder in confusion. Much as we must speak of their failures, however, we as evangelicals should not exhaust our energies in simply deploring their plight. A Christian phalanx, however much a minority, can impart a sense of purpose to a nation and to the world no less than the early church did in a former dark age of paganism. God is calling evangelicals to a greater sense of responsibility in the arena of education, and also in that of the mass media and of politics. By not speaking up in the present cultural debate, we will fail not only the church and society but God as well. If those of us who bear the burden of evangelical intellectual engagement withdraw, the renegade world will continue unchallenged in its caricature of evangelicals as either political extremists, snake-handling revivalists, or cultural dinosaurs.

Some leaders foresee in the 1990s an extraordinary opportunity for restoring Christian perspectives in at least some of the universities. They envision also a remodeling of evangelical education that manifests itself to be both academically powerful and faith affirming in the highest sense. I agree with them. I would not be faithful if I did not hope for a positive resurgence of valid evangelical education. All evangelical Christians, I believe, are duty-bound to participate convictionally in today's pluralistic dialogue concerning American education. The burden of this engagement comprises also an extraordinary and unique opportunity for evangelical intellectuals.

Unless Christian education publicly expounds its way of knowing God, strenuously proclaims universally valid truth, and clearly identifies the criteria for testing and verifying the knowledge-claims we make, then the Christian view of God and the world will survive as but a fading oddity in an academic world that questions its legitimacy and appropriateness. In secular universities religion departments teach the great religions of the world merely as historical phenomena exerting no universal truth-claim. We do not ask them to engage instead in Christian evangelism. We simply ask them to tell the truth about Christianity and to present it on its own grounds and not as twentieth-century relativists reconstruct it.

The late Charles Malik, former chairman of the United Nations General Assembly, held that no task is currently more crucial than to examine the Western university and to maintain an evangelical presence and participation that offers a viable alternative to its erosive naturalism. Future generations will look back and ask why, amid a colossal culture crisis torn by furious thunderclouds of conflicting minds and wills, American evangelicals—fifty million of them—were so intellectually ineffective while the outlook of modernity swayed in the balances. We who live in this greatest world power in all human history seem to be embarrassingly and incredibly silent amid the deeply divided soul and heart of this nation.

For more than a century—in fact until about a hundred years ago—American higher education was largely Christian. Richard John Neuhaus remarked that the now dead founders of great Christian institutions have become disenfranchised and their constituting visions have been betrayed. Even the thesis that theology is something that has to do with God is now an embattled premise on some of those campuses. The loss of initial orientation has involved an enormous shift in student values. Some dormitories are hardly a home away from home; students talk openly about shacking up on campuses where counselors and deans often take permissive sex for granted.

In Britain, Parliament has made religion an indispensable part of the national educational curriculum; it has stipulated, moreover, that Christianity be taught, not for reasons of evangelism but rather to define the inherited culture. As recently as a century ago, no one in England could be admitted to Oxford University without subscribing to the Nicene Creed. Today in America a graduate student who affirms Nicene christology would, on some campuses, be considered past his or her mental prime. Religion as taught on some American university campuses reflects the non-Christian religions and bizarre modern cults as much as, if not more than, Christianity; even if not discounted, Christianity is crippled by higher criticism and historicism. Sociologist Peter Berger has remarked, and rightly, that no world religion has ever had to cope with so insistent an attack on its fundamental beliefs as has Christianity by those who profess to be its adherents.

Enlightening indeed is the comment of a one-time fervent American evangelical whose mainline denomination was grooming him a half-generation ago to become an ecumenical Billy Graham. Speaking of doubts nurtured in the classroom and of his waning faith that characterized the experience of many university students, he observed:

> God took ill, slowly wasted away, and then one day was gone. Intellectual doubts would rise, and I would cover them over with prayer, devotion, service. There would be a wisp of smoke, a flicker of flame, then a blaze,and I would have to fight the fire, and I did it many times, but finally I could no longer believe in a God who by any stretch of the imagination-could be described as Father. What the universe said was nothing like that. It seemed that the universe was as indifferent to us as to beetles, sharks, butterflies. I came to the conclusion that we do not matter, except to each other.[1]

As the post-Enlightenment generation sealed off religious concerns as matters of private preference, the West sought to build a culture without God and on the basis of science and technology. A secularized doctrine of church and state segregated religion from public affairs and implied that God had nothing to do with the historical destinies of a nation. Despite the grim specter of Hitler and the Nazis, we seem to have learned little about the high cost of abandoning God and moral absolutes. The religion of the Bible is largely expunged from the public arena; the universities, the mass media, and the political realm have become largely nontheistic if not atheistic.

Yet the modern world, alongside its loss of the Judeo-Christian heritage, is becoming more religious while it becomes less godly. Human beings are by nature religious; if revealed religion is obscured; they will simply pursue false religions. Worse yet, many intellectuals are no longer sure just what religion is. Some consider communism a religion,

---

1. Sylvia Fraser, "The Real Charles Templeton", *Chatelaine*, February 1975, 77.

others speak of drug-induced psychedelic experience as religious. Some intellectuals cannot seem to differentiate God from the devil.

For all that, evangelical Christianity is experiencing some gratifying gains on secular campuses. Here and there concessions are being made toward a balanced pluralism that reflects historical Christianity more fairly in professional posts. The Society of Christian Philosophers has come into being and sponsors a significant journal, *Faith and Philosophy*. There is growing conviction that in the clash of ideas a reintroduction of the Judeo-Christian tradition may alleviate the lost excitement of liberal arts learning. Moreover, evangelical student movements continue to report noteworthy evangelistic success.

The fact remains, however, that evangelical professors on secular campuses are often isolated and that a curious hostility is frequently directed toward qualified evangelical applicants by academic colleagues who support radicals for faculty posts. Evangelical scholars are bypassed because their personal commitments are considered nonobjective and a threat to the supposed objectivity of the faculty. Secular universities have become mission fields where the conceptual initiative still lies with secular humanism or, as is increasingly the case, with raw naturalism.

There have been no comprehensive reversals of the trends that elicit many of the complaints about secular academe; in fact, the chorus of criticism expands. Today's continuing shift from classical learning has pushed aside academic interest in the great literary works of the past that focus on the perennial problems of philosophy and give shape and substance to the West's cultural inheritance. The tendency to turn to community involvement to recover the excitement of liberal learning allows reformists and political concerns to dwarf the importance of ideas and their consequences. Under way is a counterbalancing effort that seeks to train the mind but dismisses the volitions and emotions as extracurricular concerns; it abandons students to a misdirected quest for self-fulfillment, be it in Yoga or Zen or other consciousness-raising substitutes for spiritual authenticity. What results is a fragmented view of the self, one that disconnects the intellect from faith and so stunts the soul that learning becomes but a faint shadow of what education at its best has to offer.

The bond between university leaning and Christian heritage has been severed. What we see at most on secular campuses is a return to faith by some who admit a realm of mystery or transcendence beyond the world of technocratic science and who break with the unrelieved relativism of the recent past by speaking vaguely of the significance of Judeo-Christian values. In a context where individuals seek mainly their own self-interest and in which entrepreneurial ambition dwarfs the sense of call, there is little sense of community and of a society in which deference to the will of God overarches competitive instincts.

Early Christianity provided an impetus for universal education; it had an imperative message for every last man, woman, and child on the face of the earth. Today secular education is prone to overlook the very realities that gave it a universal initiative. It conceals the importance of biblical theism for Western culture and strips from students any remaining link to enduring truth and a fixed good.

Why then, you may ask, do I as an evangelical spend so much time discussing secular higher learning and so little on the Christian alternative? The fact is, of the twelve million university and college students in the United States, only about ninety thousand are enrolled in the seventy-seven member schools of the Christian College Coalition. What is more, over 97 percent of evangelical Christian young people attend not Christian but secular universities where they find little incentive to align intellect and faith even on campuses that once heralded an explicitly Christian origin. The total number of college students enrolled at religiously affiliated campuses is no larger than the student enrollment of two state universities. Only about 3 percent of the college students in the United States attend Christian colleges that reinforce their faith commitments.

It is imperative that evangelicals mount an alert, conceptual witness that transcends a merely privatized faith. Instead of resorting to a strategic retreat in a humanistic-naturalistic age, we need to launch a comprehensive outreach that enlists otherwise "wasted" young minds as humble and devout but active participants in a culture wide mission. We must rally them to join us in the incomparably vital and sacred task of rescuing our children and their children and generations yet to come. We need to remind a disillusioned materialistic generation that it is not too late, as C. S. Lewis put it, to be "Surprised by Joy."[2] We need to train first-rate scholars to live and speak as Christian astronomers and physicists and historians and psychologists and artists. We must so formulate and verbalize the truth that the world will want to listen. We must translate theology into the vernacular of our day, even if Madison Avenue considers words but a manipulative means to a materialistic end. Let us declare and demonstrate what a real education is all about. Let us reinstate an abiding concern for truth and the good, declare the awe of God as the cradle of wisdom, and reaffirm God's saving work in human life.

If true to its calling, the evangelical college offers the best prospect for elaborating, promulgating and exhibiting the Christian world life view in a comprehensive and consistent way. In their promotional literature, evan-

---

2. C. S. Lewis, *Surprised By Joy* (New York: Harcourt, Brace, Jovanich, 1988).

gelical colleges have always flaunted this world-life academic perspective as specially distinctive of evangelical education. Unfortunately, not all evangelical schools fulfill this high promise. Sociologist J. D. Hunter questions whether evangelical colleges and seminaries do, in fact, effectively transmit evangelical orthodox views to the oncoming generation.[3]

No campus—however evangelical—can be wholly isolated from cultural influences. Is it not a matter of "bait and switch" for a professedly evangelical institution that promises in its public relations to expose students to the central beliefs of biblical Christianity to dilute those beliefs in the classroom by concessions to the secular philosophies that it professes to critique? Is it not both an academic and a spiritual tragedy if students, parents, and donors are encouraged to think that an institution is firmly committed to the evangelical faith when students in one or another department of that school are presented instead with neoorthodoxy or some other distortion of an authentic scriptural stance? Slowly but surely the inherited commitments are put under pressure and are spared suffocation only by a thousand qualifications, until finally they collapse under the weight of alien compromises and logical inconsistency.

In *The Closing of the American Mind*[4], Allan Bloom pictures the college and university life of American young people as an escape from the authoritarian rigidity and ethical sterility of the home and as a final opportunity for permissiveness before being thrust into a world that will hold them publicly accountable. In this amorphous interlude, says Bloom, the universities bear at least some responsibility for civilizing the American student. Yet the sad fact remains that universities have forfeited the very transcendent realities that make possible the maturing of the human mind and the sensitizing of the human spirit. The classroom accords no significant role to the God of the Bible, to fixed and final truths, or to changeless moral imperatives. The radical moral rebels are not alone in holding ethical realities at a distance; they are joined by more and more mainstream academicians who ask whose morality is to be taught if students are to be morally instructed and imply that no universally valid truth claim any longer attaches itself to ethical commitments. If the campus is to reshape the life of American youth, it is clearly the Christian campus that must rise to the task.

It is absolutely astonishing, however, that in a land where two-thirds of the population is Protestant, and fifty million persons profess to be born-again evangelicals, so few believers champion any program of

---

3. James Davison Hunter, *Evangelism: The Coming Generation* (Chicago: University of Chicago Press, 1987).
4. Bloom, *The Closing of the American Mind*, 346.

higher education other than what currently exists; the specifically evangelical campuses they support reduce, moreover, to a handful of evangelical colleges and seminaries. Unfortunately, even these evangelical campuses now often inherit young people who at home have acquired little moral and theological instruction over and above the most elemental restraints; even many churches and Sunday Schools leave our youth grossly unprepared for constructive moral and intellectual participation in an increasingly pagan society.

Over and above an evangelistic appeal that often hurries over the crucial intellectual issues, can we as evangelical Christians respond effectively to the present crises in education? Can we engage seriously in the battle for the human mind and will in a society that uncovers our assumptions about the truly real world? Can we confront an academic phalanx that boldly claims to have demolished evangelical presuppositions when for the central beliefs of biblical theism it has, in fact, merely substituted a rival set of presuppositions dictated in advance by the naturalistic creed of a radically secular age? Shall we merely direct our peals of thunder and flashes of lightning against secular educators, or shall we step into the gap that even some of the best young student minds wish we would fill?

Not long ago a graduate of a denominational college wrote me out of the blue to say that during his campus studies he had been shaken head to foot by biblical criticism and that "Ungodly religion majors made me fight for my faith. The intensity of the world situation," he continued, "soon led me to cop out. I sinned a lot—sex, alcohol, drugs. Some of my Christian fellow students were soul-winners who considered intellectual endeavors unspiritual; they were better at proclaiming truth than at defending it on rational grounds." My correspondent conceded that he himself was "more of a prophetic fire than a philosophical incinerator," as he put it. "But I believe we need preachers today who are also theologians and theologians who are also preachers. I wish we evangelicals," he added, "could get away from populism and use our whole persons rather than just appearance and emotion." Next he thanked me—I add this modestly—for lifting him above "irrational complacency over secularistic society" and for calling him to put his whole life on the line in the present culture crisis. "Your essays deal with an evangelical world-view and urge an application of the Word of God to the whole of life," he wrote. "I have begun to suspect that good books are to be prized more than food and lodgings."

We must go beyond mere negative disdain for secular humanism and steamy neopaganism, so that we are perceived as on the side of reason and not as hostile to reason and as supportive of liberal arts education and not as opposed to it. Let us promote positive criticism that grasps the motivation and intention of the nonevangelical views for what they are without caricaturing and maligning them, yet noting their serious weakness and incoherence. Let us exhibit the cognitive and moral power of the Christian alternative, showing how in proposing to rescue the human race from moral alienation it also rises above the devastating inconsistencies and ethical compromises of our secular society.

We have no mandate to impose Christian beliefs upon a pluralistic society. We do have a mandate for presenting evangelical realities in a winsome spirit, and in an intellectually and morally compelling way. That is why we cannot be content with a merely comfortable evangelical coexistence of polite silence in a secular society. A reduction of the Christian mission is a betrayal of our task in a culture victimized by theological and ethical erosion. That task is more urgent now that Western youth turns to consciousness-exploding chemistry for life's supreme thrill and treats a drug-induced hallucination that escapes rational and moral inhibitions as a quasi-religious experience of the Transcendent. It is all the more urgent now as Western philosophy flirts with deconstructionism, the view that no Logos, no reason, no purpose structures the universe and human life.

We need to protest the premature closure of the university mind, which excludes Jesus Christ from its universe of discourse even while it relates all its assumptions about persons and society and human destiny to philosophical conjecture and ideologically loaded causes by disavowing the Christian agenda, the university refuses to transmit the biblical heritage to a younger generation. We need to lift a banner for God's truth and for the good precisely where others disown it as discredited and restrictive when, in fact, it is comprehensive and liberating.

We can still contribute to the right ordering of the world in our own special moment of history. We can show our continuing devotion to the *Veritas* (truth) that Harvard and other venerable institutions have forsaken. We can make a bold stand for God's rightful priority in modern life and for truth and virtue. Only if it rightly perceives the Way, the Truth, and the Life, and grasps anew the possibility and plausibility of spiritual regeneration, will our fragmented society rediscover its lost coherence.

We can applaud the honesty of once-Christian universities that now publicly admit their radical shift to secularization and no longer claim to be Christian or to reflect the Christian heritage. They deserve more credit than do institutions that continue a profession of evangelicalism, but are concessive in their commitments. Every sincere effort to clarify institutional purposes, to foster a sturdy Christian world view, and to reinvigorate a distinctive way of life deserves commendation.

For an evangelical campus, belief in the centrality of the self-revealing God, the singular divine incarnation of Jesus Christ, and the Bible as the norm of Christian truth must be not merely one characteristic among many others, but the unmistakable comprehensive and integrating fact. As committed participants in the world of learning, we must manifest a commitment both to intellectual integrity and to evangelistic compassion. The evangelical affirmation is not that Jesus Christ is simply a way of truth and life for a beleaguered segment of humanity, but that He is *the* Way, *the* Truth and *the* Life for all people.

We do not see human culture as salvific for it has no resources to impart redemptive grace. Yet culture at its best can, nonetheless, be a seawall against rising tides of barbarianism. Unfortunately, however, much of contemporary academe no longer serves this function; efforts to identify and to preserve timeless truth and enduring ethics are scorned by many of its influential voices. Surely education has run amok when a prestigious university will seek out and pay an exorbitant salary to an atheistic professor, when undergraduates are deliberately taught to disparage the reality of true knowledge, when university classrooms refuse to integrate theological nuances and secular emphases, when students for the sake of doctorates write dissertations on what they do not necessarily believe, and when the grip of the enemy motivates scholars to treat God as a term of contempt.

To challenge the naturalistic tide in a society that has forgotten what soul searching is all about, we need evangelical faculties with cognitive and communicative power to quicken and to nurture the great spiritual concerns of life. If ever this generation is to become a generation of virtue, it needs to be dramatically confronted by those who smell the acid, enveloping smoke of our pagan age, and who will share the incomparable realities and rewards of new life in Christ that alone can lift the pall of darkness. We need in our midst a postapostolic vanguard to speak afresh of a still possible Damascus Road experience even in today's wretched existence. We need the sharing of those who by the grace of God have personally moved from disenchantment with secular humanism and its looming abyss of nihilism. In its preoccupation with self-analysis and self-image our generation is reaching for changes and values that promise release from the cluttered and clogged mind of an unpromising modernity.

Under God it is not too late to restore to collegians a hunger to pursue truth and right in the context of the inspired Word of God. It is not too late to challenge faculty to dedicate themselves to fresh exposition of the Christian view of God and the world in their various disciplines of study. It is not too late for a campus of administrators, faculty, and students who share a corporate vision of the Christian mandate to bring all learning and life into the service of Jesus Christ through personal and group commitment. It is not too late through such evangelical centers to reach out to a cognitively confused and volitionally wayward society. It is not too late for Christian education to claim all the realms of culture for their noblest use to enrich and uplift humanity. It is not too late for academicians grateful for divine revelation, for the divine gift of grace to penitent sinners, and for the life- transforming power of spiritual sanctification, to extend Christ's own victory over injustice and evil and to herald the ultimate triumph and lordship of Christ over all peoples and nations.

In today's anti-intellectual climate can we foresee an evangelical campus that would fully expose entering freshmen to Plato's *Republic* to see how the classic Greek mind held ancient naturalism at bay, how it wrestled such priority concerns as the nature of the ultimate world, the durability of truth and the good, and the ideal content of education, how it confronted the perils of political democracy in its struggle for survival against the narrow self- interests of the people it served? Shall we not immerse young minds in the best insights of philosophical reasoning and then exhibit revelatory biblical theism with its timeless claim upon the mind and heart of humanity in all its generations? Why not teach our students logic and a respect for the universal significance of reason at the very outset of their studies? Why not, on a background of the timeless affirmations of Scripture, introduce them as well to what is best in the humanities and to the space-time tentativities of modern science? Is there any longer an evangelical campus that ventures to resist today's perilous tide by crowning collegiate studies with a comprehensively integrating course in the Christian world-life view? Is there any longer a senior requirement that applies the claims of God the Creator, Redeemer, and Judge of life to the predicament of the self and of other selves who populate this wounded cosmos? An associate of the Carnegie Foundation has suggested that just as colleges and universities have final graduating exercises, they might also sponsor entrance dedicatory exercises that mark the serious entry into the world of learning. It is a challenging idea indeed. Is there an evangelical school anywhere that is not primarily driven by size and numbers, not given to the bait of diversity that attracts ever wider constituencies for the sake of student enrollment and financial support, at the eventual cost of the school's doctrinal affirmations? Do these affirmations pose in the catalog like some dust-covered monument from the remote past? Do they now count for less as a statement of faith or credal commitment than do the swirling nebulous winds of contemporary evangelical opinion?

Is there a campus where evangelical professors are recognized in the extended world of learning for their prowess in particular fields of concentration? Are students excited by their professors' engagements in the secular arena that so desperately needs to know the relevance of a biblical faith? Do their professors take time to hone the God-given gifts of the younger generation? Are professors respected and revered not only for their academic contribution but also for their participation in the life of the church?

The student family and faculty community must reenforce one another in the Christian virtues, demonstrating a collegial relationship that bonds administration, faculty, and students. Its goal will be the preparing of devout and culture-sensitive alumni who represent and can elucidate the cause of truth and right in an appealing and logically compelling way. The faculty will be spiritual and intellectual role models that students can emulate.

The needed reformation in evangelical education will not emerge under its own inherent initiative. It requires biblical incentive, volitional determination, intellectual insight, creative imagination, and sacrificial dedication. Thirty years ago evangelicals lost a golden opportunity to launch a great Christian university. Today many people are asking if it is possible to launch even a modest evangelical college that is unswervingly true to the Protestant Reformation and that, if relatively small, can gain national respect for its academic achievement, its moral strength and its spiritual vision.

There is no need to dream wildly of throngs of graduates confronting the forces of secularism and paganism, or graduating hundreds of Augustines, Calvins, and Wesleys. All we need to pray and work for is but one contemporary Augustine, one contemporary Calvin, one contemporary Wesley. Better yet, instead of trying to clone some past star, let each student reach for God's image in Christ, each to be like Him and to serve Him to the fullest with his or her peculiar gifts. We need also to stimulate a highly qualified laity; the fact is, that all leaders of the Protestant Reformation were university trained and often had better academic credentials than did the clergy.

Stemming the present tide is obviously not our responsibility alone; the future of America, the West, and the Third World, too, is in God's hands. Our role—and it is major—is to bring to this present hour minds and hearts illumined by God's mind and heart and knees bent before Him in intercession. Our calling is to obey and to remember that His special intelligible revelation to a small people in a small sector of the ancient world became, in His special providence, the resource that lifted the West above its pagan mires. The dynamic power of that revelation remains available today to reverse contemporary neopaganism as well, if we but release it to mold and maintain the vision of our evangelical schools and colleges.

# The Shrouded
# Peaks of Learning

*It is difficult to imagine a more awesome culture-context than our own in which to debate what constitutes a truly great civilization. Evangelical colleges have an inescapable duty not only to focus the awareness of students and of the entire academic enterprise on the current civilizational crisis, but also to discuss and debate the crucial issues of truth, goodness, and freedom as life and death matters for our generation.*

Like many career journalists, I was thrust earlier than most young people into the mentality and life-style of the secular world. When in 1935 I arrived at Wheaton College at the age of twenty-two, I had behind me some seven years of journalistic engagement, first as a high school sports reporter, then as a general reporter and relief editor, and finally as editor of Long Island weekly newspapers and suburban stringer for leading New York dailies.

After my conversion to Christianity, my goal was to learn and to live the Christian world-life view. From the day of my spiritual conversion I knew that evangelical faith differed radically from the modernistic religious sentiment that prevailed in the 1930s. Modernism had overtaken most of Protestantism's mainline leadership, had severed evangelically founded institutions from their inherited creedal commitments, and had turned many churches simply into podiums for book reviews, travelogues, and moral idealism.

**103**

My secular editorship had left me quite unaware of evangelical academic options. When a Christian headmaster told me of Wheaton College in Illinois, I applied with alacrity, even though its published code of conduct (no smoking, no gambling, no card-playing, no dancing and no moviegoing) seemed amusingly odd (for, among other things, I had been cinema editor for a chain of seven papers). I mention this not to downgrade evangelical institutions. Their refusal to capitulate to the way of the world in thought and behavior was and continues to be commendable. Separation from the world in those days, however, was widely translated into a list of legalistic negations at the expense of an all-embracing biblical ethic. To be sure, hindsight often disclosed many of the strictest prohibitions to be prudent, but the absence of a comprehensive program of personal and social ethics left Christian sanctification largely as an obscure doctrine. Evangelical agencies withdrew from secular society to concentrate on evangelistic and missionary concerns that theological modernism had abandoned. Evangelicals had no vision of cultural penetration to counter modernism's optimistic Social Gospel.

Convinced that all truth is God's truth, literate Christians had in earlier generations founded great American universities like Harvard, Princeton, and Columbia. By the late 1930s Christianity had virtually lost an evangelical presence in mainstream academe. Philosophical idealism had weakened the theological stance and witness of the once-great Christian universities and also of many denominational colleges and seminaries. In some American graduate schools evangelicals were denied advanced degrees unless they conformed to the new thinking. Teaching posts were denied to evangelicals because compromised schools espoused empirical scientific method as the supreme source of trustworthy knowledge and dismissed miraculous theism as obsolescent. On the Continent, as well, most young doctoral scholars were influenced similarly against evangelical orthodoxy, first by devotees of modernism and then by champions of dialectical neoorthodoxy; both religious trends rejected specially revealed truths and an objectively authoritative Bible, although for different reasons.

Leading American evangelical liberal arts colleges abandoned mainstream secular education as theologically irrecoverable, in view of its growing infatuation with logical positivism and naturalism. Secular higher education was perceived as essentially antievangelical, especially in the realms of theology and philosophy; evangelical educators shaped no strategy, however, for permeating this secular arena. This first period of evangelical reaction stretched into the mid-1940s. To provide an alternative to such secular learning, and in order to preserve and promote Christian education, a variety of private religious schools were founded, such as Bible institutes, Bible colleges, evangelical liberal arts colleges, and theological seminaries.

Moody Bible Institute, which the evangelist Dwight L. Moody had founded in 1886, enrolled thousands of young Christians directly after high school either for undergraduate studies as an end or to solidify their faith before entering liberal arts colleges. It became a prototype for similar efforts, as did Bible Institute of Los Angeles (BIOLA), where evangelist R. A. Torrey served as dean from 1912-24. The Bible institutes made the Bible their basic text and viewed the liberal arts as a secular diversion if not a pagan pursuit. In 1900 only nine such Bible institutes existed. There were twenty-three by 1910, thirty-eight by 1920, fifty-eight by 1930, and ninety-three by 1940. By 1950, only one generation ago, there existed in the United States and Canada 150 "Bible institutes" and/or "Bible colleges," the terms by then having become roughly synonymous. An accrediting association formed in 1947 and recognized by the U.S. Office of Education had by 1952 conferred accreditation on the collegiate division of twenty-three such schools.

Bible colleges gradually enlarged their curricula and selectively incorporated liberal arts offerings. Although they respected university learning, they nonetheless distrusted it as erosive of Christian beliefs. They drew their own faculty members from graduates of a small circle of approved independent seminaries. Instructors were often oriented more activistically than academically. Few had a sense of calling to scholarly concentrations that would best secular contemporaries; most had little interest in a Renaissance breakthrough into secular scholarship.

However different the stance of the Christian liberal arts colleges and evangelical seminaries may be, they, too, are essentially paraculture. Both exist alongside secular education, and both seek to protect students from and against it. My own exposure to evangelical undergraduate and graduate education extended from 1935-42, first as a student in the nation's largest and most prestigious Christian college and then in the Northern (now American) Baptist Convention's largest conservative seminary. At Wheaton College I earned the bachelor and then master of arts degrees, the latter in theology, and at Northern Baptist Theological Seminary, the bachelor of divinity and doctor of theology degrees. The instructional tenor on both campuses was largely theologically assertive, over against the current open-endedness of secular education that questions the absolute truth of any worldview while casting about for an alternative to evangelical orthodoxy.

Across the Atlantic, neosupernatural transcendence had already gained the initiative and the Barthian dialectic had stalemated liberal rationalism. In the American universities evolutionary naturalism continued to rear its head and to protest the loitering influence of absolute idealism and personalism. On evangelical campuses much of the intellectual conflict still echoed the modernist-fundamentalist conflict that similarly reverberated ongoingly through denominations and their churches. This conflict centered on the cognitive credibility of supernatural creedal commitments and left evangelical theology generally on the defensive.

Most of my college courses involved the mastery of a textbook, usually a well-chosen secondary source. My interest in truth and validity inclined me toward a philosophy major, which I combined with an anthropology minor. These were then the most popular majors on campus, in contrast with Wheaton's current preference for business and economics, followed by literature. My precollegiate preparation had been less than ideal. As the oldest of eight children in a poor family, I had no expectation of attending college and hence opted in high school for the commercial course which substituted typing, shorthand, and business law for literature, composition, and creative writing.

My major Wheaton professors, fortunately, were more interested in classic and mainline thinkers than in secondary sources. Gordon H. Clark, who had come from the University of Pennsylvania faculty, not only confronted us sequentially with the claims and counterclaims of Plato, Aristotle, Augustine, Anselm, Kant, Hegel, and many others, but in methodology he assumed also to speak for them in class and thus pressed us to challenge, to commend, and to criticize. Alexander Grigolia, the anthropologist, kept the primary sources on assigned reserve reading. The Latin requirement of those days thrust Cicero upon us, and the optional Greek course included readings from classical Greek poets and dramatists as well as the Fourth Gospel. A graduate level elective course called for summarizing a major work on theology. I chose Calvin's *The Institutes of the Christian Religion*. While several professors interacted with major sources, we were seldom required to work in them. My most memorable (because unproductive) research effort was a disappointing fifty-mile train trip from my Long Island home to the New York Public Library for reference material on the image of God in men and women.

Seminary studies followed the same textbook-lecture-examination routine. Discussion was usually a detour devoted to clarifying some textual obscurity. The ablest teachers taught theology and church history. One lone faculty member, William Emmet Powers, sparked intellectual fireworks in the wake of his discovering Emil Brunner and Edwin Lewis. Powers prodded us to hone our questions razor sharp although his answers were often circuitous, since he was less a systematic thinker than a strange blend of Thomistic, Reformed, and neoorthodox components. Seminary graduate studies consisted largely of students' presentation and defense of papers on specific topics, augmented by professors' critical comments, and periodic lectures.

In those seven years two aspects of my Wheaton studies most promoted cognitive cohesion for me. One was the three-hour required senior course in theism based on James Orr's monumental work, *The Christian View of God and the World,* a sweeping theological vision that vigorously set Christian postulates over and against rival worldviews. The other was the three-day written comprehensive examination for the master of arts in theology degree, in preparation for which I read most of the major articles in the five-volume *International Standard Bible Encyclopedia.* If Orr's work provided the canopy, these essays provided the pillars of a broad and deep evangelical perspective.

Looking back, I wish that my undergraduate learning had thrust me more fully into primary sources, that the liberal arts had more cohesively shaped my overall course of study, and that there might have been more private or at least semiprivate conferences with mentors about the quality and nature of my work and possible future. Something is to be said for the British system that does not look upon classroom attendance and successful examination over lecture content as one's essential course fulfillment but which involves small groups of students tutorially in the preparation of weekly reports for discussion and evaluation by a don.

I have two recollections about these years of evangelical education. One is that my epistemological moorings were not finalized until well after the undergraduate years. To be sure, Gordon Clark's philosophy classes stressed both the role and the limits of human reasoning and focused such issues as the mind's identity with, distinction from, and dependence on divine reason, and whether humans can achieve anything of intellectual finality at all if we exclude divine revelation. I was persuaded that God's revelation in Christ does not contradict the divine revelation in the cosmos and in the generic consciousness of humanity. Moreover, that special revelation is not merely the completion, fulfillment, or perfecting of that universal revelation but is, rather, a uniquely salvific expansion of it, and God's corrective for religious profligacy. General and special revelation are not rival activities; one presupposes the other, although general revelation does not of itself imply or demand special revelation. Such ruminations accented revelation-and-reason concerns on which I had not yet finalized a verdict, and my evangelical environs, in fact, placed me under no great pressure to do so.

It took a secular university environment to challenge this lack of urgency, first in 1944 in summer sessions at University of Indiana and then from 1945-49 in summer sessions at Boston University while pursuing the doctorate in philosophy. At Indiana the head of the philosophy department, W. Harry Jellema, plunged us shoulder-deep into Plato's *Republic* and then, in effect, mounted a lively exchange between Plato and Paul, or Plato and Calvin, while preserving their mutual confrontation of naturalism. Also at Indiana the distinguished Thomist philosopher Henry Veitch submerged us in Thomas Aquinas' fivefold proof of God's existence. To think or speak about God and redemption was not prohibited, but what now became crucially important was how to think of them and how to speak of them. Wrestling the primary sources left its mark. Classroom lectures and dialogue constantly pressed upon us their contemporary relevance, unmasking pretenses of philosophical neutrality as implications were related to what was taught elsewhere on campus in the history and science courses, as well as in other disciplines.

At Boston University Edgar S. Brightman and Peter Bertocci ardently promoted personalism; they considered it a preferable alternative to biblical theism, absolute idealism, and naturalism. Yet in addition to familiarity with their own distinct views—Brightman's finite God and Bertocci's growing interest in panpsychism—they demanded from students a comprehensive knowledge of the entire modern philosophical movement from Kant through Hegel and the absolute idealists. Gordon Clark had earlier prepared me well in the modern empirical thrust from Locke, Berkeley, and Hume through Kant and his Ritschlian successors; now I pursued the post-Hegelian rationalists and their critics. The most demanding aspect was a summer course in which every week I had to read, summarize, and constructively critique one of the Gifford Lectures. Thus I was lifted out of mere secondary sources to confront influentially formative thinkers at close range.

In the educational context of this larger intellectual perspective, I wrote two volumes in 1948, *The Uneasy Conscience of Modern Fundamentalism* and *Remaking the Modern Mind.* Christian theology, I now sensed increasingly, can exhibit cognitive strength with great power in a university atmosphere riddled by rival truth-claims. Furthermore, lively competition in the free market of ideas constrains Christian believers to identify precisely what Christianity approves and disapproves and why. They are required to probe opportunities for establishing the cognitive coherence of truth among those who have prematurely eclipsed its larger horizons.

It would be unfair to evangelical colleges, of course, and even to my own maturation, to view today's schools through uncorrected lenses of studies fifty years ago, or even to assess them by the twenty or more years I taught on one or another of these campuses. Already in the late 1930s President J. Oliver Buswell, Jr. strove to move Wheaton toward a

Christian university. Numerous evangelical colleges stressed the intellectual importance of Christian world-life tenets. Contrary to the secular perception of them as culture-negating, the evangelical schools identified themselves rather as faith-affirming. More and more, they drew new faculty from graduates of prestigious secular universities toward which they had nudged their ablest students for further studies. Student movements arose—Inter-Varsity Christian Fellowship, Navigators, Campus Crusade, and International Students among them—to advance evangelism and devotional piety amid the secular academic environment. In time evangelicals served here and there on secular campuses in administrative and teaching posts. As these schools lost metaphysical and moral consensus, however, and exotic and erotic cults vied for student participation, some of these gifted evangelicals thought nostalgically of the long past "glory days" of the early Christian universities.

The May 9, 1960, issue of *Christianity Today,* which I then edited, carried to two hundred thousand readers my leadoff editorial titled "Do We Need a Christian University?" Echoing conversations with evangelical academicians teaching in secular universities, the essay was publicized widely by *The New York Times,* national radio, and the religious press. The immediate context was Billy Graham's impending evangelistic campaign in Madison Square Garden. Here many thousands of college and university age students were likely to make spiritual decisions. Lacking a local evangelical alternative, they would be studying on secular campuses permeated by naturalistic philosophy. The envisioned Christian university would differ from existing evangelical institutions in several respects. A complex of numerous related colleges whose faculty would consist largely of evangelical professors already established in mainline universities was projected. Its inner-city setting would allow hands-on training and vocational opportunities in journalism, radio, television, business and finance, the arts, and other fields.

In two meetings—one comprised of leading evangelical academicians and the other of financially gifted evangelical laymen—the fortunes of a great evangelical university were debated, romanced, and eventually forfeited. The main obstacle was not money. Missing, rather, was a lack of consensus among potential supporters over whether American Christianity really needed a first-class university. Would, perhaps, another major Bible institute be preferable, or an expansion of Wheaton or perhaps Calvin College to offer a doctorate in one or two specialized fields? Or, perhaps ought not a conservative Presbyterian seminary be launched to forestall the inroads of ecumenical pluralism into Protestant ministerial ranks?

In September 1966, as a fallback from the goal of an evangelical university, a Christian higher education consultation at Indiana University projected what is known as the Institute for Advanced Christian Studies. Its initial objective was to establish an evangelical center like Dumbarton Oaks or Airlie House in the metropolitan Washington D.C. area. Here perhaps six mature scholars might be supported in rotation during a year's academic leave to complete books in their fields of specialization. The research and study center was to be located accessibly to a prominent university, whether on the East coast, West coast, or in the Midwest. Funding for such a think tank was not forthcoming, however, even when the Haverford Hotel in suburban Philadelphia might have been secured for about $350,000. Evangelicals by and large responded more readily to evangelistic efforts with immediate tangible results than to long-range educational efforts seeking to challenge and alter the secular intellectual climate of our times. In certain instances where evangelical leaders attracted resources for educational use they enlarged existing facilities safely removed from the centers of cultural influence. Scaling new peaks of learning for long-range recovery and dissemination of Christocentric culture-changing education had limited appeal.

The Billy Graham Center at Wheaton College, with an annual income of over $1.5 million, stresses world evangelism and missions; its related Institute for the Study of American Evangelicals pursues mostly sociological and historical studies. The Center operates a 250-watt FM station although communications is the college's fourth most popular major.

In 1976 Calvin College of Grand Rapids, Michigan, established the Calvin Center for Christian Scholarship for research on theoretical and practical issues. On a budget of $100,000 to $150,000, teams of scholars comprised of several faculty members, several visiting fellows, occasional adjunct fellows, and a few students have so far issued each year a book-length publication of their work and conclusions.

Hillsdale College in Michigan, a onetime evangelical school no longer religiously affiliated, has partially implemented its recently projected Christian Studies program. Instead of isolating Christian Studies as a special degree program, the college hopes to add a conservatively-oriented scholar, whether Protestant, Catholic, or Jewish in each academic discipline. Each discipline will then reflect the Judeo-Christian heritage in tandem with the views of secular learning.

The previously-mentioned Institute for Advanced Christian Studies (IFACS), founded in 1966 after the collapse of the Christian university vision, hoped as its ultimate goal to lift the Christian world-life view as an intellectually valid banner against the tide of secular education. Except for myself as editor of *Christianity Today*, the directors were respected faculty members at mainline universities. In 1971 the Lilly endowment provided a $75,000 matching grant; later grants brought $235,000 to the resources for one phase or another of the effort, including invitational scholars' conferences. IFACS currently sponsors a series of volumes that relate the Christian world-life view to the various university disciplines.

IFACS was a major factor in the emergence of the Christian College Coalition that in 1982 allied seventy-seven evangelical colleges with an enrollment of eighty-five thousand students. Some alumni of these schools, after pursuing doctorates, now serve on secular university faculties and hold places of importance in government and science; others have achieved distinction in ecclesial vocations.

Evangelical colleges as a whole, despite their emphasis on Christian world-life concerns, exhibit little curriculum wide integration of the biblical perspective. One criticism of the evangelical classroom is a preponderance of teaching methodology that promulgates systematized doctrine in a way unrelated to the immediate life struggles of students and thus discourages their critical interaction. Efforts to recover the excitement of education by enlarging students' sociopolitical involvement simply shift the locus of academic vitality from the clash of ideas to community activity, and do not cope with course content and teaching method as being responsible for poor learning motivation. Substitution, as it were, of community involvement for reading and research in pursuit of ideas and concerns of truth may—as in the case of praxis-liberation theologians—relocate the excitement of "education" in radical social engagement. College is hardly a kind of Peace Corps operation. The importance of life-regulating ideas can be seen, for example, in how Liberty Foundation and Sojourners project quite divergent public goals and, even where they agree, differ over approved means for implementing those agreements. Does such diversity call for wrestling with the underlying divergent principles? If no such principles exist, should collegiate courses oriented to social involvement be offered at all? Unfortunately, a phrase like "the pleasures of the intellect" arouses little applause on many evangelical campuses; the substantive discipline basic to cognitive gratification is not specially popular. Some evangelicals even deplore as Hellenic or Greek rather than Christian and biblical the traditional focus on the primacy of ideas. Noting an increasing evangelical disposition to take the secular university as a model, sociologist J. D. Hunter questions whether evangelical central-beliefs are, in fact, being persuasively mediated to the present student generation.[1]

---

1. James Davison Hunter, *Evangelicalism: The Coming Generation* (Chicago: University of Chicago Press, 1987).

Efforts to launch a research center in America similar to Tyndale House in England have failed thus far. Established by British evangelicals at a site within easy walking distance of Cambridge University, Tyndale's 35,000-volume library has resources in biblical studies surpassing those of the university and is the only facility in Cambridge that allows the use of computers in its carrels. Fifty study desks accommodate specialists from many countries. Besides offering computer searches of over two thousand nine hundred ancient Greek and Latin texts, facilities that turn New Testament research toward linguistic studies and away from preoccupation with more speculative approaches, the library also stocks 100 scholarly journals. British evangelicals have also established similar if more modest efforts at Latimer House, Oxford, and Rutherford House, Edinburgh.

Meanwhile the inauguration in America of religion departments in state universities has complicated the fortunes of theology. The decision to teach only *about* religion, more especially the history of religions, is widely correlated with *Religionsgeschichte* presuppositions that disallow any absolutely unique revelation. Religion departments have become increasingly unable to escape the entrenched pressures of secular humanism; the very definition both of religion and of religious experience has become more and more controversial.

It would be less than accurate of course to imply that American evangelical colleges have made no effort whatever to challenge secular education. In his day, Cornelius Van Til aggressively assailed the speculative presuppositions of secular learning, although his writings circulated mostly in evangelical circles. Besides authoring almost some forty books, Gordon Clark shared in written symposiums that were used as texts on secular campuses.[2] The naturalistic temper of university learning rendered marginal, however, his exposition of the Christian worldlife view in *A Christian View of Men and Things*.

More and more graduates of evangelical institutions completed doctorates on prestigious secular campuses, and did so with academic competence. Some wrote doctoral dissertations critical of widely held nonevangelical views. A dozen or more received doctorates from Harvard during Willard C. Sperry's deanship; among candidates for Harvard doctorates in the 1940s were Edward John Carnell, Kenneth Kantzer, John Gerstner, Paul Jewett, George Eldon Ladd, Roger Nicole, and J. Harold Greenlee. Carnell's Harvard dissertation critically appraised Reinhold Neibuhr's epistemology[3] while mine at Boston

---

2. See, for example, Gordon Clark, *Readings in Ethics*, co-edited with T. V. Smith, 1931.
3. Edward John Carnell, "The Concept of Dialectic in the Theology of Reinhold Niebuhr" (Th. D. Dissertation, Harvard Divinity School, 1948).

University simultaneously faulted the erosive impact of personal idealism on A. H. Strong's theology.[4] Soon after the founding of Fuller Theological Seminary, Carnell confronted nonevangelicals with his prize-winning work, *An Introduction to Christian Apologetics*, even as I completed *Remaking the Modern Mind* and *The Protestant Dilemma*. After midcentury no feature of American theology was more noteworthy than the reemergence of evangelical systematic theology as a viable contender.

To make the transition from the evangelical scene into the mainstream university milieu, one first must note the American evangelical confusion over what constitutes a university. The ready claim to university identity by schools such as Bob Jones, Oral Roberts, John Brown, Taylor, Seattle-Pacific, Biola, Liberty, and others reflects this misunderstanding. The concept of a university as an institution of higher learning with related graduate colleges and/or professional schools such as law, science, medicine, history, education, music, and so on, is foreign to the American evangelical scene. What is meant, instead, is an oversized college that offers some graduate courses alongside undergraduate studies and in some cases offers also a doctorate in one or two limited fields of study. This misunderstanding of the traditional European concept was compounded when the Christian College Coalition was portrayed promotionally as essentially a national university that links eighty-five thousand students enrolled in more than seventy affiliated colleges. Now that many American secular universities attract more students in extension studies than on campus, even evangelical colleges and seminaries vie with each other to establish extension centers.

The fact that Harvard, Yale, and Princeton were originally Christian colleges does not justify attributing university identification prematurely to evangelical colleges whose aspiration far outruns their present status. Alongside the limited evangelical involvement in higher education, one must note the prominence of Roman Catholic colleges and universities in America, the first being what has become Georgetown University in Washington D.C.. Catholics take justifiable pride also in Notre Dame, Loyola, Catholic University of America, Marquette, and other schools. From the history of Catholic institutions, and contrary to inferences that might be drawn from the fortunes of Harvard, Yale, and Princeton, and many other campuses established to train Protestant clergy, it should be apparent that university learning need not inevitably lose its original religious orientation.

---

4. Carl F. H. Henry, *Personal Idealism and Strong's Theology* (Wheaton, IL: Van Kampen Press, 1951); originally presented as a dissertation to the faculty of Boston University.

## The Moral Collapse of Secular Learning

If most past-generation American evangelicals could not really feel at home atop the academic heights, secular learning obscured those summits in yet another way, namely, by naturalistic erosion of transcendent, metaphysical-moral realities.

The fact that over three hundred thousand foreign students are enrolled among America's twelve million university students testifies to the continuing perception of U.S. campuses as prestigious carriers of the world's most coveted learning. Regard for these institutions as "world class" continues, moreover, despite a 1983 report titled "A Nation at Risk" that spoke of "a rising tide of mediocrity" in American higher learning. Among growing complaints especially of undergraduate American education are its preoccupation with methodology, its deference to vocational training, and its concentration in the name of "progress" on social studies that neglect reflective thought and the intellectual heritage of life-shaping ideas and ideals. The 1.8 million-member National Education Association tends to regard underfunding as the main educational problem, despite the fact that many secondary school graduates now enter college with poor writing and reading skills, and that achievement and aptitude scores are lower than two decades ago.

By the late 1960s educators in both American colleges and high schools were doubting their moral authority to impose values on students and, in view of evolutionary theory, increasingly questioned a universally fixed right and wrong. Modern academe had drifted astonishingly from Plato's representation of education as an ethical enterprise and his insistence on the inseparability of the intellectual and moral. Value clarification of individually perceived mores was the vogue, even if verbal expression of such internally felt ethics involved no universal validity-claim and, in effect, accommodated ethical relativism. Nothing now seems more offensive to educational bureaucrats than the insistence that public schools should teach at least some fixed truth and an absolutely unqualified good and evil. Professional educators view such instruction as intolerance of America's diversity and pluralism. What emerges, however, is an intolerance of all absolutes except that of intolerance!

Yet four out of five American parents still think public schools should instill not only correct subject matter but also moral absolutes and proper behavior. They think that schools have a basic duty to vindicate the ethical life and to clarify which behavior patterns merit universal support and why. They are dismayed when discussion of the good consists simply of citing current moral dilemmas and exhorting students to respect school regulations in respect to campus cheating, littering, vandalism, and so on. Under these circumstances schools merely reflect surface values of the immediate community rather than a program of principles that undergird and sustain a continuingly vigorous society.

The universities are now seemingly at a crossroads. Criticism of liberal arts learning has stimulated such works as E. D. Hirsch, Jr.'s volume on the decline of *Cultural Literacy* (Houghton-Mufflin, 1987), and Russell Jacoby's *The Last Intellectuals* (Basic Books, 1987). Allan Bloom's *The Closing of the American Mind* protests that higher education currently impoverishes the souls of collegians and breeds a relativism that cancels the pursuit of a good life. Analysts more and more link the current moral malaise of American society to the academic dilution of shared beliefs and values essential to social stability.

Government and corporate grants, often self-aggrandizing, helped lift schools out of their particular isolations, and many campuses as a result soon catered to the special interests of their benefactors. For many secular universities the great society became the social and educational mandate that replaced liberal arts by technocratic scientism in order to produce technological and commercial specialists. Some campuses may have resisted this surge but a largely materialistic culture and perspective nonetheless infiltrated academe.

The rampant individualism of liberal education today is a cancer among both students and faculties. Current criticism concerns itself therefore not only with education as a perceived discipline requiring specific administrative commitments, but also with—or especially with—students and teachers. The search for self-fulfillment that underlies much individualism, Spaeth thinks, is abetted by academics whose only interest in interdisciplinary programs is to promulgate their own perspectives. Paul Piccone comments, "For most career minded professors, teaching students in universities has become at best an irrelevant chore and, at worst, an unavoidable—but certainly containable—nuisance, while originality is a liability readily circumvented by immersion in overspecialized subfields and impenetrable 'professional' jargon."[5]

Many teachers who present the humanities do so in an irrelevant and uninspired way; they often fail, moreover, to challenge the relativism that nurtures social nihilism. Even some teachers who approved humanities courses did so for reasons other than any significant truth-claim and discussion of timelessly relevant ethical principles and of the ultimately real world. Many students consider liberal arts an unwelcome detour from required curriculum content and from vocational objectives. While

---

5. Paul Piccone, "Pathologies of Higher Education", *The World and I* (march, 1988 561.

some humanities-oriented scholars may dispute the truth and goodness of science per se, their counterparts, natural scientists, far more boldly resist the humanities as a necessary aspect of learning. More and more scholars are asking whether anything is now as important as mathematics and the natural sciences. Even high school graduates increasingly take for granted their commitment to scientific techniques as a way of life, and avoid claims of final truth and morality that secular humanists routinely assail alongside their inconsistent commitment to social imperatives. Often philosophy, history, foreign languages, literature, and the arts are considered unproductive. Students are certificated as educated even if they are ignorant of the Magna Carta, for example, and of the Reformation.

Have the Camelot days of so-called liberal learning disappeared? Many classrooms convey little about life other than its quantitative elements. The prejudice grows that values belong neither to the externally real world nor to the subject matter of knowledge, and therefore have no claim on student life and activity. Only empirically "verifiable" knowledge is considered genuine knowledge; except for the reductive mathematical formulas of physics and chemistry, all life-concerns are considered but matters of personal preference.

Liberal education is in trouble, its critics insist, because it ignores the ultimate issues—the meaning of life, the nature of truth, the identity of justice and the good, the content of love, the role of power. As Allan Bloom writes: "The crisis of liberal education is a reflection of a crisis at the peaks of learning, an incoherence and incompatibility among the first principles with which we interpret the world, an intellectual crisis of the greatest magnitude, which constitutes the crisis of our civilization."[6] Worse yet, says Bloom, many leaders now lack the capacity to recognize, let alone discuss, this crisis. Many Protestant and Catholic critics share Bloom's dim view of present-day liberal arts education. Emergence of secular humanism as the masked metaphysics of Western university learning has nurtured growing demand for an alternative view that disputes rather than enthrones contemporary relativism.

To help forestall the cultural triumph of naturalistic empiricism and technocratic scientism, Mortimer Adler and Robert M. Hutchins in 1945 projected a campus core list of great books. During his presidency of the University of Chicago, Hutchins introduced the study of these books at various levels. The so-called great books maintain a focus on persistent issues of philosophy, indicate alternative ways of facing them, and underscore the inescapability of decision. They were considered the

---

6. Bloom, 346.

agenda for permanently relevant reading and a catalyst to lifelong learning. As a promising alternative to John Dewey's experience-oriented
education, the great books program challenged those academics who
would allow every discipline unchallenged while assuming that such
diversity somehow promotes cognitive coherence and stimulates holistic
unity of the self.

American education has no ancient or medieval "classic" tradition of
its own. It therefore faces the problem of setting convictions in long-
range context. According to former U.S. Secretary of Education William
J. Bennett, 86 percent of all American colleges and universities offering
bachelor's degrees require no study in classical Greek or Roman civilization, 75 percent require no study of European history, and 72 percent
require no study of American literature or history.[7] The "bachelor's
degree," notes the National Institute of Education, "has lost its potential
to foster the shared values and knowledge that bind us together as a
society."[8]

Amid these crosscurrents stand faculty members unsure of heritage,
and administrators in doubt about the foundations of a quality education. Stated curricula define the purpose of educational institutions and
indicate the place they assign in human life to liberal arts, intellectual
order, metaphysical beliefs, moral earnestness, religion, and democracy,
in short, to the nature and character of alumni they envision and hope
to nurture.

Indispensable to any shared learning experience is a central core of
content. This core implies a verdict on the need and value of academic
coherence. It identifies which competencies are expected from scholars.
If education is truly education, the course of study must urge, if not
impel, students toward scholarly creative work, lest they inhibit the vitality of learning and the ongoing cognitive life of their communities. A
mind unhoned by relevant intellectual resources can hardly be alert to
formulating the right questions and supplying worthy answers.

Those who regard history as but a collection of mostly past dates and
events, and therefore stress preoccupation with the present, are surely
mistaken. As the Archives building in Washington reminds us, "Past is
prologue." History reminds us that the present is but one moment in
time whose distinctives are not necessarily either permanent or better
than what has been known before. It reminds us also that precisely
because of neglect of the past and its lessons, the present may be

---

7. William J. Bennett, *To Reclaim a Legacy: A Report on the Humanities in Higher Education*
(Washington: The National Endowment for the Humanities, 1984).
8. See *Involvement in Learning* (Washington: U. S. Government Printing Office, 1984) 10.

doomed to insignificance. The status of free-floating opinion, Socrates warned, is tenuous. The West's intellectual and spiritual structures build on Jerusalem and Athens, Rome and Geneva. Efforts to establish a decisive link not merely between the Graeco-Roman era and modernity, but also and especially between the medieval era and modernity, often tend to eclipse the Reformation. They tend to concentrate instead on the Enlightenment with its radical materialistic components, while the Renaissance with its Christian humanists like Calvin and Zwingli is overlooked.

Some critics asked why the Hutchins-Adler selection of great books, heavily weighted with medieval scholastics, omitted classics of the Protestant Reformation like Calvin's *Institutes of the Christian Religion* and Luther's *Christian Liberty* or *The Bondage of the Will*. Furthermore, any list of only past masterworks runs the risk of neglecting important contemporary books, including those by African, Asian, Latin American, and other ethnic writers.

Recently the Western culture program at Stanford University survived a year of controversy by tapering the required core list of reading sources to only six: Plato, the Bible, Augustine, Machiavelli, Rousseau, and Marx. Although open to future supplementation and revision, the present list supposedly highlights perennially crucial concerns of Western civilization and is therefore considered basic to a shared intellectual experience. In addition freshmen may be required to study ancient and medieval culture and all students must take a course in non-Western civilization.

The revised Stanford list of six reading sources is a marked cutback from the program's previous core list of fifteen works supplemented by eighteen "strongly recommended" sources. Included in the earlier readings was Luther's *Christian Liberty;* Freud's *Civilization and Its Discontents* was also listed, although Shakespeare's works were bypassed. The earlier list of over thirty required and recommended works was excessively European, observed certain critics who thereby implied a geographical determinant of literary greatness. Other critics deplored an apparent overemphasis on the past at the expense of preparing students for the pluralistic nature of today's society. Still other faculty noted an absence of works that recognize concerns of racial minorities and of women. Some critics proposed adding Jane Austen's novels, Emily Dickinson's poetry, and some of Martin Luther King's sermons. Some favored a concentration on topical themes rather than on entire texts. Others wanted relevant provision for the 60 percent of today's college students who pursue nonhumanities vocational programs.

What moderns mean by an educated person is obviously both at stake and unclear. The timeless classics—not least of all the Old and New Testaments—are important for their insistent claim to tell the truth about reality and man; for their refusal to capitulate to even the most ferocious attacks against those claims; for their cross-questioning of metaphysical and epistemological counter-assaults; and for their confrontation of rationalistic efforts to disfranchise the long-addressed concerns about God, existence, freedom, goodness, and truth. The classics powerfully confront a generation given to pelting the humanities with historicism and relativism, a generation generally disdainful of tradition and ever seeking what is novel. However much one may seek to reduce the great books to mere culture-creations, or pervert them by superimposing contemporary culture-prejudices, they nonetheless remain a challenge to regnant naturalistic explanations of reality of life, and of ourselves as well. They resist easy reduction to the fluctuating mind of modernity. Not least of all they dispute the bold claim of natural science to have a corner on truth, even while the very nature of truth is held to be ambiguous.

Many combinations of curriculum content are possible without necessarily impairing the quality of educational offerings; no detailed curriculum need be exclusively approved for all institutions. The only necessary norms are unity, cohesiveness, and coherence of the educational goals that underlie book selection. Variations must, however, escape the trivial and mediocre and avoid a patchwork of components that holds nothing together. The St. John's College/Annapolis program involves four years of seminars based on great books in literature, philosophy, history, and religion. There is no need to consider this particular program as normative.

No doubt professors and students are more important than curricula, since no course of whatever kind is self-implementing. We can hardly speak of cognitive community where consensus consists mainly of faculty-shared antipathies—the scorn of fundamentalism, or of orthodox theism for which fundamentalism becomes a ready aspersion, or even of any supernaturalism more articulate than a vague transcendence or some mystery fringe of reality. Beyond a shared commitment to academic freedom and faculty tenure, what common program is there for addressing the intellectual chaos of our foundering and unfocused campuses? What cohesive view of learned discourse can emerge where some departments are scarcely on speaking terms in respect to substantive concerns and share no awareness of an overarching cognitive totality. What real community exists in pursuit of shared truth or a common good where a massive conglomerate of learning lacks a synoptic intellectual canopy?

Ideally a faculty is more than a cluster or cloister of academic colleagues who appreciate each other's labors; it is a community of mind and heart that throbs with awareness of an intellectual heritage and that hungers for and thrives on broad cognitive communication and debate. Philosophy is less than love of wisdom if Heidegger is its patron saint and Plato, Aristotle, Aquinas, Calvin, and Kant are forgotten. Political theory is impoverished without an awareness of Pericles and Hobbes, not to mention Lincoln and Churchill. Physics is impoverished if taught without recognition of Newton and with reference only to Heisenberg, Einstein, and Oppenheimer. It is specially noteworthy how zealously modern secular educators avoid reference to Jesus of Nazareth. A contrived conspiracy of silence best seems to safeguard against any discussion of creedal claims made in His behalf. Is Jesus not at very least one of the great teachers of the world? Does dishonorable nonmention perhaps say something important about the secular evasion of the enduring realities?

## The Evangelical Challenge

Whether the existing evangelical colleges can effectively confront the cultural landslide is uncertain. Less than 1 percent of the nation's college students are enrolled in evangelical colleges. Many evangelical programs seldom engage primary sources; some deliberately avoid exposure to critical or hostile secondary sources and opt for mediating texts. To be sure some professors pose the right questions nonetheless, but the temptation is strong to concentrate on isolated volatile concerns. Not even so-called "Christian counterproposals" may be welcomed uncritically. A culture-critique is surely inadequate if it simply elevates school prayer as the most critical issue or insists only that creationism be taught in science courses.

The evangelical movement must resist a declining interest in the disciplined theoretical life. Little is schematically taught at home or in most churches today that the evangelical classroom can reinforce or extend. Many a student looks to college or university as a welcome flight to intellectual autonomy and as an escape to moral laxity from spiritual aridity and ethical repression at home. College is a resort stop before looming vocational and financial responsibilities of the long future expose the venturesome spirit to public view. Yet, as Allan Bloom reminds us, this campus hiatus is "civilization's only chance to get to" the young student and to challenge him or her to the higher intellectual life.[9] "The indispensable fact," says Bloom, concerning the present student generation, is "that the students who enter are uncivilized, and that the universities have some responsibility for civilizing them."[10]

It is difficult to imagine a more awesome culture-context than our own in which to debate what constitutes a truly great civilization. Evangelical colleges have an inescapable duty to focus the awareness of students and the entire academic enterprise on the current civilizational crisis. They also are responsible to create an environment where students and academics can discuss and debate the crucial issues of truth, goodness, and freedom as life-and-death matters for our generation. Is anything more contemporary than the absolute denial of absolute truth, the claim that moral distinctions merely reflect one's preferred cognitive framework, and that social cohesion depends not on universal ethical authority, but on the superior might of rulers and tyrants? Would it too much threaten departmental turf, for example, if the collegiate curriculum was revised to introduce students academically by studying Plato's *Republic?* Here they would witness the cognitive concern of a noble pagan who wrestled civilizational decline with apostle-like zeal. What has Plato's energetic enlistment of young Athenian intellectuals, his analysis of the debilitating implications of rational and moral relativism and his warning against the unconfronted weaknesses of democracy to say to moderns whose evangelical leaders profess a new social concern and cultural engagement? We all need to remember Plato's challenge to Protagoras who insisted with all the audacity of modern relativists that truth is not objectively the same for everyone and that all judgment is a matter of individual perception.

Would not also the Judeo-Christian Scriptures show their abiding relevance anew by comparing and contrasting them with classical world wisdom as well as with contemporary secular theory? For Christianity few doctrines are as decisively important as that of humanity's creation in the divine image. Should we not at least know what Hebrew prophets and Christian apostles say in principle not only to Plato, but also to Kant who insisted that the *human mind* universally imposes interpretative categories on sense data, and to Hegel who championed the developmental transformation of concepts, and to Darwin who suspended humanity's cognitive apparatus on evolutionary chance? Is all human conceptuality simply forced by nature or demanded by culture? Are all truth-claims and frameworks merely relative to a preferred worldview?

---

9. Bloom, 336.
10. Bloom, 341.

The Bible can, of course, be studied, and it is now often studied in a way that automatically devalues its truth-claims. The humanities today, Bloom comments, "almost inevitably" subject the Bible "to modern 'scientific' analysis, called the Higher Criticism," or use it in comparative religion courses mainly for its supposed contribution to "the very modern, very scientific study of the structure of myths."[11] Comparative religion merely relates Scripture to a universal "need for 'the sacred.'" Speculative criticism channels interest into how the books are structured and concludes that they are "not what they claim to be. . . . A teacher who treated the Bible naively, taking it at its word, or Word, would be accused of scientific incompetence and lack of sophistication." The secular campuses are prone to detour the Judeo-Christian scriptures, Bloom complains, to a department that teaches " 'the Bible as Literature,' as opposed to 'as Revelation,' which it claims to be."[12]Evangelical colleges, by contrast, tend to reserve its content mainly for Bible majors; they shape no "oppositional culture."

While most alumni escape moral pollution, few are able to formulate an alternative more coherent than what can be obtained in many neighborhood churches. Many are quite incapable of addressing an irrational postmodern age where Enlightenment-oriented modernity is on the defensive, cultural relativism is promoted, and nihilism is accommodated. Many media personalities of our day are intellectual and moral nerds, and as such they do little to combat the prevalent historicism and relativism that impede forceful presentation of biblical claims upon society and mankind.

Most evangelical faculty and administrators are convinced of the organic oneness of truth. They know that the so-called contemporary worldview really dissolves into a plurality of multiform views; they are aware that secular learning offers no coherently integrated learning content. What baffles these faculty and administrators is what curricular reforms to make and how to make them. Is there truly a determination in American evangelical circles to confront in dialogue and by curricular supports the current onslaught on metaphysics and morality, one that boldly reaffirms the reality of the supernatural, the universal significance of reason, and the meaningfulness and purposefulness of existence? Is there the needed conviction and passion to tell 12 million college or university students that Christianity remains a religion of truth for all minds?

---

11. Bloom, 341.
12. Bloom, 341.

In an address delivered three-quarters of a century ago J. Gresham Machen lamented the fact that students in America's great Eastern universities showed little vital interest in Christianity. He attributed this disinterest to the fact that "the thought of the day, as it makes itself most strongly felt in the universities . . . [and] from them spreads inevitably to the masses of the people, is profoundly opposed to Christianity, or at least—what is nearly as bad— . . . is out of all connection with Christianity. "The Church," he added, "is unable either to combat it or to assimilate it, because the Church simply does not understand it. . . . What more pressing duty is there," he asked, "than for Christian scholars to make themselves masters of the thought of the world in order to make it an instrument of truth instead of error?."[13] In his *Christian Critique of the University*, the late Charles Malik located the weakness of modern education in its defection from Christian control beliefs. Loss of the truth of God has led in turn to what Malik called "the great heresy of this age," the reduction of man to material, economic, and sociological factors.[14]

Meanwhile the secular universities' loss of the cognitive unity of the sciences has evaporated the unity of the humanities and forfeited the unity of liberal arts learning as a whole. This fact is all the more awesome in that, as Andrew Hacker reminds us, the proportion of young people attending college increased in the twenty-three years between 1960 and 1983 from 34 percent to 58 percent, or from three to almost ten million.[15] During that same period enrollments in private colleges dropped sharply from 40 percent to 21 percent. Less than half of today's students now expect college to help them develop "a philosophy of life." About 85 percent of all enrollees in the humanities are freshmen and sophomores (a considerable number, incidentally, are also enrolled in remedial English).

The Huchins-Adler great books appeal made almost forty years ago is not widely honored and has not succeeded in arresting educational fragmentation. It has merits, even if it need not be implemented precisely in its original form. Whatever curriculum reforms are made, the themes that now confound secular learning must be engaged, including the reality and will of God, the role of mankind as a responsible cosmic

---

13. J. Gresham Machen, "Christianity and Culture", in *Education, Christianity, and the State, Essays by J. Gresham Machen*, ed., John W. Robbins (Montville, NJ: The Trinity Foundation, 1987), 52.

14. Charles Malik, *The Christian Critique of the University* (Downers Grove, IL: InterVarsity Press, 1982).

15. Andrew Hacker, "The Decline of Higher Education", *New York Review of Books* (13 February 1986), 35-41.

steward and the wickedness of sin as moral ruination. We must not simply skirt the omnipresent relevance of the issues of truth and falsehood, good and evil, life and death, man and society. The term love, moreover, needs rescue from ancient and modern erotic misconceptions. The value of an unquenchable pursuit of truth, of the desire for goodness, and of a life lived as fit for time and eternity must all be exhibited and made compelling.

Proposals for C. S. Lewis College reflect a growing conviction that the time is opportune for pilot projects and educational ventures that point toward a renaissance, or if one prefers, a new Reformation in education. Its goal is to avoid nonacademic and vocational erosion of liberal acts learning. It more or less presupposes a high school foundation in English, American and world literature, writing and speaking, foreign language, science, and social studies pertaining to Western civilization and American history. The proposal stems from and builds on several convictions, namely, that authentic faith does not require shielding Christian commitments from public scrutiny, that the secular university need not be abandoned to relativism, that educational content is enhanced by attention to the classical heritage of great books of the past, and that among the greatest of the great texts, the Hebrew-Christian Scriptures tower supreme.

Good education, Edwin J. Delattre remarks, is evidenced by intellectual interactions and dialogue with mentors that prepare students for lifelong involvement in the larger public arena.[16] Its goal is the achievement of a logical, analytical, and decisive mind, one that can engage the Hebrew prophets, the New Testament apostles, and the Greek philosophers, as well as modern communicators in ongoing conversation. Not only by reading but also by listening and by intelligently counterquestioning and affirming will such minds be honed. Education that is oriented to the durable distinctives does not end with a sheepskin or degree; it continues lifelong not only because information expands but also because true learning involves far more than mere accumulation of information. It involves orientation into and exercise of mind-expanding conversation with oneself and with others that challenges the will and apprehends what is perennially valid.

Yet we must not romanticize learning oriented to the great books as being self-evidently superior. They do not, as such, provide a unified and consistent view of life or of the nature and content of truth. However one may alter a core list, reading great books will not in and of itself yield a

---

16. Edwin Delattre, *Education and the Public Trust* (Washington: Ethics and Public Policy Center, 1980), 144.

Christian philosophy of education or an educated person. Much as these volumes focus upon enduringly important issues and indicate well-reasoned answers, only some of them—and these in the borrowed light of the Great Book—emphasize unequivocally that "the fear of [Yahweh] is the beginning of wisdom" (Ps.110:10). Bloom notably refers in the same breath to Moses, Jesus, Homer, and Buddha as "creators . . . who formed horizons" and then comments, "it is not the truth of their thought that distinguishes them, but its capacity to generate culture."[17] Can a stable and enduring culture be generated without attention to the nature and content of truth? To be sure, myths exercise a bonding influence in every culture; without shared ideas and ideals its main supports are lacking. Even Plato and other reflective pagans would have fled cognitive relativism. Does not Bloom's verdict simply underscore the need to include, for example, Calvin's *Institutes* and Luther's *The Bondage of the Will* in any ideal list of great books? A consistent Christian philosophy of education cannot be predicated on a smorgasbord of even great books, but rests supremely on the Scriptures. Unwise as we would be to neglect the classic writings, they do not as such provide a specifically Christian or unified theistic outlook that reflects a fully informed biblical world-life view. No view can claim to be authentically Christian if it ignores transcendent divine revelation, the Kingdom of God as the created world's enduring concern, Jesus Christ as the pattern of what humanity was divinely intended to be, and the indispensable role of the new redeemed society in addressing the historical fortunes of mankind.

The framework for America's earlier vision of "the order of the whole of things," was the Bible, Bloom remarks. Today's loss of such public indebtedness to Scripture is what blurs an acknowledged need for and possibility of biblical world-explanation. When John Dewey wrote that "despair of any integrated outlook and attitude is the chief intellectual characteristic of the present age," he proposed—unavailingly—to remedy such intellectual chaos by replacing theism with naturalism. Can educators any longer forcefully challenge the culture crisis, evangelicals ask, without squarely facing the theme of divine revelation? Secular philosophy has so confused ultimate issues that we cannot ignore the threatened closure of the human mind and will to the divine transcendent.

The ideal beginning for a joint Catholic-Protestant educational venture would be affirmation of the articles of both the Apostles' and Nicene Creeds. Such a cooperative venture need not, nor should it, prematurely close the debate over faith-and-reason relationships and the

---

17. Bloom, 201.

Augustinian, Tertullian, and Thomistic alternatives. A theologically-sensitive college could, in fact, examine the issues significant for medieval scholasticism, Reformation dogmatics, and recent modern theology as vital contemporary concerns. The role of the Bible would be an issue for frank and open discussion. Catholic scholars tend to disparage evangelical proneness to plunge headlong from the Bible to a facing of modern problems without an intervening authoritative tradition; they smile politely, but disdainfully, at "fundamentalist" moves that appeal to the authority of Scripture and bypass the normative wisdom of an ecclesiastical magistracy. Evangelical scholars may indeed tend too much to disparage an illuminating role for tradition. After all the Bible does not speak directly to many pressing contemporary concerns, however much its ethical norms and principles implicate all human decision and behavior. On the other hand Jesus and the apostles set a precedent for an immediate appeal to Scripture and for skepticism concerning much ecclesiastical tradition. Evangelicals in principle prize "the wisdom given us" (2 Pet. 3:15) above the church fathers, the medieval scholastics, and contemporary papal, ecumenical, and even evangelical affirmations.

To be sure, Richard John Neuhaus is rightly critical of the direct appeal by some evangelicals to the Bible alone for legitimating legislative proposals and for neglecting the rhetoric of a republic. He looks to Catholic natural-law theory for mediating concepts and language on which to predicate a broad consensus and thus promotes natural-law possibilities that the Reformers would have questioned. Reformation evangelicals would be just as foolhardy, however, to predicate cooperative university education on an infused Reformational epistemology. Neuhaus promotes a wider pattern of Christian unity and action for which many evangelicals are probably unprepared. His widely publicized conversion from Lutheranism to Roman Catholicism is understandable given the unfolding of his arguments over the past decade. The declining influence of mainline Protestant ecumenism and the sporadic character of evangelical public engagement, he holds, combine to create "the Catholic moment," one not to be abandoned to the American Catholic hierarchy's vocal left wing. Neuhaus advocates the retention of diverse religious traditions within a comprehensive concord on Christian basics in which the Catholic Church sets the pace in shaping public philosophy and national life.[18]

Projection of C. S. Lewis College comes at a time when all likely sponsors—independent evangelical, ecumenical evangelical, and Catho-

---

18. *Postmodern World* (San Francisco: harper and Row, 1987).

lic evangelical—represent conflicting and even competing ecclesiastical alignments. Some evangelicals will doubtless view so broad an effort as the first step of an evangelical return march to Rome. Others, for whom the Reformation remains normative, will welcome new possibilities of conversation and association that may lead to a larger evangelical exodus from Rome. Yet the Catholic Council of Bishops' warning against fundamentalism (which has in view evangelicalism also) shows deep and continuing differences with Protestantism concerning, for example, the normative authority of church teaching and tradition, the scope of biblical inerrancy, the inspiration of so-called apocryphal books, the salvific nature of sacraments, the veneration of Mary, and the primacy of the church over Scripture.[19]

Meanwhile pluralistic Protestant ecumenism increasingly accommodates itself to Catholicism in ventures that in return offer but token welcome to evangelicalism. Numerous Protestant ecumenical seminaries now minimize differences, emphasize commonalities, and promote a mixture of Protestant and Catholic faculty, students, trustees, and funding. Evangelical disappointment over pluralistic Protestant ecumenism continues to encourage an exodus of large denominational churches, although here and there mediating evangelicals are drawn into affiliation in hopes of reorienting ecumenism conservatively. Additionally, more and more young independent evangelicals desire the deeper worship and ritualistic sensitivity as well as culture involvement evident in more ecumenical circles. They welcome a larger role for pageantry and the arts and often uncritically blend this interest with analogical theories of knowledge; they little suspect or know the problems inherent in an epistemology that renounces univocacy.

C. S. Lewis College proposals are therefore not without risks and problems. Questions remain whether a mediating or adjunct educational program, as C. S. Lewis College is initially projected, can really cope with the deficiencies of modern liberal arts learning. If prestigious Catholic universities have been unable to stem the secular tide, it is asked, can success really be expected for a hybrid venture that, in contrast with an independent Christian university, has but a broad supplementary or complementary role? Can a Christian college in an adjunct position hope to redirect an associate secular campus, or serve as an effective lighthouse amid dense didactive fog, or even long hold its own ground in a prestigious climate of confusion?

---

19. *Statement of the National Conference of Catholic Bishops ad hoc Committee on Biblical Fundamentalism*, 26 March, 1987.

The risks should not be quashed or unstated for they are real. They need not lessen the importance of a coordinated, strategic witness to confront the naturalistic tide now inundating our culture and yielding it powerlessly toward paganism. Even if such cooperative confrontation does not, in fact, achieve all that is meant by intellectual penetration, it should not, for all that, be disparaged as merely an act of desperation. When education is in crisis it is better to venture something than to do nothing. Fear and anxiety are neither the only, nor always the best, foundations on which educational strategy should be based. There is much to do, and we must do what we can. Evangelicals dare not abandon or leave unchallenged the wasted minds that roam the secular campuses; they must recharge the conviction that the biblical worldview can indeed recapture the commitment of a resistant student-generation unaware of or estranged from the values of its heritage.

Whether the unstable epistemology of a conservative Catholic- ecumenical-evangelical effort can provide a convincing alternative to the relativistic tide of contemporary education must yet be ascertained. If evangelical institutions manifest a growing tendency to moderate their emphasis on biblical inerrancy, can they consistently criticize a cooperative venture where inerrancy is considered an open question? True intellectual comrades can disagree and even disagree vigorously, yet in those very disagreements reflect a shared concern over the survival of a great civilization. A community devoted to reconstruction needs a friendly climate in which ideas can be exchanged and evaluated, and it needs time to reflect on a long view of history and of the history of thought. It requires resumed conversations with Plato and Paul, Augustine and Thomas Aquinas, and Luther and Calvin whose insights bear on human nature in our time.

The personal projection of intellectual bondfellows in ventures such as C. S. Lewis College should be that of academicians known for educational vigor and commitment to the pursuit of truth and goodness. Given to disciplined study as an expression of devotion to God, they form a covenant community of scholars dedicated to keeping faith with the truth of God, to upholding special divine revelation as the cornerstone of historic Christianity, and to maintaining confessional integrity with the ecumenical creeds of Christendom. If truly under God, such a faculty will exemplify personal godliness and demonstrate compassionate social concern as intrinsic to the church's evangelistic and missionary outreach. Through such representatives of God's mission could come a heroic new era of Christian education, a theological revitalization of the love and pursuit of truth. In a generation of moral ruin and intellectual confusion their championing of biblical wisdom could help nurture once again an authentic Christian character and turn renegade seekers to transcendent anchorage in Jesus Christ. Across the centuries would resound once again the call of Moses and Plato and Paul, of Augustine and Calvin and Luther—to name but a few—to scale with them unshrouded peaks of learning for visions of theocentric wisdom that restores the valleys of daily life and culture to their pristine purpose and joy.

# The Renewal of
# Theological Education

*In a time when many long-standing institutions are unsure of their identity, evangelical seminaries must maintain faith with the biblical heritage and affirm New Testament orthodoxy. They must remove any doubt at the crucial point where many religious ventures today are failing, namely, that of the unambiguous evangelical approach to theological education.*

Education in general, as we know well, is undergoing severe criticism. Some critics deplore the whole enterprise as an instrumental far too slow and speculative to assure the necessary transformation of society, and instead promote violence and revolution as preferred mechanisms for social change. Many others, who defend education, lack consensus over its ideal core content and acknowledge a loss of fixed norms of knowledge and of morality to which they would orient liberal learning and the social order.

The enterprise of theology is by no means exempt from involvement in this academic turbulence. Indeed, theology's very survival value is questioned. Some may say that to speak of "The Renewal of Theological Education" is to presuppose a dire situation in theological learning that some moderns unfortunately consider permanent and irreversible. Champions of so-called theology-of-revolution and theology-of-liberation invoke scriptural themes that lend a larger aura of biblical legitimacy to their proposals than they actually deserve. The term "theology" is, in fact, retained even where some speak God-language while they renounce supernatural divinity. Yet the secular city is largely untouched by such sophistry. The long-respected terms "theologian" and "theology" are now used by political pragmatists in Washington as synonyms for nitpickers and hairsplitting. On secular university campuses some religion departments connect the discussion of divinity with so many metaphysical novelties that their gods seem to be here today and gone tomorrow. The claims of the New Testament upon the modern mind are too readily deflected by calling them fundamentalist beliefs that ignore the supposed critical undermining of Judeo- Christian principles. Never has it been more clear than today, when speculative religious theories are often stillborn, that not every wind that "blows where it listeth" (John 3:8, KJV) is the Holy Spirit.

Tentativity and revisability have left their stamp upon every aspect of contemporary culture. We live in a time when the very future of civilization sways uncertainly in the winds of change. Our planet has soared into the era of space travel and global mass media visibility. What planet Earth has meanwhile lost is a pervasive trust in the self-revealing God and a shared sense of truth and goodness. Secular scholars increasingly venture to explain history and nature and even the human species itself in terms only of natural processes and energy events. Classrooms in our most prestigious universities leave the impression that all affirmations of truth and right are culture conditioned and that humanity's final end is the grave or crematory.

Between 350,000 and 500,000 able young scholars from Third World and other countries annually swarm to America in quest of scientific learning. Many are soon indoctrinated in scientism through the emergence of naturalism as presumptively the only credible worldview. As these world scholars return to leadership roles in their various countries, their trained minds are inclined sceptically not only toward their own inherited religious culture but also toward the great theistic verities that Christianity espouses; they harbor the presumption that the modern scientific worldview of reality is objective and unrevisable truth. Our revered institutions, many of them founded and funded at the outset to teach the essentials of the Judeo-Christian heritage, thus disengage the gifted leaders of the oncoming generation, both foreign and American, from the core beliefs of evangelical religion. Besides international students, our nation also hosts thousands of foreign diplomats, yet there is little about the welcome they receive to imply that the principles of Christianity are in any way significant for the political order and for history and the cosmos. As Bernard Williams would have it, "nothing is important to the universe"; "we read our values into the world"; at best, ethics commends an individually preferred life-style as "most satisfactory for human beings in general."[1]Our century seems almost insensitive to profound culture shocks in the recent past that ought to have awakened us to the looming dark night of paganism that already shadows even Western nations long exposed to vast spiritual blessings associated with the Judeo- Christian heritage. In Germany, homeland of Martin Luther and of the Protestant Reformation, a neopagan ideology embarked a generation ago on a deliberate policy of brutally exterminating all Jews. Its naturalistic assault on Old Testament religion also undermined in principle the supernaturalism of the New Testament in its affirmation of a Christological fulfillment of the prophets. Elsewhere on the European continent the fortunes of Christianity plummeted to unthinkable depths. The Soviet sphere nations all but drove underground a virile Christianity and directed unspeakable persecution against those who courageously carried on evangelism. Simultaneously in so-called Free Europe an encroaching secular materialism so displaced the postwar generation's spiritual vitalities that church attendance sank to incredible lows. Buddhists and Muslims called secular Westerners from the seductions of materialism, and in England some of them acquired redundant church properties for use as mosques and temples.

In the United States, now the vaunted lifeline of evangelical world missions, worldlings have, in a single decade, slain an estimated 15 million fetuses on the altar of sexual indulgence, and the moral permissiveness of secular society tightens its grip even on many churchgoers. Despite the remarkable recent growth of theologically conservative churches, which shelter some fifty-million "born again" believers, the heady spirit of evangelical triumphalism is giving ground as evangelical, cultural impact lessens and evangelism slackens. Prominent televangelists, basking in their network visibility as global voices for revealed religion, revived the lengthened shadow of Elmer Gantry and encouraged the secular city to nationalize its indifference to evangelism by charging exploitation and manipulation. Political confrontation by the religious right has failed to achieve basic legislative changes in the public arena, although it put family values firmly on the national agenda. Some major denominations, meanwhile, have startled the religious realm by a denominationwide controversy over a fully-authoritative Bible.

Any institution which intends to foster the renewal of theological education must signal at once that it has no desire to promote cognitively deviant religious experience. In affirming divine revelation as an authentic way of knowing, it must consider intellectual clarity in theology desir-

---

1. Bernard Williams, *Ethics and the Limits of Philosophy* (Cambridge: Harvard University Press, 1985), 152ff, 182.

able and possible rather than futile. It must not demean the importance of universal reason as a test of truth. It aims to prepare a cadre of devout scholars who "with gentleness and respect," in keeping with the Apostle Peter's exhortation, are "always . . . prepared to give an answer to everyone who asks . . . the reason for the hope you have" (1 Peter 3:15).

When modern writers speak of religious experiences that are beyond conceptual clarity and indescribable in words, and declare religion intelligible only if we postulate new ranges of meaning in which conscious and unconscious factors intersect each other, we had best beware. New currents in both theology and religious art displace the contrast of the supernatural with creaturely life, stress human continuity with the divine, and connect the spiritual with the mysterious rather than with intelligible ideas. Such novel expositions treat as polluted all the inherited expositions of Judeo-Christian religion. In a time when many long-existing institutions are unsure of their identity, evangelical seminaries and divinity schools must maintain faith with the biblical heritage and affirm New Testament orthodoxy. They must remove any doubt at the crucial point where many religious ventures today are failing, namely, that of an unambiguous evangelical approach to theological education.

Among America's more than seven hundred colleges and universities, many of the most prestigious were originally founded, as were Harvard and Columbia and Duke, to school young intellectuals both in the liberal arts and in the basic principles of the Christian religion. Loyal alumni of such institutions, who proudly send their offspring to their *alma maters*, now share a rising tide of indignation because, instead of learning biblical essentials and Christian morality as part of their campus instruction, they return home with cheapened ethical standards and with greater distance between themselves and the Judeo-Christian heritage than when they enrolled.

Timothy George rightly points to the Reformation as our model for a movement to recover the apostolic purity of essential Christianity. His emphasis on the abiding validity of Reformation theology contributes to the current theological debate against those who would dismiss the Reformation on the one hand as archaically medieval, or on the other as merely the first flash of secular modernity. The leaders of the Reformation, George reminds us, "were captive to the Word of God. Their gospel of the free grace of Almighty God, . . . and their emphasis on the centrality and finality of Jesus Christ stand in marked contrast to the attenuated transcendence-starved theologies which dominate the current scene." The Reformation was not, as modernist scholars held, a deliverance from all fixed theological norms; it was a reassertion of the foundational dogmas of the Early Church, one that challenges us to listen anew to what God has once-for-all said in Scripture and once-for-all done in Jesus Christ.[2]

Christianity has survived the external assault of naturalistic philosophers whenever evangelical scholars have unmasked its reductive prejudices and inner contradictions. Inside the professing church itself concessive theologians and fainthearted clergy have at times so diluted the essence of Christianity that not even Jesus and the apostles would have recognized themselves in their representations. A few have even affirmed that God is dead while others, not quite so radical, nonetheless have considered Him terminally ill and an early candidate for philosophically administered euthanasia. Some have denied that the Gospels are historical accounts, and that Jesus of Nazareth was virgin-born, or that He arose bodily from the dead. We need no testimony beyond that of recent modern theology to the fact that a fragmented faith soon involves a piecemeal surrender of Christian truth to rapacious critical lions eager to consume it.

Underlying this theological turmoil is a broken doctrine of Scripture. Critical repudiation has varied from fractional to radical, and it swiftly prepared the way for an endless succession of doctrinal modifications. The manuscript manipulators' shared concern was to achieve an authoritative revision of the canon, yet their partition and patchwork lacked unanimity. After three generations of unfruitful documentary dissection, a courageous cadre of exhausted scholars conceded at last to what evangelical leaders were long saying on their own, that no convincing case had been made by critics who sought to discover earlier, more reliable sources that the biblical writers supposedly used to refurbish legends and myths in the special interest of Hebrew religion. Yet some professional religionists who drew their salaries from the churches, supposedly out of missionary concern for the survival of Christianity in the present age, surrendered even the minimal postulates of biblical theism. Nowhere in the history of great literature have professed experts dissected a classic work into so many diverse and conflicting reconstructions as have critics of the Bible. Under their tutelage divinity students have frequently invested more energy learning novel and often stillborn critical theories than they have given to mastery of the Scriptures and of the central tenets of the biblical revelation. The result is that no great world religion exhibits as does Christianity the spectacle of a ruthless attack on its charter documents by scholars who at the same time profess to clarify the essential Christian message. Never until the present century have those who live by the church's hard-won offerings spoken with such contempt of the church's heritage and pursued so deconstructive a theology to the Word.

---

2. Timothy George, *Theology of the Reformers* (Nashville, TN: Broadman, Press, 1988).

The unwitting consequence of this critical activity is that the Judeo-Christian Scriptures have withstood the most searching scrutiny of any religious tradition. To this day the Bible offers the most compelling revelation of the supernatural order. Its disclosure of the living God and of His ongoing purpose in creation and history challenges the stifling spirit of secular society. Scripture's insistence that every human being bears the *imago Dei* (God's image) disputes modern views that erode the equality and dignity of all humans. Its exhibition of divine moral imperatives confronts the ethical relativism of our age with a call to transcendent authority. The Bible's portrait of Jesus of Nazareth even today motivates hundreds of millions of all races and cultures in their quest for healing, meaning, and new life and to personal repentance on the ground of Christ's mediatorial redemption and to dedicate their lives and talents to Him. This critical hour demands that some truths call for particular theological emphasis in order to note their special contemporary importance. The Christian movement needs to clearly exhibit the authority of Holy Scripture, the missionary and evangelistic implications of evangelical commitment, the integration of intellect and piety in theological learning, and the high relevance of the Christian witness to secular society.

The European theologian Emil Brunner once remarked, quite rightly, that the fate of the Bible is the fate of Western civilization. If the Bible goes, the best of the West goes also. The church must give witness to the following convictions about Scripture: first, that no movement can influence society in general if its leaders continually undermine its charter documents; second, that no movement can impact culture if its scholars exhaust their energies in defending Scripture and fail to unleash it in society-at-large for which it was intended; and third, that the effort by critical scholars to distinguish trustworthy and supposedly untrustworthy segments of the Bible lacks consensus and poses a greater crisis of critical authority than it does a crisis of biblical authority.

The one book above all others that a twentieth century scholar should study remains the Bible; among all the great books with which one should be familiar, the Bible stands tallest. Timothy George rightly reminds us that the Reformers were "master exegetes of Holy Scripture." Indeed, "All of the Reformers, including the radicals, accepted the divine origin and infallible character of the Bible."[3] The churches today need a vital recovery of the authority and comprehensive truthfulness of Scripture and its application to all dimensions of life.

It is now widely acknowledged that the New Testament would never have been written, and that the Christian churches would never have

---

3. George, 315.

come into existence, except for a firm belief that the crucified Jesus arose bodily from the tomb. The critics' efforts to ground this resurrection faith in a childlike illusion have been shown repeatedly to be logically uncompelling. It takes more unfaith to believe the grotesque claims of the skeptics than it requires faith to stand on the side of the New Testament witness for which the apostles unhesitatingly gave their lives. We need to respond to the evangelistic and missionary mandate of the church with a sense of urgency. While we may be grateful that new mass media techniques in the space age enable us to reach vast multitudes, there remains no better way of evangelizing and discipling than one-on-one relationships in one's home community.

We must deepen our personal and institutional commitment to evangelism. Perhaps our local churches would shame us for the sin of silence if they placed on probation any member who had not during the work week spoken to someone about receiving Christ as Savior and Lord. I greatly esteem our missionaries who have invested their lives in an evangelical witness that has made Christianity the only religion with a world presence. It now costs five times as much to support a Western missionary abroad than a national worker, and we may be grateful that the Third World is awakening to its missionary mandate.

For all the disconcerting facts of the current religious scene, there remain gratifying signs of Christian breakthrough. One who listens can hear the rustling of refreshing winds amid the dry branches of a parched society. A generation that turned to materialism, to sexual indulgence, and to drugs for an infinity of pleasure, has found that bleak level of life to be so bitter that even the rate of teenage suicides is mounting. Ours is a generation reduced to living on the raw edges of death, not merely of physical death, but moral and spiritual death. Yet C. S. Lewis emerged to hold off almost single-handedly snide intellectuals who disparage Christian theism and to remind them that their reasons for rejecting Christ are mere rationalizations.

Christianity has brought new hope to the bleakest segments of society. Mainland China, where Red Guards brutally sought to destroy the surviving remnants of Christian witness, nurtured house churches through which millions have come to a devout commitment of faith. Soviet Russia, which virtually confiscated the Bible and intolerantly imprisoned Jews and Christians, has fallen as a victim of its own totalatarian illusion. In the Asian country of Korea 25 percent of the population now affirms a Christian identity. In the African country of Kenya churches are growing so swiftly that many lack trained pastors. Even in Romania, until recently a police state with one of the most intolerant socialist regimes, there has arisen the Second Baptist Church in Oradea whose twenty-five hundred members make it the largest evangelical church in Europe.

The intellectual vanguard of the Christian movement needs today, as in the early church, to be the moral vanguard also. In a day when discipline has virtually disappeared from the churches, and when pastors and televangelists become victims of a carnal culture, we need to embrace truth and piety by living a godly life. A generation ago Western society spoke of the French vices and of barbarians only in the context of totalitarian Eastern Europe or Red China. New moral barbarians have permeated the West and more and more wish to set the agenda in terms of new patterns of conduct and family. Worse yet, even some religious leaders wink their way past deviation from inherited Judeo-Christian values, as if God is a God we can domesticate, manipulate, and acculturate. Is it any wonder that Satanism comes to the fore in a time when many professing Christians seldom pray, have only a surface knowledge of Scripture, and give themselves to the heightened temptations of television soap operas?

We need piety on the Potomac, but do we really have a right to demand it unless we treasure piety in the big cities and in rural America also, and especially in the churches of our land? The Reformers not only believed in prayer; they prayed. They not only promoted worship; they worshiped. If the lack of devout leadership today is itself a judgment of God upon our light view of sin, should we not ask whether the call to repentance must be directed also to those of us who have made church-going the sterile thing that it often is, before we urge the unregenerate world to bring itself under the will of the living Lord? Can we train a vanguard of young minds and hearts for whom the mastery of theology means also, as the New Testaments suggests, to aspire to the mind of Christ who withstood the fierce temptations of His day while He spoke of loving God with one's whole mind?

If ever society stood in desperate need of the Christian message it is today's society. We are now experiencing the twilight of Western civilization. Although I speak of Western culture's approaching doomsday, I do not imply that impersonal forces hold the cosmos and human history unrelentingly in their grip, or that capitalism as the Marxists claim is foredoomed because of the supposed superiority of socialism, or that a fanciful economic determinism renders certain the triumph of an already failed communist revolution. None of that propaganda has the weight of wisdom going for it. The crisis of the West is a moral and spiritual crisis. Education has been unable to halt the billows of injustice; science and technology have bestowed upon us neither wisdom nor happiness. Too much was expected of them by a generation that had misplaced its trust. Nor will a universal proclamation of biblical truth of itself achieve a millennium. It is a consequence of the fall of humanity that little in our history works out precisely in the way in which it is supposed to. The Gospel of Christ does offer transcendent criteria and a view of the dignity as well as the depravity of humanity and promises redemptive rescue and a life transforming dynamic.

To be sure, before God's own final judgment falls upon human history no Christian can insist that every last hope is now already gone for the West and for America. Twilight is not yet midnight, but it may be sunset for America, twilight for the West. Into this very darkness the light continues to shine: Jesus Christ who towers over all human existence as the sinless Son of God, Light of the world and Redeemer of the penitent, the living Head of a new society, the Just and Holy One, who through the body of believers seeks to extend His personal victory over sin and injustice. He, moreover, will return in great power and glory to consummate the energies of all who serve His holy cause in obedient love.

Life is draining away from the secular city, increasingly unmindful as it is of the very realities that make for meaningful survival. Yet, despite the throwaway rhetoric of a generation near intellectual and ethical bankruptcy, we can still reach for God's "good news" for those millions now living on the borders of spiritual death. The gospel of Christ has something to say to totalitarian tyrants and to terrorists, to a world of materialistic greed and of mass starvation, to a world of drugs and sexual license and AIDS. It has something to say to all generations, because it deals in depth with the issues of sin and death, and points the way to the forgiveness of sins and new life and joy. Let us call anew for a recognition of the sovereignty and righteousness of God, whose judgment looms over a prideful technocratic society and over a religiously hollow culture impervious to His demands for truth and good. What can cut across human self-confidence and self-justification more decisively, I ask you, than the doctrine of divine election, of God at work both in judgment and in deliverance, and of supernatural grace that alone can truly free a deeply-flawed humanity?

Let it be said that American evangelicals and their institutions were constantly alert to ultimate spiritual and moral realities, were in daily touch with the great doctrines and precepts of revealed religion, were concerned for the life of the mind and were aware of the profundity of the Christian worldview. Let it be said that they faithfully expounded its implications for human life in the twentieth and twenty-first centuries, and amid their intellectual confrontation of a crumbling naturalistic culture were engaged in character building that shapes a life fit for time and for eternity. That is the demand of evangelical integrity and the opportunity for evangelical effectiveness.

# Part III
# Maintaining
# Evangelical Integrity

# Seizing an
# Evangelical Opportunity

*Something seems basically amiss or lacking in the evangelical enterprise. A problem remains despite entrepreneurial enthusiasts armed with newly coined catch-phrases on jet-set missions, and who operate with highly paid public relations staff and computerized mailing lists. The basic problem is one of indifferent enthusiasm for mental application and liberal arts engagement. We seem to support stringent learning far less than other options*

We are trusted and honored guardians of the next generation's evangelical minds. Much of the intellectual and moral leadership that Christianity will provide in the looming twenty-first century will reflect the priorities we nurture in this fast-closing twentieth century. I am persuaded that evangelical colleges and institutions of higher learning still face perhaps their best opportunities. Some of our academic efforts, to be sure, may falter and fail. Will we nonetheless reach for higher options, or will we lose them by default?

## What Special Opportunities Lie Before Us?

Tens of thousands of alumni of mainstream universities that were founded and funded to enunciate biblical truth and morality are not disillusioned over the sad condition of many of those campuses. Syndicated newspaper columnist Michael McManus says that droves of parents who patriotically pay high tuition fees to send their youngsters to a now-secularized alma mater are currently distressed. Their teenagers, they complain, graduate with little exposure to Christian realities and return home more confused and morally compromised than when they left. Evangelical colleges stand to inherit a great deal of approbation and goodwill if they offer a respectable alternative.

Today's compartmentalized character of secular learning is provoking new interest in an integrative world-life view. No sound mind is long satisfied with shuttling between conflicting worldviews—with what Richard Mouw depicts as "rather constant trans-world-view traffic."[1] Amid present-day liberal arts studies, evangelically-integrated education can offer a convincing option. The world needs to know that the Christian faith is not a form of philosophical vagueness. Do our schools effectively portray Christ, the Logos of God, as the source and monitor of creation life, of redemption life, and of resurrection life? Do they persuasively portray the Logos of God as the coherence of all reality and existence? As Stephen Toulmin reminds us, philosophers of science are increasingly penetrating today's metaphysical vacuum to postulate their own principles explaining life and existence. Evangelical education, if it determines to do so, can and ought to speak comprehensively and compellingly to such worldview concerns.

Naturalistic theory readily caters to self-interest. Is it not remarkable that our courts now impose community service as a redemptive activity for criminal offenders? In today's drug and AIDS ravaged society, evangelical education can nurture personal involvement in community service and in the public order to help mitigate social injustice and to exhibit Christian compassion. Thank God, the evangelical movement has commendably reversed its earlier withdrawal from cultural engagement. What is needed, however, especially in our Christian colleges is clarification of principles and programs that effectively unleash evangelical engagement in the social arena. A conjunction of currently existing relief and development agencies with the Evangelical Foreign Missions Association, for example, could conceivably stimulate an international Christian service corps that leaves its mark overseas and in America.

Evangelicals continue to neglect the doctrine of the church and at high cost. Something needs to happen on evangelical campuses to help students realize that they are not merely the church of tomorrow but rather, as Tom Rutherford puts it well, the church of today.[2] Nine in ten persons are under age twenty when they receive Jesus as Savior and

---

1. Richard Mouw, "Evangelicalism and Philosophy", *Theology Today*, 44 (October 1987), 334
2. "Where Have All the Students Gone?", *Acts 29* (November-December 1989), 2.

Lord; before them lies a half century of Christian life and work. Even during college they should experience active church involvement alongside the usual school religious activities. In communities where many people find survival empty of worth and meaning, spiritually committed collegians can exhibit winsome and exemplary personalities and lifestyles. Over against the futility and devastation of self-indulgence they can witness to the freedom and joy of God-oriented living. The idea that the old self is a lost cause is an evangelical maxim; only a new order of life and a new constellation of values can lift human beings to new selfhold. The church of Christ is a new society of regenerate believers. The presence of dedicated evangelical youth in that regenerate society can rejuvenate struggling churches and enlarge their community impact. Young-blooded participation in church life before graduation will help establish and solidify lifelong patterns of spiritual engagement.

## Are Evangelical Colleges Up to the Challenge?

Are such expectations excessive? Do not evangelical campuses already face many serious challenges? For some administrators no question is more crucial than whether evangelical parents are any longer willing to sacrificially underwrite a Christian education for their children. The fact is that some who are raising crucial and unnerving questions are not scholars hostile to religious colleges but rather constructive critics who ask whether our colleges live up to their distinctive claims.

After thorough and unprecedented research, Professor J. D. Hunter concludes that many evangelical institutions no longer transmit the biblical outlook effectively enough to achieve a compelling transfer of the evangelical heritage. No longer is the Christian worldlife view imparted on a curriculum-wide basis. Cognitive bargaining with nonevangelical academe, Hunter affirms, results in a dilution of Christian distinctives. He observes on various campuses a moderation of the Bible's unbroken authority and compromise of the view that Jesus Christ's mediation is the sole ground of acceptance with God.[3] Hunter's verdict rests on an examination of seminary and college campuses thought to be representative of the Christian College Coalition. Not given to self-analysis or self-criticism, few of these schools have invited Hunter for dialogue and discussion, even though he is an evangelical believer and full-ranking University of Virginia professor. Many merely dismiss his sampling as unscientific. Those of us who have taught or still teach evangelical

---

3. James Davison Hunter, *Evangelicalism: The Coming Generation* (Chicago: University of Chicago Press, 1987).

alumni in graduate courses are quite aware of holes in the dike of evangelical consistency.

Many evangelicals have applauded Allan Bloom's *The Closing of the American Mind* for its exposure of the intellectual and moral relativism that now pervades secular campuses. On the other hand they have said little about Bloom's protest against the dilution of liberal arts education, and his plea to reinstate great books and primary sources into classroom learning. To be sure, Bloom has been censured by those who dislike an emphasis on classical literature and on the history of philosophy, and even more for his generalization than were their predecessors.

It is no secret that many evangelical campuses face increasing curriculum pressure on the humanities. Just as some critics consider approval of the money-making Doctor of Ministries Degree to be the American Association of Theological Schools' worst mistake, so others consider today's emphasis on student social and political activism to be the culprit in the decline of the humanities in education. A generation ago evangelical colleges were differentiated from Bible colleges by their unapologetic commitment to the liberal arts; now theology and the humanities alike generally face curriculum pressures.

Evangelical lay leader Robert Case II, who in 1987 was named to the National Council on Vocational Education, thinks that evangelical colleges should rethink curriculum requirements in order to prepare Christian students for the trades and technical vocational opportunities. Classical education, he holds, leads to baccalaureate degrees but fails to train craftsmen of ability and integrity for the work force; vocational opportunities will consequently go by default to Japanese, Korean, Taiwanese, German, or other foreign workers. Case would have evangelical colleges offer not only special degree programs in nursing, as some already do, but also in laser technology, machine operation, computer training, paralegal and stenographic vocations, and dental hygiene. Even the few philosophers that evangelical education currently produces, says Case, won't repair our roads and bridges; someone must work with concrete as well as with ideas. In short, Case urges Christian colleges and high schools to reassess the orientation of their present curricula.

Sadly, the prospect now seems remote for an evangelical university in a great metropolitan center, where students could also find hands-on training in all their special disciplines. Whereas Jewish and Catholic minorities established major universities in some of America's larger cities, the numerically greater evangelical community failed to do so. Ironically, in Japan where evangelicals comprise less that 1 percent of the population, God's special providence has recently shaped the emergence of Tokyo Christian University with its new $50 million campus fully paid. The president of this complex, a convert from Buddhism, serves also as president of the Japan Evangelical Theological Society, and himself teaches the campus course on the Christian world-life view.

## The Clash of Worldviews

In the 1970s I warned of two emerging specters, namely a blurring of evangelical identity and the emergence of neopaganism in the West. Not so, said friends who disagreed and possibly disowned me; America, they insisted, is experiencing a great spiritual awakening.

Nonetheless, it seems to me that three worldviews are currently on an inevitable collision course that will decide the spiritual and moral fortunes of modern civilization. These are: first, biblical theism (a summary term for the Judeo-Christian heritage); second, naturalistic scientism (which substitutes empirical verification for divine revelation); and third, Eastern occultism (belief in an all-compassing hidden spiritual reality, with emphasis on feeling rather than on either revelation or laboratory observation).

Today with its overthrow of communist tyranny, Eastern Europe confronts a generation of intellectuals indoctrinated from elementary through university studies in Marxist materialism with the problem of finding and choosing viable alternatives. Despite Eastern Europe's disavowal of socialist economics for a free market and its welcome pursuit of religious liberty and of political self-determination, I see no reason to reverse my verdict, namely, that naturalism is overtaking the Judeo-Christian heritage that for centuries lifted the West from its past paganism. The hunger for freedom from a communist yoke remains largely a hunger for "this-worldly" things. The Western idols of money and power and sexual lust offer the human race no enduring hope or reason for being. The West has not internalized the truths and values that can spare not only itself but also Eastern Europe from ultimate disillusionment. The formative cultural enterprises of the Euro-American world—whether public education, the mass media, or politics—are shaped by humanistic influences that increasingly deteriorate to self-seeking naturalism.

Beleaguered and persecuted Christians mustered much of the courage to withstand totalitarian encroachment, most notably in Poland and Romania. Spiritual believers know that the source of true joy is not material goods, needful as they are for survival, and however much the hungry and poor must be a continuing concern of social injustice and a call to Christian compassion. The biblically virile churches can mediate spiritual and moral vitalities that preserve and restore the sense of transcendent worth. In the face of tyrannical oppression pockets of spiritual faith have indeed been honed to lofty courage in Eastern Europe.

The largest evangelical church on the European Continent is 2,500 member Second Baptist Church of Oradeo, Romania, which engaged in a standing confrontation with the Ceausescu regime. Everywhere, in fact, evangelicals grew stronger under persecution and imprisonment. In Poland the Roman Catholic Church forged a line of resistance to the communist regime. In other former Soviet-bloc countries the Orthodox Church survived mainly by accommodation. The Romanian Orthodox Church, which sheltered the Graham meeting in 1987 in Timisoara with government approval three days after the recent December revolution erupted, had the previous month congratulated Ceausescu on "unanimous reelection" as Communist party chairman. Yet, even here in the Romanian Orthodox Church we find a new life movement of dedicated believers called the Lord's army. Evangelical churches, that faced government hostility in a way that the Orthodox Church never did, now seek religious freedom from Orthodox influence no less than from Communist restriction. If a spectacular revival of Christianity is to emerge in Eastern Europe, it will likely come in churches emboldened by confidence in God and His Word, churches that boldly withstood communist tyrants amid both material hardship and religious persecution.

What, you ask, has this to do with American Evangelical education? A great deal. Despite fundamentalism's return to the political arena and rampant evangelical triumphalism, I have felt for more than a decade that evangelicalism might again soon be isolated and barricaded in a modern Dead Sea cave. In his *Against the Night: Living in the New Dark Ages*, Charles Colson states that, were Western culture to disintegrate, many churches in their present unspiritual state are unlikely to rise phoenixlike above the ashes of ruination.[4] The very culture in which we presumably have some duty to stand spiritually on guard has so enmeshed us in its tawdry values and cognitive ambiguity that we may be blown away along with it. Is it inconceivable that most evangelical colleges might fifty years from now survive only as academic museums? In any event, if the present naturalistic-scientistic culture is not to outflank the enrollment of only ninety thousand Christian College Coalition students within the larger total of twelve million American collegians, is not something more required of evangelical education, dispersed and diverse as it is, than its present contribution?

Doubtless it is fair to say that never since I entered Wheaton fifty-five years ago have evangelical colleges faced as much criticism as today. The criticisms are many and wide-ranging and some are hazardous gen-

---

4. Charles Colson, *Against the Night: Living in the New Dark Ages* (Ann Arbor, MI: Servant Books, 1989).

eralizations: for example, that fund-raising and public relations seem to be a campus administrator's main qualification; that the secular media seem unaware of these campuses or seldom find its leaders quotable; that evangelical academe is so diverse that its cohesive identity is hard to focus except in generalities; that students are middle-class sophisticates driving cars their parents could not afford; that more and more students lust for ultimate business success as their world-mission; that no truly consistent campus morality replaces the disavowal of the fundamentalist "don'ts"; that the excitement of liberal arts learning seems to have faded.

To meet such complaints, defenders sometimes point to impressive attendance at student prayer meetings and to growing interest in practical religious assignments or in missionary careers. Gratifying indeed as such considerations are, they involve the appropriation of conviction more than the victory of truth itself for which the colleges were founded. Parents understandably welcome a shelter from personal vices and the pursuit of constructive career goals in a society addicted to drugs, alcohol, and sex, even if candid administrators must admit that even here an evangelical campus cannot give absolute guarantees. A Christian college or university can function neither as a surrogate parent nor as a surrogate church. It has its own mission: to articulate the Christian perspective in relation to the history of thought and to contemporary culture. Much as the present predicament of academe involves a crisis of will not less than as crisis of mind, Christian learning in the present cultural conflict can least of all afford to leap over the question of the cognitive credibility of evangelical theism.

Before the recent Romanian revolution, on invitation of evangelical leaders (aware that the secret police could imprison them for not reporting conversations with a foreigner and for holding meetings unauthorized by the Securitate), I taught and ministered in five key cities of Romania. University graduates holding secular jobs who became Christians in mid-life told me in clandestine meetings before Ceausescu's fall how their entire schooling was steeped in materialist philosophy. Long before university years, they were schooled in the ancient Greek cosmologists, in the Platonic-Aristotelian myths, in "the Christian myth" as well, and in the myths of pre-Marxist moderns from Descartes through Hegel, and finally and climactically in Marxist materialism. For them it is imperative, they told me, to learn the implications of Christian theism not only for experiencing personal regeneration, but for properly grasping the history of philosophy as well. On their own initiative they have begun translating my six-volume *God, Revelation and Authority*, among other works. Although believers are a minority, dedicated university graduates seek to mount a bold witness to their atheistic peers in a nation of twenty-three million people. Five hours a day after their daily secular work we met to explore the Bible and its implications for the Christian worldview, so they could serve weekends as lay ministers in some of the more than nine hundred churches for which Ceausescu refused to approve pastors. By contrast, have our evangelical campuses lost the excitement of theologically oriented learning.

Recent world developments promote a dramatic clash of ideas that involves all the disciplines of learning. By no means is this impact confined to the creation-evolution debate with its identification of ultimate reality either in terms of a personal God or of impersonal processes and quantum events. Rejection of the long-regnant critical projection of an earlier, more reliable text behind the Bible and the recent emergence instead of canonical and narrative theology, for example, open exciting interactive possibilities in history and literature. Recent discussions of Scripture as literature more and more misidentify its genre as mythico-logic and undermine its objective truth and uniqueness. Do the sacred writers identify biblical meaning simply as whatever readers individually "find" there? What does the loss of textual authority and objective truth by deconstructionist philosophers imply for Christian faith? No less important is the nature of history and the role of historical criticism in respect to crucial biblical events like the Exodus and Jesus' incarnation and resurrection. The great divides of history are not merely chronological but more notably intellectual or logical. What does that imply for modernity and its view of the past and present?

The issues the Bible raises are as contemporary as today's newspapers. The collision of ideas and ideals it engenders remains as crucial as ever for the fortunes of cultural survival and for personal meaning and destiny.

The non-Christian religions are no longer distant oddities; their temples and mosques are settling in our cities, and their devotees are taking courses in evangelism. Yet much of the evangelical community lives a life of banality. Those who simply condemn the culture in the name of God can easily become its victims at the expense of God's cause. Nor is the roster of compromise exhausted by the fund-raising techniques of certain televangelists, the sexual dalliance and self-enrichment of others, or the repudiation of church discipline by still others. Instead of serious theological learning, some evangelicals now prefer sensational fiction that portrays the world's end or that depicts occult forces seeking to capture a college town while obscure demons and angels engage in spiritual warfare.

Few colleges any longer offer the academic world a clear metaphysical perspective. Can the Christian college hope to influence secular learning, and if so, how? The addition of eminent Christian faculty known to secular academe would tell its own story, so would active participation of faculty in professional societies compromised not solely of evangelical scholars but of all scholars engaged in the various disciplines. Whenever a secular text becomes standard in any discipline, should not our best minds identify its presuppositions and assess its handling of subject matter and its conclusions? Better yet, should we not indicate credible alternatives, applying rational test and adducing appropriate evidence for a preferable option? Cannot a competent faculty member writing a definite textbook in his discipline be funded for a year of postdoctoral research on secular campuses, while he or she completes that effort? Can we encourage and reward faculty research and writing of journal articles that will be read by secular counterparts and pressing them to examine their presuppositions and to consider alternatives? Must our colleges function adjunctively to secular campuses and in some relation maintain vital dialogue with them? Can the college venture cooperative workshops with evangelical and other quite sympathetic professors who teach on nearby secular campuses? Shall we groom outstanding evangelical students to become doctoral candidates who will write significant dissertations? Does not the whole process of campus teaching involve molding each learner into the best possible student he or she can be? Should honor students, invited once or twice a year to sessions where faculty debate the significance of some recent publication, be asked to summarize agreements and disagreements?

Our two hundred forty million American population includes fifty million evangelical Christians but only six million Jews. Yet despite their minority, the cultural impact of the Jewish mind and of Jewish influence in America is nothing less than remarkable. American Jews manifest a remarkable presence in science and mainline academe, in publishing and the mass media world, and in the arts as well, not to mention in the business world and Wall Street in particular. The proportion of American Jews in professions like law and medicine far outruns that of evangelicals. Jews also dominate the entertainment, fashion, and clothing industries. In their social emergence many American Jews have become Reform Jews; the culture has impacted on their spiritual heritage no less than they themselves have impacted on society. Indeed despite vigorous support for a Jewish homeland in Israel, most American Jews prefer to live in America.

Relatively few of the most highly regarded leaders in public life today, whether in education, politics, or the mass media, have emerged from the evangelical colleges. Billy Graham stands unrivaled among contemporary evangelists. Yet from our ranks has emerged neither another Alexander Solzhenitsyn as a champion of human rights, nor another C. S., Lewis as an eminent write, nor another Charles Colson as a leader and champion of prison ministries and reform. One can, of course, point to philosophers like Alvin Plantinga, originally of Calvin College and now of Notre Dame, as the only American evangelical invited to deliver the Gifford Lectures, and Keith Yandell who for three years chaired the philosophy department on the long-radical University of Wisconsin campus. Other evangelicals are indeed represented at secondary and tertiary levels.

Yet something seems basically amiss or lacking in the evangelical enterprise. A problem remains despite entrepreneurial enthusiasts armed with newly coined catchphrases on jet-set missions, and who operate with highly paid public relations staff and computerized mailing lists. The basic problem is one of indifferent enthusiasm for mental application and liberal arts engagement. We seem to support stringent learning far less than other options.

In the forepart of our century, mainline denomination colleges were enticed by the speculative religious philosophy that reigned on secular campuses. Evangelical education, on the other hand, resisted such culture conformity, emphasized biblical faith and objective truth and goodness, and increasingly championed the ideals of academic excellence. In time when classic liberal arts learning began to give way on campuses generally, mediating religious campuses could nonetheless still voice some generalities about God and man and the universe, take pride in their more stringent sex codes, avoid alcoholic excesses, and manifest a certain indifference to the rising sports craze. Yet among these religious schools the smaller ones read mostly secular textbooks with which teachers differed only now and then. Apart from endorsing Sunday church attendance, faculties became increasingly secular-minded. In time denominational ties gave way except for "covenant" relationships whose presence was important for periodic fund-raising.

It was to forthrightly evangelical colleges that one looked for a comprehensive assessment of the history of thought in terms of Christian philosophy. Habits of the mind were nurtured to present and defend the Christian faith. Campuses were concerned with manifesting a consistent statement of doctrine and a program of integrated learning that prepared students for cognitive leadership. The time had not yet arrived when evangelical campuses were unsure how to cope with the intellectual anarchy of secular society. Gradually, however, the unifying principle of academic learning began to fade. While new faculty still espoused certain Christian beliefs, they lacked an in-depth knowledge of Christianity even in relation to their own disciplines. To be sure, they valued an inner private interaction with the reality of God and from time to time gave devout personal witness to the salvation that God offers in Christ. They insisted, furthermore, on the deep distinction between good and evil, on the dignity of human selfhood, and on the importance of personal choice; they relied more and more on theology and Bible departments in particular to define and elaborate doctrinal concerns. It became difficult to maintain the excitement of evangelical education while avoiding two extremes—that of the authoritarian teacher who reads well-worn lecture notes as if they were Holy Writ, and that of the open-headed conversationalist who stimulates classroom discussion as if it were a modern rock-band performance.

Student interest meanwhile multiplied for entrepreneurial business as a life vocation. Some of the best evangelical colleges, whose most popular major a generation ago was philosophy, now listed business and economics as their leading degree courses. Students came under increasing pressure to forego costly college studies for vocational pursuits that could help them more quickly to realize dreams of a marriage, a family, and owning a home.

## The Life of Learning

The summer after graduation from high school holds increasing importance as an important work station. It can and should be no less important as an academic and spiritual threshold. In such an atmosphere evangelical colleges can make completion of high school an opportunity, a rite of passage, if you will, to disciplined Christian learning. Some schools have already acted on the suggestion of Ernest Boyer of Carnegie Institute that, in addition to concluding their four-year program with commencement services, colleges should also initiate incoming freshmen into a solemn service of dedication to evangelical learning.

For what ought to constitute that four-year period of learning I claim no heaven-sent agenda. Today's available evangelical education offers a variety of options, although they should be linked together by an overarching canopy of mutually shared goals. I would not venture to reeducate the educators; I have as much to learn as anyone else, if not more, about how to improve what we currently do. Surely, however, both high school and college graduates should learn enough about modern technology to make it in today's competitive job market when an information and service economy depends more than ever on formal education. Evangelical leaders are as sorely needed in business as in the professions, in science and the arts, and in ministerial and missionary careers.

The Bible claims the whole man, mental and spiritual no less than emotional and physical. Every graduate therefore should be assured of the credibility and consistency of Christianity and its claims and be able to relate those claims confidently to the current culture crisis.

For that reason as a threshold course for incoming freshmen—either in an August preliminary term or as part of the regular fall quarter—a study of Plato's *Republic* could well be required. Here a great Greek mind charts weaknesses in a merely naturalistic view of existence and life, yet elaborates a tenuous supernaturalism apart from transcendent divine revelation. Plato puts before us the issues of justice and injustice, of objective truth and the good, of the perils of democracy, and of the ideal content of learning. The classic Greek philosophers invite us to the very universe of discourse in which much of public life today is still discussed. Some parents will doubtless complain that they do not subsidize their children in a Christian college to have them learn about a pagan philosopher. The fact is, however, that early exposure to classical literature, to a primary source and to a crucial link in the history of philosophy, is integral and foundational to liberal arts learning; such study, moreover, stimulates habits of disciplined inquiry that are serviceable throughout life.

In addition to this august introductory course—or paralleling other studies if students begin in September—should be classes in Old Testament Theology and in New Testament Theology. If properly taught, these classes would relate and contrast the biblical mind with classic and ancient as well as modern and contemporary thought, and would foster revelation-and-reason concerns. Such issues as the eternity or evolution or creation of matter, the nature of the cosmos and of history, and of human life and destiny, and the nature and limits of reason, would be faced in the context of both evangelical orthodoxy and modernity. Because of the Bible's importance as Christian education's overarching textbook, it must not be displaced by books merely about the Bible, important as familiarity with a supportive evangelical library will become. Ranged between this panoramic freshman philosophical overview and a final senior course on the Christian world-life view or biblical theism, and, of course, the climactic comprehensive examination in one's major field, would be required courses in one's chosen discipline that grapple related world-life-view considerations.

The recent discrediting of the Graf-Wellhausen documentary theory of biblical origins, and the nature of literary inspiration, for example, become no less significant in the study of literature than do the variety of genres in which revelation is expressed, and the question also of what constitutes a literary classic. In science the discussion of methodology and the nature and limits of empirical explanation is as important as are laboratory achievements and prospects. In history the nature of historiography and of historical verification becomes significant; how history gains its meaning, and whether or why biblical history is a distinct species of history are crucial concerns. In addition, each discipline would involve the reading of primary rather than merely of secondary sources and opportunity for pertinent and stimulating class discussion. The aim of such a curricular approach is not to minimize usual course content, but to provide a context of presentation that promotes academic integration from a Christian perspective. The aforementioned senior course in evangelical theism and the comprehensive examination in one's major discipline would bring together in a cohesive way the numerous, often disparate aspects of today's collegiate learning.

Actually very much akin to this vision is what the founders of many of our Christian colleges projected, namely, learning that embraced the entire collegiate experience, and not merely one special segment of campus life. No better use could be made of a million dollars if venture capital, it seems to me, than nurturing a Christian Studies program that channels competent faculty and gifted students into its orbit. John Hopkins University was initially funded by a railroad magnate; the University of Chicago by an oil magnate; Carnegie-Mellon University by steel and aluminum and oil tycoons; and Stanford University by a railroad baron. In our time the Lilly Endowment and Pew Memorial Trust are among agencies that have aided evanglical higher education. In *The Third America*, Michael O'Neill tells us that contribution of the nonprofit sector "has more to do" with ideas and ideals than with money, structures, and media expertise. Some of this sector's greatest accomplishments, including "creating theories and research that have revolutionized modern life—happened with, at first, little money and few structures but a great deal of courage, passion, intelligence, and energy."[5]

Unless the original vision of evangelical education is similarly implemented, evangelicals will survive only as a rear guard reaction to the cultural assumptions of modernity, assumptions promoted by humanists and other naturalists. The tragic consequences of such social withdrawal are easy to foresee. Religion will continue to be privatized. Self-gratification will outweigh community interest. A civilization already destined for the ashheap of history will supply the governing premises for our age and its agenda. Yet the liberal humanist knowledge-class is a minority, no less so than the evangelical community. We allow it to dominate and distort the educational arena, the mass media, and political dis-

---

5. Michael O'Neill, *The Third America* (San Francisco: Josey-Bass Publishers, 1984), 52.

course. The realities of God the Creator, of moral first principles, of human dignity and rights, and of shaping values basic to effective survival of a constitutional republic are being eclipsed. Those of us who protest this disaster are being increasingly viewed as sinister devotees of some outworn religious myth. The one sure way to extend such contemptuous dismissal of the Judeo-Christian heritage is simply to keep on doing what we are now doing, and no more.

# Cognitive Bartering on Evangelical Campuses

*If the universities are the intellectually incisive and critical centers of society, then the evangelical colleges and seminaries have a high responsibility for presenting, preserving, and protecting the biblical heritage at its best. The question arises whether the evangelical campuses have borne this burden well, or whether they have even accepted it.*

What is the cognitive integrity of evangelical higher education? That is the essential question posed by Professor James Davison Hunter in his provocative treatise, *American Evangelicalism: Conservative Religion and the Quandry of Modernity.*[1] His research demands to be taken seriously, for it reveals the most fundamental issue concerning the future of evangelical education. Will evangelical institutions of higher education continue to educate students in such a manner which can lay legitimate claim on the evangelical heritage? Is evangelical higher education still distinctively *evangelical?*

Professor Hunter is largely concerned with the dynamics of the encounter between modernity and the evangelical worldview and how this encounter is perceived by the man and woman on the street more than by the professional theologian. This distinction, of course, need not

---

1. James Davison Hunter, *American Evangelicalism: Conservative Religion and the Quandary of Modernity* (Chicago: University of Chicago Press, 1983). This chapter is a running response to Hunter.

imply irreconcilable or radically divergent perceptions, although it may suggest that conceptual assumptions and implications in his survey are more implicit than explicit. Nonetheless, Professor Hunter does indeed, to some extent, deal with theoretical as well as experiential and moral aspects of the evangelical movement.

In a decade when an exuberant evangelical triumphalism has characterized many evangelical enterprises, and when some conservative religious leaders basked in the confidence that a new and greater evangelical awakening is already underway, Hunter's research points instead to noteworthy concessions that attest to an erosive impact upon the evangelical movement by the very secular culture that evangelical forces sought to change. Hunter declares it "reasonable to predict that the evangelical world view will undergo still further mutations that will make it even less similar to the historic faith than it already is." Given the contemporary trend, he foresees on the horizon no likelihood of a great evangelical awakening that reaches beyond a much more modest "private sphere renewal."

Behind this verdict lies a firm conviction that in emerging from cultural isolation, evangelicals—while adhering to a literal interpretation of Scripture—have engaged in costly "cognitive bargaining" in order to participate in a rational-functional world of modernity. Ongoing cultural dialogue is maintained, Hunter contends, by concessions in the evangelical movement's epistemic commitments, by subtle modifications of doctrine and strategy in quest of synthesis with the modern outlook, and by an apologetic stance that amalgamates evangelical and secular motifs and goals and thus moderates the differences between them.

*American evangelicalism* aims to indicate why evangelical orthodoxy continues to survive amid secular modernity. Hunter does not presume to tell us what self-consistent evangelical people ought to affirm, or how to chart a superior intellectual program or strategy. He judges the contemporary movement by conformity or nonconformity to its own heritage. He is aware that the evangelical movement in its history incorporates considerable diversity, and also that, whatever religious movement one might survey, "cognitive bargaining" with the reigning culture is unavoidable except by total withdrawal and isolation.

Hunter's later work *Evangelicalism: The Coming Generation* statistically confirms his insistence that the evangelical movement is undergoing significant changes whose consequences for the next generation are of high importance.[2] His research is grounded in the Evangelical Acad-

---

2. James Davison Hunter, *Evangelicalism: The Coming Generation* (Chicago: University of Chicago Press, 1987).

emy Project, an attitudinal survey of students and faculty in 1982-1985 in nine liberal arts colleges (including Wheaton College, Gordon College, Westmont College, Taylor University, and Houghton College) and seven Evangelical seminaries (Fuller Theological Seminary, Gordon-Conwell Theological Seminary, Westminster Theological Seminary, Asbury Theological Seminary, Talbot Theological Seminary, Wheaton Graduate School, and Denver Conservative Baptist Theological Seminary).

Evangelical reaction to Hunter's investigations have been mixed. On some campuses the effort was greeted with stony silence; neither trustees nor constituencies were informed of the report. On other campuses Hunter's methodology was criticized as inadequately scientific, although front-line sociologists like Peter Berger and Robert Wuthnow strongly commended it. Some readers complained that questions could have been framed less ambiguously. Evangelical publications profiting from extensive school advertising by and large were protective of established institutions and failed to raise deep concerns. The Christian College Coalition virtually overlooked the effort. A growing number of educators and other leaders are convinced, however, that an avoidance of self-evaluation and self- criticism would be costly for the future of the evangelical movement.

Let me indicate at once my own evaluation of Hunter's investigations. His analysis is, I believe, highly important, and the evangelical movement cannot afford to overlook it. All empirical study halts short of absolute demonstration; scientific method deals at best in high probability. Yet our judicial system rests precisely upon such evidence, as does our adversarial political order. No doubt the Evangelical Academy Project might have improved its phrasing of some questions, though most were adequately framed. In a very few instances what might appear on the surface to reflect theological deterioration might actually be viewed as simply a shift from too rigid a view to a more representative one. On the whole Hunter's survey raises the right questions and elicits illuminating responses.

More importantly, the evangelical campuses surveyed, when one focuses not on marginal but on centrally important control-beliefs, do as a group reflect disconcerting theological deterioration. Moreover, in my graduate teaching on numerous seminary campuses, I have confirmed to my own satisfaction the accuracy of Hunter's indications; for example, even on some of the best evangelical college campuses, some professors have taught their students that Jesus Christ is not the sole ground of human acceptance by God, and that the entire human race need not have descended from Adam.

Other important theological modifications have wider currency, not the least of which is the growing acceptance in evangelical seminaries and colleges of a neoorthodox view of Scripture that accepts biblical teaching as fallible witness at the expense of its comprehensive authority and reliability. Since the dialectical view excludes propositional revelation, and Karl Barth consequently holds that the Christian revelation does not involve a given worldview, the consequences for revealed doctrine and for evangelical worldview exposition are enormous.

Hunter offers three incisive criticisms of evangelical worldview exposition: (1) much of the movement, he says, has concentrated on spiritual piety more than on conceptual cultural engagement, thereby inviting belittlement of that engagement as intrinsically anti-intellectual; (2) even its academic institutions now sometimes present the evangelical world view too weakly to enlist the oncoming generation for its control-beliefs; and (3) in confronting secular culture it yields to cognitive and strategic approaches that purchase secular interest at the cost of evangelical diminution.

Hunter observes that "Conservative Protestantism as a whole has been slow, even reluctant, to accommodate the pressure to rationalize its worldview. The recognition of this reluctance has prompted the popular accusation of anti-intellectualism."[3] This emphasis on experiential over theological facets has been most conspicuously true of charismatic and pentecostal religion. It is also true that American fundamentalism historically has shunned theological and philosophical formulation of its beliefs and that many Southern Baptists have tended to be anticreedal. It is also the case that some contemporary Wesleyans minimize the importance of the evangelical emphasis on the comprehensive truthfulness of Scripture by insisting that personal piety is the deepest commitment of the holiness movements. It should not be overlooked, however, that Reformation-oriented evangelicals, including many Baptists, have stressed worldview concerns for many decades. Hunter may somewhat understate the matter when he considers the 1942 formation of the National Association of Evangelicals as the first significant effort by American evangelicals to rationalize the evangelical world view in terms of conservative apologetics.

In the early 1930s Wheaton, then already the leading Evangelical college, required every student to take a senior course in theism, with James Orr's *The Christian View of God and the World* as the textbook. During the mid-1930s, Wheaton's then-president Dr. J. Oliver Buswell, Jr. had the announced goal of moving Wheaton toward a Christian uni-

---

3. *American Evangelicalism,* 74.

versity. To that end he added evangelical professors of Phi Beta Kappa from mainline campuses to the faculty. Among those chosen was the philosopher Gordon H. Clark who came from the faculty of the University of Pennsylvania and made philosophy the most popular campus major. At the same time Calvin College, Christian Reformed in orientation, aggressively asserted Christian world-life concerns. Other evangelical institutions—including some Bible colleges—reflected a growing ambition to promote Christian worldview considerations throughout the curriculum.

The influence of Orr's writings is evident in the recently published biography of the Scottish apologist by Glen G. Scorgie.[4] Orr edited the initial edition of the prestigious five-volume *International Standard Bible Encyclopedia* (ISBE) and he enlisted scholars like B. B. Warfield and Melvin Grove Kyle as key distributors. While Orr did not affirm biblical inerrancy, he adhered to propositional revelation, stressed the Deity, virgin birth, and bodily resurrection of Jesus Christ, and vigorously assailed the piecemeal theological concessions of critical scholars on the left. Orr's writings, in fact, and those of his scholarly contributors to ISBE, offered a considerably more formidable exposition of evangelical corebeliefs than had the popularly written conservative series, *The Fundamentals*.

Instead of accelerating this comprehensive intellectual thrust, the National Association of Evangelicals (NAE) somewhat moderated it by admitting the Assemblies of God and other denominations whose emphasis is more experiential than cognitive, and who in time came to comprise about 25 percent of the movement's membership. Wesleyan or Holiness denominations also tend to emphasize spiritual pietism more than theology and apologetics. When organized in 1942, NAE formulated a minimal doctrinal statement, including an article on the infallibility of Scripture that member organizations affirm. This statement is sufficiently broad to accommodate both Calvinists and Arminians, in addition to a diversity in respect to baptism, church government, and eschatology. Evangelicals have been willing to make such accommodations for over a century for the sake of evangelistic and missionary cooperation while at the same time they resisted modernist and pluralist theological penetration. More significantly, NAE's doctrinal statement serves as a ready abridgement of and substitute for the more comprehensive historic creeds and confessions of faith espoused by many of

---

4. Glen G. Scorgie, *A Call for Continuity: The Theological Contribution of James Orr* (Macon, GA: Mercer University Press, 1989).

the member bodies. At one time NAE commissions were said to reflect the views of twenty million evangelicals.

Early on, many NAE leaders regarded social action with distrust in view of the modernist banner of the social gospel; the movement, in fact, very gingerly handled my own jeremiad on *The Uneasy Conscience of Modern Fundamentalism.*[5] The NAE soon established a commission on higher education, although its interests were often more pragmatic than academic. Yet the NAE's official publication, *United Evangelical Action*, carried book reviews and featured selections that gave theology and apologetics an important role.

The fact remains, however, that evangelicals were engaged in "cognitive bargaining," as Professor Hunter affirms. Wheaton in the thirties and forties was quite open to a six-day twenty-four hour creation week and to a world flood theory and had very limited sympathy for theistic evolution. Orr's *The Christian View of God and the World* was, however, firmly committed to the latter. Moreover, Orr's text made much of empirical evidences for God's existence. Both Cornelius Van Til at Westminster and Gordon Clark at Wheaton opposed this empirical stance in the interest of presuppositional theism, which begins with God in His revelation and from this axiom deduces the core beliefs of biblical theism. Clark differed from Van Til, however, in insisting that our knowledge of God objectively coincides with God's knowledge of himself, and that rational consistency is a test of truth. Neither Van Til nor Clark resorted to empirical argumentation in quest of a logical demonstration of God's existence and nature.

"Cognitive bargaining" among evangelicals came with a younger generation of scholars. From Fuller Edward John Carnell's *Christian Commitment: An Apologetic*[6] gave more ground to experience in formulating theological and moral principles, from Wheaton Arthur Holmes' *Contours of a World View*[7] reflected a larger role for empirical factors in elaborating the case for theism and presented theistic evolution that ignored serious criticisms of Darwinian evolution expressed even by contemporary scientists. Wheaton modified its earlier statement on divine creation to accommodate theistic evolution but continued to refer human origin to miraculous divine intervention. Somewhat less influential writers than Carnell and Holmes promoted cosmological, teleological, and moral arguments and, as Hunter indicates, pursued "proofs" by correlating theological and scientific method and couching "theology in

---

5. Carl F. H. Henry, *The Uneasy Conscience of American Fundamentalism* (Grand Rapids: Eerdmans, 1948).
6. Edward J. Carnell, *Christian Commitment: An Apologetic* (New York: Macmillan, 1957).
7. Arthur Holmes, *Contours of a Worldview* (Grand Rapids: Eerdmans, 1983).

the grammar of empiricism."[8] Contrary to Thomas Aquinas, some conceded that the evidential arguments did not wholly succeed as logical proofs. For all that, these approaches still gave evangelical theology an empirical focus, as did J. Oliver Buswell's *Systematic Theology of the Christian Religion*.[9] On the other hand, the emphasis on deductive theology, prominent from Origen to Schleiermacher, was reaffirmed in the present writer's *God, Revelation and Authority*.[10]

It is true that many conservative campuses have been much more interested in Christian *life* views than in worldview concerns. Even here, however, it was fundamentalist "don'ts" rather than an agenda of biblical principles that detailed the essence of a moral life. In due course, with pressure growing by students increasingly interested in worldly success, business and economics replaced liberal arts as leading majors in many evangelical colleges. The adjustment of curricular schedules to a changing core content, and the importation of skilled professors trained in secular institutions and not really at home in Christian world-life view concerns, worked against an interaction with Christian world-life concerns on a curriculumwide basis; except in a modicum of general or required Bible courses, serious theology received little attention other than by preseminarians and philosophy or religion majors. Moreover, students from fundamentalist and charismatic backgrounds were—at least until a decade ago—not much interested in doing theology in-depth. Many fundamentalists were satisfied with a polemical content, while many charismatics considered theological study an alternative to experiential Christianity.

Professor Hunter locates other facets of cultural concession, with some cause, in the simplification of creedal formulas and evangelistic guidelines. Youth for Christ, for example, was far more prone to send up "a cheer for Jesus" than to repeat the Apostles' Creed. The "regeneration formulas"—the four spiritual laws, for example—seem mechanical and supercondensed to intellectually oriented Christians. One might protest that it is somewhat unfair to distill the essence of a regeneration experience from popular evangelistic formulas instead of from the writings of theologians. Even more to the point is the lack of proposed alternatives by some critics of the status quo. Even the New Testament writers offer succinct summaries of the gospel; one thinks of Romans 3:21-26, 1 Corinthians 15:3-4, or John 3:16. These summaries do not

---

8. Hunter, *Evangelicalism*, 72-77.
9. J. Oliver Buswell, *Systematic Theology of the Christian Religion* (Grand Rapids, Zondervan, 1949).
10. Carl F. H. Henry, *God, Revelation, and Authority*, 6 vols. (Waco: Word Books, 1976-1983).

stand in isolation, and even as abridgments they are theologically more profound and less culture concessive than contemporary contractions that simulate advertising blurbs and media blips. Nonetheless, the evangelistic formularies of today offer a larger window on core doctrines of orthodox theism than did modernistic theology a century ago. Some of us who came into evangelical orthodoxy through the side door of the Oxford Group (in the context of Episcopal ritual) know that in God's providence even a diluted dose of the biblical dynamic can turn a life right side out.

Professor Hunter discerns still other evidences of cultural concession. Although, he observes, evangelical spokesmen—in contrast to inclusive modernism—hesitated to find truth in all religions, some at the same time also increasingly hesitated to declare all nonbiblical religions false; they spoke rather in terms of the "superiority" of evangelical orthodoxy. In short, in deference to the growing mood of tolerance and for the sake of civility in dialogue, the Christian belief-system was packaged for greater marketability. References to eschatological damnation and hell as the final destiny of the impenitent wicked were evaded, abridged, or introduced semi-apologetically. The term "heresy" vanished from inter-religious dialogue. Even leading evangelists in their preaching avoided negative doctrines—which recital of the Apostles' Creed, for example, would have surfaced—in order to emphasize the inner psychological utility of personal commitment. This doctrinal rearrangement accommodated a doctrinal stance more aligned to experiential interests than to metaphysical clarification and inevitably invited theological imbalance. Even the doctrine of the "new birth" was sometimes preached in a way that modernists and humanists a half-century ago might have welcomed. Pulpiteers called for a new life, a new character, undergirded by spiritual forces that transcend the human self; and they called their congregations to integrate a personality otherwise plagued by tension and discord, and enlist the self in new and outgoing commitments. All too often minimized was the miraculous atonement and bodily resurrection of the incarnate Christ as the rebellious sinner's only possible ground of salvation.

The enlarged interest in psychology did not stop there. Psychological techniques in witnessing and modern sales methods promoting evangelism sought to dull the offense of the gospel. During the last Billy Graham crusade in the District of Columbia newspapers carried a large advertisement featuring a big picture of Graham but no reference whatever to God. No less significant is the deluge of evangelical publications whose writers deal with psychological problems such as stress and depression, and whose treatises propose remedies redolent with psychologized scriptural language. This shift of focus from Christology to anthropology, from Christ as "the man for others," and from oppressed and needy outsiders to self-examination and self-fulfillment, has significant theological as well as psychological implications. The new generation, in Hunter's words, is overturning the inherited perception of "the nature and value of the self."[11] While evangelicals now, as in the past, shun narcissistic self-infatuation, they ignore self-denial and asceticism in deference to self-indulgence and self-promotion. Whereas the past generation had a rigid agenda of proscriptions that defined Christian virtue, the new generation, emphasizing spiritual liberty, has no prescriptions to replace the prohibitions of the past.

The sum and substance is that much of contemporary evangelicalism is endangered by a hedonistic, culture-embracing self-interest. It states its own differentiae in a way that muffles the offense of revealed religion in a pluralistic setting; it engages increasingly in "cognitive bargaining," that is, it "buys into" culturally commended views in order to sell its own positions. The traumatic consequences of such trends seem not to be apparent to popular evangelical leaders who themselves incorporate some of these concessions even as they attribute numerical success and financial viability solely to spiritual considerations. Evangelicalism is still notably institutionalized in the Bible Belt (that is, the Midwest and South). Yet wherever the modern world view dominates the culture, modernity is likely to override the evangelical inheritance. Modernity's victory among American evangelicals is not likely to result from external political repression of religious liberty or from academic restrictions on freedom of expression. More likely it would eventuate, Hunter observes, through the movement's shift of meanings and aims and a convolution of statistics that lessens identity with the enveloping culture.

If the universities are the intellectually incisive and critical centers of society, then the evangelical colleges and seminaries have a high responsibility for presenting, preserving, and protecting the biblical heritage at its best. Instead of ignoring cultural slippage, or worse yet, tolerating and accommodating it, evangelical academic institutions bear the duty of identifying competing and contrary trends; theirs is the even higher task of systematically formulating the Christian inheritance and exhibiting it consistently and powerfully in the academic arena. The question arises whether the evangelical campuses have borne this burden well, or whether they have even accepted it. As for the initial task of identifying cultural inroads, are not scholars on secular campuses more than those on evangelical campuses presently focusing on critical con-

---

11. Hunter, *Evangelicalism*, 65.

cerns? How well do the religious institutions actually guide and guard the cognitive commitments of the movement? Some readings of the current religious scene seem to imply that evangelical colleges may be as much a part of the problem as of its solution.

Many campuses—some more than others—have curtailed the inroads of alien culture; they have nurtured a vanguard of students not only for pastoral and missionary effort but also for secular vocations in which to serve God and mankind. One must applaud the deep commitment of evangelical campuses to serious academic learning, their provision of a morally superior campus environment, their emphasis on the indispensability of spiritual and ethical concerns to sound character, their devotion to family values, and their announced aspiration to integrate faith and learning. At the same time many evangelical campuses are abandoning their cherished claim to offer all students a comprehensively biblical world-life view. This loss is a by-product not simply of students' increased preference for economically rewarding majors at the expense of traditional liberal arts learning, but it is due even more to a lack of intellectual and curricular cohesion.

The concessions made by evangelical colleges to secular society cannot be offset merely by smart public relations, by faculty additions from major secular universities, by campus lectures or conferences featuring prestigious nonevangelical scholars, by massive fund-raising for endowments or student scholarships, and least of all by sales pitches announcing less expensive degree programs. If evangelical institutions do not boldly interact with contemporary intellectual theory, if they make no compelling public case for the evangelical option, if they merely voice slogans like "values that endure" and "Christ-relatedness" (claims, incidentally, that Protestant modernists would eagerly have made a half-century ago), and if they do not equip prospective alumni with an articulate Christian world-life view, then they have not identified or taken seriously their academic priorities. When *none*evangelical universities and colleges invite unapologetically evangelical scholars as lecturers and seek to add to them faculties—and a few have—we will have clear evidence of academic achievement, although prevailing prejudice still limits such opportunities.

Writing of articles and books that not only address the weakness of contemporary secular learning, as did Allan Bloom, but that in addition sketch the outlines of a comprehensive evangelical alternative, is a task that Christian scholars can hardly expect nonchristians to assume. Instead of withdrawing from professional societies and organizing more compatible alternatives, evangelical scholars should participate in the opportunities for dialogue at the conceptual flashpoints of the culture crisis.

The excitement of collegiate life needs once again to be found in vindicating the truth and the good amid the clash of current perspectives. The classroom is to the college what the operating room is to a hospital. The students who take their assumptions so for granted that they show up only for anesthesia might as well have their head amputated.

Not more than 1 percent of the twelve million American college and university students are in evangelical colleges affiliated with the Christian College Coalition, an organization that represents a total enrollment of 90,000. Southern Baptist universities, colleges, and junior colleges—most of which are not members of the Christian College Coalition—enroll 105,000 students, hence about 12 percent more than Coalition colleges. Evangelical colleges cannot hope to compete with secular campuses solely on the basis that they are Christian efforts. Most college students now come in expectation of future career advantages. Despite what evangelical educators say about nurturing "a richer life," Christian colleges have largely capitulated to the student reach for material success as reflected in the popularity of business and economics as major fields while the humanities increasingly struggle for prominence.

There is a double irony in the forfeiture of curriculum wide, world-life view concerns, for Protestant denominations have a remarkable propensity for losing the Christian orientation of their colleges. George Washington University was once a Baptist institution; Hong Kong Baptist College is a recent loss to the Christian orbit. Brown University was originally a Baptist institution, University of Chicago was originally a Christian university, and its divinity school had Baptist beginnings. Evangelicals have no program for tapping into the discontent of alumni of the many once-Christian but now secular universities to which alumni send their teenagers with increasing reluctance. There has been so much mattress-hopping on some campuses that one is tempted to call them "bediversities" rather than universities; the *uni* or oneness lasts only for the night. Harvard, Duke, Yale, Vanderbilt, and Columbia, among others, were founded as Christian colleges.

The ability of evangelical colleges to profit from current discontent is limited by the fact that some evangelical colleges increasingly emulate the secular institutions, and eagerly invite from them competent church-affiliated professors who have had little interaction with integrative Christianity. Their participation in Christian education is made easier by the current emphasis of evangelicals on cosmopolitan diversity as an asset while theological distinctives become wafer-thin. To emphasize diversity at the expense of an institution's historic doctrinal basis may serve the purposes of popular evangelism and of public relations and fund-raising initiatives. The collapse of doctrine into experience as a prime emphasis is a costly development. Discerning churchgoers consider experiential primacy and pragmatic openness in doctrine a weakness. The charismatic movement has already paid heavily for its emphasis on a deep inner work of the Spirit that renders one virtually immune to temptation, a doctrine on which Jim Bakker and Jimmy Swaggart and the rest of us sinners are all living commentaries. Some evangelical institutions are now more hesitant than even a decade ago to profess loyalty to a comprehensively truthful Bible. One unconfirmed report is that in promoting their schools, only a minority of the presidents of colleges in the Christian College Coalition are currently disposed to champion this historically basic epistemological premise.

The growing interest in alternatives to the evangelical campus and in pilot projects probing new academic possibilities arises not so much from a disaffection for historic Christianity as from a disappointment over present evangelical academic engagement. To be sure, some projected ventures hold a broad view of biblical authority, and some anticipate a conservative Protestant, conservative Catholic, and even conservative Jewish alliance against secular modernity. An evangelical institution that hedges its commitment to biblical authority is hardly in a position to protest such cooperative ventures.

As the cost of education rises, a new possibility looms for area community colleges related to evangelical churches and interested centrally in the conceptual, moral, and spiritual aspects of the culture-conflict. Such efforts would not be known primarily for sports that draw a much larger attendance than do commencement exercises, but it may well attract devout Christians to leave half their estates to implement the vision—as did John Harvard who little suspected that a prestigious university would soon be named for him. Another possibility is suggested by off-campus programs of education already underway simply on a secular basis that involves books, microfiche, computers, cable television, and videocassette recorders (VCRs). The PBS adult Learning Satellite Service is already used by 1,400 colleges. New communications techniques make possible receiving assignments and returning them to distant instructors whose comments are also relayed by computer. A program of evangelical learning might well emerge that overcomes the need for a massive investment in campus real estate and buildings and that is basically centered in printed media and accommodates home learning as part of a supervised effort. Presently existing church properties, often little used throughout the week, could preserve much of the face to face professional and student interaction that is a vital part of a learning experience.

Currently, existing evangelical colleges are still best positioned in terms of assets, personnel, and other resources to address a culture that is sinking below the horizon. They need to reassess their intellectual role and responsibility. Campuses where students take their faith for granted now often lack the cognitive excitement that one finds among Christians on secular university campuses where one must swim vigorously to keep from drowning. An evangelical college today might well plunge its entire freshman class into a sustained initial study of Plato's *Republic*. Students would cope with the best of the classic ancient minds in its critique of naturalism and postulation of a speculative alternative and would debate the ideal content of education and the risks of democracy. Enlivened by such confrontation students might well be thrust next into the Old Testament and New Testament for a grasp of the revelatory alternative to philosophical reasoning and its implications for both naturalism and idealism, ancient and more recent. In this context students could then be dispersed into liberal arts learning, there to be called to account again in a required senior course in the Christian worldview and its implications for modern man and society.

A massive body of learning awaits assimilation by our generation. The newly-discovered space-time relativities often seem to our generation its most exciting facets. If the West's Christian heritage holds intellectual importance in our age, it will not do so because neopaganism born of the rejection of Christianity vindicates that significance. The responsibility falls squarely on evangelical academe, which must first firm its own hold on the Christian heritage. We are faced by ideological adversaries in the cultural challenge. Evangelicals must first determine that their own house is in order.

# Besting the
# Cultural Challenge

*Evangelical Christians dare not isolate themselves from the cultural mainstream. They are obliged to call human beings everywhere to a personal salvific experience of Christ, and to declare also all humanity's answerability to the God of history, and to proclaim the standards by which the returning Lord will judge the social and cultural developments of all nations by the criteria of revealed religion.*

Western culture, is now governed by a false creed. That creed says people are made for self-fulfillment apart from God . . . and apart from the ends for which God created us. If we screen the gospel of Christ through this culture-context, it is soon stifled, negated, and nullified.

There is still much to applaud about Western culture, especially when it is viewed alongside the existing alternatives. We had better qualify the enthusiasm of evolutionary optimists and utopian technocrats who revel in scientific inquiry and in humanistic consensus on human rights. These features, after all, seem powerless to contain today's unbridled naturalism that nurtures brutality and immorality on a colossal scale. The current creed is that "in the beginning" was not the Word but rather the world (or at any rate an infinitely condensed fireball). In that case the final future of our planet may well be an infinitely exploded fireball. Scientific research increasingly outruns moral legitimation. The last word—the only word that matters, we're told—belongs to empirical science.

Life is allegedly governed by the DNA molecule, not by a Creator-God. Neither government nor society nor one's private life is held accountable to Deity; indeed, whatever gods there be are depicted by the naturalists as but the copious imagination of the human race.

Humanitarianism is now evaporating from secular humanism. In our generation the West is again approaching the plight of its pagan past, when human existence at the center of world civilization was characterized not only by moral corruption but by spiritual degeneracy as well. Radical terrorists scorn all the laws of civilized society by holding innocents hostage and by destroying passenger-laden airliners to advance their arbitrary political goals. In the name of their skewed causes, the savages audaciously renounce both legality and morality.

Rejection of the prevailing culture is now popular among deviant young people who repudiate established institutions and whatever procedures may define "the system." Moreover, they disdain and defy contemporary society, not indeed from the spiritual standpoint of a deservedly radical Christian critique, but rather from the standpoint of a reactionary divergence that elevates itself above universal reason, universal law, and universal morality. The streets of many of our big cities are overrun by alienated youth whose dress, language, symbolism, and behavior all suggest a deliberate disavowal of accepted norms and point to a rebellious detachment from humanity as a whole. Sociologist Jack Katz notes that many violent criminals now justify even murder by moralizing their crimes and convincing themselves that they pursue a higher calling by rejecting legal and social norms.[1]

Around us today live a multitude of seething and tormented minds, souls lashed by furious winds and waves of a drug culture, and a society threatened by AIDS. They are disinherited spirits, cognitive wanderers, feeble characters whose dutiful selfhood has almost expired and whose agitated hearts seem steeled against the truth. Except for an eerie sense of ultimate catastrophe, a bewildering chaos chills their sense of future. Because they are alienated from the supernatural, they are unstable struts of an insecure society in an uncertain time, bereft of a shiftless center. They readily accommodate this feeling of exile from spiritual realities. Their religious impulses are more a matter of superstition than a power that exerts internal or external influence. They speak now and then of right and wrong, but never of absolutes. They live in a world no longer sure of definitions. Some occasionally churn up the vocabulary of values, but their values take on the sense of mere wants and desires. Their rhetoric cannot conceal the homicides, violence, drug addiction,

---

1. Jack Katz, *Seductions of Crime* (New York: Basic Books, 1988).

alcoholism, and broken family patterns that shag and scar the surface of society.

The present generation refuses to admit that it is coping with demons; its teachers were unhelpful in confronting the ghastly terrors that stem from a paganism born of their rejection of Christianity.

The children of degeneracy often come from broken homes with divided values and are often products of value-free schooling. They are vexed by the emptiness of teenage life. Some expressly worship Satan and practice his life-style of deception and murder; now and then they even deliberately sacrifice one of their number to the Tempter. This they do even in an age when many professing Christians have moved the doctrine of Satan underground and when a secular society that stands ever closer to the Evil One nonetheless refuses to believe that the archfiend of iniquity inhabits our spiritual and moral vacuums. More than they know, many in our generation are already marching toward the hapless neopagan fringes of our culture. They are those for whom the only remaining purpose in life is death—whether spiritual, moral, or physical. Some are virtual corpses with a nagging consciousness of what once might have made human existence meaningful. For them life that is truly life seems now almost beyond reach. The disaffirming dogmas of modernity shape a perfunctoriness about religion that actually breeds a kind of irreligion in which one is but a disinterested spectator and postpones as long as possible any contemplation of death. Such irreligionists are on an ebbing civilization's death row; they bear faces of these already reckoned dead and waiting to be buried. This predicament they owe in part to an intellectual elite that tries to explain all reality by natural processes and events; all that is spiritual—the living God, eternal truth and good, the soul and its afterlife—it classifies as mythology and superstition.

One mark of our times is that multitudes of moderns now find human life interesting only if it is touched by scandal. Network newscasters preoccupied with the bedroom and living room sins of televangelists and others may actually reflect a growing tendency to view evildoing as socially normative. Hollywood has extended moral perversion to ultimate reality by its cinematic distortion of "The Last Temptation of Christ," in which writers and producers transfer to the Son of God the steamy sensuality of the wicked soap operas they conceive. Irreligious modernity thus ventures to nullify Jesus' moral challenge by implying that He participated in our vices, or that He is outmoded if He did not do so.

Alongside alcoholism and drugs, television has become in some respects one of America's worst addictions, one that now seems to worsen by the year. Nothing is any longer too sacred for the indelicate media to pervert. Seldom do the networks question the cognitive and ethical concessions of a vagabond society. The main complaint is not simply that their undergirding philosophy connects happiness only with material things although that is no small matter. The media prizes entertainment more than meaning, image more than reality, and readily pushes supernatural concerns outside the pale of enduring interest. Profit-thirsty corporations rely on seductive materialism to peddle their products. Worse yet, some sponsor advertising that enlists whorish fashions, unchaste sensual images, and provocative glimpses of carnal night life to connect indulgence with enchanting deviance. Christendom's hallowed music and most reverent traditions are frequently trivialized to enhance a materialistic sales pitch. The tobacco and beer giant Philip Morris, now the nation's biggest advertiser, spends over one and one half billion dollars annually for promotion despite the link between cigarette smoking and cancer and the rise of alcohol addiction.

Given the commercialization and secularization of Christianity's sacred seasons, believers may well be tempted to call for a moratorium on present patterns of Christian observance. Some public schools are more prone to feature Little Red Riding Hood and Snow White and the Seven Dwarfs than to refer to Jesus and the twelve disciples. Thanksgiving fares little better than Christmas. The lead editorial in *The Washington Post* for Thanksgiving Day 1988 managed not to mention God at all. Our lottery age secularizes religious semantics by substituting the notion of luck for that of divine providence. The political arena, as former Federal Appeals Judge Robert Bork notes, now reflects the bias of an intellectual "knowledge class" that promotes the privatization of morality and minimizes the public significance of religion. The prime point at issue is not whether public schools should become evangelistic podiums—whether for Christian, humanist, or existential commitments. The basic issue is whether the younger generation—cut off as it is from comprehension of the Judeo-Christian cultural heritage—can any longer truly understand itself and the distinctive principles and values that shape the American vision of life.

If we are alarmed at the heritage our present generation is leaving to future generations, there is good reason to be so. Many public schools steer clear of religious values and now often speak of moral values in a way that casts doubt on the existence of absolutes, except for administratively administered dictums like "Don't cheat on examinations" and "Don't litter the campus." Many contemporaries translate our treasured freedoms into an existence without God and without duty. The transcendent moorings that make ethical imperatives compelling are gone. Christianity, the religion of Jesus, is depicted as anti-Semitic. Even some clergy scorn any emphasis that humans are spiritually lost and divinely doomed apart from regeneration *as incompatible with religious freedom.* Religious liberty becomes a rationale for subverting transcendent meta-physical concerns into subjective preference. "Character" becomes a code-word for a minimum of moral violations. Marital fidelity is no longer an absolute requirement of public leadership, and experimental drug use is likely to be winked at if one indulged in it in one's early years. Seven million American boys between the ages of fifteen and eighteen are said to have had sex with a girl. It takes more than socio-logical research or well-intentioned pleas for their postponement of pleasure to deal with this torrent of immorality. Our generation has lost value consensus. Masses fear AIDS mostly because it limits sexual indul-gence; they want a cure for AIDS much more than a cure for immorality.

The culture-context in which we live therefore seems hardly propi-tious. For this dire predicament Christianity is not to blame; if anything, Christianity comprises a seriously neglected antidote. Yet the world's sorry condition is no more unpropitious than was the global scene in which Christianity first appeared with a salvific mission. In some ways, in fact, evangelical Christians face an opportunity greater than that of the apostolic age and of the Protestant Reformation, unless the coming of the transcendent Judge of all history should return to cancel that possi-bility. If God mercifully offers the season for repentance, this planet is not yet inescapably doomed unless Christians refuse to be light, leaven and salt.

## The Evangelical Confrontation

It is desperately urgent, then, that the Christian community compas-sionately confront this cultural catastrophe with a moral conscience and with a spiritual energy informed by the Scriptures. Evangelical Christians can hardly challenge the culture-context if they themselves are over-whelmed by the very social forces that need correction. Already in a former time, when Lord Shaftesbury sought allies to confront the seven-teenth century cultural drift in Britain, he lamented, "I know what con-stituted an Evangelical in former times," but "I have no clear notion of what constitutes one now." What would he say today, when all varieties of conflicting positions are affirmed in the public arena by those who claim evangelical legitimacy and biblical authority for their views? The Bible is invoked to approve contrary and contradictory views over the desirability of democratic government, the serviceability of nuclear power, the worthiness of socialist or capitalist economics, the propriety of legislating morality, and South African sanctions.

Despite these disconcerting developments, I stand by the main thesis of my jeremiad of forty years ago, *The Uneasy Conscience of Modern*

*Fundamentalism.*[2] Evangelical Christians dare not isolate themselves from the cultural mainstream. They are obliged to call human beings everywhere to a personal salvific experience of Christ, to declare also all humanity's answerability to the God of history, and to proclaim the standards by which the returning Lord will decisively judge the social and cultural developments of all nations by the criteria of revealed religion.

American evangelicals have emerged, fortunately, from the cultural underground into the cultural Main Street. The day is long past when secular media can snidely dismiss the evangelical phenomenon as anti-intellectual and subcultural fundamentalism and characterize its political activists in terms of Kentucky snake handlers and Islamic terrorists. Those who speak of evangelicals as if they were fossils recently unearthed from a cultural trash site have little sense of the deep controversy now underway over mainstream values and the role of large droves of evangelical activists who place those issues permanently on the public agenda.

Christians have no need to apologize for promoting particular proposals, especially when others aggressively crusade for their preferred alternatives. Even were others not to do so, Christians have every right to engage conscientiously in public affairs. We may even admire the active public engagement of many non-Christians, some of whom boldly challenge the corruption of our culture while all too many churchgoers still reserve moral principles for the secluded practice of a private cult. If Christians mean it when they say that Christian truth is public truth—truth to which all humanity is accountable—they must realize that biblical principles stand virtually no chance of being recognized as significant if those of us who are obliged to proclaim these principles remain silent. In that case, others with less intellectual legitimacy will sooner or later rush into the vacuum in a desperate effort to offer guidance in this decisive turning time in Western intellectual and moral history. Sad to say, secular culture has permeated evangelical loyalties more than many of us realize. We have eagerly freed ourselves from those legalistic fundamentalist "don'ts," but this has not occurred without significant loss. As J. D. Hunter notes, no new "don'ts" have arisen to replace the abandoned ones. Meanwhile church discipline has all but disappeared even from evangelical congregations. A church that is no longer under divine commandments is not the church that God envisions or the church that Christ founded.

To be sure, our Christian mandate in the world in no way justifies a politicization of the churches. The heart of the good news, which believ-

---

2. Carl F. H. Henry, *The Uneasy Conscience of Modern Fundamentalism* (Grand Rapids: Eerdman, 1947).

ers are commissioned to proclaim worldwide, is the living God's salvific activity accomplished for us in external history, as the Scriptures author- itatively attest. As the apostle Paul writes, "Christ died for our sins according to the scriptures; and that He was buried, and that He rose again the third day according to the scriptures" (1 Cor. 15:3-4, KJV); If the sinless yet crucified Jesus is not risen, this so-called good news is "null and void, and so is your faith" (1 Cor. 15:14, NEB). Personal faith, which is a gift of God, enables the penitent sinner to appropriate these redemptive realities savingly. There is a legitimate way of viewing social ethics as part of the "good news." This is not because our flawed human works can contribute in any way to our salvation. Yet Jesus' resurrection from barbaric crucifixion attests and vindicates God's good creation. Moreover, His resurrection claims penitent sinners for moral commit- ment and spiritual renewal, as creatures sharing in a creation whose eth- ical goals God will fully validate. No human being anywhere need submit to the crush of evil forces as finally decisive for his or her exist- ence. The risen Jesus has already in His own person and life won the victory over all unjust powers that would destroy Him and His cause in this world. Christ will return in climactic judgment upon impenitent humanity and the nations, for the full enthronement of righteousness and the final subjugation of evil. In this interim church age the Exalted Lord and present Head of the church seeks through the energies of God's regenerate people to extend His personal victory over sin and injustice. We have a mandate not only to win lost sinners everywhere to the Savior, but a mandate also to light, to leaven, and to salt the earth.

We have an immense opportunity in the area of Christian social eth- ics, one that evangelicals have almost let slip away by default. That opportunity to illumine and confront the cultural predicament is enhanced by the fact that many mainline denominations have made an incredible mess of their message. Liberal churchmen forfeited the task of evangelism and replaced the gospel by sociopolitical and economic pro- posals for cultural rescue. They promoted "the salvation of our planet" by concerns of ecology and international relations. Worse yet, they bap- tized their proposals as genuinely Christian. This switching of priorities and confusion over authentic biblical content has led to a revolt in the churches that *U.S. News and World Report* reflects in striking statistics: "Since 1965, U.S. evangelical churches have won new souls at an aver- age rate of eight percent every five years, while membership in liberal Protestant denominations has declined at a five-year rate of nearly five percent."[3] Methodists have lost 1.4 million members since 1970, and the

---

3. *U. S. News and World Report* (December 19, 1988).

United Church of Christ has lost a half million. Since 1958 one out of three Episcopalians has defected in protest against liberal views of politics and sex.

Evangelical Protestants now number over forty million. Their opportunity to neutralize the errors of the ecumenical bureaucracy and to reshape Christian social involvement is unprecedented. It is no gain if Protestant ecumenism collapses and carries down with it mainline churches whose drooping memberships we might still recover for constructive social engagement and restore to evangelistic vitalities. A danger exists that some misguided evangelicals may duplicate costly ecumenical mistakes. Nothing can be gained by emulating modernists who routinely commute to the newest theological shopping malls trying to stay a week ahead of the social fashions only to promote markdowns a decade behind the times. Whether in Christology or sociology, those who chase novelty in order to be in the forefront of truth usually end up two millenniums behind it.

It is distressing that some marginal conservatives do not discern the handwriting on the wall. They too consider it newfangled and smart to embrace socioeconomic notions of world-regulation that all but hardcore liberals are slowly abandoning. They run the risk of perpetuating outworn liberal social proposals and do so allegedly as evangelicals rather than as avowed proponents of speculative social theory. At the same time a highly vocal band of conservatives promoting highly desirable objects has aggressively entered the public arena in a somewhat objectionable way. Often motivated by specific legislative proposals much more than by articulate biblical principles, they shaped no comprehensive philosophy of public engagement. If recent neoorthodoxy rejected divinely revealed principles and truths, fundamentalist activism acknowledged but neglected them while promoting—quite unsuccessfully—particular legislative changes. The social arena thus gained the aura of a rodeo where conservative cowboys sequentially sought to lasso and rope one undomesticated issue after another. The fundamentalist right cooperated with the Catholic right on specific concerns, most notably pro-life hostility to abortion under virtually any and all circumstances. Catholic political involvement meanwhile reflected a canopy philosophy of church tradition and natural morality theory.

The fundamentalist program took the course of public confrontation more than consultative cooperation with duly elected legislators. Moral Majority greatly overstated its membership, and religious spokepersons who stationed themselves between the masses and their elected government officials exuded a spirit of political triumphalism and threatened to run rival candidates to challenge those who resisted the fundamentalist agenda. Protestant Christians were left without a canopy political philosophy; evangelicals were untaught in the biblically disclosed principles of social ethics; political activists overlooked the implications of democratic pluralism for public involvement. No less important is the fact that the political particulars strongly championed by the religious right and promoted as consistently Christian commitments often were presented as if their biblical supports the self-evident. Recent studies have shown that the religious right and the religious left both claimed biblical legitimacy for positions on foreign and domestic policy whose precise scriptural authentication was obscure. Most often they merely christened the thrust of the secular left or of the secular right as the Christian approach. Seldom was it openly acknowledged that the resolution of political particulars have no absolute certainty and rested on possibly fallible inferences from revelatory principles. Legislative proposals were not transcendently given legal pillars of the divine kingdom of God but were revisable statute law.

The ambiguities of evangelical involvement unwittingly encouraged the notion that no moral foundation for public policy decisions exists other than natural law or church tradition. It makes a world of difference whether political decisions are arrived at in terms merely of culture preferences, tradition, or authenticating biblical principles. All Christian legitimacy is lost if an appeal to the Bible reduces to the skeptical notion that the Bible means all things to all interpreters. In the political arena the Christian must wind his or her way between the view that the Bible is completely untranslatable in respect to political particulars and the view that Christians must equate the sense of Scripture with the majority view disclosed by a Gallup poll.

For example, although it is rife with risks, the growing Southern Baptist involvement in the public arena provides a remarkable opportunity to strengthen the role of law in society, to shape moral conscience, to stimulate godly behavior, and to exemplify Christian sociopolitical engagement at its best. As the nation's largest—numbering some fifteen million members—the denomination can wield enormous influence both in the religious arena and in the secular sphere. The denomination needs prudent guidance in respect to critical concerns, legitimate goals, and proper methods; it needs to learn where to properly draw the line between involvement of the Convention, of local churches, and of individual Christians in public affairs.

The question of legitimate political goals has become urgent. Evangelical ranks include some who insist that the churches' only task should be personal evangelism awaiting Christ's apocalyptic return, and who consider most social involvement a misguided effort to refurbish a satanic environment from which the people of God should isolate themselves. Essentially premillennial-dispensational in stance, this wing has recently accommodated a modified approach. Reflected by Moral Majority, this newer division seeks to "recover" or to promote Judeo-Christian values in national politics and to champion a long list of legislative specifics. It offers no master political vision or conceptual blueprint for reorganizing society, in large part because it still regards overarching eschatological commitments as more decisive.

At the other end of the spectrum are the highly vocal theonomists. They too seek to transcend cultural withdrawal and venture an aggressive condemnation of public immorality; they are determined to defeat all proposed legislation that would undermine biblical values. The distinctive of Christian Reconstructionism is that it considers the Mosaic law a divinely intended framework for all civil government throughout human history, not for the ancient Hebrew theocracy only. Its champions therefore deplore democracy as a heretical form of government, one unacceptable to a Christian vision of society. Its ready appeal lies in its commendation of Christian world dominion. It combines its commitment to miraculous supernatural theism with the expectation of a dramatic historical impact and spiritual advance through Christian evangelism and government. Calvin in Geneva, the New England Puritans, and Abraham Kuyper in the Netherlands are all invoked by Reconstructionism because they promoted a Christian ordering of society, although they projected no global takeover. Today's so-called "dominion theology," essentially post millennial in stance, would gradually reinstate capital punishment as the Hebrew theocracy applied it to a whole range of crimes and would "Christianize the world" in expectation of Christ's return in power and glory. The movement readily enlists the enthusiasm of charismatics, who in their own recent proliferation see a sign of the kingdom.

Transcending these alternatives is the more customary evangelical orthodox view, as exhibited in earlier centuries by the Evangelical Awakening an eighteenth-century England and by American evangelicalism before the fundamentalist withdrawal from sociopolitical engagement under the pressure of historical pessimism. This traditional evangelical approach considers both radical withdrawal from public affairs and theonomic reconstructionism as biblically unjustifiable. As do other views, it insists on the imperative of personal evangelism and of sociocultural engagement as well wherever the people of God are scattered worldwide. In contrast to the theonomists, however, it emphasizes that Christians in the present church age are divinely and purposely distributed under a variety of forms of government. Many traditional evangelicals would now consider a democracy or republic a preferable form in view of their approval of political self-determination in a flawed society prone to dictatorial totalitarianism. The people of God are in any case citizens of two worlds, and they are to serve God obediently in evangelistic engagement and in public affairs. The public goals of the churches are differently viewed if they have no conscious covering philosophy, if they espouse radical church-state separation or radical church-state conjunction, or if they consider the American experiment a precious inheritance compatible with biblical ideals.

The American founding fathers would consider utterly repulsive the Soviet view of absolute church-state separation which enthroned the state as the ultimate source and stipulator of human rights, denied the public significance of religion, and prohibited public evangelism. The American Constitution, by contrast, embodies the two great principles of nonestablishment and of free exercise.

It is likely that no state can entirely escape a measure of "establishment"—whether that be humanistic, theistic, or whatever—because every legal system has religious implications. Many framers of the Constitution probably considered Protestantism the preferred religion. They did not, however, constitutionally ensure a Protestant America. Most would doubtless be greatly astonished to discover that secular humanism has become the orthodox metaphysics of American education and politics. They would be astounded that a ten-year-old student's voluntary prayer in a public schoolroom could raise a public outcry. They would also ask why a misplaced fear of a Christian establishment had so stifled evangelical free expression that a humanist establishment had triumphally exploited the vacuum.

It becomes all the more important that the churches be exhorted to examine their presuppositions, their goals, and their methods, and be urged to debate and defend them on biblical grounds. No less important are the reasons that Christians adduce in the public area to support their legislative preferences. In the political realm are evangelicals to make metaphysical appeals to the revelatory authority of the Bible and Catholics to ecclesiastical authority and Jews to the Torah and humanists to the humanist manifesto? Or ought all of us to use public reason and the rhetoric of a republican in espousing our views? Richard Neuhaus reminds us of the critical importance of this matter in *The Naked Public Square*,[4] an issue that I addressed earlier in *The Christian Mindset in a Secular Society*.[5] For citizens to rely on public reason in championing

---

4. Richard John Neuhaus, *The Naked Public Square* (Grand Rapids: Eerdmans, 1987).
5. Carl F. H. Henry, *The Christian Mindset in a Secular Society* (Portland: Multnomah Press, 1989).

legislative particulars need not mean that public life should be con-
ducted on the premise that religious beliefs are irrelevant.

In our decade divisions in the churches readily become the occasion
of ruinous rumors. Believers are sometimes perceived by the world as
fighting like wolves and hyenas instead of striving cooperatively for
social renewal. This is a time to reach for shared convictions, not a time
to publicize the worst about each other. I know that factions tend to
exploit such pleas by pointing accusing fingers at everyone but themselves. We must not minimize the basic importance of scriptural authority, for once we lose that we are left only with ourselves and other
unscriptural authorities. Let us remember, however, that in Paul's day
certain sincere Christian Jews defamed him for accepting believing Gentiles without their first becoming Hebrews; Paul himself, moreover, had
disconcerting differences with Barnabas. Yet all parties resisted a pragmatic openness which would have cast the apostles as theological
nomads unsure where to pitch their tents. The time has come for regenerate Christians to bridge and close ranks, aware that the redeemed
community has little integrity unless it is unified in its worldwide mission. The studied correlation of Christian social action with biblical core
beliefs and biblical controls should go far to make Southern Baptists and
other evangelicals an effective force and a commendable example in
public affairs.

## Needed: New Credibility in Evangelical Initiatives

All this, though necessary, is not yet sufficient. Our projected solutions must be authentically Christian. We Christians need not and must
not shun the use of power. But Christians dare not use power merely in
the world's ways and for the world's ends. A Christian should use power
under God to serve Him obediently and to promote justice in society.
The morally disciplined use of power requires us to view God Himself
as the supreme power in the universe and Jesus Christ the risen Head of
the church as the one on whom God has already conferred all power.
The new society or fellowship of the twice born therefore has an important role in world history; it bears notably on the futures of nations and
the destiny of cultures.

In their witness to the world powers, the scattered people of God
have often experienced persecution, suffering, and even martyrdom. Yet
more Christians exist today on mainland China than when Communists
overthrew Chiang Kai Shek and evicted Western missionaries. In Europe
today the largest evangelical church is in Oradea, Romania, where Baptist believers were for years engaged in a courageous standoff confrontation with hostile authorities in a socialist police state. Under many

forms of government dispersed Christians bear their witness to the God of justice and of justification. They have had to cope more often with the beast state of Revelation 13 than with the so-called God-state of Romans 13. If despite its constitutional safeguards the United States declines into a beast state, it will not be only because atheistic humanists have captured its public institutions but equally because theists— and not least of all, evangelicals—have allowed the naturalists to preempt the citadels of power.

In God's beneficent providence Third-World Christians are awakening to their global missionary outreach precisely at a time when many European and Anglo-Saxon Christians are preoccupied mostly with themselves. Today new possibilities exist of enlarged evangelical engagement in erstwhile communist countries and even in some Moslem areas. To be sure, we do not know the ultimate course of religious liberty in Eastern Europe, or of the Three-Self patriotic church for the fortunes of the house churches in mainland China. We do know that, with the all-too-tardy withdrawal of Soviet troops from Afghanistan, Koranic religion has renewed its bitter hostility to Christians who are again being persecuted despite American help in resisting and repelling Soviet aggression. Even so, Christianity remains the first and only religion with a world presence; many lands, America among them, hold a high potential for dramatic evangelical advance. Alongside the distant evangelical thrust for world missions "over there," the importance of the evangelical future "over here" becomes increasingly evident.

Despite the evangelical resurgence in the United States, all formative cultural arenas—education, politics, and the mass media—are presently dominated by nonevangelical influences. It is futile to try to force evangelical commitment upon those centers of power that reflect a naturalistic outlook on life. Evangelicals need a strategy that effectively rivals and then aims to transform these arenas by penetrating them. Our goal should be the dynamic transformation of individuals and, as far as possible, the penetration of the culture. Only when the culture permeates and engulfs the church is the church really in danger, and we had better not underestimate that risk today. If we do not succeed in restoring biblical concerns to secular society, and Western culture continues its impenitent way to irreversible ruin, such eventualities need by no means imply the end of Christianity. Nowhere does a New Testament link the fortunes of the church with the fortunes of a particular civilization or culture.

The new society must on its own terrain sponsor educational, media, and governmental efforts predicated on Christian principles, and demonstrate the truth, justice, and *agape* over pragmatism and *eros*. We can hardly do so if we withdraw from the larger world in which God has stationed us as witnesses and fellow citizens. It is high tragedy that American evangelicals, who have commendably established and funded many biblically oriented schools, have acquired on obvious proclivity for accommodating takeover by nonevangelicals; when challenged, these usurpers would rather destroy those enterprises than restore them to their original intent. If churches cannot or will not safeguard their own religious heritage, why should the secular city consider Christians reliable guardians of society's conceptual and moral fortunes?

It is high tragedy, likewise, that conservative Christians, who have commendably helped to elect godly candidates to political office, should have left so many of their own representatives untutored in the relevance of biblical principles, so that in shaping programs of action these candidates have sought and found inspiration mainly in nonevangelical sources. Let us train a generation of young leaders with a twofold vision—first, the nurture within the church of a scripturally oriented vanguard of competent professionals in every area of expertise—evangelicals able to articulate the Christian world-life view and its implications for every realm of world endeavor; and second, the formulation of a powerful intellectual and moral challenge to our collapsing secular society and offering our confused culture compelling options that escape the ever-looming chaos of present patterns of thought and life.

The current social predicament calls for much more than single- issue patchwork; it requires a comprehensive canopy outlook that deals with the mind and will of a collapsing culture at every level of its struggle for survival. Evangelicals need not enter the cognitive debate by the back door. By no means has the so-called "steamroller of modernity" demolished God and the supernatural and moral absolutes. A generation ago logical positivism ran rampant and intimidated any and all interest in metaphysics; today positivism is derided and God is doing remarkably better than expected. The early church and the Reformation lived by much more than rumor about the good and the true, and moderns, too, can learn to rely on divine providence and prayer, and be taught to reach for fixed truth and right. Social critics may hesitate or even refuse to learn from Scripture. They cannot refute the witness of Western history, however, which shows that values lack permanence apart from supernatural norms, and that a loss of absolutes presages a loss also of human meaning and worth.

A loss of human meaning and dignity is precisely what marks this season of civilizational decline. The posture evangelicals assume—and the convictions they make known—may not determine success in the public arena, but they will determine whether or not evangelical Christians show themselves faithful.

# Evangelical Cobelligerency: A Next Step?

*Participation in a pluralistic republic poses for Christians the basic question of whether they are to concern themselves in the public arena mainly with their own interests as one of the numerous faith-communities, or whether their first obligation is to identify and to promote the common good of society.*

After a long period of political withdrawl, evangelicals are now considering a response to the call for "chartered pluralism" as called for in the recent statement, *The Williamsburg Charter.*[1] Some evangelical spokesmen are now probing possibilities of enlarged political cooperation with culturally concerned Catholics and other American conservatives.

Straggling far behind are fundamentalists of the 1930-1950 era whose premillennial dispensationalism involved a pessimistic view of history. Expecting Christ's imminent return, they devalued political and cultural engagement and concentrated on personal evangelism. Written in 1948, my *Uneasy Conscience of Modern Fundamentalism* pleaded for their return to evangelical public involvement instead of merely operating energetic rescue missions and voting once every four years.

---

1. *The Williamsburg Charter* is a major statement on religious liberty in a pluralistic society. It was released by the Williamsburg Charter Foundation in 1988.

Across forty years the American scene has changed remarkably. A recent conference of active evangelicals of diverse perspectives discussed the evangelical movement's present cultural role. Interestingly enough, the only unrepresented perspective was that of social isolationists whose apolitical stance and public withdrawal dominated American fundamentalism a half century ago. To be sure, this viewpoint still has support in circles such as Bob Jones University and *The Sword of the Lord*, and among an older Dallas Seminary constituency, convinced that the end-time apostasy is already underway and still pessimistic about historical involvement and change. The impact of "Amish evangelicals" and traditional fundamentalists has been quite negligible since Jerry Falwell's Moral Majority shaped a politically active conservatism by the Religious Right. Even many Mennonites no longer insist that the regenerate church as "a new society" should wholly avoid world engagement.

Signs of a significant shift of attitude among conservative Protestants can be detected by all who have eyes to see. At a recent seminar sponsored by the Washington-based Ethics and Public Policy Center, every conference participant assumed that evangelicals *must* be strenuously involved in public affairs. Some stressed this as a matter only of political necessity, since to withdraw from public life yields the battle uncontested to unbelievers who sponsor contrary values. Most, however, declared active public involvement to be a matter of moral duty implicit in the Christian's dual citizenship, and hence divinely mandated. The Christian is to beam light, sprinkle salt, and knead leaven into an otherwise hopeless world.

The most intensive form of this Christian penetration is sponsored by Reconstructionists, who advocate some form of ecclesiastical imperialism. Their biblical model is the ancient Hebrew theocracy where God mandated His covenant people to separate from pagan society and to live according to Mosaic legislation. In the Middle Ages Roman Catholicism projected the Holy Roman Empire that gathered not only a covenant people but all society politically within the context of Christian belief and conduct.

Unlike recent modern fundamentalism that confines the relevance of Mosaic legislation to an earlier and now superseded dispensation, so-called Christian Reconstructionism proposes that the United States enforce Judeo-Christian legislation. This transformationist view considers theonomy—that is, civil government rules by the Mosaic code—the divinely intended norm for political authority in all times and places. It correlates the Mosaic legislation not only with a covenant people, as did the Hebrews, but it proposes to bring all society everywhere within its orbit and to treat all mankind as part of one faith-community. Theonomists proclaim the political lordship of Christ over the nations and regard any form of democratic government as heretical.

The theonomist view has understandably stirred vigorous debate. Was the United States, as some theonomists claim, originally a Christian state? Should Christian principles be legislated upon a pluralistic society? Is a revival of certain ancient Hebrew theocratic legislation feasible today? Do theonomist proposals reflect a profound misunderstanding of the biblical view of church- state relationships during the present church age? Some critics observe that instead of trying to impose Christian legislation on society, theonomists are actually promoting a remodeled Hebrew political order. Theonomists are themselves divided over whether some ancient Hebrew legislation—for example, the menstrual laws—are to be carried forward. Most critics argue that it would lead to unbelievable chaos if society today were to reimpose the theocratic death penalty and execution (by stoning, moreover) of offenders guilty of any of a dozen or more types of crimes.

Promoters of theonomous reconstructionism are mainly postmillennialists who think that Christians must aggressively extend God's kingdom on earth in order to bring humanity and all the nations progressively under Christ's sovereignty in expectation of His climactic return. Evangelical Christians of earlier generations were also eagerly concerned to extend Christ's lordship over all spheres of life. They were convinced, however, that the Hebrew theocracy has been divinely superseded. They found no biblical basis for trying to establish a theonomy or universal society controlled by the Mosaic judicial code. In the New Testament era, they insisted, God purposely scattered Christians around the world in countries that embrace many forms of government; within these countries they were to witness to the Risen Lord and seek to extend the claims of biblical justice. They rejected the notion that "God commanded the Hebrew covenant community to do it; therefore Christians must do it." The New Testament era nowhere involves a program of civil government predicated on the assumption of a single, universal faith community or of a political revival of theocracy.

Given the tyrannical use of power by totalitarian regimes, many Christians have in modern times preferred alternative forms of government that assure political self-determination. Beneficent totalitarianism is a concept that they associate only with the coming reign of Christ; any concentration of absolute political power in merely human rulers in fallen history they consider fraught with risk. To be sure, many Christians would not deny that democracy may through lack of consensus fall into chaos, or that now and then a benevolent monarchy may rise. They do not, however, view democracy as heretical, as do Reconstructionists;

rather, they see theonomy as an illegitimate proposal for civil government in the present church age. For them a republican or democratic alternative is compatible with legitimate evangelical concerns, especially in the American context of church-state separation.

Participation in a pluralistic republic poses for Christians the basic question of whether they are to concern themselves in the public arena mainly with their own interests as one of the numerous faith-communities, or whether their first obligation is to identify and to promote the common good of society. Many evangelicals are disinterested in, or neglect, formulation of a public policy. They exhaust their energies primarily in what they oppose, or in promoting single-issue concerns. Few church members are taught that political developments are important; some are untaught even about private morality. Emphasis on the importance of an evangelically shared view of a common civic good may, in fact, seem odd to them.

As a result, many evangelicals tend to face and enter the political arena primarily in terms of a particular faith community's special interests, and they justify their involvement and goals solely by appealing to the revelatory authority of the Bible. Their civic involvement consequently centers in high-profile confrontational activism that promotes Christian legislation and a Christian state, and does so, if not under the banner of theonomic Reconstructionism, then under that of a moral majority. Since they exhibit little, if any, concern for a public philosophy, they are readily perceived as a threat to pluralistic democracy. In this development the political involvement of evangelicals has acquired an identity different from their role in England in the eighteenth-century Evangelical Awakening. Departure of recent American political activism from the earlier evangelical stance is a major reason for growing emphasis on the evangelical need of a public philosophy, and beyond that of a strategy of cobelligerency.

Earlier evangelicals were concerned for public justice, not simply for an agenda of special evangelical interests. In the effort to promote civic righteousness they identified themselves with the entire body politic. They championed a public philosophy and addressed a national conscience. Their political convictions were not grounded simply in a private vision of civil decency. They sprang as well from a divine compulsion to speak of public affairs in the context of transcendent justice and of a universally binding social good. Such convictions are what pulsated through Wilberforce's plea to the English Parliament to end the slave trade, though to be sure he did not hesitate to refer to the God of the Bible and to scriptural considerations.

The distinction between public interest and partisan interest is reflected in differing attitudes toward religious liberty concerns. The Religious Right, for example, eagerly appealed to religious liberty and increasingly acknowledged it as basic to all other human freedoms. Yet it invoked religious freedom in a special way to protest encroachments on evangelical freedom, and to advance legitimate evangelical concerns. A more disciplined public philosophy would have avoided such selectivity, however, and would have first of all stressed religious freedom for all persons of whatever faith. Had the Religious Right paid attention to this distinction from the outset, its critics could not so readily have considered its insistence on the relevance of religion to public affairs as a civic threat to nonevangelicals. To transcend this initial misperception of religious intolerance, conservative Protestants invited participation by like-minded Catholics, Jews, Mormons, and others, thus leading a pluralistic image of sorts to the Religious Right. This broader constituency diminished suspicions that conservative Protestants were trying to impose an agenda of Christian sectarian legislation upon the state. Even if they promoted a multireligious agenda, however, they nonetheless stopped far short of articulating a public philosophy.

The need for evangelicals to be involved publicly in justice issues was addressed not only in *The Uneasy Conscience of Modern Fundamentalism* (1948), but also in my *A Plea for Evangelical Demonstration* (1971), *The Christian Mindset in a Secular Society* (1984) and *Twilight of a Great Civilization* (1988). In the latter three books the basis for such involvement is located in God's creation-ethic and in His universal revelation, including the *imago Dei* (image of God) that, however sullied, nonetheless survives the fall of mankind. Some Reformed scholars appeal also to common grace in expounding general revelation. Calvin propounded the doctrine, and Charles Hodge, Herman Bavinck, and Abraham Kuyper relied on it in expounding a philosophy of history and culture. Common grace, no less than saving grace, presupposes total depravity. Its role is limited to a divine restraint of the effects of sin and to humanity's enablement of civil righteousness and human culture.

Other Reformed writers reject the doctrine of common grace, while still others—notably Valentine Hepp, Kuyper, and Bavinck—developed it into a natural theology and apologetic based on general truths supposedly shared by all humans. In doing so, the latter disregarded Calvin's insistence that unregenerate humanity suppresses its own inescapable knowledge of the Deity. Roman Catholicism appeals to "natural law," the theory that despite the fall of humankind there survives a universally shared body of moral truths. The Protestant Reformers disavowed this doctrine as involving too optimistic a view of the consequences of original sin. Calvin, indeed, spoke of "natural law," but by it he did not mean that a universally shared body of ethical and theological truths survives the Adamic fall, or that revealed ethics and theology can or should be superimposed on such a philosophical edifice. What the Reformers stressed was that the light of general revelation universally penetrates the mind and conscience of unregenerate humankind, but that humans deflect it in a way that nonetheless renders them guilty for their defiance and distortion of it.

An evangelical public philosophy of involvement must not be located onesidedly in a sectarian religious tradition but must also embrace, even if it is part of that tradition, universal revelation and public reason, albeit without disavowing the crucial importance of special revelation.

Evangelical forfeiture of a public philosophy through the Religious Right's shortsightedness together with mainstream evangelicalism's overall indifference has led to the present opportunity for and growing emphasis on "a Catholic moment." Thomistic scholars devoted to natural-law theory propose to articulate a canopy-vision under which Evangelicals in league with other Christians might pursue public justice and at the same time focus attention on traditional community values.

Some Thomists confuse the Protestant emphasis on general revelation and/or on common grace with natural-law theory. In recent years a number of lesser Reformed scholars have controversially and confusingly depicted Calvin as devoted to natural law and have pursued an evidentialist apologetics highly compatible with empirical Thomistic theology. Whereas evangelical orthodoxy has stressed God's rational propositional revelation and the importance of biblically revealed principles of morality, some contemporary Catholics adapt the discussion toward natural-law theory and church tradition by questioning whether the Bible does in fact give us much in the way of revealed ethical principles. As Richard John Neuhaus observes, conservative evangelical co-belligerency with conservative Protestant ecumenists and conservative Catholics need not involve an implicit commitment to natural-law theory; indeed, it would be a costly theological mistake were Protestant evangelicals to conjoin a public political philosophy essentially with natural-law arguments and a natural theology.[2] This philosphical and theological retreat was rejected by the Reformers, and it must be rejected by American evangelicals as well.

Despite its somewhat theonomous beginnings, the Moral Majority moved in a pluralistic direction by enlisting nonevangelicals and non-Christians, although its purpose was much more limited than formulat-

---

2. Neuhaus, *The Naked Public Square.*

ing a pluralistic public philosophy. More recently, however, proponents of the so-called Williamsburg Charter have emerged to champion "chartered pluralism." Shaped by Os Guinness, the Williamsburg Charter project is not predicated on shared beliefs; it assumes that American pluralism has now moved beyond that possibility. The fact is that, alongside traditional Christian (Catholic, Protestant, Greek Orthodox) and Jewish groups, enlarging clusters of Muslims, Buddhists, and Hindus are emerging in America. American society now also includes 4 percent of the population who are completely irreligious, who never attend church, and who consider religion to be of no value and irrelevant to public affairs. Another 6 percent disavow any religious preference, yet grant that religion can be important in national life.

Chartered pluralism, it must be emphasized, involves neither a general dilution of belief (for example, to Judeo-Christian theism) nor a fluctuating civil religion. It comprises a compact whereby pluralistic society embraces "the *3'R's* of religious liberty: rights, responsibilities and respect." It is "chartered" in that it accommodates no one interest group and is "pluralistic" in that it is not merely majoritarian. Moral and religious consensus is not a *given*, but rather a *goal*. Instead of focusing on the more narrow rubric of "church and state" the Williamsburg Charter focuses on religion and government with a shared vision of religious liberty within a pluralistic society.

Some critics insist that since participating constituencies mean different things by rights and by responsibilities, the stability of the compact is at risk. Some observers have misrepresented the charter as a betrayal of evangelical or Christian theological loyalties and as an heretical and pagan alternative. It is neither. Its import is more formal than substantive. It affirms universal religious liberty, universally obligatory rights and duties. To citizens as individuals it leaves the establishment and vindication of specific content, whether on philosophical or revelatory ground. The Charter has much in common with John Courtney Murray's emphasis some decades ago that Roman Catholics should enter the political arena not through attempted ecclesiastical controls but through projection of a public philosophy. Their subsequent public emphasis on "distributive justice" no doubt soon advantaged a number of Catholic institutions and some Protestant spokesmen were prompt to protest. Many evangelical agencies simply got in line for similar benefits.

There is little doubt that, armed with the Vatican II emphasis on religious liberty and with natural-law tradition, Catholics will continue to expound the content of public justice consistently with their own participatory interest. If evangelical Protestants do not carefully identify areas of consensus and difference, that will be their loss, deservedly so. The stranglehold of secular humanism, and increasingly of raw paganism, on public life is so erosive of biblical values that a shared effort in the political arena is increasingly imperative. America's people and its religious disposition will be even more diverse in the 1990s than now. Religious liberty is an important evangelical theme and evangelicals should be its foremost heralds. It is incumbent upon them to demonstrate that the case for public justice rests not solely on special revelation, but also and no less upon God's moral purpose in creation. Natural law or no natural law and despite the fall, humanity is not unaware of answerability to God for public behavior.

Cobelligerency will be an increasing fact of political life in the years ahead. Participating groups will experience both gains and losses and preferred ends will necessitate frequently shifting alliances. Nothing in scriptural revelation or in general revelation precludes even evangelicals and secular humanists from joining forces, for example, against race discrimination or ecological pollution. Philosophically, a humanist may not want to stand with a theist any more than a theist would prefer to stand with an atheist. If the issue at stake is human rights and duty or pollution of the planet—not supernaturalism or naturalism—each can ignore what he or she perceives to be the other's shaky epistemology in order to cooperatively commend right action and public justice.

In *A Plea for Evangelical Demonstration* (1971) I stressed the importance of evangelical public identification with the body of humanity no less than with the body of Christ. Nothing precludes an interreligious or ecumenical cooperative public witness against injustice or for justice. If evangelicals were to take the initiative in setting such an agenda then nonevangelicals would have to ask themselves whether or not they can "afford" to cooperate. We ask ourselves the question simply because we too often forfeit the initiative to others.

# Part IV
# Contemporary Theology and the Battle of the Gods

# Will Christianity
# Outlive Its Critics?

*Today it is not Christianity but rather so-called modernity that is being judged. The final choice is not between an ancient religion and modern science; it is between spiritual good news and no good news at all.*

No world religion has been abused and assailed by foes within and without more than has Christianity. Yet it is the first of the great world faiths to attain a global presence and enlists almost a billion adherents even in the present generation. Is its future secure? Do we speak only of a cultural oddity when, two decades after Mao, we note that more than ten million Christians now populate mainland China rather than the some seven hundred thousand who were counted before hostile Red Guards desecrated churches and banned Bibles? Or when after two generations of communist virulence, evangelical Christianity in Eastern Europe is today more vigorous than ever? Or when African churches in Kenya are multiplying so quickly that not enough pastors can be found to lead new congregations? Or that in Korea 25 percent of the inhabitants of that Asian country eagerly declare themselves Christian?

Do such phenomena merely reflect a momentary culture swing or culture lag? Must we view evangelical resurgence in the United States within a larger philosophical and historical framework that destines biblical theism to inevitable obsolescence?

## Background: The Critics Within

Early in this century religious modernism trumpeted worldwide its confident verdict that evangelical orthodoxy represented a stage of religious senility that invites euthanasia. To be sure, modernism found in the Bible much that surpassed rival ethico-religious outlooks. It paid tribute to Jesus of Nazareth as the supreme moral example and model of personal trust in a providential Father's care for His creatures.

Modernism nonetheless repudiated miraculous theism on the premise that scientific laboratory observation and duplication was the superlative way of knowing. "Once-for-all" facets of Christian confession—special revelation, singular incarnation, Jesus' virgin birth, substitutionary atonement, and bodily resurrection—it disavowed as pious myth. It welcomed Christianity only as the "highest" expression of "religion-in-general"; it commended Christian regeneration only for its reduction of the inner personality conflict of those who modeled Jesus' dependence on the Father. Western universities and mainline seminaries eagerly joined modernism's defection from evangelical orthodoxy. They viewed miraculous theism as outdated and modernism as its perpetual replacement. They championed academic freedom even while they consolidated modernist bureaucracies to exclude so-called "fundamentalist" scholars from faculty posts. They wrested denominational institutions from their original positions and deployed evangelical endowments to promote doctrines that the founders would have opposed.

No religion in history has had to contend—and yet survived stronger than ever—with the phenomenon of professional scholars who dismissed central elements of its heritage as legend and myth, while they professed to speak as friends of that movement. In many cases such revisionist critics drew salaries from institutions originally established on the premise of the credibility and reliability of inherited core beliefs. Confidence in philosophical reasoning now eclipsed faith in transcendent divine revelation. Speculative philosophy of religion displaced revealed theology. The case for theism was argued not on the basis of divine disclosure but through the search for God in the "not-god," that is, in nature, history, and conscience.

Students of philosophy and of history should not have been much surprised by modernism's subsequent collapse. Its optimistic emphasis on man's essential goodness and on the inevitability of progress could not be squared either with the drift of history (most notably World War II) or with human nature (especially Freudian analysis and the Nazi terrors). Nor, as Karl Barth and his neoorthodox followers emphasized, could it be reconciled with the Bible's insistent witness to once-for-all revelation grounded in the self-disclosing God. Nor, as religious humanism rightly noted, could it be dignified as philosophically consistent: modernism did not and could not validate by the scientific criterion it espoused its own belief that trust in Jesus is incomparably integrative of a discordant self. Other religions offered alternatives and the finality of Jesus could not be established within the limits of the scientific method on which modernism professed to rely.

European neoorthodoxy brought new excitement to doctrinally pluralistic seminaries that welcomed its theological mix: rejection of the Bible's objective authority, alongside insistence on the absolute uniqueness of redemptive revelation and on internal volitional response to an essentially nonpropositional divine confrontation. The view attracted even backsliding evangelical seminarians who under incessant critical fire wearied in their defense of the Bible. Much as neoorthodoxy penetrated denominational seminaries and religious colleges, its impact on secular university campuses was negligible except in religion departments that mainly welcomed any and every novelty while they largely excluded evangelical orthodoxy. As a formative cultural influence neoorthodoxy was less potent than modernism.

## The Agenda of Secular Humanism

Secular humanism reaped the fruit of modernism's collapse and later of neoorthodoxy's deterioration. More than any alternative, radical humanism shaped the worldview gifted by public schools, colleges, and universities to the younger generation. Belief in God was assuredly neither disallowed nor caricatured. It was considered a merely private opinion without public significance. The campus curriculum allowed God no role in science, in history, or in much else. God emerged in literature classes where the genre of fiction could easily contain Him. Humanist premises supplied the masked metaphysics of Western university learning: reality is reducible to impersonal processes and quantum events; all existence is time-bound and perishable; theological, philosophical, and moral principles are culture relative and subject to revision; human beings autonomously and creatively impose whatever values history and the cosmos bear.

Despite this supposedly thorough empirical bent, secular humanism nonetheless insisted on an agenda of social ethics—most notably, human equality and rights, ecological concerns, and in many cases, concern also for the poor (usually to be expressed through political response). Yet fixed social imperatives have no objective standing in the context of comprehensive evolution and change. Less sentimental naturalists therefore considered this social schedule an emotional lag in a philosophy that excludes absolutes. Evangelical Christians recognized it as an inconsistent retention of fragments of the Judeo-Christian inherit-

ance; some declared it to be an unwitting deference to the created
*imago Dei* which, despite the Adamic fall, survives in all humanity.

Humanism's decline into raw naturalism is currently evident in an
awesome slump of humanitarian concern toward barbaric patterns of
thought and life. Human life is increasingly regarded as animal flesh to
be exploited for sexual pleasure, private greed, or political gain. The
abortion of 15 million fetuses by Americans in a single decade is but one
of many indications of present-day infatuation for the pagan god Eros.
Major universities have not learned the lesson of Hitler and the Nazis;
once again they specialize in the advancement of technical science
while moral concerns remain on the margin. Human existence continues
to decline in special value and meaning, and a sense of melancholy
more and more overtakes contemporary life.

## The Collapse of the Christian West

While the conflict between Christianity and non-Christian religions
remains highly significant in Asia and Africa, the Western world's spiritual struggle is now mainly posed between Christian theism and deteriorating humanism or raw naturalism. In the decisive European and
Anglo-American culture centers, humanism remains the most formative
influence in education, the mass media, and politics. Gradually evaporating from the cultural context are many symbols and supports that in
the past made Christian faith seem outwardly credible even in a society
governed by hostile influences. The doctrine of church-state separation
has been widely interpreted in the United States so as to discourage an
overt Christian presence in public education and in the public square.
For all that, despite an evangelical resurgence that now enlists some fifty
million "born again" believers, the mass media, educational arena, and
political sphere mainly reflect radical humanist premises.

Much as it was largely ignored or disparaged in the classroom, biblical theism nonetheless stimulated dynamic student movements like
Inter-Varsity Christian Fellowship, Navigators, Campus Crusade for
Christ, Young Life, and International Students. In professorial philosophical circles, moreover, where a positivist analytic temper long held sway,
cognitively competent theists now identify with the increasingly influential Society of Christian Philosophers. Many biblical critics still pursue
negative theories. A growing cadre of scholars now rejects as futile the
unsuccessful research behind the Bible for supposedly earlier, more reliable manuscripts that the canonical writers revised by adding legendary
and mythical flourishes in the special interest of miraculous Hebrew-
Christian theism. Evangelical scholars meanwhile have given themselves
to writing major commentaries and other texts that reflect the rational

strength of biblical claims. Christian schools—day schools, colleges, and seminaries—have drawn maximal enrollments and channel a steady stream of candidates into the arena of expanding church growth.

The evangelical thrust is not, however, without its somber side: entrepreneurial rivalry, commercial opportunism, some televangelists' fall from grace, experiential engrossment more than intellectual interest. Although it lives on moral levels significantly above the shoddy mean of secular society, the American evangelical movement is not without need of spiritual and ethical renewal. On balance the movement remains both an evangelistic lifeline and a vast support system for global missionary effort with evangelist Billy Graham as its popular voice.

Evangelicals have forfeited major opportunities—not least of all, establishment of a quality university in a major metropolitan center. What they lacked in intellectual cohesion was by many leaders thought to be outweighed by their numerical strength and diversity. The eventual cost of such trade-off may yet be higher than appears on the surface. Few evangelical colleges now fulfill their long-standing promise to teach the Christian world-life view in a way that integrates all the branches of learning. Business and economics majors are displacing philosophy and the other humanities courses as leading majors. Some erstwhile seminaries now flaunt an evangelical label but hesitate to affirm comprehensive biblical truthfulness and lack a stable epistemic base.

The evangelicals' growing interest in political affairs was channeled by Jerry Falwell into the Religious Right which sought, unavailing, to re-Christianize or to christianize America by legislative change. A highly vocal but much smaller group of Christian Reconstructionists sought to co-opt evangelical political involvement for their emphasis that Mosaic legislation remains the divinely intended framework for all civil government and that democracy is heretical. Political confrontation outran conversation and cooperation with established political channels. Confrontation tended to insert aspiring religious leaders between voters and their elected representatives and accommodated Pat Robertson's run as a presidential candidate. In the absence of an overarching philosophy, evangelicals concentrated mainly on special issues and tended to favor concerns that especially lent themselves to financial promotion. Despite the expenditure of tens of millions of dollars, these efforts by the Religious Right did not achieve passage of a single piece of preferred legislation or solidify political power.

The present religious vacuum in the public square is now probed by some who see a propitious opportunity for Catholic-Evangelical cooperation both in public affairs and in spiritual impact. Their proposal distinguishes rhetoric appropriate to a pluralistic republic from the rhetoric of revealed religion, and it relies mainly on the assumptions of natural law theory. Its confusion of general revelation and common grace and natural law poses difficulty for many Reformed evangelicals, as does the prospect of a resurgent Roman Catholic religiopolitical force.

As recently as January 1989, in a statement of concern presented at the Global Consultation on World Evangelization by A.D. 2000 and Beyond (GCOWE 2000) in Singapore, Latin American participants protested that Roman Catholicism remains "the most fierce opponent to all evangelistic efforts on our part." Lausanne II, held in July, was ambivalent; it welcomed Catholic participants from countries whose evangelical leaders approved. American Catholics emphasize that Latin American Christianity should not be considered normative; uneasy evangelicals reply that it provides evidence of what does and can happen when and if Catholicism controls the political scene.

Yet evangelical resurgence achieved very limited gains in public education, the mass media, and politics, and its leaders welcomed an informal alliance with Catholic forces in the interest of shared cultural and political objectives. The inclusivist Religious Right, in which conservative Catholics were active, has placed moral values prominently on the agenda of public debate. Catholic leadership largely shaped shared pro-life concerns. Conservative Catholic and Protestants, evangelicals among them, effectively promoted common or compatible ends through such agencies as the Ethics and Public Policy Center and the Institutes for Religion and Democracy. At a time of rampant ethical relativity and religious scepticism, their general emphasis on religious and moral concerns gained a noteworthy following. A program of cobelligerency for limited objectives might well involve not only an Evangelical-Catholic alliance (engaging Protestant ecumenists interested in traditional values) but Jews and Mormons also—and perhaps even some secular humanists—in respect to shared pubic concerns.

The reception by President Bush at the White House of Cardinal Agostino Casaroli, who in the Catholic bureaucracy ranks second to Pope John II, and of the six active American cardinals, accelerated some evangelical anxieties about church-state separation, although such apprehensions are wearing thin. Leading evangelical evangelists and religious entrepreneurs have for a generation prized a photo opportunity with incumbent presidents. Billy Graham has during several regimes been an overnight White House guest.

Yet the danger of politicizing evangelical Christianity itself remains, particularly if, beyond cobelligerency, projection of a Christian political party should be a future step.

## The Limits of Knowledge

A privileged meeting of scholars including historians and political and social scientists fell into an unscheduled discussion of the present condition of America. In a momentary reference one participant thought my recent *Twilight of a Great Civilization* too pessimistic, despite its emphasis that twilight is not yet midnight.[1] Another observed that irregular cultureswings may suggest that a nation is declining when in fact it is on the threshold of unprecedented advance. Several commentators reflected the confident evolutionary premise that, in the end, change means progress. Soon the conversation shifted to a regard for knowledge as the chief factor in forestalling the decline of a political world power. Knowledge, it was stressed, makes for less gullibility; it gives decision makers more leverage. Technical progress can contribute to security; America can now send whole documents to European allies instantaneously.

Rebuttal was underway *in media res.* Conventional wisdom may reflect only a political fad. Knowledge is important, but how do we know what knowledge is relevant? Much information that might be helpful is secret and is available only to privileged persons. Bits of data are not necessarily analytic knowledge. Even so, policy making can and sometimes does override both intelligence and historical memory. Our inferences are not infallible; sheer luck may at times be as important as other factors. Worse yet, our predictions are repeatedly overtaken by surprises. Not even historians can forecast the future. The only thing that is assuredly predictable, one observer comments, is that our predictions are subject to surprise.

We cannot even assuredly foresee what parts of the world will be important a generation hence. None of the self-styled futurists predicted the world petrol crisis. Who a generation ago foresaw the remarkable tenacity of the North Vietnamese, the Iranian shah's overthrow, Marcos's exile from the Philippines, Lech Walensa's successful defiance of Polish communist leaders, a key role in world affairs for Islamic Shiites—not to mention the collapse of the Soviet Union? Who can now tell the PLO's eventual role in Israel? What of the mainland Chinese? Call our megaprojections what we will, they sooner or later run into trouble.

Discussion turned next to moral and religious matters, even if briefly. Many contemporary scholars refer now and then to an ethicoreligious dimension, but they avoid sustained discussion of it much as the Victorian era avoided open talk of sex. Despite the importance of knowledge, volunteered a learned historian, education per se is no sure solution: a more highly educated communist leadership is not necessarily "a good thing." Moral and religious developments, it was granted, are no less difficult to

---

1. Carl F. H. Henry, *Twilight of a Great Civilization* (Westchester, IL: Crossway Books, 1988).

foresee than other developments. What social scientist two generations ago would have foreseen the collapse of theological modernism or of pluralistic ecumenism and have predicted the resurgence of evangelical orthodoxy? What historian would a generation ago have foreseen either the rise of the Religious Left in Latin America or of the Religious Right in the United States?

Whether economists, historians, statespeople or futurists, the most farsighted scholars somehow turn out after all to be nearsighted. Problems of morality are not susceptible to simple solutions either by knowledge or by political power. No amount of even ideal knowledge will assure its proper appropriation.

The Greek sages optimistically held that if a person knows the truth, he or she will do it. They did not cope with the unregeneracy of the human will, with humanity's resistance of light and need of a regeneration of character. We can study conditions and trends, engage in research, evaluate careful inquiry for its adequacy, weigh anticipated results, explore new possibilities that illumine empirical data, but we can neither decisively predict the future nor demonstrate cause-effect relationships. Factors are at work in history and society that are not comprehensible by empirical method.

## The Permanence of Truth

The previous bit of banter spurred reflection on my part about what the classic ancient philosophers and the early Christian apostles might have said about these same concerns. Even the pagan philosophers Plato and Aristotle identified as life's most important intellectual priority what is now least and perhaps often only grudgingly mentioned, the theologicoethical dimension. For the Graeco-Roman idealists no less than for the Hebrew prophets and Christian apostles, the sense and value of human life and the very possibility of a cohesive culture turned upon the logical priority of the eternal supernatural world to which humanity stands in a privileged relationship. Beyond that, what distinguished Judaism and Christianity—among other things—was their insistence on the transcendent Creator-God who takes a self-disclosive initiative in history, and their precision in expounding the nature and work and word of God. The Apostles' Creed is astonishingly more specific about supernatural realities than any summary of Plato's *Republic*.

One plank in apostolic preaching strikes a dramatic point of contact with this discussion of prediction and surprise, and it provides the basis for an academic admission that our finite projections about the future are constantly vulnerable to sudden overthrow. An insistent emphasis of the Bible is that God decides and alone knows the far future and that human beings know it only to the extend that God reveals it. In stark contrast to the notion that history is open-ended, and in line with the teaching of Jesus, the early Christians expected no unending sequence of historical upward and downward swings or repetitive cycles, but stressed instead an approaching climax and termination of history. The final end of history, moreover, would come suddenly and unexpectedly, in striking reversal of conventional wisdom and ordinary human prediction. "The day of the Lord," writes the apostle Paul, "will come like a thief in the night" (1 Thess. 5:2, NIV). The apostle Peter reiterates the emphasis: "In the last days scoffers . . . will say . . . , 'Ever since our fathers died everything goes on as it has since the beginning . . . ' But the day of the Lord will come like a thief" (2 Pet. 3:3,4,10, NIV).

New Testament Christianity also denied that the terminus of history will have the character of evolutionary utopia; history will issue, rather, divine moral judgment that separates two strands of humanity for contrasting destinies.

In accord with their incarnate and risen Lord's teaching, the early church centered the end-time in the personal return or second coming of Christ. A band of current critical scholars, the so-called Jesus Seminar, holds that Jesus predicted neither an end to earthly history nor His personal return. First-century Christian creedal commitments are not derived by a majority vote of preselected skeptical scholars. There is no assurance, in fact, that critics comprising the Jesus Seminar would wholly approve even doctrines that a majority attribute to Christ.

The Bible insists that God is the sovereign judge of history and that He alone—not skillful social scientists or ethical idealists or textual critics—will decide just when history has run its course and when divine judgment is to fall. Although His comprehensive judgment occurs only at the end of all ends, Christianity insists also that the living God is even now judging the nations. God is saying something about present human history through the circumstance that every earthly civilization, however pretentious, is moving toward ruin and rubble.

The Western secular mind more and more concedes that empirical observation has limits. It even admits that we should prepare for surprise through an unexpected inversion of our inferences from past and present experience. Revision can suddenly become the order of the day. One surprise is intolerable: a final termination of human history in divine moral judgment, centering in the risen Lord's triumphant victory over evil and injustice. The contemporary West may now and then assign some activity in the turning times of history to ethical and spiritual forces. In deference to its basically naturalistic stance, it considers inadmissible any ultimately decisive role for theologicomoral referents. The secular West has given up on universally valid religious truth, and in doing so it has unwittingly forfeited all objective truth and good. Not only does it thereby nominate itself as a prime candidate for the final judgment that Hebrew-Christian revelational religion affirms, but it deprives itself of the regenerative and redemptive powers of grace. No less importantly, it disqualifies itself from a determinative role in the climactic interreligious dialogue of our lifetime.

## Truth and Its Witnesses

The irony of this situation is exposed by recent international furor over Salman Rushdie's *The Satanic Verses*. The Iranian ayatollah Ruholla Khomeini called for Islamic murder of Rushdie on the ground, allegedly, of blasphemy. Whatever might be said about the propriety or impropriety of that religious perception, Shiite fundamentalists voiced a basic concern over religious truth, and they were unashamed to tell the world so. Rushdie had allegedly reflected on the purity of Muhammad and his mission as Allah's exclusive prophet. The great nations of the West replied only at the level of freedom. They condemned the appeal for violence as an appropriate response to criticism of Islamic theology.

It was indeed morally imperative that the freedom issue be raised—both freedom of expression and religious freedom. That is all the more the case because Muslims have repeatedly sought to soften United Nations religious liberty guarantees and because radical Koranic religion has relied on violence to extend its power. Muslim leaders still threaten to kill or to maim Muslim converts to Christianity. The freedom issue is undeniably of crucial importance. Not even freedom remains a significant conception if truth is irrelevant. Religious liberty is fundamental, but it is not a self-validating principle.

With an eye on Soviet ambitions in the oil-rich Persian Gulf, the West has cultivated Sunni Muslim countries (which comprise 90 percent of Islam), especially Bangladesh, Egypt, Indonesia, Pakistan, Saudi Arabia, and Turkey. Several of these countries—not least of all Saudi Arabia and Turkey—have a long history of religious restriction and repression. Even Afghanistan, where American aid to resistance forces hastened the withdrawal of Soviet troops, currently provides Muslim Afghans a fresh opportunity to persecute ex-Muslim Christians.

When the forty-six-member Islamic Conference Organization met in Saudi Arabia earlier this year, it halted short of encouraging the Khomeini-sponsored murder of Rushdie, but it joined in condemning Rushdie for blasphemy and called for a book store boycott. World image momentarily got the better of truth concerns. In opening the Islamic conference, Saudi Arabia's King Fahd referred pointedly to "our tolerant religion" (of Islam), while an associate identified "respect for each other's beliefs" as a cornerstone of international relationships. Most Muslim governments attending, as *The Economist* of London commented, had "no particular tender concern for the principle of freedom of expression"; many, in fact, seem not to distinguish between freedom and license.

The fact is that the Islamic world refuses, contrary to the secular West, to forego a universal religious truth claim. It insists, moreover, on the comprehensively valid truth of Koranic religion, not just some vague "truth" of "religion-in-general." The point is not that civil government should be the arbiter of metaphysical counterclaims. It is rather that the Western intellectual establishment has neither mind nor heart for ultimate religious truth; the West's intellectual elite has given up on universally valid truth in religion. Its loss of God is in fact the loss of unchanging good and truth. The most relevant observation on Rushdie's comments mustered by humanists is that tolerance ought to preclude insulting people's religious beliefs.

A society that abandons transcendent truth and right has less hope long-term than a society that insists on them, even if the legitimacy of this or that particular religious claim may be in debate. A world that seriously wrestles with the Hebrew view, the Christian view, and the Muslim view does not shred the ultimate concerns. The questions whether Yahweh is merely an ancient critical reconstruction, whether Jesus of Nazareth is the Christ, and whether Muhammad is the Prophet are today foreclosed by secular humanism's reduction of religious truth to internal psychological significance as much as by radical Islamic intolerance of rational consistency as a test of religious truth.

Every world religion has its unique interpretation of the facts of existence, its own way of accounting for nature and history and its own explanation of man and of final outcomes. Stoics postulated world cycles which, when reabsorbed into primal fire, then reduplicated whatever had gone before. Buddhists too espoused successively appearing and disappearing world ages. The Hindu theory of reincarnation assigned many successive bodies to the one soul. Today some frontier philosophers of science speculate anew about comprehensive cosmic chaos. Secular humanism reduces all views (except its own) to culture-conditioned preference.

Evangelical Christianity insists that religious liberty is the basic human freedom which shelters all other legitimate liberties. It holds together religious liberty and the universal truth claim of biblical Christianity. Within that framework its growth often remarkably outpaces an official religion or state church. It has no need of a politically entrenched ecclesiasticism, whether a Jewish state (Israel), a Shiite state (Iran), or a Sunni state (Saudi Arabia).

The God of the Bible is the Sovereign Creator and the God of truth. He is not alone truthful in His deeds and judgments; He is the very ground of truth. All truth is therefore God's truth. Truth is what God thinks; in this sense, all truth is revelatory truth. All treasures of wisdom and knowledge, the apostle Paul writes, are hidden in Christ, the eternal Logos. Christianity resists the modern reconceptualization of truth as a product of perpetually revisable scientific empiricism. It does not dispute a role for tentative human inferences based on limited experiential data. It does distinguish opinion, theory, and truth. Christianity does not promote a spiritual truth different in kind from what truth at its best means elsewhere. Its metaphysical and moral affirmations belong to the same logical universe as do other universally valid truth. Its historical claims involve the same history as do other legitimate historical statements that Jesus of Nazareth was crucified under the Roman procurator Pontius Pilate belongs to the same conceptual category that Julius Caesar was murdered by a company of men including Brutus does. The truth of the gospel is not some vague type of veracity that escapes universal truth conditions. The neoorthodox notion that Hebrew-Christian "truth" differs in kind from Graeco-Roman truth is a recent modern misconception. Christianity does not teach that its message is true because one personally subscribes to it, nor even because it is reliable; rather, Christianity holds that the message is reliable because it is true. The New Testament conception connects truth at once with rational revelation and public reason.

Even major encyclopedic works today carry articles on "Christianity" that evade the question of truth in religion. *The Abingdon Dictionary of Living Religions* discusses truth, remarkably, only in connection with non-biblical religions.[2] The term "truth" does not appear at all in the index to John Noss's *Man's Religions*.[3] Indeed, Noss tells us that Christianity is "not a retreat into ultimate truth, but a redemptive mission" as if the Christian mission is to be sealed off from universally valid truth claims.[4]

Religion scholars grant Christianity's "uniqueness" and "universality"; some concede that Christianity is "highest" in the class of world religions. Critics hedge the question of truth as if pursuit of this concern would *a priori* manifest intolerance and pretense. The current critical mood resists representations of Scripture as "the Word of God written"; it disputes that Jesus Christ is singularly the Logos incarnate. It avoids speaking of any one true religion, even when it portrays Christianity at its best.

To be sure, absoluteness does not belong ultimately to Christianity as a religion. Christianity as a world religion has had fanatic and tragic chapters, including ecclesiastical imperialism. Absoluteness belongs at

---

2. Keith Crim, ed., *The Abingdon Dictionary of Living Religions* (Nashville: Abingdon Press, 1981).

3. John Noss, *Man's Religions*, (New York: Macmillan, 1964).

4. Noss, *Man's Religions*, 711.

best only to the God of the Bible. But modern critics affirm "partial truths" in all religions; even these "partial truths" are then often treated as different in kind from universally valid truth. The term "partial truth" is itself ambiguous; it may designate a mixture of valid and invalid propositions, or suggest partisan or prejudiced and hence not objective claims. In the long run, a forfeiture of its truth claims is not only a forfeiture of human interest in Christianity's ultimate importance but a foreclosure of its essential nature as truly redemptive revelation.

Christianity, the largest and most widespread of the great world religions, has a missionary movement from the first. Although the rapidly multiplying global population poses problems for all religions, the present coincidence of the missionary mandate with mass communication and space travel provides an unprecedented opportunity for world outreach. Ralph Winter of the U.S. Center for World Mission notes that in A.D. 40 there were 40,000 unreached non-Christians for each committed Christian believer. By 1900 the percentage was down to only 100 per evangelical believer. In January 1989 there were less than ten non-Christians for each believer.[5] In fifty countries mission strategists have projected an acceleration of world evangelization between now and A.D. 2000. Attention is shifting from expensive international conferences to cooperation and coordination in regional and national outreach.

Some fifty million evangelicals comprising the "born again" movement in the United States attest the remarkable virility of Christianity in the secular Anglo-Saxon West. In the formerly-communist lands, the churches are growing. In Africa the number of Christians has multiplied from 5 million to 200 million; in Nigeria the church has quadrupled in twenty years. Even in Asia where the unreached are more numerous, spiritual gains in South Korea and on mainland China indicate a notable turning of the tide.

Protestant ecumenism has so much idealized the megachurch and its sociopolitical impact that the biblical narrative seems painfully irrelevant when it depicts Jesus conversing alone with Nicodemus or with the woman at the well, or even Paul's solitary conversion on the Damascus Road. Yet whether their main agenda item be church unity, evangelism, or social activism, major denominations with their ecumenical priorities continue to fragment.

The Protestant Reformers launched the modern era of theological development by renewed emphasis on basic apostolic doctrines, notably the authority of Scripture and justification by faith alone in Christ's salvific work. The Roman Catholic Church has in recent decades pursued less rigid alternatives and has ventured a biblical movement involving interest

---

5. Ralph Winter, *Mission Frontiers*, 11 (January-February 1989), 3.

in evangelism also. Especially among the laity—whether Catholic, charismatic, or traditional evangelical—there is growing awareness that the
world must not be permitted to set the Christian agenda. The New Testament church's marching orders were given by the Risen Lord. This circumstance indicates that humanity's deepest need remains the forgiveness
of sin and reconciliation with God through Christ's mediatorial work.

The rescue of Western culture from moral shame is not the church's
prime duty. Nor will Christianity be a failure if Anglo-Saxon civilization
collapses in hideous disgrace. It is not by the transformation of social
and cultural institutions that the success of the Christian mission in fallen
history is ultimately decided. Ancient Roman culture was not transformed; it toppled under its own weakness. The ethical fortunes of that
age were carried forward by what the proud Roman nobility could only
have viewed as a motley assembly of enthusiasts. The apostle Paul himself conceded that in the world's eyes not many were wise, mighty, or
noble (1 Cor. 1:26). They loved God, lived honorable lives, and exuded
compassion in a cruel and barbarian society. They responded to the
needs of neighbors, and they bore testimony to their spiritual life in
Christ the risen Lord. Roman society meanwhile sank into oblivion; its
ruins remain even today for curious tourists to see. Christians knew
themselves to be "more than conquerors" (Rom. 8:37). The middle ages
were to yield a new culture in which art, literature, music, philosophy
and all else found a new center in the God and Father of Jesus Christ.

Today it is not Christianity but rather so-called modernity that is being
judged. The final choice is not between an ancient religion and modern
science; it is between spiritual good news and no good news at all. The
testimony, life, and activity of Christians still speak eloquently in local
communities where townspeople know redeemed sinners for what they
have been and are. It is still the case, as in the past, that virtually all the
enduring humanitarian movements take their rise in the biblical heritage.
Try as critics may to discredit Christianity's claims, in each successive generation they pose a crisis of critical authority more than a crisis of biblical
authority. Each generation buries its critics; the Bible—speaking in 1,500
languages—outlasts them all. Christianity's best days are not only in the
far distant past; they lie ahead as well. If human history disintegrates, the
Decalogue will remain; if civilization crumbles, Christ will stand tall above
the ruins. The kingdom of God is not held together by mortar and mam-
mon; it is where life is truly life, love is truly love, the good is truly good,
and right truly right. The people of God have the best of both worlds;
those who opt for pseudo-values lose out both now *and* then.

# Reformed Theology in the Post-Christian Age

*The Christian ontological axiom is the living, self-revealed God. The Christian epistemological axiom is the intelligible divine revelation. All the essential doctrines of the Christian world-life view flow from these axioms: creation, sin, and the fall; redemption by promise and fulfillment; the incarnation, substitutionary death and resurrection of the Logos; the church as the new society; the approaching divine consummation of history; the eschatological verities.*

The designation of our age as post-Christian is critically important. It reflects the resignation of modern Western learning to the scientific method of empirical observation and verification as the only legitimate way of knowing any and all reality. Upon this method Protestant modernism relied earlier in this century to discredit miraculous theism and the biblical claims for once-for-all divine revelation and once-for-all divine incarnation. Modernism held that an immanent causal continuity of nature and of history excludes all miraculous incursions. Consequently it declared evangelical orthodoxy unscientific and archaic.

Modernist theology did not rule out an emphasis that the Bible contains more noble and more lofty spiritual and ethical sentiments than other religious literature,nor did it nullify the claim that Jesus of Nazareth lived in closer intimacy with the Father than did founders of other religions, or that Christian religious experience may be more self-fulfill-ing than its rivals. What theological modernism did exclude, however, in view of its anti miraculous stance, was any singularly absolute inspiration of the Bible, any claim that Jesus Christ is the "only one of the Father's kind," or that Christian redemption differs qualitatively or essentially from the spiritual dynamic of all other religion.

The scientific method and its accompanying technology resulted in an historically unprecedented secularization of culture. Its impact turned modernity into what one sociologist describes as "a great relativizing cauldron." Much as we may commend the global dispersal of evangelical missionaries who traveled from America, Britain, and the Continent to establish a world presence of Christianity, two stark developments in the twentieth century nevertheless overarch this spiritual effort. One is that atheistic worldviews have become dominant, whether in the form of totalitarian ideologies or rampant secularism. In the very century that began with an evangelical determination to win the world for Christ in a single generation, no perspective has grown as astonishingly as has atheism in its number of adherents or in its political power. The other development is the pervasive secular humanist penetration of the cultural milieu. The educational centers of the West are entrenched in scientific naturalism as the unofficial metaphysics of Euro-American liberal arts learning.

Third World nations and other countries now eagerly welcome Western learning, envy Western technology and aspire to rival it. Scientific naturalism has become the philosophical core of Western education. Wherever it penetrates, this naturalistic view tends to call in question the validity of religious claims by weakening the plausibility structure of belief in the reality of the gods. More than that, it tends especially to erode the credibility of Christian supernaturalism. James C. Hunter remarks that "Protestantism is the world religion that has confronted the modern world longer and more intensely than any other religion."[1] The Christian world and life view that Reformed and other evangelical expositors gave a global presence is under widening academic assault. The secular Western outlook now encircles the evangelical witness. Its academic thrust into the intellectual bastions of the modern world in effect relativizes and nullifies the Christian creeds. Its impact reinforces the agnostic disposition of teachers who are skeptical of their inherited religions, and it nurtures an antitheistic outlook among students who in the coming generation will be national leaders in the major professions and in academic disciplines.

---

1. James D. Hunter, *Evangelicalism: The Coming Generation* (Chicago: University of Chicago Press, 1987), p. 214.

There has indeed been a gratifying resurgence of evangelical scholarship in the free world. The escalating evangelical contribution to theological literature is perhaps the most remarkable theological development of the past half generation. Even in the context of the American Philosophical Association a Society of Christian Philosophers has emerged. The metaphysical mainstream seems nonetheless to be funneling into neopaganism. This is evidenced by the West's staggering moral decline in the wake of its loss of metaphysical anchorage. It is seen as well in the deterioration of secular humanism to sheer naturalism as humanism loses its humanism and approaches self-assertive animalism.

No less important for the deepening entrenchment of a post-Christian outlook is modern consciousness, that is, the secular mind-set or interpretative grid. This operates internally in tandem with external cultural pressures that dilute and secularize religious institutions that have long lent public plausibility to faith. As sociologist Peter Berger says, modern Westerners no longer live in a society whose beliefs and values are uniform and where one's choice is whether to be orthodox or heretical. Instead, a staggering array of options exists and one is forced to make personal decisions in a pluralistic society that no longer reflects a collective solidarity of human ideas and ideals.[2] From this historically unparalleled plurality of social norms and competing public institutions contemporary persons turn inward, reaching individual decisions in the context of a modern consciousness that renders inherited spiritual beliefs problematic.

One might be tempted to consider this analysis of modern consciousness one-sidedly Euro-American, and to dismiss it as simply another intrusion of primarily Western concerns into the larger world scene. It is true, of course, that some great world centers still exist where modernity does not undermine religious claims and where pluralism does not erode inherited spiritual traditions. The rigidly Islamic countries of the Near East exemplify this. Yet modernity has become a major problem for all religious traditions, and even Islam must sooner or later engage the scientific revolution.

The twenty-first century will thrust upon almost the entire globe a need to reflect on the pluralism of religion and on the validity of religious truth claims. As long as an overall ethical consensus prevailed, religious pluralism in recent generations seemed no great problem. The emergence of rival views of justice, of the good life, and even of holy war and religious terrorism, threatens social stability. The significance of religion and of the rival gods has staggering consequences not only for

---

2. Peter Berger, *The Heretical Imperative* (Garden City: Anchor/Doubleday, 1979).

the private world of worship but for all of life and history. The West's own concessions to secular affluence have prompted Buddhist and Hindu missionaries to maintain a growing presence in the Occident and to shape an enlarging literature to the English-speaking world. Muslims are already becoming a political force in parts of England. Pluralism and secularism, the concomitants of modernity, exert "cognitive pressure" so that any and all religious commitment is readily perceived as a matter only of personal preference. Reformed theologians will not minimize the urgent need for a reflective encounter between exponents of the great world religions and for theological dialogue in quest of understanding and truth.

The spreading influence of scientific naturalism now bids everywhere for the mind-set of the intellectual community and impacts formatively on the student generation. As the early Western missionary outreach often moved in tandem with political and economic imperialism, so secular naturalism today traverses the path of technocratic science, which penetrates global frontiers no less spectacularly than does Christian missionary transformation. In assessing the implications of naturalistic scientism "for religious thought in the pluralistic situation," Peter Berger stresses that three basic options exist: reductive, deductive, and inductive.[3] Since these options helpfully illumine the current religious crisis, we do well to reflect on them.

The reductive option substitutes the authority of modern consciousness for all other authority. Instead of *Deus dixit* (God speaks) it stresses *modernus dixit* (modernity speaks) modern consciousness legislates validity. Its intellectual program tapers religious heritage to modern secularity and translates the inherited tradition into contemporary alternatives. Rudolf Bultmann is the paradigmatic reductionist figure. He considered scientific method cognitively supreme and held that a closed system of empirical causalities engulfs nature and humans. He dismissed as mythological all representations of supernatural forces penetrating the empirical world. Bultmann's retention of transcendence to depict God's internal activity involved a failure of nerve in his program of demythologizing. In any case he allowed for the reality of God only in a nonfalsifiable way grounded in subjective decision.

The deductive option, in contrast to the reductive, reasserts "the authority of a religious tradition in the face of modern secularity" and affirms "a religious reality sovereignly independent of the relativizations . . . of one's historical situation." It stresses *Deus dixit* and provides objective criteria of validity.

3. Berger, 61.

Reductionist claims are self-liquidating. For one thing, empirical epistemology cannot establish the epistemological absoluteness of the scientific method. Reductionists do not even agree, moreover, on the definition and content of experience. They often disagree over whether religious experience is distinguishable from general experience, and if so, whether there exists an ontologically identifiable transcendent being or whether religious experience has only functional importance. Although Berger aims to reject "the particularly oppressive authority of modern secular consciousness," he does not find in deductive theology a promising alternative to the final authority of modern consciousness.He declares traditional authority "no longer plausible." Its problem, he notes, is the difficulty of sustaining credibility in the modern era. He rejects "any external authority (be it scriptural, ecclesiastical or traditional)." Berger opts therefore for the inductive option, "a deliberately empirical attitude" that sets out from one's own experience and ventures "open-minded hypothesis." He affirms "The human as the only possible starting point for theological reflection."[4] He professes to advance the superiority of Christianity by depriving Christianity of objective revelatory authority and by making fundamental concessions to an empirically limited epistemology. Berger acknowledges that to focus centrally on religious experience is to follow Schleiermacher and Protestant modernism in the disavowal of Christianity as a once-for-all revelation and to adopt its characterization of Christianity as a developed form of religion-in-general. Berger locates the essence of religion, as did Schleiermacher, in a universal and continuing feeling of absolute dependence viewed as immediate self-consciousness of the Infinite. The authority of Scripture is said to lie in its witness to this experience. Berger identifies the core experience of all human religion in terms of a transcendent reality's impingement on or invasion of ordinary human life. The nebulous character of this religiously experienced realm is implicit in Berger's assurance that "religious experience insists that . . . the gods inhabit a reality that is *sui generis* (in a category by itself) and that is sovereignly independent of what human beings project into it."[5]

Berger's approach leads to a pallid notion of deity, one in which among the many gods some, or one at least, may be superior to others, but none can be rejected as false, or for that matter dignified as exclusively the true God. This methodological inability to distinguish true from false religion (Jonestown? Satan worship?), to regard any religion or religions as counterfeit, or any as objectively true, diametrically

---

4. Berger, 154.
5. Berger, 123.

opposes the New Testament representations of religion. Berger leaves us with the possibility that logically contradictory religious claims can be equally authentic, valid, and true. He hesitates to call anything "unbelief."[6] The apostle Paul did not deny that human beings have a vast variety of religious experiences, but he did not hesitate to pass a truth judgment. Paul writes the Christians in Rome that pagan religionists did not "honor God as God," but "exchanged the truth of God for a lie, and worshiped and served created things rather than the Creator" (Rom. 1:21-25). There is no room here for a common religious experience expressed ideally in the form of doctrinally divergent religions, especially not for any religion that confuses the Creator/creation distinction and views everything as a manifestation of the Divine. Biblical theism explains religious pluralism without baptizing it in pantheistic terms.

It is not self-evident that the multiplicity of worldviews and plurality of religions embarrasses the absolutist claim that only one religion is true. The presence of many alternatives does not necessarily mean that all are false. Rival truth claims may relativize the claims of many or most, but not necessarily all. Religious pluralism poses no intellectual problem whatever, of course, if one contends that doctrinal affirmations are wholly marginal to religious experience. Following Schleiermacher, Berger holds that all doctrinal attribution is subsequent to experience. Calvin would have disputed the thesis that theology moves from the human to the metahuman. Only in knowing God, he said, do we properly know ourselves.

Specially noteworthy is Berger's deliberate choice of neoorthodoxy to exemplify the deductive option, with Karl Barth as the paradigmatic figure. Actually, neoorthodoxy cannot be considered to be as genuinely representative of Reformed theology as was J. Gresham Machen a generation ago or Gordon H. Clark in our generation. To be sure, in line with historic evangelical orthodoxy Barth emphasized that God's Word posits itself, that experience of God's Word is rooted in the Word and not in human reason, conscience, volition, or feeling, and that religious experience is not the starting point of theological reflection. No doubt, Barth's religious epistemology is burdened even in these respects by his rejection of objective, propositional revelation and his concentration on our volitional response to internal confrontation. Berger's criticism of Barth rightly focuses on the main issue: Barth rejected the relevance of logic and public reason, and of any and every external criterion including historical science, as a test of revelational content. Barth requires a

---

6. Berger, 169.

leap of sheer faith in response to an internal divine address, a leap unsubject to any rational test.

Although once a champion of the Barthian view, Berger abandoned it because Barth considers reason marginal to revelatory disclosure. Even if Barth later sought to modify this disjunction of revelation and reason, he nonetheless doomed neoorthodoxy to be merely a temporary diversion from twentieth-century liberal theology.

Berger could have presented the deductive view on an authentically Reformed basis, and his refusal to do so betrays his antipathy to biblical Christianity. Much as he professes not to bow to the final authority of modern consciousness, Berger considers the social and psychological weakening of external authority to be destructive of the plausibility of any deductive option.[7] Berger presents scientific reductionism through one of its strongest voices, namely, Bultmann, and likewise empirical induction through Schleiermacher, whereas he presents deductive orthodoxy only through the Barthian model of revelational irrationalism. He considers a reductionist dismissal of deductive orthodoxy so inevitable and necessary that he does not even present a fair case for it. As Charles Colson pointedly observes in another connection, "Those who resent that Christians make exclusive claims may be practicing the very kind of intolerance they profess to resent. The essence of pluralism is that each person respects the other's right to believe in an exclusive claim to truth." Every tradition, Berger holds, implies the exclusive finality of its revelation as its doctrinal reflection transforms a general human experience into a preferred specific version. This theory may account for Berger's own conferral of crown rights on empirical induction as an explanatory principle, but it does not provide empirical induction with objective philosophical validation as a universal and final referent.

If Berger seeks to avoid marginalizing reason, moreover, his insistence on a universally shared, pretheoretical religious experience, to which diverse traditions only subsequently attach conflicting doctrinal explanations, is hardly helpful. More profound is the Reformed challenge to the secular mind-set's pretensions of final authority. Reformed theology disputes the inviolable cognitive force of reductive secularism by exhibiting the logic and dynamic of biblical theism. It disputes the neoorthodox connection of Judeo-Christian revelation only with volition or subjective decision at the expense of rationality and logical consistency. It affirms the relevance of the laws of logic to religious truth and it predicates the superiority of deductive orthodoxy on intelligible divine

---

7. Berger, 69.

revelation. The orthodox revelational option invalidates the mind of modernity as arbitrary and presumptuous.

Berger is surely right when he now and then stresses that modern consciousness is not a deterministic and irrevocable "given." It is not the pinnacle of human consciousness but only "one moment" in man's historical development.[8] Berger even grants, and appropriately so, that "in certain respects modern man may be cognitively *inferior* to human beings in earlier periods of history."[9]

Berger's own empirical-inductive approach to truth cannot in any event rise above tentativity and revisability. He welcomes the emergence of experientially oriented evangelicals who, instead of defending their Christian orthodoxy on a strictly biblical basis, seek to justify it empirically. Some even champion scriptural authority on empirical grounds and regard a born-again experience as legitimizing Christian doctrinal claims. Since Berger professes by empirical considerations to level all absolutist views to religion-in-general, he understandably welcomes this trend, confident that the empirical method will not identify a transcendent reality that conforms to the religious understanding of traditional orthodoxy. In any case, evangelicals who fall into the trap of religious empiricism should be forewarned if they think that on the basis of empirical induction any secure case can be made for once-for-all revelation or for any authoritative doctrine.

Berger complains that traditional orthodox deduction from scriptural revelation asserts its positions *a priori* (as self-evident). Yet his own conclusions from empirical religious data are not strictly inferred from such data but reflect presuppositions on Berger's part. He insists that an inductive approach leads to a spiritual reality transcendent to the physical universe. If there are experiences of the supernatural distinct from experiences of the natural, then, as Stan D. Gaede says, the naturalistic methodology is not wholly adequate to pursue such truth, and one ought to develop a methodology that justifies knowledge of the transcendent.[10] In short, what transcends the physical world can be assured only by a method that does not assume in advance that the physical world is the only reality.

To his credit, Berger insists on the need of a category like the supernatural if the transcendent is not to be dissolved into an amorphous phenomenon like Tillich's "ultimate concern." Berger commendably rejects Barth's exemption of revelation from any test by universally

---

8. Berger, 7ff.
9. Berger, 122ff.
10. Stan D. Gaede, "Symposium: The Heretical Imperative." *Journal for the Scientific Study of Religion* 20 (1981), 185.

shared reason. Berger himself promotes a particular religious under-standing of transcendent reality without justifying it in terms of universal validity. When Berger speaks of the reality of the transcendent, faith seems to have a logic of its own beyond the limits of his self-imposed empiricism. If a transcendent supernatural reality truly exists, can one consistently insist, as Berger does, that a universally shared religious experience with a doctrinally indefinable core underlies all historical forms? Surely reductionists who demand a replacement of traditional orthodoxy disagree widely over what revised meaning modern con-sciousness requires. Berger invokes Bultmann's "Gospel myth" as the model, but others insist that Christianity must be recast repeatedly in successive myths reflective of the contemporary world view. Berger's proposal to revive Schleiermacher's quasi-pantheism in terms of signals of transcendence therefore seems an *a priori* imposition on experience.

In affirming an ontology in which all religious experience partici-pates, Berger moves around both a naturalistic-functional view of reli-gion and a kerygmatic disavowal of the objective, propositional intelligibility of the religious object. Does fervent emphasis on universal religious experience in and of itself bridge the gap to a supernatural ontological reality?

Berger's emphasis on a universally shared religious experience enables him to look more appreciatively at religions which emphasize divine interiority in contrast to God's transcendent address to us "from the outside." This way of putting it is somewhat confusing, however, since Christianity stresses both divine transcendence and divine imma-nence. The essential point is that the God of Israel is other than the nature gods identified with the rhythms of the cosmos and the human self. He is not the inner ground of nature and humans. Berger recasts human consciousness universally in terms of self-awareness of immedi-ate dependence on the All. He depicts all religious experience as an encounter with the "reality of the Unseen," as supernatural and sacred, moreover, in view of a quasi-pantheistic notion of experience.

Berger writes in a Western context in which plural religions increas-ingly impinge on religious consciousness. His interest in the world reli-gions is accelerated by dialogues promoted by the Vatican Council and by the World Council of Churches. Berger reaches for a blend of Eastern and Western religion, a comprehensive merger that preserves the interi-ority of Eastern religion and the personal autonomy of Western liberal-ism. The evangelical orthodox cause is forfeited before the dialogue begins, however, if in interreligious dialogue Christianity is to be repre-sented on Berger's prejudices of a common religious experience com-bined with postexperiential theological differentiation, . The notion that experience is the ground of all religious affirmation no doubt accommodates a shift of focus away from secular reductionism. It involves at the same time a shift away from historic Christianity, which does not rest its case on universal experience but rather on special transcendent revelation. Much as Berger claims to avoid making Christianity palatable to modern secular consciousness, his rejection of revelatory deduction reflects a basic compromise with contemporary cultural *a prioris*. His phenomenological-sociological analysis of religion excludes the orthodox deductive model, an exclusion that says more about Berger's presuppositional commitments than about evangelical orthodoxy. Berger prejudicially assumes that no basis exists or can exist in public reason for considering traditional orthodoxy credible or compelling. He presumes to validate religious truth claims by experience rather than by an appeal to authority, and he does so on his own authority.

Berger desires to discuss religious truth claims in view of the historical and social sciences, but he does so on the prior assumption that all religions are doctrinal variants of one and the same non-intellective experiential substratum. "Religion is not, in its essence, an intellectual enterprise," Berger tells us. He wants no shift from an experiential to a theoretical level for purposes of apologetic confrontation. However much more religion may be than an intellectual enterprise, if intellectual concerns are marginal, Berger should not complain when Barth considers logical tests irrelevant. Evangelicals complain that Berger himself smuggles certain intellectual presuppositions into his theory. Berger leaps from supposed experience of the transcendent to the ontological factuality of the Transcendent. Berger does not tell us how an uninterpreted feeling of dependence accommodates truly objective evaluation. His own religious preferences dictate the framework within which a solution is sought. Yet observations provided by the sociology of religions cannot do service for normative theology. For Berger, revelation-in-experience is a possibility everywhere and always, yet revelation, he insists, can never be objectively given once-for-all. He opts for a general revelation of sorts, yet he cannot distinguish true from false revelation. He cannot insist that revelation everywhere and always implies a personal deity, and he cannot legitimately make objective truth claims either for the Other or for revelation.

Berger grants that the empirical approach cannot "ever prove the truth claim of an alleged revelation in the way a natural science proves or validates its hypotheses"; religious experience is internal and interpretation will "always entail faith."[11] This is more damaging to Berger's

---

11. Berger, 141.

approach than he allows. For since not even natural science escapes tentativity, religious science has multiplied vulnerability. If the experiential core is prerational and faith is decisive for interpretation, how does Berger escape sharing in Barth's "sacrifice of the intellect"? Equally to the point is another consideration. When Berger insists that "the inductive possibility is the most viable . . . indeed . . . the only viable option," he is as absolutistic and exclusivistic as is Barth.[12] Berger's verdict can only be a private faith certainty and not an empirical judgment. Berger may have reservations about many articles of the Apostles Creed, but he apparently has dogmatic certainty about the validity of Schleiermacher's religious theory and method. To be sure, Berger concedes that his approach does not involve "a Christian faith commitment."[13] Whether Christian or not, it nonetheless involves a strenuous leap of faith. Against a Barthian deductive approach Berger may oppose faith that has "immunity against rational and empirical criticism."[14] This is precisely, however, what is involved in his own commutation and objectification of religious experience into transcendent objective reality.

## The Detour of Empiricism

Modern consciousness is not a giant guillotine that sovereignly determines the survival rights of particular beliefs. It is not the ultimate criterion of admissible religious affirmations. Its absolutistic pretenses have no justification. It can give no final ruling on validity claims. It is, as Berger himself says in one of his better moments, "one among many historically available structures—no more, no less."[15] It is not the climax of human historical evolution but reflects only a particular temporal phase.

One therefore confers an undeserved authority on modern consciousness if one legitimates any imperial claims made for religious experience. We can and must challenge arbitrarily imposed boundaries, not least of all empirical authoritarianism. An appeal to human experience as the starting point in identifying God cannot as such effectively transcend modern consciousness. Human experience is incomplete. It yields only tentative conclusions. Moreover, study of religious experience is not a study of transcendent religious reality. Unless one affirms that we are part of God, God is other than human experience, however religious that experience may be.

Contemporary consciousness, we are told, poses two basic problems for Christianity. First, there is the difficulty of maintaining credibility for

---

12. Berger, 154.
13. Berger, 181.
14. Berger, 181.
15. Berger, 120

the supernatural in the present cultural setting of secular naturalism and religious pluralism. Second, there is the problem of exhibiting the objective validity of any religious truth-claim whatever. Berger's invocation of inductive experience will not help us much in either respect for he promotes an inadequately revised version of modern consciousness as the criterion of validity for religious reflection. He defers to modern Western secular consciousness except for its atheism. Human experience, he insists, includes religious signals of transcendence. This critique of modernity is too concessive. Berger permits modernity to invalidate any deductive revelatory alternative to the inductive method, and then interprets experience in a partisan way in order to promote his own alternative.

Berger encourages open-ended reflection on religious experience. Many details of his view are sketchy. If a "common core" universal religious experience is not actually an *a priori* given, then Berger arbitrarily superimposes this theory on his own experience, and ours as well. In truth the theory has no more universal validity than do other doctrinal interpretations of supposedly pre-theoretical experience. The dogma that all dogma is a later optional interpretation of a universally shared pre-theoretical religious experience confers a surface plausibility on innumerable pluralistic views, while at the same time it deprives once-for-all normative biblical revelation of credibility. It promotes the plausibility of religion-in-general at the price of discrediting the claims of Judeo-Christian revealed religion.

Viewed in this context, Berger is really a "closet" reductionist. It is surprising to be told that universal experience validates Schleiermacher's approach to religion, since no experience is universal and limited experience in fact conclusively validates nothing. Berger's appeal to fragmentary religious experience no more avoids a counterthrust by secular modernity than does Barth's appeal to internal divine confrontation. Berger's resort to induction as the alternative to reduction and his abandonment of theological deduction from intelligible divine revelation is in fact a concession to reduction, one that capitulates to modern secular consciousness by giving the palm of victory to experience. Hence Berger's view becomes a carrier of modernity rather than an alternative to it.

Berger opposes "uncritical" acceptance of secular presuppositions. He proposes to "relativize the relativizers" who limit the pluralistic possibilities of experience. He argues that universal human experience includes distinctive experience of the sacred. He opposes reduction of the supernatural to immanence, but his approach nonetheless unwittingly reinforces the privatization of religion, since to universalize his thesis Berger must rely either on the authority of his own experience or on a mere faith interpretation of experience in general.

## Secular Modernity and Revealed Religion

The poverty of modern secular consciousness calls for a strikingly different reappraisal of the human situation, one that recognizes mankind's created nature and present historical predicament and final destiny.

Evangelical orthodoxy champions a more profound role for rationality in religion than either Barth or Schleiermacher or Berger affirm. Christianity does not stake its claims on a fideism that disallows all relevance of reason to religious reality, nor does it present its case by leaping from a universally shared, pre-intellectual experience to an experience-transcending Reality. The deepest fact about humanity is that all human beings are universally locked into the general revelation of the one true and living God. By creation all humans bear the image of God. We are born into this life with certain ontological and epistemological givens. We accept the existence of other selves and of the external world; it is unnatural to doubt them. In view of the Christian doctrine of the *imago Dei* (image of God) Calvin would say that in knowing God we know ourselves by contrast. The Judeo-Christian view of mankind, gifted creationally with rational and moral capacities, flows from the revelation of the Creator-God as the living source of truth and the good. In knowing truth and the good we know the living God; in knowing the living God we know truth and the good.

Rebellious humans have sullied the divine image. Nobody escapes a responsible relationship to his or her Maker, despite the fact that fallen humans hide themselves from the true Transcendent, postulate reductive alternatives, or affirm that there is no god at all. Adam is humanity's paradigmatic figure, fashioned in God's image, fallen into sin by voluntary rebellion, substituting human autonomy for divine authority, yet called to inescapable moral and spiritual account for attempting a reorientation and reconstruction of good and evil. This is every last human being's case history whether his or her religion be Buddhist, Confucian, Hindu, Shamanist, Taoist, or whatever. To be sure, Adam's role is also unparalleled; he is federal head of the race, a participant in the promise of specially revealed redemptive religion and archetype also of the second Adam.

Despite the Adamic fall, rebellious humankind remains everywhere answerable to the living God, who makes Himself known in universal revelation as Creator and Judge. Moral revolt has sullied, but not totally obliterated, the divine image. Lighted by the Logos of God, human beings even in their ongoing disobedience continue in responsible daily relationships to their Maker and Judge. The biblical doctrine thus disputes Berger's evolutionary assumption that at birth humans are unfinished and develop gradually, and through interaction with society and culture, ideally reshape the sociocultural milieu.

The crucial matter here is that all religious truth and reality have their source solely in the one self-revealing God, the living God who by creation inscribes His image upon the human species, makes Himself known universally and perpetually in general revelation, and objectively publishes His special once-for-all redemptive disclosure in the Hebrew-Christian Scriptures.

For both the plural world religions and for modern consciousness the implications are far-reaching. Through God's universal interior revelation, alongside His external self-disclosure in nature and history, a "creational" consciousness of God is indelibly perpetuated in the mind and conscience of every person. The world's religions and philosophical systems are therefore not simply historical accidents. They incorporate diverse responses to the living God's ongoing revelation, responses to the light of the Logos inescapably reflected in and through the *imago*. Even if in their fallen condition humans seek to suppress its content, this creational consciousness is a fundamental fact of human existence.

Creational consciousness takes epistemic priority over each and every historically contingent cultural consciousness to which supremacy is now often arbitrarily accorded. Creational consciousness is not translated by fallen humans into an unsullied representation of the living God and religious reality. The medieval notion that a universally shared system of truth, or universally shared body of law or of morality, survived the fall does not deal realistically with the depth of human revolt. The consequences of the fall are staggering. Human beings strive to suppress the truth; they no longer think God's thoughts after Him. The human will is set against its Maker. Humans reconstruct the reality of God more compatibly with their preferences. Nonbiblical religions take shape as ingenious "works religions" whereby fallen mankind by human initiative seeks to mollify God's demands and to overcome a long-compromised relationship. The pluralistic nonbiblical religions are the end result. They are a joint product; on the one hand they are a response to universal divine disclosure, on the other a deflection and dilution and distortion of it that constitutes a warped effort to bridge the gap between an alienated God and his alienated creatures.

Schleiermacher therefore seriously misread the reality when he judges all religions to be a joint product, a universally shared, pretheoretical religious awareness subsequently shaped by post-experiential doctrinal individuation. Biblical theism inverts both prongs of this verdict. Every human being stands always and everywhere in responsible relationship to the truth of the living God disclosed in general revelation. Humanity's theoretical reformulations of God in His revelation universally presuppose the priority of a relationship in which the true and living God, despite humankind's rebellious response, nonetheless exerts a truth claim upon the conscience and mind of every last person. The divergent nonbiblical religions—deprived of special revelation—obscure general revelation by blending and subordinating it into diverse speculative schemas that espouse competing and conflicting divinities. Secular philosophical systems and nonbiblical religious systems stand in broken cognitive continuity with general revelation, and so they distort it. The secular idealist or theistic philosopher and the proponent of a nonbiblical religious outlook revolt against the living God no less than does the atheist who deflects general revelation in his or her own preferred way. A proper exposition and true interpretation of general revelation requires more than the discard of atheism. The mere insistence on an amorphous transcendent, even on a vague supernatural reality, or on deity creatively redefined or depicted as growing, can falsify the living God, the Creator and Judge of all. Speculative theisms can be as hostile to biblical theism as are naturalism and polytheism.

For all the pluralistic deformity of religious reality, however, general divine revelation remains in place. The perspicuity of the living God's universal disclosure remains undimmed. It is not the ambiguity of general revelation, but the response of humanity in sin, that translates religious reality into a nondescript spiritual realm or into imaginative reconstruction of reality such as those of the pagan Gentile world that the apostle Paul indicts in Romans.

To reduce universal religious experience to pretheoretical feeling already reflects sinful human's rebellion against the light of the Logos conveyed both externally in nature and history and internally in and through the rational and moral *imago*. Nature ever since creation has manifested God's eternal divinity and power, and the heavens even now lucidly declare the glory of God (Ps. 19). To depict the rational particularization of universal religious experience as a *superadditum* is to conceal the fact of God's intelligible self-disclosure in general revelation and also to minimize sinful humanity's reduction and attempted suppression of the rational-moral-spiritual content of general revelation. The obscuration of general revelation is not due to divine hiddenness or to a deficiency in divine disclosure or to a lack of revelatory lucidity that render's God's existence and nature problematical or merely probable or highly probable. The obscuration is a consequence of the Adamic fall of human revolt, of volitional rebellion. There is no logical or epistemic necessity for confusion in grasping the self-revelation of the living God. Sin is the source of the havoc that humankind has made of general revelation. Sin also underlies the contention that human doubt over God's existence is due to a lack of revelatory data. God is not an elusive presence. There is no rational excuse for doubt that the Creator God lives. Much as the various particular religions may and do distort the light of general revelation, every human being nonetheless remains personally and inescapably related to universal divine disclosure. That disclosure penetrates individual experience everywhere, however much rebellious mankind may seek to minimize it. The *imago Dei* (image of God) in the individual worshiper links him or her in direct continuity with the Logos.

Nor can be it legitimately contended that God is not revealed in the not-God, that is, in and through historical events and natural phenomena. That He is so revealed, even in and to humans, is an essential emphasis of general revelation. God created and controls the universe and reveals Himself throughout it. His unyielding omnipresence indicts the atheist. The sensually perceived universe conveys divine revelation. The scientist is not confronted only by sense phenomena, but also by phenomenal reality that is dependent upon God and in and by which God makes Himself known. Against scientific empiricism our complaint is not that God is unknowable in sensory phenomena; sensory realities are revelational of God. In every aspect of human experience humankind is under pressure of God's universal revelation.

The scientistic interpretation of sense phenomena is reductionistic. The naturalistic contention that only sensually verifiable phenomena exist or are meaningful is perverse. God is not an object of sensation; without Him as Creator and Preserver, the experienced universe would not even exist. The subjective distortion of universal revelation does not exclude the possibility or actuality of an objectively given special once-for-all divine revelation. The Bible provides at one and the same time an objective literary statement of the content of both general revelation and of special redemptive revelation. The Bible is God's intelligible revelation of His own nature and will for His creation and constitutes the normative exposition of God's creational and salvific purpose in the universe. It exhibits Jesus Christ as the divine agent in creation, in redemption, and in judgment.

Contemporary secular consciousness, much as it reflects a particular historical stance, is not to be dismissed as wholly irrelevant. Scientific naturalism is so deeply embedded as the covert metaphysics of the modern mind that it derogates the plausibility of any intellectual alternative, but then, the shared ideas and ideals of any culture function in much the same authoritarian manner. Reformed theology explains the human search for meaning as *imago Dei*. Humanity is made for God and for meaning. From the dawn of creation humans are trust-disposed creatures who worship either the true God or false gods. If humans turn aside from the living God, they will postulate counterfeit ultimates and invest false gods with life. Humans are engaged in a continuing quest for a comprehensive explanatory principle. They seek to comprehend all existence and life in an orderly way. Reformed theology explains the misdirection of the human's search for meaning by pointing to demonic influences and sin. In the course of spiritual rebellion humanity voluntarily excludes the ultimacy of the Creator-Redeemer God and romances speculative alternatives.

The Protestant Reformers criticized medieval theology not only for soteriological misconceptions, but also for epistemological novelties, especially the Thomistic attempt to prove God's existence apart from reliance on divine revelation and by empirical inference from the finite universe. The Reformers sided instead with Augustine's insistence that "faith seeks understanding," predicated on the priority of divine revelation, rather than on Aquinas's formula, "I understand in order to believe," with its excessive confidence in human reasoning.

It is not theologically disreputable to begin the presentation of one's worldview with *a priori* affirmations grounded in intelligible faith. An intellectual is wholly within the bounds of epistemic propriety if he or she affirms God's existence even in the absence, and deliberately in the absence, of empirical proof. What is objectionable about Berger's insistence on the reality of the superempirical Transcendent is that he professes to derive and validate it by empirical methodology. *A priori* affirmation in and of itself might constitute sheer fideism, or naively taking for granted all that one affirms on the premise that faith inevitably contradicts reason, but Reformed theology disavows theological fideism as strenuously as it disavows philosophical empiricism. The demand for evidence is illegitimate only if it requires evidence inappropriate to the religious object. That demand is wholly appropriate if it solicits evidence appropriate to the reality and existence of God. Reformed theology does not rule out any and all relevance for public reason.

To begin with, we should stress that presuppositions are legitimate and in fact unavoidable. All scientific, philosophical, and theological views begin with assumptions or they could not even get underway. Modern science at first pretended to be assumption free and sought to discredit theology because theology began with assumptions, but the complaint was self-discrediting and had to be abandoned. Then modern empiricists sought to impose their own highly debatable assumptions on theology. They held that only the empirical method can validate truth claims, theological truth claims included. The empirical method, however, is incompetent to judge questions of metaphysics and miracle. Since such concerns fall outside its scope, it cannot adjudicate the reality and nature of the supernatural. In any case, empiricism can render no fixed and final verdict on anything.

Christians put Christianity at high risk if they suspend the case for biblical theism on empirical considerations, not only because of the limits of empirical method but because of the nature of God. The God of the Bible is not a sense-perceptible reality, nor is He related to the universe in an absolutely uniform way. Reformed theology rightly resists the effort to speak authoritatively about God on the basis of religious experience. That effort covertly substitutes anthropology for theology. Empiricism conceals Christian theology's deductive status and substitutes induction; instead of beginning with God in His revelation and deducing the content of theology from this controlling axiom, it begins with religious experience and seeks to demonstrate God as a distillate of anthropology.

Such a method postpones at great cost an immediate appeal to the self-revealing God who has made Himself universally known in general revelation and whose redemptive revelation is objectively accessible in Scripture. Furthermore, it tapers the Christian world-life view to an arbitrary demand that it justify its claims in accord with the demands of an alien philosophical theory, that of empiricism.

No metaphysician is required to taper the basic axioms of his or her world-life view to the requirements of some competing speculative theory. Plato, Kant, and Whitehead presented their explanatory principles without any antecedent necessity of conforming their views to the tolerances of competing systems. It is arbitrary to require the Christian theologian to justify the axioms of biblical theism at the bar of empirical verification. Axioms are never validated by extraneous considerations; they are basic postulates from which all other theorems are derived and upon which they rest.

The Christian ontological axiom is the living self-revealed God. The Christian epistemological axiom is intelligible divine revelation. All the essential doctrines of the Christian world-life view flow from these axioms: creation, sin, and the fall; redemption by promise and fulfillment; the incarnation, substitutionary death and resurrection of the Logos; the church as the new society; the approaching divine consummation of history; the eschatological verities. The basic axioms imply each other; we speak authentically of God only in view of His intelligible self-disclosure. That revelation, inscripturated, attests that humanity bears by creation the rational and moral image of the Creator and expounds the essentials of biblical theism.

Christian presuppositions are not scientific hypotheses. If they were, they would be subject to empirical verification and to a method that cannot in any case adjudicate the reality of the supernatural or rise above tentativity. Christians do not view these axioms merely as arbitrary assumptions that offer only a conjectural explanation of all existence and life. Rather, they know the axioms to be assumptions rationally necessary for all intelligible thought. Human reason is not the source of divine revelation; God is. Human reason is a divinely ordered instrument for the recognition of revelation. Humankind is made in God's image; reason and logic have ontological significance.

To the pluralistic religions we do not offer an accommodating restatement of Christianity on their preferred presuppositions. We do not expect them to restate their basic principles so that they conform to Christian tenets. We have our presuppositions; they have theirs—only let us be clear about what these respective presuppositions are. Because we differ radically in our assumptions about God and much else does not mean that religion reduces to everyone's private preference. The question of which presuppositions are preferable and why remains a burning issue. The evangelical Christian repudiates relativism and confidently appeals to the laws of logic and to the rule of sufficient evidence. The Christian axioms are the reality of God the self-revealed Creator of all, and intelligible revelation as the way of knowing Him. The Christian's verifying principle is divinely inspired Scripture. The Holy Spirit is the source of personal faith in Christ.

In the so-called post-Christian age Reformed theology retains its reformational power to confront the world and to revitalize the churches. Modern consciousness is powerless to halt its own decline to pagan perspectives, yet the secular mind-set lacks finality and authority. It strives against the creational image of God in humans and it is now confronted also by the specially revealed Word of God. That Word is objectively inscripturated and is addressed to the wicked heart of rebellious humanity as a message of God's elective grace.

# Reformed Theology and the Molding of Christian Culture

*If we speak of Reformed theology and its shaping influence in the molding of culture, we must be keenly aware that the church as God's elect society is the primary sphere of Christ's lordship. It is imperative that the people of God stand apart from the world as an identifiably distinct society, a holy or separated people, whose life and dynamic are supernatural, whose ruling head is the crucified and risen and no-glorified Jesus.*

The shaping ideas and ideals of Western culture are now increasingly questioned. The long-cherished theological foundations undergirding law, ethics, psychology, history, and other disciplines of learning are widely distrusted. Scientific empiricism identifies the ultimately real world in terms of impersonal processes and energy events. Phenomenology emphasizes the creativity of the human knower while existentialism stresses autonomous personal decision. The outcome, in either case, is the denial of any supernatural Being, the elevation of humanity as the measure of truth and goodness, and the affirmation that the grave is humanity's final destiny.

Across almost two thousand years the Christian revelation of God shaped a culture of unparalleled spiritual and moral power. Its roots lay in Hebrew monotheism. The Mosaic law given at Sinai nurtured a society whose ethical standards, already at its very outset, towered far above the standards that other nations gradually attained through long centuries of historical development. In the Christian era the larger incarnational revelation of the living God inverted Graeco-Roman paganism even as in earlier Hebrew history the message of the prophets had inverted ancient Near Eastern paganism.

The distinctive contribution of Christianity to the Western cultural mainstream is not difficult to identify. It included the convictions that God by His sovereign Word created and sustains the space-time universe in its orderly relationships, that at the climax of creation God fashioned the human species in His personal image for knowledge, righteousness, and love, that human beings are divinely designated moral stewards of the cosmos, and that history is linear, and under God's control moves toward an all-encompassing spiritual goal.

Both evangelical and secular scholars concede that these basic premises shaped a Western worldview dramatically distinct from its rivals. The humanitarian concerns that Christian missionaries carried to Asia and Africa, the development of modern empirical science, the expectation that history will consummate in a final triumph of the good in vindication of the kingdom of God, the confidence in Christ's church as a new society that conveys enduring hope for sinners alienated from God and from each other—such cherished core beliefs and values lifted the West far above its ancient pagan moorings.

In recent generations the naturalistic mind-set has steadily eroded these theologically grounded convictions. The great priorities of the Protestant Reformation—that the Bible is God's authoritatively revealed Word and that God, by divine grace and apart from any human merit, justifies otherwise lost and doomed sinners through faith alone in Christ's saving work—are eclipsed by the scientistic worldview. The metaphysics of modernity is that impersonal processes and quantum events comprise the ultimately real world, that all reality is time-bound and dated, and that truth claims and moral imperatives are man-made in a universe that originated in a cosmic explosion.

Much confusion of religious terminology prevails even in Christian circles today, not least of all over such descriptives as fundamentalist, evangelical, pentecostal, charismatic, and so on. The tendency to use the term "evangelical" as inclusive not only of Arminian and Reformed Christians, but of charismatic believers as well, and more broadly still of whoever claims a "born again" experience, has diluted its cognitive force. In view of this confusion many scholars are prone to distinguish themselves more precisely today as Reformed. Contemporary Reformed circles are not exempt from costly compromise with the theology of Karl Barth and Emil Brunner, nor are they immune to liberal or other incursions. Neoorthodox and liberal overtones weaken the historic Protestant authority principle and the validity of Christian truth claims. If Reformed theology is to challenge an amorphous evangelicalism, it can do so effectively only in terms of a comprehensively consistent doctrinal witness.

I do not use the term "evangelical," as some now do, for non-Reformed Protestants. The historic Reformed faith champions evangelical orthodoxy, with much focus on the early ecumenical creeds and historic confessions. By the term *evangelicals*, I mean Protestants of broadly Reformed commitment, whether identified with Reformed denominations or not. The theological orientation and doctrinal sensitivity of the Reformed churches lend them a special serviceability in confronting the confessional weaknesses and ambiguities of many Protestant communities. The primarily experiential orientation of many professedly evangelical churches is a conspicuous weakness. Even in fundamentalist circles, which are often caricatured as preoccupied with doctrine, what passes for serious theology today is often remarkably thin. Contemporary Christianity is overdue for theological emphasis on God's claim upon the whole person, intellect, will, and emotion, and on the New Testament importance of the mind of Christ for obedient service to God.

If we speak of Reformed theology and its shaping influence in the molding of Christian culture, we must be keenly aware that the church as God's elect society is the primary sphere of Christ's lordship. It is imperative that the people of God stand apart from the world as an identifiably distinct society, a holy or separated people, whose life and dynamic are supernatural, whose ruling head is the crucified and risen and now glorified Jesus. The moral virtues that the Holy Spirit gives to believers constitute an earnest of the coming age, a sampling of eschatological finalities. It is for the people of God that the Christian world-life view provides first and foremost an integrating perspective, one that stretches throughout time and is vibrant with eternity. Yet the church is called to exhibit to the whole world the blessings of serving the true and living God.

The temptation to which Protestant modernism yielded, to think of the unregenerate world as potentially a global brotherhood of peace and love, a macrocosm of which Christ's church is a dynamic microcosm, led to tragic theological misunderstandings. One such misunderstanding viewed the social gospel as a message of socioeconomic redemption. The perverse notion arose that salvation has only a cultural form, that the task of Christianity is to save not individuals but society, and that this redemption of culture could be achieved by techniques that efficiently reorganize world structures. Here, the church's "good news" is politicized while the indispensability of the new birth is ignored.

This is not to say that the church has no message for the political and economic arena. The church is to speak to the world first and foremost concerning the self-revealing God and His incarnation in Jesus Christ, concerning redemption from sin and the victory of divine truth and righteousness. Without that overarching canopy, all condemnation of evil lacks good news and merely multiplies pessimism over human existence. It is remarkable that so many writers who today appeal to the Old Testament prophets to advance their theology of social revolution and political liberation seem unheeding when those same prophets protest against false gods and emphasize the need of spiritual conversion.

It is we ourselves as believers who must invest our creationally bestowed gifts and talents in every discipline of life and learning. Science and the humanities, literature and the arts, and the other arenas of life are to reflect the glory of God. Christian education aims to penetrate society with distinctively biblical convictions. It seeks the cohesive integration of all learning and life. It witnesses to the world of the joys and rewards of serving the self-revealed God. These are indispensable facets of our evangelical mission in society.

The question is now often asked whether separate Christian schools are really necessary or whether they merely encourage a withdrawal of Christians from the prevalent culture into private ghettos. If supposedly Christian institutions themselves compromise essential Christian commitments and obscure their relevancy, as sometimes is the case, then separate institutions of learning do double harm. On the one hand they cloud the fundamentals of a Christian world-and-life view. Worse yet they accommodate or promote subchristian alternatives in the name of Christian education. When the prevailing culture mentality intolerantly or arbitrarily dismisses a theistic alternative as unworthy of consideration and registers an inevitably erosive impact on evangelical beliefs, then it becomes imperative to present the biblical revelation on its own platform. This is best done where all contenders are evaluated on merit, rather than on prejudice.

Such Christian learning, giving proper attention to the systematic interrelationship of the basic Christian doctrines, and stressing their implications for life in the contemporary world, is doubly necessary. It is indispensable for the public's proper grasp of Christianity's controlling principles, and for a balanced Christian assessment of rival views. If the Christian community is itself in doubt over what conformity to the mind of Christ implies for moral and spiritual life in the world, it cannot confidently live by the truth of Christ that sets us free for the service of God and humankind.

The Protestant Reformers regarded the doctrine of vocation, that is, a view of work as a divine calling, as the natural bridge linking the community of faith with the larger world. Insisting as they did on the universal priesthood of all believers, they rejected the medieval notion of a celibate, male priestly class which, in contrast with ordinary laborers, was held to be exclusively in divine service. This medieval distinction erected a sharp divide between the common worker and the priest ordained to the service of God. The Reformers insisted that all children of God have direct access to the Father through Christ, that all are to employ their gifts and talents vocationally to the glory and in the service of God, and that under God are to serve fellow believers, neighbors, and society in general. The custodian whose vocational calling is janitorial work is no less in the priestly service of God than a clergyman presiding at the Lord's Supper. The consequence of this view is that the believer makes the transition daily from the arena of personal ethics into the larger realm of social ethics by way of personal involvement and service. This emphasis contrasts dramatically with a modern ecumenical and denominational tendency to adopt and publicize a verbal resolution on social issues and to rely on such symbolism to effect social change.

The Christian view of work appears in tandem with a special view of "recreation," a term that most moderns equate with play, an activity about which Scripture says little. To be sure, there is room in the scriptural view for relaxation, but the main biblical correlation concerns work and worship, work and rest. On the one hand, the Old Testament contrasts the workweek and Sabbath rest; the creation account strikingly notes God's rest on the seventh day. Work is not viewed as an evil to be endured for the sake of leisure or play, but as a meaningful moral engagement sheltered by worship of God whose wonderful works are known to the community of faith. Recreation speaks not of secular indulgences, but of spiritual and physical renewal. In the New Testament the Lord's Day did not at first provide in a pagan society the larger opportunity for spiritual activity that Christians enjoy today. It nonetheless reinforced the priority of worship. In the Bible what we consider play activities, such as dancing and singing, could be channeled into the worship of God, yet New Testament Christians would have rejected as objectionable much that moderns consider recreation. Television is largely preoccupied with the transitory. It profanes and trivializes life and tends to devote special attention to religion only when its spokesmen are in moral or financial trouble. The mass media are not wicked, per se, and Christians should strive to place them in the service of culturally constructive spiritual and moral concerns. The glory of God overarches concerns of work and recreation alike in the biblical view.

The creational ethic included a work ethic. Human beings are made not simply for play, but for responsible activity in the created cosmos. Before the Fall, and not as a consequence of it, Adam was given a task to do, that of keeping and dressing the garden. The creation account establishes the propriety and necessity of work, a principle that the apostle Paul echoes in his linkage of "work" and "eat" (2 Thess. 3). Sin impacted catastrophically upon humankind's creationally given task in two ways. Work became arduous and grievous, and humans readily stripped and raped nature to gratify selfish desires.

The biblical revelation therefore rebukes the growing modern tendency to regard work as an evil that an ideal society will eliminate. Instead, Christian conscience views culturally constructive work as a divine provision. In the face of large eruptions of unemployment, the people of God will be alert to job opportunities for fellow-believers, who in turn, by the quality of their work, will commend their service. Scripture is concerned about justice for the worker. "Pay fair wages" is a theme found in the Old Testament books of the Prophets, in the Gospels, and in the Epistles.

The Protestant work ethic has in recent generations been blamed for modern society's obsession with affluence, but social critics disagree over the extent to which capitalism itself can be considered a derivative of Christianity. In any case the Bible is not to be blamed for the infractions sometimes attributed to capitalism. What is incontrovertible is that at only one point in the long history of human poverty have multitudes of persons risen from the lowest economic strata to middle-class status and that through free market economics. The Protestant virtues of thrift, diligence, and hard work promoted such economic achievement.

The Bible, no doubt, encourages free-market economics. Its emphasis on human sinfulness and fallibility translates into a distrust of bureaucratic power and pretensions of human omnicompetence to manipulate economic outcomes. Twentieth-century Nazi Socialists and Soviet and Chinese Communists, all of them aspiring to cultural domination at the supposed height of humankind's evolutionary development, became instruments of unprecedented violence and demonic destruction. Champions of the welfare state illusion that economic determinism guarantees the ultimate emergence of a Marxist utopia are now gradually conceding that not even their unlimited bureaucratic control of economic forces has been able to make that system work. Many socialist economies are now in such deepening difficulty that they have begun to accommodate principles of private property and profit, proper to capitalist economies. The failure of the communist revolution to achieve its utopian goals, and the bleak economic predicament of many socialist countries, reflect the soundness of scriptural emphasis on the limits of world wisdom.

The motif of freedom has implications far beyond the economic realm. Even if the Reformers may not have fully grasped the dimensions of religious liberty, Reformed theology stands as a bulwark of human liberty. Jesus Christ stressed the importance of voluntary faith; never did He coercively impose on anyone faith in His deity and salvific significance. Religious liberty is in fact the ground of all other liberties. The apostolic imperative, "We must obey God rather than men" (Acts 5:29), preserves each person's right in good conscience to resist all arbitrary authority in the name of the living God. When totalitarian rulers or dictators require us to refrain from doing what God requires, or to do what God prohibits, we have a clear biblical mandate for standing on the side of God, the King of kings. The church is not to render to Caesar what belongs to God. Nothing is more embarrassing to a modern government in the eyes of the world than when it imprisons a godly person for doing what God commands or for refusing to do what God prohibits. The tide of public prayer for the victims of tyranny publicizes throughout the heavens and the earth the pretensions of tyrants who act as gods.

At the same time the Christian community is mandated to render to Caesar all that is Caesar's. The legitimate and necessary role of civil government in a fallen society is a firm Reformed emphasis, even if civil government is limited in its prerogatives. Through the instrumentality of the state, God wills the promotion of order and public justice, just as through the organism of the church God wills the universal proclamation of the gospel and the bestowal of new spiritual life.

The very foundation and meaning of justice is debated in our generation. Rival claims are set forth in the name of biblical justice, Soviet justice, Islamic justice, modern liberal justice, and so on. The Reformed insistence on transcendent law in terms of the revealed will and word of God is of crucial importance to the present-day human rights crisis. Ever since the Enlightenment, modern scholars have sought to displace supernatural revelation by some other foundation of law, but "natural law" theory has crumbled. Its philosophical supporters from ancient Greek to modern times differ somewhat over its supposed content. Its critics emphasize that no universally shared system of truth and morality can survive the fall of humankind.

Calvin insisted that general revelation remains in place and that nobody is without some light. Indeed, human beings are sinners universally because they revolt against light both in Adam and on their own account. Calvin did not, however, hold to a natural law ethic. Law is increasingly doomed to impotence apart from a revival of its divine revelatory foundations. A Swiss jurist, Peter Saladin, acknowledges that the philosophical foundations of law postulated by modern scholars are not cognitively plausible; indeed, we can no longer espouse these undergirding assumptions, he adds, "without sacrificing our intellectual and moral honesty."[1]

The biblical doctrine that at creation God bestowed the divine image upon the human species anchors a transcendent basis for law and morality and supplies an absolute foundation for racial equality. The doctrine illumines the modern controversy over women's rights and over minority rights and provides a cognitive justification for claims of universal human dignity and worth. It does so, notably, in the context of divinely stipulated human duties. Major architects of the United Nations Declaration of Human Rights traced its roots to the Ten Commandments. The Decalogue is often seen not only as a Hebrew covenant ethics but as a restatement of creation ethics addressing human revolt. Historian Paul Johnson stresses the dramatic conjunction in the Hebrew legal system of the two declarations that law has divine origin and that all mankind is made in God's image. He comments: "The fact that God ruled meant that in practice his law ruled. And since all were equally subject to the law, the system was the first to embody the double merits of the rule of law and equality before the law."[2]

Biblical monotheism grounded law and morality alike in the transcendent Creator's will and word. The doctrine of creation *ex nihilo* sharply distinguishes biblical theism from the ancient Near Eastern polytheistic religions, from living religions like Buddhism and Hinduism, and from modern religious process metaphysics. Mesopotamian polytheism nullified the absoluteness of a divine will. Divine cosmic order was affirmed, but the gods were not its source. The plural gods not only contended against primordial, cosmic evil, but also competed among themselves and sometimes acted arbitrarily; yet the gods mandated the king to translate the general principles of cosmic order into articulate moral and legal particularities that govern human life. The king's authority was further limited by an earthly political assembly. By contrast, Egyptians viewed their pharaoh as intrinsically divine. Each pharaoh stipulated

---

1. Peter Saladin, "Christianity and Human Rights: A Jurist's Reflections", in *How Christian are Human Rights?*, ed. Lorenz, 29ff.
2. Paul Johnson, *A History of the Jews* (San Francisco: Harper and Row, 1987).

divine law without any answerability to a higher source or to previous pharaohs.

In Hebrew religion, the one sovereign Creator-God Himself stipulates all human duties and holds all persons—earthly rulers included—responsible for discerning and doing His will. Unlike the polytheistic gods, moreover, Yahweh is not an embattled part of nature. He is the transcendent Legislator, and His covenant with Israel stipulates his will in verbal specifics. The United Nations Declaration of Human Rights (1948), lists human liberties that civilized modern nations affirm, but it makes no mention of God as the supreme and sovereign source of law and morality. Nor does it deal with human duties. It does not even obligate member nations to enforce these rights. The Bible by contrast presents God as the transcendent source and stipulator of human duties, and as the final judge of all humanity and of the rulers of this world. It is true, of course, as John W. Montgomery says, that not even "the most intellectually sophisticated catalogue of human rights, policies and goals" guarantees that people and government will observe them.[3] The Bible supplies a potent force for social betterment by its assurance that final judgment awaits us, that the risen Christ is even now judging unjust nations and unjust rulers and wicked civilizations in present history, and that God's patience with injustice has moral limits.

The biblical insistence on the divine image in persons universally has important implications for the increasingly urgent dialogue among exponents of the plural religions whose rival claims call for constructive and critical appraisal. Some spokesmen predict that all religion will soon disappear only to reemerge in some secular guise. Others hold that belief in the supernatural will survive into the twenty-first century as energetically as ever and in many forms. Intellectual centers more and more sense that a major dialogue about religious realities is indispensable if not inevitable. Are the ontological claims made by the world religions mythical, so that they tell us nothing about external or transcendent realities? Has religion at best only functional significance? Does it serve only internally to integrate and unify an otherwise discordant self? Or do the world religions carry overlapping truths and values, some more than others, but all of them nonetheless providing access to one and the same God? Or is there one at least among the religions of the world that tells the normative truth about God, and if so, on what basis can we affirm this?

---

3. John Warwick Montgomery, *Human Rights and Human Dignity* (Grand Rapids: Zondervan, 1986)., 13.

The divine creational image endowed the human species for worship of the living God in obedient rational and moral fellowship with the Lord of life. The warping of God's image is evident from the many diverse religions that represent God in notably different ways and from their conflicting truth claims. So great is the span of divergence that God is depicted as nonexistent, or as everything that exists, or in terms of one or another of countless intermediary options.

Although the divine image is seriously flawed by sin, the Bible insists that the image nonetheless survives. This has major consequences for interreligious dialogue. However conflicting and contradictory the world's living religions may be as divergent, creative systems of belief, an ineradicable link survives between every human and his or her Maker in both his conscience and mind. The Bible teaches that, irrespective of religion or race, all human beings have sufficient intellectual and moral light to hail them anticipatively before God's judgment throne.

The Reformers took the volitional and noetic consequences of the fall too seriously to accept natural-law theory. They did not accept the Thomistic view that human beings universally, despite the fall, embrace a shared body of truth and morality. The Reformers emphasized that general revelation remains in effect, and insisted that it penetrates and convicts every human person despite his or her spiritual rebellion. Quite apart from the conflicting religious systems fashioned within the framework of revolt, general revelation is still internally operative and is objectively given in the cosmos as well as in conscience.

Even the rival systems, both philosophical and religious, which seek by ingenious alternatives to bridge the spiritual gulf between humans and God, may here and there retain apparent glimmers of light. Their metaphysical and epistemic presuppositions tend to distort the cognitive content even of such affirmations. So, for example, Jesus and Hegel each insistently affirm that God is Spirit, yet the God and Father of Jesus is vastly different from the Hegelian *Geist*. The verbal equivalent, taken alone, obscures the rival truth claims involved. Without special revelation in inspired Scripture, people in revolt against God do not infallibly distinguish between what assuredly belongs to general revelation and what reflects human suppression and distortion of that revelation. No longer do human sinners love God with their whole selves; instead, they evade thinking God's own thoughts after Him. No longer do they will to do the will of God; instead, they tend to attach an internal revelation claim and salvific import to one or another of the conflicting philosophical or religious schemes. These speculative options promise to fill the spiritual vacuum of the self, and they require less in the way of moral decision than does the candid confession of one's horrendous guilt and one's absolute need of transcendent rescue. Human pride routinely probes the self-gratifying possibilities of works salvation. Special revelation not only clarifies and reinforces general revelation to the rebellious spirit of humans, but it also does so in the momentous context of God's offer of redemptive grace.

We do not need simply to accelerate interreligious conversation; we need to compare fairly and contrast truth claims and world-and-life view affirmations. We need to ask where and why synthesis is or is not possible. We need to assent to truth and to follow wherever it leads, to press for clarification where truth is obscure. In every land we must relate this concern to philosophies and religions that bid for the loyalties of the masses. In Korea, for example, Christianity must be set alongside Buddhism, Confucianism, Taoism, Shintoism, the folk traditions, shamanism with its appeal to occult powers, and to newer religions such as that of Sun Myung Moon. Although Confucianism is now declining in attraction, it provided, at least until recently, the moral basis of large segments of society. The same temptations apply in every culture, though the gods may masquerade under any number of names and guises.

Theology genuinely rooted in the Bible refuses to minimize the matter of truth, whereas truth is not a primary concern for some major religions. The comment of one-time dean of theology in Yonsei University, Tai-dong Han, is noteworthy in this regard. "Confucianism accepts truth as true and falsity as false," he writes, "whereas Buddhism considers that neither truth nor falsity is a valid criterion for judgment. Taoism claims that truth cannot exist without falsity" but holds that they are "two phases of one reality."

Professor Han's further reference to the Christian religion is disconcerting in view of biblical representations of the singular and exclusive truth of Judeo-Christian revelation. Christianity, says Professor Han, "accepts paradox as the ultimate form of truth."[4] Christianity can hardly hope to make its way by thus exempting its theology from all rational answerability and from the law of contradiction. Only in its recent neoorthodox forms have Christian and Reformed scholars sacrificed the relevance of reason and logical tests of faith. While some early church fathers spoke of the doctrine of divine incarnation and of the Trinity as paradoxes, they did not mean thereby to deny, as does neoorthodoxy, that such revealed doctrines give us objectively valid information about God's intrinsic nature.

The doctrine of divine creation is of crucial importance in discriminating between the great world religions and the spiritual experience they

---

4. See *Encyclopedia Brittannica*, 15th edition (1974), X:530.

foster. Speaking broadly, the major faiths are basically distinguishable by whether or not they affirm the transcendent ontological reality of God. Christianity insists that God is the transcendent Other, not ontologically identical at any point with the universe, that is, with humans and nature.

The great religions of India (and Western and Oriental mysticism) affirm that deity is experienced as the ground of consciousness of all humankind. Buddhism and Hinduism are both compatible with this emphasis that the Divine is ultimately to be found in the depths of human consciousness, or at any rate in an experience of our unity with the cosmic universe.

By contrast, traditional Judaism and orthodox Christianity—and Islam as well—view God as the transcendent Creator, who confronts His creatures from above and without, that is, as the Other. The revelation of the transcendent Creator nullifies any identification of the human self as a part or aspect of God.

No one need deny that as a matter of historical confluence, these transcendent and immanent approaches have intersected and in some expressions influenced each other, and continue to do so. One can find Hindu versions of confrontational religious experience no less often than medieval Catholic, neo-Protestant, and liberal Jewish versions of mystical interiority.

Before evolutionary naturalism saturated twentieth-century thought, Christian theology unhesitatingly viewed God's creation of humans and the world as the beginning point of divine historical revelation. Reformed theology stresses the sovereign act of God who transcendently called the universe into being for His special ends. Wherever one turns, the biblical emphasis is that the time-space cosmos is dependent on a sovereign mind and will; creation is not merely an inner existential experience of dependence. This nurtured confidence in the intelligible behavior of nature and prompted empirical investigation of the detailed behavior of the universe. This runs counter to modern theories that ultimately the real constituents of the universe are impersonal processes and energy events, and that a quantum fluctuation played the major role in the origin of the universe. Reformed theology insists that the order and meaning of the universe is grounded in the Logos of God.

The Oriental pantheistic outlook did not encourage human experiment with natural processes. Such Oriental religion typically regards the Divine as the All of which we are parts. The Christian doctrine of God's once-for-all incarnation in Jesus Christ stressed both the ontological otherness of God and the pliability of the created universe as a sphere of rational divine purpose and activity. It challenges the humanistic tendency to view science as redeemer by conferring an authoritative role on tentative empirical observation and by professing to derive normative values from human experience.

This survey of theology and culture is too wide-sweeping to yield a detailed agenda of areas that Reformed theology can helpfully illumine and reinforce today. Beyond emphasis on the civilizational importance of general revelation, and on the burning relevance of biblical authority, and of redemptive revelation, three important last points should be made clear.

The doctrine of divine sovereignty and of divine providence in history is of foremost importance. The history of nations in our generation is not a matter of divine indifference. The sovereign Lord of history and of the church is working out a comprehensive purpose for His own glory and for the supreme good of all who trust Him. We are not to abandon history, to lose interest in the affairs of the world, and to become irrelevant to public affairs. If we do, Christians must resign themselves to a ghetto survival. We are to help reshape society. If all the Reformers regarded any doctrine as in harmony with a true and living faith, it is the doctrine of divine predestination. The modern eclipse of that doctrine has cast costly doubt on the convictions that God reigns by His providence in everything that transpires in the universe, and that our personal experience of His grace is anchored in divine election. Intermediary notions, that God's election is predicated on foreknowledge and that He does not know so-called contingent events, unwittingly encouraged the secular view that humankind autonomously determines the present and the future.

Too much pulpit proclamation today recalls God's redemptive acts in ancient biblical history without bringing forward into the present generation the emphasis that God is everywhere and always active either in grace or in judgment, and that all the events of our times are firmly anchored in His sovereign purpose. Evangelical sermonizing often reaches its climax by interiorizing all doctrinal referents so that the appeal for personal decision obscures God's strong hand in external history and nature.

Culture shaping is not the church's only task in the world, nor even its main task. It is a legitimate and necessary task if we are to be salt, light, and leaven. Often it requires our rejection of ideals that the world esteems or the culture idolizes. Still, however much we reshape culture, it will not become the kingdom of God. The kingdom of God remains always transcendent to our socio-political-cultural achievements. The church as the society over which Christ rules is doubtless the nearest approximation of the kingdom that history offers. The Church is not the kingdom, nor are our sociopolitical achievements to be confused with the kingdom. Yet we are to be involved publicly to the limit of opportunity and ability, and competent Christians should fill leadership posts as the door opens for service to God and to society. Every victory for justice is a victory for God's kingdom, as is every victory of grace. Only at Christ's personal return in power and glory will the Lord of history and of the church inaugurate the kingdom of God in its fullness.

A second critically urgent doctrinal issue is justification by faith without works. In evangelical churches concentration on the "new birth" has largely eclipsed preaching on this doctrine. Meanwhile, some ecumenical reformulations of justification doctrine involve compromises making it more acceptable to concessive Anglo-Catholic and Lutheran scholars. The presently applauded formula affirms the salvation of sinners through Jesus Christ by grace alone. What is left obscure is whether justification must be complemented by works and requires works to be efficacious, or whether, as Paul writes to the Galatians, justification is by faith alone in Christ's all-sufficient atonement.

A further area of immense importance concerns Christology. Here the crucial concerns are twofold. One is growing representation of Jesus Christ, as by process theology, in terms of one nature, that is, a divine-human nature. A second concern is the widening acceptance of salvific universalism and neo-Protestant openness to ways of salvation other than faith in Jesus Christ. If one abandons the apostolic insistence that there is "no other name . . . whereby we must be saved," one inevitably undermines the urgency of the Great Commission.

Despite efforts by secular humanists and by other atheists to push Christianity to the periphery of serious intellectual discussion, biblical theism remains a profound influence in modern civilization. It is not currently the mainspring of modern learning and life, and secular society seeks constantly to crowd it into a ghetto of mere personal religious preference. Yet the fact is that whatever may be the fortunes of Western culture, and whatever may be the fate of influential present-day cultures in Asia and Africa, the Christian revelation championed by the Protestant Reformers will remain a vigorous missionary enterprise on a world scale. It will continue to offer to the bankrupt spirit of contemporary society a dynamic life-transforming faith. More than that, Christian theology puts a premium not only on experience, but also on truth as its firm undergirding source and support. Reformed faith has never given comfort to the foes of Christianity who claim that biblical faith lacks rational credentials. Rationalization may be on the side of unbelief, but reason and truth, it insists, are on the side of faith. All the supposed reasons for rejecting Jesus Christ are rationalizations. In the academic arena, no value takes priority over the concern for truth, and truth is what biblical religion esteems, what the Reformers sought to preserve, and what we are called to restore as the fortress of the human mind and spirit. The revelatory truths anchored in the living God of the Bible, which historically influenced the thought and life of Occident, confront the Orient as well with a logically compelling alternative to the meaning-draining options and conjectural mythologies to which much current philosophy deteriorates.

In presenting Christian truth claims we nonetheless have both reason to be heartened and reason to be troubled. The world does not see what we are thinking, but it sees how we are living. Reformed doctrine avoids perfectionist theories of Christian behavior and does not confuse sanctification with glorification. It emphasizes sanctification nonetheless as a doctrine of crucial importance for the individual believer, for the church, and for the life of the church in the world. How the Christian lives and acts in a world of social injustice and warped values has a bearing on the way in which secular society perceives the God of the Bible and His concerns. Our behavior and misbehavior can obscure Jesus Christ and His cause, almost as much as the sin of verbal silence about the Redeemer.

The point should not be overstated, and the temptation to overstate it is close at hand in our time. For some say the time has come for action, not for words, and that the church should forego preaching and concern itself with social change; the world will draw the proper inferences, it is said, from our activities. Such an emphasis is greatly flawed. Even if the world had observed the behavior of the Christian apostles night and day, it would never, nor could it, infer from their deeds the divine incarnation of the Logos in Jesus Christ, His sinless life and substitutionary death, His bodily resurrection, and His anticipated return in final judgment. The essentials of the kerygma are divinely revealed truths, and they are to be proclaimed to the world as such. The fact that the Hebrews were sent into Babylonian captivity for their moral and spiritual disobedience did not invalidate the truth of biblical theism, nor does the misbehavior of Christians today invalidate the truth of the gospel. What it does is to give needless comfort to secular worldlings in their rationalizations of their rejection of Christ.

In bearing public witness we are the messengers of hope. That hope is grounded on the risen Christ. He has already passed through death and into the eternal order, from which He rules the church as its living head. Where genuine hope survives in the modern world it is nurtured by the living Lord, who rescues an otherwise hopeless humanity for life fit for time and eternity. The conventional dogma of the day is that human existence and survival has neither purpose nor meaning, that we face death with all beasts as our final end, and that the life of mankind is without enduring personal or social value and is lived on an uncaring and unresponsive planet. We live in a society which seems no longer to know what real love means, yet multitudes long to be loved while they live a tasteless existence, and inhale the dust of death. Relativists have relativized themselves out of relevance. Rationalists propose so many meaning-giving myths that they jeopardize the very meaning of meaning. Even the secular spirit is losing heart. What passes for worthwhile human existence and for social cohesion is almost everywhere a mockery in the very century that evolutionary naturalists heralded as the pinnacle of human development.

The axioms of the Christian world-life view retain their enduring power. It is God in His revelation that this earth needs to know. The knowledge of God and His will can teach us anew what life is all about and how tragic it is to give ourselves over to the demonic. To us falls the task of conveying ethical monotheism to the modern world along with its great correlatives, the dignity of the human person, equality before the law, the sinfulness and social responsibility of humankind, the prospect of divine redemption, the incarnation of God in Jesus the crucified and risen Savior, love as fulfillment of the law, and peace and justice as God's intention for history. In ancient Hebrew times a small nation with a divinely gifted metaphysical and moral vision exercised for God and for good an influence far exceeding its demographic status. Today, in the face of neopaganism, the Christian task force can impact directly and indirectly upon world fortunes far beyond the numerical strength of a globally dispersed church. Evangelicals now have an unprecedented opportunity to witness to the world of the lordship of Christ not only in evangelism, but also in science and technology, in philosophy and education, in literature, music, and the arts, and not least of all, in history and even in political life where Christ exerts His claim as the Lord of the nations and King of truth and justice.

# The Doing and Undoing of Theology

*The proper task of theology is to exposit and elucidate the content of Scripture in an orderly way, and by presenting its teaching as an orderly whole to commend and reinforce the worship and service of God.*

It should surprise no one that theologians, instead of theologizing, are now asking how to do theology, and are wondering if, in fact, it can any longer be done, or even ought to be done. Churches are dismayed, and rightly so, that technicians isolated in Essene-like caves have perverted theology into some kind of speculative enterprise undertaken by professionals only. Not a few churchgoers disdain theology as an activity whereby imaginative seers turn God into a myth and promote an earthly utopia instead. Is it any wonder even many of the clergy neglect theology and focus more and more on day-to-day "practical" concerns?

With this aversion to theology marking the present age, evangelicals should take seriously their responsibility to engage serious theological contributions where they can be found. Among those contributions is the sturdy work of Paul Holmer, the late professor of theology at Yale Divinity School. Like Professor Paul Holmer, I long for intellectuals to rediscover the vital aspects of the biblical heritage, and I deplore the radical disagreements that divide theologians and, consequently, encourages religious skepticism rather than spiritual faith.

The early volumes of my work on *God, Revelation and Authority* appeared just before and simultaneously with Dr. Holmer's volume *The Grammar of Faith* or it would have been quoted at numerous places with full appreciation.[1] I, too, offered an alternative to the recent theological approaches that grounded historic Christianity in emotive or volitional factors. My counteremphasis that reason is on the side of evangelical orthodoxy drew full-page notice from *Time* magazine. My volumes also drew a somewhat questioning look from some scholars who professed to speak for evangelical faith. Gracious person that he is, Professor Holmer wrote a cautious commendatory blurb, aware that we both were trying to enlist our readers for the community of faith. Yet, for all our agreements, were we not somewhat apart on what theology is and does?

My agreements with Professor Holmer far outrun my disagreements, a rare experience for any two theologians engaged today on theological frontiers. I salute his insistence that one of theology's main goals is to instruct us in the art of living and to make us godly and Christlike, that Scripture is its antecedently given norm and that historical criticism, however useful, is too limited to explain the past, that "to understand the religious themes of the New Testament" it may be "far more important . . . to learn to hunger and thirst for righteousness, to learn to love a neighbor, and to achieve a high degree of self-concern" than to have historical-critical understanding of the text; that there are no bare uninterpreted facts; that theology interprets the Scriptures from a special perspective and proposes "a deep and abiding truth" as "a criterion and standard for all human life."[2]

I concur moreover that theology ideally communicates in the contemporary vernacular; that it prods us to first-person, present-tense relationships of the love and fear of God; that it affirms that "I am no longer I, but Christ lives in me"; that it is cognitive, but that imagination can promote obedience, facilitate compassion and romance new possibilities; that the meaning of Jesus is not exhausted in theories about Him and His work; that knowing the creeds is not the same as knowing God; that the Bible as it stands, apart from the imposition of philosophical schemes, enjoins a particular behavior; that the biblical doctrines require a new quality of heart and imply a distinctive life of virtue, piety, and action in the world; that the temptation of professionals is to refine our understanding of Jesus and Paul rather than to obey them; that being a great theologian is not the equivalent of being a good Christian; and that

---

1. Paul Holmer, *The Grammar of Faith* (New York: Harper and Row, 1978).
2. Holmer, 9, 12.

genuine theology is a correct speaking about and worship of God and not a substitute for prayer, worship, and praise.

I agree also that the meaning of Scripture is found not above or behind the text but in it; that the Bible has a distinctive perspective; that theology is not to be a way of discovering nonbiblical meanings for biblical representations; that it is not some extraneous neutral metaphysical system that makes the Bible intelligible; that the refutation of philosophical theism is not the demolition of Christianity; that the task of theology is not to be God's revelation but to help people to believe in God; that the working language of Christian faith already exists in Scripture and need not be invented by modern philosophers; that we must return to scriptural ways of speaking about God, grace, and Jesus.

Finally, I agree that theology as a schematic imposition "has a subservient but crucial role in producing the consciousness of God;" that thought, worship, and obedience sustain each other; and that theological systems are subject to revision.[3]

But with all this in mind, I would like to offer a sketch of my own convictions about the doing of theology.

1. We begin at the wrong end, I believe, if we suggest that theology is something human beings produce and perform. *God* does theology, and we are to think after him his thoughts that are not our thoughts, and we are to emulate His ways that are not our ways. Unless the concept of God originates with God, rather than with us, all theology is a lost cause.

2. God's universal revelation was in place long before we were, and from our first conscious moments we did not and cannot escape it. Though fallen humankind may be on the run from God, every human being nonetheless has a theology, shoddy though it be. Theology is implicit not only in a devout prayer, but also in a profane Gentile's hushed "Goddam" and in an aggrieved Jew's outburst "Jesus Christ."

3. The outside world leaves its imprint upon our theologizing through its theologizing—the household idols of the family, the street theology of friends, and the religious dialogue of the larger community. There is for us no culture-free theology. All human theologizing is by culture-specific persons living in definite historical contexts and speaking particular languages to culture-environed persons. Rival religious doctrines and practices attest that theology is extensively influenced by its cultural horizons.

4. The crucial question for Western civilization and for world history is whether all theology is culture derived or whether amid the multiform

3. Holmer, 146.

theologies one at least has its basis in transcendent divine revelation. Does the historical and contextual involvement of theology require the acculturation of all theological propositions? Are any theological categories universally applicable? Modern academe, the intellectual guardian of culture, tends to reply negatively: no theology is cross-culturally valid; all is a product of culture. Biblical redemptive religion, by contrast, was born and nurtured in a conviction that the self- revealing God of covenant has "once-for-all" delivered a singular core theology.

5. We usually learn this Christian "good news" first from the church, comprised of believing parents or devout friends and townspeople who relay the great tradition worldwide and ongoingly manifest its vitalities.

6. Only the canonical text reaches around and behind that testimony. The Bible is the church's authoritative norm. It is remarkable that recent approaches notably move away from radical critics who find no revelatory truth and no real redemptive events in Scripture and reconnect the Bible once again with literal and historical elements. Professor Brevard Childs is right: "the canon of the Church is the most appropriate context from which to do Biblical Theology," even if he too much loosens the canon's linkage to inspired prophetic-apostolic autographs and to a scripturally given Word of God.[4] The Bible has come not from the church but through the church, and it is addressed to the church.

7. Yet all of us who now read that sacred text bring our presuppositions to it. For better or worse, we read from a Western, feminist, black, liberationist, or some other perspective. Are the interpretative lenses equally valid, equally valuable, equally justifiable? Are some lenses distortive, forcing a speculative mold upon what we read? Nobody has warned us more eloquently than Dr. Holmer that the besetting sin of theologians has been to propound extraneous metaphysical constructs through which they propose to impart "meaning" to Scripture and to give Christianity a new lease on life, instead of deferring to a definitive life and meaning that Scripture carries.

8. The prime goal of theology is the worship and service of God, and under God comes our love and service of humankind in the name of the risen Jesus. There is growing disavowal, and rightly so, of theology whose only interest is objective truth to be stored like "canned doctrine" only for future emergency use. Biblical theology is given within a context of divine covenant that addresses the community of faith and seeks the dynamic transformation of its life-styles and a new society. The Bible does not promote a pursuit of truth that does not include on its agenda also a pursuit of sinners and their salvation. God's revelation flares with

---

4. Brevard Childs, *Biblical Theology in Crisis* (Philadelphia: Westminster Press, 1970), 99.

personal and social relevance; it embraces an evangelical imperative for a lost world, a message for humanity estranged from God in its affection, thought. and deeds.

9. Scripture speaks first to *me* in the seething throng, not to society in general. It addresses *me* as a handicapped and disqualified contender in the human race, one whose own plight needs desperately to be rectified. God addresses *me* amid the global mass of four billion humans and serves His transcendent summons: "I made *you;* I died for *you;* I own *you.*" He points to Jesus Christ on Golgotha to indicate an escape from my resignation to an indifferent cosmos and an engulfing culture. The Creator-Redeemer confronts us not only for new birth but also for new creaturehood, for a new value system, a new society, and a new mission. God Himself stands watch over a developing personal-life story, not an experience dated like some paleontological fossil, but a life of ever-new prospects and possibilities. The Lord of life would live out in me daily and hourly the same intimate spiritual drama exemplified in Jesus of Nazareth on earth, whose dependence on the Father, obedience, and fullness of the Spirit we are to emulate.

10. Yet theology is not to be confined to Ivy League towers sealed off from the world. Theology should be done in empathic solidarity with the world for which Christ died. It must have an eye to the morally wicked and bankrupt, the spiritually lost, the centers of power and the destitute and oppressed, and even philosophers and theologians (in Jesus' day they were called scribes) who substitute the traditions of people for the revelation of Yahweh. It must dispute the prevalent notions of self-fulfillment and of creative individuality, which shun the evangelical call to new birth and eternal life as regressive and snub the pearl of great price for a Wellington diamond or other material value. It was that way in Graeco-Roman society, which sought the good life by rearranging its natural human propensities, and in our own recent past we too shared the fallacy.

The gospel speaks not only to the whole self, but to the whole world also, although it may not always say what theological ventriloquists vocalize. We need a missiological theology alert to all the frontiers of human need, alive to the vast world that God so incomparably loved in gifting His one and only Son, and abreast of the confused cultures and competing worldviews of our time. We must be doing theology not only for one continent whose sin is specially focused in material aggrandizement and sexual libertinism, but for a larger world that accommodates unmitigated famine and unrelieved destitution, copes with Islamic terrorism and Koranic or Soviet expansionism, and practices ancestor worship, polygamy and other evils. We need missiological theology for a global population that in the year 2000 may number half again what it is today with many struggling under authoritarian rule, and perhaps no more than 15 percent of that population identifiably Christian. We need missiological theology aware that, at this century's close, given present trends, fewer Christians may live on the northern half of our planet than in Africa, Asia, and Latin America. We need a missiological theology that is braced for the collapse of contemporary civilization while it races to outflank that prospect by the powerful proclamation of the gospel that enlists people of God for their distinctive role in the world. It will not matter one iota how contemporary our missiology is, if its center is not Jesus Christ the incarnate Logos and risen Lord, and if the substance of its message is not the biblical evangel.

11. For those of us who respect Scripture as the norm and verifying principle of legitimate theological affirmation, the appeal to reason can never imply the exaltation of the human mind as divine, the elevation of human reason as itself the source of divine revelation, or a plea for speculative metaphysics through which the Bible is thought to gain its meaning or credibility. What is at stake, rather, is the question whether God is the ultimate source and stipulator of truth, whether the forms of reason in human beings belong to the *imago Dei* (image of God) or are merely an evolutionary development, and whether divine revelation as biblically attested is propositional, that is, communicated in logically formed sentences.

None of this is a plea for Platonic rationalism, Hegelian idealism, or Brightmanian personalism. The laws of contradiction and of excluded middle were not invented by Aristotle but merely formulated by him. Philosophical efforts like those of Kant and Spencer to explain the forms of thought other than as divinely bestowed aptitudes soon fall victim to illogical alternatives. The ontological axiom of Christian theology is the existence of the God of the Bible, and the epistemological axiom is divine revelation. All the truths of revealed religion flow consistently from these first principles. Human reason is not the creative source of truth but is a divinely fashioned instrument for recognizing truth, nor is a demand for verification of theological claims inappropriate to Christian theology. The Christian verification principle is not inner faith or sense experience or moral effect or cultural consensus. It is revealed Scripture. The inspired Bible is the proximate and universally accessible statement of the cognitive content of divine revelation.

The truth of revelation can be cognitively known prior to conversion. An atheist or a moral profligate can know that Scripture teaches that Christ died for sinners even if he or she refuses to appropriate the benefits of Jesus' atonement. Human beings are culpable for their rejection of

God's revealed truth. If one must be converted before one can know divine truth, one could hardly be culpable for rejecting it.

I consider logical consistency a negative test of truth, but not a ground of faith. The Holy Spirit alone gives faith. What is logically contradictory cannot be true, or truth and error would be equivalencies. Logical consistency will invalidate spurious alternatives to revelation; it unmasks reasons that are adduced for unbelief to be in fact nothing but rationalizations. The logical consistency of a claim will protect the believer from a commitment to absurdities.

The proper task of theology is to exposit and elucidate the content of Scripture in an orderly way, and by presenting its teaching as an orderly whole to commend and reinforce the worship and service of God. Believers are to present themselves as a living sacrifice, "which," says Paul, "is your reasonable service" (Rom. 12:1, KJV). The New Testament speaks of the regenerate believer in terms of "the new man, which is renewed in knowledge after the image of Him that created him" (Col. 3:10, KJV), and exhorts the believer to "be renewed in the spirit of your mind, and . . . put on the new man, which after God is created in righteousness and true holiness" (Eph. 4:23-24, KJV).

The evangelical theologian must not, however, presume to shape a "theology of glory." His special temptation may be to forget that he too is culture-scarred, that evangelical theology lives by grace and not by works, that we run the risk of sketching God's autobiography as if it were our own. Only in glory will the devout theologian be vocationally redundant, for then all "shall I know even also as I am known" (1 Cor. 13:12, KJV).

The Pauline insistence that "For we know in part" (1 Cor. 13:9, KJV) serves as a protest against the emphasis that all human thought forms and affirmations are culture conditioned. If no transcultural truth exists, then we can say nothing whatever that is permanently and universally true—nothing at all, including this presumptive negation of transcultural truth. The fact that we live individually within a twentieth-century skin does not mean that we think and know only twentieth-century prejudices.

Christianity may not offer many revealed truths, but it does offer some—that circumstance, centering in the truth of God's incarnation in Christ, lifts Christianity head and shoulders above its contemporary rivals. It is part of the strength of biblical theism that it champions the centrality of the Logos in the Godhead and affirms the ontological significance of reason, that it rests on intelligible divine revelation and affirms the comprehensive unity of scriptural doctrine, and that it nurtures a rational faith rather than an experience that is antithetical to reason.

12. Never has it been more important than now to hear what Dr. Holmer says about the theological tendency to spin speculative theories aiming to provide a definitive meaning for the Bible in order to make Christianity more palatable to the world. Our generation has been plagued by a plethora of such proposals—existential (Rudolph Bultmann), existential-ontological (Paul Tillich), process philosophy (John Cobb), and future of God theology (Jurgen Moltmann). Like Mary Baker Eddy's *Science and Health with Key to the Scriptures*, they offer extraneous expositions intended to identify a meaning that will render Scripture relevant to modernity. Alfred North Whitehead at least had the candor to openly declare his process metaphysics an alternative to biblical theism, rather than projecting it as the ideal Christian conceptuality. The failure of process theory to accommodate convincingly the Christ of the New Testament should of itself have put Whitehead's successors on guard. The speculative "Bible-salvage" efforts that today offer the greatest temptation to evangelical theologians, as I see it, are those which focus on the material plight of mankind and warn us that Christianity can gain credibility only through a massive program of economic redistribution.

I am not here devaluing the very commendable role of Christian compassion in the world. The community of faith has through its global outreach to impoverished masses set an example of neighbor love that has motivated even secular society, however belatedly, to respond to human need on a grand scale. The fact that the secular initiatives are often frustrated by the lack of on-site mechanisms for final fulfillment tributes in its own way the operational effectiveness of the long-standing religious agencies.

Nor do I devalue the salt-light-leaven role of the Christian community in the political arena as it strives to identify public injustice, to improve inadequate legislation, and to promote sounder alternatives. Such efforts can only boomerang, of course, if the church as the new society does not incorporate and exemplify within her own body and structures the patterns she commends to the world. One of the sad misconceptions of our generation is that Christian imperatives are best written into history by media publicity for verbal ecclesiastical proclamations. Religious bureaucracies seem most prone to forget that the church is a globally dispersed vanguard scattered for mission, a male and female charismatic community filled and refilled by the Spirit, a new society maintaining its diverse gifts in outreach that evidences a liberated life-style. Theology must be done by all the people of God, and not just by a cluster of professional clergy who presume to speak to and for the church (all too often in one-liner politicoeconomic pronouncements and who readily view the church, apart from themselves, as a subordinate and supportive flock). Theology must engage, educate, and edify believers for their culture-engaging mission, one that reduces neither to mere secular political involvement nor to mere private individual rescue, but involves the self in society in a genuinely biblical way.

In contrast to churchly involvement in the world as an exemplary new society, much recent theology proposes a politicization of the church in order to salvage the world and, indeed, to salvage the church's credibility as well. This is especially the case in the theology of revolution, which so much relocates the meaning of Scripture outside the Bible that it reads Scripture through Marxist lenses, justifies violence, and considers revolution the historical frontier on which God is now acting redemptively. Revolution theology is poor economics and worse theology; or, better put, it is no theology at all, but the baptizing of an ideology.

Liberation theology differs, it is often stressed, because it justifies violence only as a last resort. This only temporarily postpones the social conflagration it precipitates. It too discusses social justice in terms of a hidden economic and political agenda that is not drawn from Scripture. Seldom does it question aspects of liberation for which modern humans struggle by asking whether all that is sought is legitimate or even an earthly possibility. Instead, all discontents are made to fuel indignation over the existing structures. What God is "doing in the world" is repeatedly equated with *ad hoc* positions that are largely socialist in nature.

The questions that are central for the Third World today were central already for Palestine in New Testament times—power and oppression, wealth and poverty, and if not white and nonwhite, then Jew and Gentile. I do not find in the New Testament the response characteristic of today's political theology, which has much more in common with radical Anabaptists and Marx than with Jesus and Paul. Dr. Holmer is right, "the political focus of Christian concepts is something altogether new and, on the face of it, quite questionable."[5]

Much as theology must be done through a sense of solidarity with the estranged and enslaved, we must justify its analysis of the human predicament and its counter proposals of freedom and justice and peace at the bar of biblical teaching. In the 1960s Jesus was heralded as a revolutionary and Christians were declared people of a revolutionary life-style. More careful exegesis and reflection have countered that Jesus was the nonviolent champion of a spiritual kingdom and that His primarily involvement was not in worldly political decisions and deeds. The besetting flaw of the political theologies is their encouragement of the

---

5. Holmer, 146.

notion that human felicity can be achieved through a reorganization of the material environment. The church's involvement with and for the poor and oppressed is not in debate. What is in debate is the conditioning of that involvement by the modern sociocultural context more than by Scripture.

The emphasis on *praxis* (daily practice) as the mark of Christian legitimacy has notable weaknesses. It has led to profound misunderstandings other than political theology. Some *praxis*-oriented theologians have insisted that the time has now come to live the Gospel and not to preach it. Not by one iota should we resist a call to do the truth (see 1 John 1:6). The notion that a cognitive orientation suspends doing the will of God (See Matt. 6:10, 7:21) inverts the biblical realities. The apostles are our exemplars in commending good works and our performance of them. Had even the keenly watchful Roman imperial guard watched the disciples day and night, it could not have inferred from their behavior the content of the apostolic *kerygma* (preaching): the once-for-all incarnation of the divine Logos, the resurrection of the crucified, sinless Messiah, and the gladly awaited return in power and glory of the Lord Jesus. These affirmations cannot be kept under wraps if one expects a recognition of Christian realities. Life-style is essential but not enough!

Not merely on its margins, but as an essential facet of the faith, Christian theology illumines the welcome prospect of a decisive climax of the historical drama of redemption, and of a glorious homecoming and reunion for the people of God. Eschatological verification will throughout the vast universe echo the news that believers are at home with God and that their minds and affections and wills rest in Him. Some theologies may presume to take us to nirvana or to reincarnation; biblical theology promises to escort us to the Father's house. Theology will be seen at last as that joyful pursuit which believers were made to enjoy forever in the unveiled personal presence of God. Christ who is the Logos incarnate, Christ the way to the Father's house, Christ the Truth and the Life as well, will also be the light of the eternal city where neither darkness nor defiance nor disaster encroaches. The final confirmation of whether a theology needs to be undone, or whether it has been done successfully, is whether it can even now bestow eternal life, that is, a life fit for eternity.

The question rightly arises, therefore, whether the apostle Paul or Jesus Himself did theology as *praxis* in the modern understanding of that term. To be sure, Proverbs 23:7 affirms that "as a man thinketh in his heart, so is he" (KJV). The theory that the truth is not "for the sake of" its application but "is" its consequences sounds more like John Dewey than Paul of Tarsus. Harvie M. Conn insists that teaching is not preliminary to practice; teaching is rather "the *use* of God's revelation" to meet needs. He concedes that Scripture does not equate sound teaching and godly living (see Titus 2:9), although one is necessary to the other.[6] Then is it not confusing to say that one does not "tell the truth" unless one tells it with love and piety?[7] What then is the "it" that one tells? And what happens to judicial testimony, which does not inquire into dispositions and motives?

13. Not every pattern of rationality offers criteria relevant to Scripture. Yet it is in respect to divine rationality and to revelation and reason that difficulties emerge. Theology should beware of making system and logical structure foundational. We should resist the view "that theological formulations are timeless or that theology's language must be a series of formulae." The meaning of the Bible is not to be perceived through a coherent whole to which the parts relate. True biblical faith is compatible with objective uncertainties that theories of biblical inspiration and inerrancy seem unable to banish. The religious concepts have inherent functional consequences and are mastered not by intellectual analysis but by practical appropriation.

The church's faithfulness to its theological inheritance and the task of confessional theology is a true test of its character—and its convictions. The sovereign Lord of the universe is the bridegroom of the church, and He will not leave Himself or His gospel without witnesses. The church will be judged, at least in part, on the basis of whether it contributed to the *doing* or the *undoing* of theology.

---

6. Harvie M. Conn, *Eternal Word and Changing Worlds* (Grand Rapids: Zondervan, 1984), 229.
7. Conn, 232.

# Narrative Theology: An Evangelical Appraisal

*Does the approach to Scripture merely as narrative really do justice to the evangelical orthodox view of the Bible as an authoritative, divinely inspired book? Does its notion of textual authority require or accommodate divine authority and inspiration in the historic evangelical sense?*

For two generations the hermeneutical problem has been pressingly urgent. This age is marked by a self-inflicted "hermeneutical crisis," and evangelicals cannot evade the great issues of the day. Modernism disowned miraculous theism as prescientific, rejected the authority and inspiration of the canonical Scriptures, and derailed the orthodox Christian understanding of the Bible. In its wake arose a multiplicity of hermeneutical theories which relocated religious authority in human experience, encounter, decision, psychic need, social criticism, and other referents. By its accommodation, immense differences of interpretation, modernist criticism nurtured exegetical relativism.

To cope with this hermeneutical crisis a member of alternatives have arisen. Notable among them is narrative theology, which focuses attention on the biblical text in a new way. Before the modernist impact, divine revelation was normatively identified with Scripture which, as a supernaturally inspired literary canon, conveyed propositional truths about God and His purposes and gives the meaning of divine redemptive acts. The sense of the revelation was to be found by grammatico-historical exegesis that aimed to recover as accurately as possible the intention of the inspired prophetic-apostolic writers.

The Enlightenment nurtured the notion that what can be said reliably about the supernatural differs from what the Bible teaches. It proposed to interpret Scripture without any presuppositions, thereby holding at bay all tendential exegesis. The assumption of assumptionless interpretation was highly debatable, and it soon became evident that all interpretation proceeded on presuppositions. The supposedly "neutral" historical criticism of the Enlightenment was in fact notably influenced by philosophical rationalism and speculative idealism. When the scientific method was subsequently enthroned as the supreme way of knowing, Scripture was divested of miracles and its essential content was diluted to universal moral truths. For a more trustworthy clue to religious factualities than the Bible offers historical critics sought primitive prebiblical documents on the premise that Scripture incorporates legends and myths that romanticize the Hebrew cult.

Today a schism over the nature of the Bible vexes the Judeo-Christian world. On one hand, a disintegrative stage has overtaken historical criticism because of the staggering diversity of its conclusions. A deep reaction is underway among formative scholars who reconnect Judeo-Christian concerns centrally with the Bible rather than with multiform higher critical theories. On the other hand, the secular view of history and knowledge is now so influentially pervasive that the present generation spontaneously accepts the critical mind-set. Except for evangelical Protestants and orthodox Catholics and Jews, most contemporaries simply resign themselves to humanistic assumptions about history, biblical history included. Existentialism and neoorthodox theologians divorce God from the realms of nature and history and consider miracle claims a matter of internal faith beyond either cognitive verification or disconfirmation. The assaults of criticism, however negative, are shrugged off as irrelevant to personal belief.

A variety of contemporary hermeneutical theories have arisen among mediating theists who have looked to factors outside the Bible to illumine the biblical heritage and whose striking differences from each other threaten to engulf Scripture in hermeneutical relativism. More recently some influential scholars have proposed narrative hermeneutics and canonical hermeneutics as constructive alternatives to these rival contemporary approaches. The newer options reject the higher critical dismemberment of the Bible into segments of differing historical value. Despite their own significant differences, the narrative and canonical approaches agree that the Bible should be taken as it stands and not partitioned and reconstructed in search of some primitive version of which we have only a prejudiced late reaction. The church has transmitted the Bible in its present canonical form, which Christians should value as the authoritative text. Instead of seeking clues to the essential meaning of Scripture in extraneous pre-biblical sources or in our internal experience, we should allow Scripture to illumine all history and experience. Scripture has its own integrity apart from the question of whether we can demonstrate the historical factuality of events to which it refers. The authority of the biblical text is independent of confirmation or disconfirmation by historical critics.

Champions of narrative hermeneutics emphasize that the techniques of literary analysis are more appropriate than those of historical criticism for understanding the Bible. Highly influential source of the narrative approach is the Yale scholar Hans Frei, whose seminal work *The Eclipse of Biblical Narrative* set the stage for subsequent discussion.[1] Narrative theology has diversified, however, into numerous hermeneutical types, as Gabriel Fackre attests.[2] Questions of precanonical sources and of historical investigation and factuality do not illumine textual meaning as significantly they, as do the shape and function of the biblical literature. The text would be as meaningful as Shakespeare's Macbeth is independently of the question whether Macbeth is a real historical person. The linguistic authority of Scripture "brackets" historical questions by focusing simply on the text and its articles of faith.

Emphasis on the Bible mainly as a literary construct can and does imply remarkably different assessments of its significance. To affirm storytelling as a central methodological motif that focuses on canonical literature as the vehicle of meaning does not automatically settle the question of whether it matters if its content is fiction or history. Some narrative theologians concentrate on story structure; some focus on story substance, determining whether it conveys morality or an alternative. Some view the Bible as a semantic myth whose meaning is found in existential new being. Others see it as an amalgam of legend, myth, factual data, and lofty spiritual sentiment. Some insist that only biography or autobiography can lay claim to historical validity. Some compare the Bible to a nineteenth- century realistic historical novel in which interaction with the social milieu brings characters to life. Others speak of the Bible as classic literature wherein the church's imagination can find imagery that can be creatively elaborated as the basis for theological reflection. Many disregard the theological function of the canon.

---

1. Hans Frei, *The Eclipse of Biblical Narrative* (Yale University Press, 1974).
2. Gabriel Fackre,"Narrative Theology: An Overview," *Interpretation* (October 1983), 340-352.

A more recently fashionable approach is political interpretation by which the meaning of the Bible is said to emerge only in social criticism. The Old Testament is made to model a sociopolitical struggle and this conflict is then usually stratified in a way that calls for Marxist alternatives. By contrast, Jane Schaberg offers a feminist interpretation in *The Illegitimacy of Jesus.*[3] The opening chapters of Matthew and Luke, she insists, are not about a supernatural conception without a human father, but are about an illegitimate pregnancy, and God's subsequent identification with a socially rejected woman and acceptance of her illegitimate babe into divine sonship.

Narrative theologians propose (and claim) to let the Bible speak on its own terms. Realistic narrative, they stress, conveys a surface meaning evident to all, and does not suspend meaning upon the perspective or response of the reader. The Bible is a unified narrative about God's redeeming work through Christ. By focusing on the text, narrative hermeneutics stresses the adequacy of human language to convey meaning, and hence its serviceability as a carrier of divine revelation. It emphasizes that the entire book is important to the meaning, and not just preferred sections as in nonevangelical criticism.

Hans Frei contends that the "history-likeness" of the gospel accounts seduced modern critics and precritical evangelicals into the belief that the gospel writers intended to give a reliable historical report. This misunderstanding, he says, led to the further assumption that the scriptural genre is that of a historical chronicle whose meaning lay in historical events. Apart from historical veracity there could be no meaning; only what historical investigation could accredit was relevant to belief. Modernism dispensed with the historical veracity of miracles and along with this any abiding significance of the related discourses for faith.

In some respects this representation glosses nuances that distinguish evangelicals from modernist critics. Evangelicals consider the Gospels not as mere historical chronicles but as a distinct genre that combines history and interpretation; moreover, they lean on inspired Scripture more than on historical research for assurance of past salvific acts. They insist, however, on the historical factuality of the divine redemptive acts, and they are confident that historical research will not disprove the factuality of redemptive history.

Frei's thesis is that "a realistic or history-like (though not necessarily historical) element is a feature . . . of many of the biblical narratives that

---

3. Jane Schaberg, *The Illegitimacy of Jesus: A Feminist Interpretation* (October 1983), 340-352.

went into the making of Christian belief."[4] In realistic narrative Frei emphasizes, "characters and individual persons in their internal depth or subjectivity as well as in their capacity as doers and sufferers of actions and events, are firmly and significantly set in the context of the external environment, natural but more particularly social."[5] The narrative content is not for this reason historical, Frei observes. He holds even historical writing at a distance from critical negation by emphasizing that modern historians are prone to discredit supernatural and miraculous elements. Much as that is the case, however, the comment leaps the relevant question of whether the professedly historical events of Scripture (supernatural or not) are in fact historical.

Frei contends that if exegesis is not to continue on a wrong course, the realistic quality of many scriptural representations requires a companion interpretative method which he calls "realistic reading." He forecasts a decline of interest in divine revelation as the central technical concept in history. To read the biblical accounts narratively, he says, is to set side the ultimacy of narrated occurrence as historical revelation. He outlines this method in *The Identity of Jesus Christ: The Hermeneutical Basis of Dogmatic Theology.*[6] He views much of the content of the Gospels, especially the accounts of Jesus' passion and resurrection, as realistic narrative.

Frei holds that scriptural narration is realistic, whether or not it includes miracles and whether or not the depicted action is factual, provided such action is "indispensable to the rendering of a particular character, divine or human, in a particular story."[7] The narrative form does not merely illustrate meaning, he holds, but constitutes it, contrary to modern biblical criticism which locates meaning outside the text. Frei emphasizes that the world depicted by biblical narrative need not be identified with the world as we perceive it, for Scripture depicts the only real world and its enduring spiritual significance. The Bible prods us to assess our experience in terms of the biblical world, instead of forcing and fitting the biblical narrative into another world on the assumption that alternatives that we construct actually constitute reality.

Brevard Childs finds this emphasis on narrative theology both helpful and disconcerting, helpful for "checking the abuses of a crude theory of historical referentiality" but "too limiting" if it restricts "the function of

---

4. Frei, *Eclipse*, 10.
5. Frei, *Eclipse*, 13.
6. Hans Frei, *The Identity of Jesus Christ: The Hermeneutical Basis of Dogmatic Theology* (Philadelphia: Fortress Press, 1967.
7. Frei, *The Identity of Jesus Christ: The Hermeneutical Basis of Dogmatic Theology*, 14.

the Bible to that of rendering an agent or an identity."[8] The prophets and apostles, he emphasizes, testify to "what God was doing in the world." Childs is critical of any theological method which speaks of the Bible as a type of literary or symbolic construct yet is unconstrained to engage in continuous exegesis of the Bible itself as the indispensable ground for all Christian theological reflection.

The term "story" is currently used of the Bible with an astonishingly meaning-span. Knowledgeable evangelicals, who have routinely sung gospel songs like "I Love to Tell the Story," are having to ask themselves whether their message in music now really communicates what they intend. James Barr depicts Israel's tradition as "story" rather than as "history," while Brevard Childs alertly asks whether as a comprehensive categorical referent the term "story" is "an adequate substitute."[9] In discussing the content of the Book of Kings, Childs thinks Frei's term "history-like narrative" needs to be informed by chronological elements, but hardly to the extent of constituting history in the modern understanding. Nonetheless, Childs thinks the term "story" may be the best designation, but "unless carefully qualified," he cautions, it "also runs the risk of losing important features which are essential to Israel's witness. . . . The use of chronology to render Israel's experience implies an element of historical particularity which strains the term 'story' almost as much as it does that of modern history."[10] On the other hand, Gabriel Fackre, who pursues a narrative interpretation of Christian doctrine (and titles his work *The Christian Story*) insists on the empty tomb and bodily resurrection of the crucified Jesus as occurring in our history and yet as lifting our history to a higher destiny.[11]

A lively debate is underway in some evangelical circles over whether narrative hermeneutics should be welcomed as an ally that is essentially orthodox. Some conservative scholars see a kinship between the emphasis of narrative proponents that the entire Book is important to the meaning and the orthodox emphasis on the authority and plenary inspiration of the whole scriptural text. The unity of Scripture, some expositors stress, presupposes a single author, God, who is present in Scripture and gives the text verbal authority.

Both Frei and Childs correlate the text with God's linguistic presence. They emphasize that historical events are not per se a medium of revelation, but function as such only in the verbal narrative of Scripture which

8. Brevard S. Childs, *Introduction to the Old Testament as Scripture* (Philadelphia: Fortress Press, 1979), 545.
9. Childs, *Introduction.*
10. Childs, *Introduction.*
11. Gabriel Fackre, *The Christian Story* (Grand Rapids: Eerdmans, 1978).

interprets the meaning of redemptive acts. Frei emphasizes that the narrative theologians' focus on the risen Jesus as the promised Savior precludes an identification of Jesus as mythical and logically entails belief that Jesus is living and risen. The argument proceeds from narrative, and logical, and factual implications of Jesus' role. No direct argument merely for the historical factuality of the resurrection is made vis-a-vis modern historical criticism, despite the fact that the New Testament itself affirms that historical disconfirmation of the resurrection would undermine the Christian faith.

By contrast with this emphasis on the scriptural communication of meaning, Paul Ricoeur relates the meaning of the biblical story to the interpreter's reaction to it. Could the insistence by some narrative exegetes on a scripturally given single meeting then be only a personal reaction conditioned by inner factors? Not all narrative theologians agree on what that single meaning is, and not all insist that any projected single scriptural meaning is unconditioned by the interpreter's presuppositions and perspectives.

Realistic novels often shape a new life-orientation for some persons by the power with which they force life concerns and issues upon readers. A noteworthy example is the enlistment as Zionists in the Israeli cause by numerous readers of Leon Uris's "historical novel," *Exodus*. Similarly, some critics emphasize, the Bible functions as a transforming power in the lives of Christians. Other exponents of narrative hermeneutics emphasize the disclosive power of metaphor in reflecting the "Wholly Other." Can metaphor convey objective truth unless it leans on nonmetaphorical language and sentences? Can scholars really establish the cognitive impact and knowledge claim of metaphors without relying on some concrete meaning which such figurative representations carry? Otherwise would not conflicting metaphors serve equally well? If no cognitive reason exists for employing one metaphor rather than another it is futile to attach knowledge claims to their "disclosive power."

If scriptural content is decisive, the canonical books incontrovertibly have, at their center, the crucified and risen Jesus and they make singular claims in His behalf. Erich Auerbach holds that the Bible exerts a tyrannical claim to truth that excludes all rival claims by placing the history of all humankind in the context of biblical destiny.[12] Scripture unfolds a worldview that lifts the reader above mere spectatorship to a captivating life-orientation so entrancing that personal beliefs emerge and rise above questions of historical factuality.

---

12. Erich Auerbach, *Mimesis: The Representation of Reality in Modern Literature*, tr. Willard Trask (Princeton: Princeton University Press, 1953).

Does this orientation approach the evangelical emphasis on the authority of the text? The evangelical belief in the divine redemptive acts does not depend on verification by historical criticism but rests on scriptural attestation. The Bible conveys the meaning of God's redemptive acts; since it is the divine salvific acts it interprets, the acts are indispensable presuppositions of that meaning. Or does the emphasis on a destiny-laden truth claim have more in common with David Kelsey's emphasis on the life-transforming function of Scripture in the believing community, than with historic evangelical formulations of its objective cognitive authority that vouchsafes and validates such personal dynamisms?[13]

Ecumenical theologian Mark Ellingsen lists as commitments common to narrative hermeneutics and confessional orthodoxy the emphasis on (1) the pursuit of a single, fixed textual meaning. Additionally, he birth overlapping assumptions concerning (2) the unity, verbal, and plenary inspiration of Scripture; and (3) an approach to factual accuracy and implications through a regard for the text rather than a bare interest in historical reality.[14] To arrive at such commonalities Ellingsen must select certain proponents of narrative hermeneutics and pass over others holding rival views. The narrative approach does not necessarily ensure a meaning content required by the hermeneutical self-understanding of the Bible and unrelated to the prejudices of the interpreter. There are numerous varieties of narrative hermeneutics and their proponents differ in important respects. Ellingsen concentrates on those who disavow certain modernist assumptions about Scripture and who in some respects at least espouse positions compatible with confessional or evangelical orthodoxy.

While orthodoxy does not suspend upon historical critical determination such biblical events as the exodus and the exile, or the virgin birth and bodily resurrection of Jesus, neither does it leave problematically in midair the doctrine that the Bible is an authoritative, plenarily inspired book, rendered divinely reliable in its autographic content and claims. Evangelical orthodoxy routinely affirms the objective inspiration and inerrancy of the prophetic-apostolic writings and their historical factuality, but seldom do even the most conservative champions of narrative theology insist on these views.

It will be well, then, to consider difficulties that narrative theology poses even in its most conservative forms:

---

13. David Kelsey, *The Uses of Scripture in Modern Theology* (Philadelphia: Fortress Press, 1975.)
14. Mark Ellingsen, "Should Philosophical Theories About History Divide Christ's Body?" *Evangelism* 3 (1985), 82-108).

1. The unity that narrative theology affirms of the Bible simply as a literary phenomenon invites scrutiny. Is the Bible unified narrative in form and/or content, and does God's literary presence specially explain Hebrew-Christian Scripture?

The theological message at the heart of the biblical literature, we are told, carries an impression of overarching unity due to God's literary presence. Yet Ellingsen remarks that by their attention to the writings narrative theologians are "inevitably led to an appreciation of how legitimate the theological variety in the Christian church is"[15] a supposed scriptural diversity that critical scholars often correlate with "the ecumenical perspective." Many biblical scholars contend, and rightly so I believe, that critics frequently overstate biblical diversity. Ellingsen insists that doctrinal diversity in the biblical narrative can be "integrated into a systematic whole" centering in God's redemption of humankind through Christ. Appeals to overarching motifs like creation-fall-redemption or alienation-reconciliation do not fit all the biblical books, nor does emphasis on God's literary presence distinguish one religious literature from another. Since it is compatible with every conceivable genre and context, it explains nothing specific about the unity of Judeo-Christian Scripture. Even so, God's literary presence is inconspicuous in the Book of Esther.

On what rational basis does narrative theology insist that the biblical narrative reflects a unified theme and orderly content? To this question canonical theology offers its own ready response: canonicity has occurred as an expression of this conviction and ongoingly implements it. Does narrative theology offer a credible alternative to classic Protestantism's emphasis on intelligible, divine revelation and the God's cognitive inspiration of chosen prophets, an emphasis that narrative theologians dilute or subordinate?

Moreover, not all of Scripture falls into the narrative genre. Consequently narrative theology must itself distinguish and account for large non narrative portions of the Bible, including the wisdom literature and letters. Frei concedes that "obviously the Psalms, Proverbs, Job and the Pauline epistles are not realistic narratives" and in some respects he exempts the Synoptics and John's Gospel also.[16] Narrative theologians tend to regard such nonnarrative segments as commentaries on the canopy theme of God's grace. The distinction indicates that categorization of the Bible as narrative oversimplifies the unity of Scripture. Is there no

---

15. Mark Ellingsen, *Doctrine and Word: Theology in the Pulpit* (Atlanta: John Knox Press, 1983), xi.
16. Hans Frei, *The Eclipse of Biblical Narrative*, 15ff.

commentary in the narrative portions? Do commentary sections alone carry the meaning? Is the Book of Esther self-evidently an exposition of divine grace? Evangelicals insist that authorial intention and grammatico-historical interpretation do not exclude a single divine Author or a single sense that permeates the diverse genres and constitutes an undergirding and overarching unity. They do so, however, on the premise that the Bible is a singularly inspired book.

The unity of Scripture has become an issue that increasingly puts narrative theologians at odds with each other. Against recent historical criticism that postulates underlying sources that editors shaped into a comprehensive unity, narrative theologians insist on the literary harmony of the whole. Some narrative theologians still espouse the validity of historical reconstruction, whether involving source or redaction criticism, and insist only that the final narrative be read as a comprehensive "realistic" unity. Donald A. Carson surfaces the flaw in such accommodation. The historical reconstruction of earlier sources is supported on the ground of a literary analysis of biblical documents that supposedly requires diverse contributory sources, whereas the narrative approach assumes the integrity of the scriptural story. To neglect the latter in contending for the former is circular. In Carson's words, "Any approach that takes the text as a *finished literary product* and analyzes it on that basis calls in question the legitimacy of the claims that layers of tradition can be peeled off the gospel in order to lay bare the history of the community." In short, if the text is judged to be a comprehensive unity, "what right do we have to say the same evidence testifies to *dis*unity, seams, disparate sources and the like?"[17] Debate notably widens among narrative theologians who would give priority to source or redaction criticism and those who leap over documentary reconstruction in the interest of comprehensive textual unity.

2. By focusing on the meaning of the divine acts, Scripture does indeed carry an independent testimony to the factuality of the redemptive acts for faith. Ellingsen therefore commends narrative theology because "it enables Christians to deal with the challenges to Scripture's credibility posed by historical criticism. When we view Scripture as literature," he observes, "Scripture's integrity cannot rightly be called into question by historical research any more than Macbeth's integrity and meaning are called into question if there were no historical Macbeth."[18] The matter can hardly be left there. We must respond with an unqualified "no" when Ellingsen asks if narrative hermeneutics affirm what con-

---

17. Donald A. Carson, review of *Anatomy of the Fourth Gospel* by R. Allen Culpepper, *Trinity Journal* 4 (1989), 122-126.
18. Ellingsen, *Doctrine and Word.*

fessional orthodoxy does when the current theory accepts the literary authority of the narrative and embraces appropriate factual implications of the text independently of historical criticism. Unless the historical data are assimilated not only to faith but also to the very history that historians probe, the narrative exerts no claim to historical factuality. What is here at stake is not simply the question whether Jonah might be a short story, or whether the parable form popularized by Jesus may not apply to a somewhat wider range of biblical data. The notion that the narrative simply as narrative adequately nurtures faith independently of all objective historical concerns sponsors a split in the relationships of faith to reason and to history that would in principle encourage skepticism and cloud historical referents in obscurity.

It may be true that questions of authorship and of relationships to general history do not conspicuously obtrude when the biblical narrative is read as a whole, although they hold a more prominent place than many narrative theologians imply. The scriptural narrative is not content to reduce questions of authorship and relationships to universal history to second order questions. While these identifications may be objectionable to many contemporary critics, the fact remains that Old Testament prophets, Jesus of Nazareth, and New Testament apostles all connect the ancient Hebrew writings with now traditional authorships. The events of the birth of Jesus, His crucifixion, and His resurrection are all related to world history. Surely the New Testament does not present the resurrection of the crucified Jesus without explicit historical claims to which it attaches first-order importance (1 Cor. 15:3- 8,17).

Representations of biblical history by many narrative theologians leave one with the uneasy sense that their commendable reservations about the historical method are correlated with a view that important aspects of biblical history belong to a different historical category than the history that contemporary historians investigate. Biblical history indeed bulks large in redemptive acts, that is, in special deeds in which God is active for human salvation. Insofar as such acts are held to be historical, must they not fall into the same category of history that legitimately concerns contemporary historical investigation? The narrative indeed gives the meaning of the acts which, as interpreted, elicit saving faith. The Bible thus provides a line to historical redemptive acts independently of historical critical investigation. Those who relied on the witness of Scripture to the exodus and exile, and to the incarnation, crucifixion, and resurrection of Christ, did so in past centuries on the basis of reliable testimony that were in no way inferior to later appeals to historical investigation. Historical method is correlated with arbitrary assumptions when it rules out past events because we cannot duplicate them in our own time, and in the case of miracles it is doubly so since questions about the supernatural fall outside the method's competence. The biblical redemptive acts are not established as historical only if historical method confirms them, nor discredited if it does not do so, for empirical investigation is always incomplete and its verdicts subject to revision. If reading the biblical accounts narratively requires setting aside narrated occurrences as historical revelation, the sense of the accounts is strikingly diluted, although their ultimacy as historical revelation is rightly questioned. Evangelism theism insists that God reveals Himself in external history and nature, and supremely in redemptive history, although human's predicaments in sin lock them up to the biblical revelation for the authentic meaning of the redemptive acts.

The revelation/history/Scripture tensions will be illuminated if one contrasts Frei's *The Eclipse of Biblical Narrative* with G. Ernest Wright's *God Who Acts*.[19] Wright insisted that an objective, divine revelation was conveyed not in the Bible but rather in external, historical redemptive events that the prophets and apostles devoutly, but fallibly, interpret in Scripture. Narrative theologians, by contrast, hold that the revelation is conveyed in and through Scripture, which, however, they categorize as realistic narrative that has a loose and unsure connection with historical actuality. While the two approaches differ radically over whether external history or scriptural narrative is the carrier of revelation, they agree in disjoining revelatory redemptive acts and revelatory Scripture, contrary to the biblical witness and the representations of evangelical orthodoxy. The disjunction of revelatory acts and "revelatory" Scripture yields, from the evangelical standpoint, more distortive consequences in the narrative theology approach, since it is epistemologically more destructive of the orthodox heritage. The proponents of historical revelation at least emphasized that a skillful methodology would uncover an objective, transcendent, divine revelation, even if confined to historical events or acts. Narrative theologians do distinguish truth from an historic revelation objectively given in external acts and from a propositional revelation objectively given in Scripture. Instead, narrative theologians concentrate on "realistic reading" that draws the reader into a narrative world where a deep insight into reality is grasped through mental moves that the reader is constrained to make.

Under the influence of the realistic narrative school even some conservative scholars are now inclined to hold on literary and hermeneutical grounds that historical actuality should be considered unnecessary to the interpretation of any narrative literature. Although, unlike Frei, they

---

19. G. Ernest Wright, *God Who Acts* (Garden City, NJ: Doubleday, 1952).

hold that biblical narrative can convey accurate historical data, such data is said to be in no way relevant to a proper understanding of the text. Here the loose narrative theology connection between text and historical actuality gives way to a fixed disinterest in the text's original reference to a particular historical context, under the misimpression that thereby one best promotes the final authority of the written text.

Ellingsen contends that the lack of a more explicit emphasis on historical factuality by narrative theologians is due to the erosive impact of historical critical theory. A prior philosophical-methodological verdict is decisive, he notes, for narrative theology which defers to the prevalent historical- critical mood and for confessional orthodoxy which resists it. If one suspends the validity of the biblical witness upon confirmation by the historical method he frustrates a vital commitment to the historical trustworthiness of Scripture. Ellingsen asks whether a basis of ecumenical unity may not exist nonetheless in the narrative hermeneutical affirmation of comprehensive biblical authority while inerrancy and scientific-historical accuracy are demoted to second-order concerns.

The counterquestion is whether faith elicited by the biblical narrative as narrative theologians encourage it involves an epistemic split, one that allegedly would retain salvific efficacy even if historical investigation were to discredit the empty tomb and Jesus' bodily resurrection? While most narrative theologians refuse to say that Christian faith produced the resurrection, it is difficult to find a categorical statement that if Christ's body disintegrated in the tomb Christian faith would be impaired.

The narrative approach unacceptably minimizes Luke's expressed concern (Luke 1:1-4) for historically reliable sources and Paul's affirmation that our faith is vain unless Christ arose factually from the dead (1 Cor. 15:17). Narrative hermeneutics embrace uncertainty over historicity. The primary interest of Christian interpretation need not be and is not historiography. A narrative-dramatic approach involving kerygmatic creativity is so open to realistic theological fiction that it readily obscures historical fact and clouds the foundations of a stable faith. The Christian gospel is inseparably dependent upon God's self- revelation and soteric sacrifice within the historical space-time continuum, and it is incumbent on those who claim that narrative story and history are not incompatible to clarify which historical specifics are nonnegotiable.

3. Narrative hermeneutics removes from the interpretative process any text-transcendent referent and clouds the narrative's relationship to a divine reality not exhausted by literary presence. For Calvin the distinctiveness of Scripture lay not in a certain literary form or style but above all else in the fact that the transcendent God Himself is speaking

to us in His Word. Hence narrative exegesis is misguided if it leaves the divine authority of its message and its revelatory identity and fails over and above literary affirmation to indicate an adequate test of truth as problematical .

Without an Archimedian lever that lifts us above the narrative, one may bask day and night in the literary affirmation of an incarnation that had eyewitnesses and insist that John the beloved would have argued even to a historian that the tomb was empty; yet simply on that basis one would not necessarily rise above dramatic literary depiction. It takes more than strenuous assertion to establish historical factuality and objective truth. Literary concentration on the risen Jesus by itself does not logically entail belief that He is alive and risen, nor does it preclude an identification of the risen Lord as mythical. Bultmann is evidence that the entire literary presentation can be welcomed as a semantic myth, wrongly convinced as he is that world history admits of no resurrection from the dead. To turn the flank of destructive criticism requires an articulate view of revelation and reason and of revelation and history, and a public test of truth.

4. Does the approach to Scripture merely as narrative really do justice to the evangelical orthodox view of the Bible as an authoritative, divinely inspired Book? Does its notion of textual authority require or accommodate divine authority and inspiration in the historic evangelical sense?

Ellingsen concedes that neither narrative hermeneutics nor canonical hermeneutics employs such terms as "verbal inspiration" and "inerrancy." Neither are these precise terms found in Christian theology prior to the modern debate over Scripture. Not even the Protestant Reformers used them. Are they therefore dispensable conceptualizations? Or are they the best terms available for making imperative distinctions in the modern conflict over religious epistemology? The incursion of the Enlightenment provoked Christians to employ new constructs to reflect and confess the Church's faith in line with what Scripture said and implied about itself. These formulations are in principle replaceable if better ones are available to express what the Bible states about its nature and authority. Evangelical orthodoxy insists that all proposed alternatives to the concepts of "verbal inspiration" and "inerrancy" are less than adequate. For narrative theology the Scriptures function infallibly in the Christian language game; they are inerrant in the sense that Scripture is received by the Christian community with all confidence that it can never deceive the community or lead it away from the Gospel and truth. Does this fully imply what evangelicals intend when they affirm scriptural inerrancy, in brief, that all Scripture is God-breathed, however diverse its human agents and their literary genres, and that in view of divine inspiration the autographs are errorless?

Narrative theologians reduce biblical historicity and inerrancy to second-order questions; historical reliability is not a basic exegetical premise, nor is biblical inerrancy. Since narrative hermeneutics focus upon the received text, questions of what lies behind the text—such as its authorship and its historical referentiality—are bracketed. These questions, it is said, are not forefront concerns for the believer living in the biblical world.

Evangelical theology roots the authority of Scripture in its divine inspiration and holds that the Bible is inerrant because it is divinely inspired. Does narrative theology understand by inspiration not the objective inspiredness of the canonical text, but rather only its "inspiringness," that is, its capacity to stimulate a faith-commitment in the reader?

If we speak of inerrant verbal inspiration simply in the literary context of narrative theology, we should be aware that Bultmannian scholars can assess the narrative as an "inerrant" myth whose meaning is anthropological-existential rather than theological, while others may view it, as does Gabriel Fackre, as a story in which the historical resurrection of the crucified Jesus is an indispensable datum. Robert H. Gundry sponsors the notion that the Gospel of Matthew is inerrantly inspired, yet catalogs much of its content under the literary genre of midrash.[20] The notion that history is not the main biblical interest need not promote a clarification of theological motifs, but it can become a pretext for escaping lucid discussion of the relationship between literary form and historical fact, between genre and historical setting.

Whatever its differences from evangelical orthodoxy, narrative theology reaffirms that the Bible persists as a harmonious unity towering above cultural and historical differences, that historical criticism has not invalidated the relevance of Scripture, and that the biblical world spanning creation to consummation is the real world wherein humankind inescapably lives. It also reaffirms that Scripture's depiction of life is challenging and compelling; that the reconciliation of humankind remains a crucial theological enterprise, and that affirmation of Jesus as the indispensable Savior remains on the human agenda as an imperative decision.

In contrast to the *canonical*-story approach that focuses exclusively on the biblical message and meaning, and to the *life*-story approach that primarily illumines personal experience, Gabriel Fackre champions a *com-*

---

20. Robert H. Gundry, *Matthew: A Commentary on His Literary and Theological Art* (Grand Rapids: Eerdmans, 1972).

*munity*-story approach that allows larger scope to tradition. Interest in the Christian "community story" in order to recover the essential tradition by a literary route (Scripture in particular), Fackre stresses, has a long history antecedent to recent emphasis on narrative theology. In Scripture a community of faith tells the God story mirrored by particular sources and reflecting distinctive life-experiences. The essential tradition is constituted by a community consensus that reads its own history in the light of transhistorical vision. Fackre does not stop there. Most proponents of narrative theology, he remarks, are more concerned with method than with theological content. Not only is "not much said about doctrine" but many question the adequacy of "the assertional language of traditional dogmatics."[21] By contrast Fackre emphasizes that the community narrative turns on a truth-claim, "the decisive singularity of the Christ event."

Fackre holds that the loss of the authority of Scripture is a key to the deterioration of much contemporary theology, and he proposes to reassert the primacy of Scripture in systematic theology and in the life of the church. Significantly, he holds that scriptural centrality is grounded in and warranted by a doctrine of revelation that entails biblical inspiration and consequently the trustworthiness of prophetic-apostolic testimony. Scriptural trustworthiness attaches itself to the authorial intention of the biblical texts and implies a unity of Scripture that invites use of the analogy of faith in its interpretation.

Whereas Hans Frei diverts attention from revelation, Fackre by contrast not only connects the identity of the Christian faith with the rubric of authority, but also expressly connects its veracity with revelation. Divine revelation is the "underside" of biblical theology, Fackre affirms. Revelation is grounded in the history of God's reconciling acts but is not exhausted by them. The events are attested and interpreted by inspired writers. "The process of revelation includes a reliable account of the definitive events in the biblical narrative, including the trustworthy interpretation of those events."[22]

The ultimate source of theological content is the Bible (apocryphal material is merely "edifying"). The Bible's authority, Fackre says, concerns only "the Gospel *substance*" and hence God's purpose and work centering in the life, death, and resurrection of Jesus Christ, but not inerrancy pertaining to "the processes and patterns of cosmic and human life."[23] The Bible is not only the source but the standard of Christian the-

---

21. Gabriel Fackre, "Narrative Theology: An Overview", *Interpretation*.
22. Gabriel Fackre, "The Uses of Scripture in My Work in Systematics", *The Use of the Bible in Theology*, ed. Robert K. Johnston (Atlanta: John Knox Press, 1983), 214.
23. Gabriel Fackre, "The Uses of Scripture in My Work in Systematics", *The Use of the Bible in Theology*, ed. Robert K. Johnston (Atlanta: John Knox Press, 1983), 214.

ology, and to this norm all theology is ultimately answerable. Apostolicity was the criterion for inclusion of the canonical books, which are "a reliable transmission of original apostolic testimony."[24]

Fackre relies on the metaphors of "vision" and "word" as specially powerful to communicate the Christian story. He holds that because of contemporary humankind's struggles, the motif of liberation and reconciliation supplies the most dramatic plot for the story's unfolding. Some critics note, however, that while the redemption and reconciliation theme is scriptural, the biblical context of creation and restoration is actually more comprehensive. The liberation motif, as Fackre says, specially accommodates "a Bible read from within the struggles for freedom and peace and in identification with the poor and the oppressed."[25] Its principle of selection and interpretation may also accommodate a restrictive framework, although Fackre holds that the Holy Spirit uses culture contexts to render patent what is latent and normative in the biblical text. Fackre does not, however, minimize either creation or revelation. At the same time, he emphasizes the universality of God's covenant. Fackre relates the world religions to a breakthrough of light and considers universal salvation a distinct possibility, but conditions it solely on special biblical revelation and redemption.

Fackre himself asks, "can 'storytelling' as a mode of theological discourse do justice to the truths claims of Christian faith?"[26] He assures us that "the truth conveyed is inseparable from the story form that comes to us" and that "the story form takes its shape from biblical faith, and we in turn are found by that faith only as we are engaged by its narrative form."[27] When one recalls the conflict between modernism and evangelical orthodoxy over whether or not Christianity is a "book religion", this verdict coalesces in important ways with the confessional insistence that biblical religion centrally involves an inscripturated Word of God. What remains to be developed more fully and precisely is the range of historical factuality and objective metaphysical truth which Fackre holds to underlie the religious faith that shapes the story form that thus engages us. A further elaboration of the doctrines of authority and revelation in connection with the biblical narrative (which Fackre considers fallible both in historical and theological affirmations) is also needed.

The texts to which theology turns to articulate its doctrines make cognitive truth claims, Fackre stresses. They embody assertions about the way things really are, in time and eternity. He prefers not to speak of

---

24. Gabriel Fackre, *The Christian Story*, 20.
25. Gabriel Fackre, *The Christian Story*, 39.
26. Gabriel Fackre, *The Christian Story*, 26.
27. Gabriel Fackre, *The Christian Story*, 8.

propositional revelation, but of textual "affirmations" (to designate a special kind of proposition which engages affect and entails commitment). The "affirmations" of Scripture involve life-and-death decision and commitment, not spectator propositions of formal logic.[28] This is a curious contrast, since logical consistency can be a life-or-death matter, and without it intelligible decision vanishes. That the prepositional revelation of Scripture seeks commitment of the whole self is not in dispute. What recent theology obscures is that the proximate goal of revelation is to convey divinely disclosed truths about God and His purposes that urgently require personal response and commitment.

Fackre connects the biblical affirmations especially with the biblical metastory, that is, with the theme of redemption and reconciliation, which he considers "the *substance* of the scriptural *source.*"[29] The revealed story, he stresses, embraces the central verities of the Christian faith—the triunity of God, the deity of Christ, justification by grace through faith, and the atoning work of Christ in His birth, life, death, and resurrection. Inspiration, says Fackre, is verbal and plenary, and as such embraces the entire historical drama and its developing plot of characters and events moving toward a climactic resolution. The Bible's literary genre of story, he cautions, must allow imagination and symbol more scope in Scripture than biblical studies and Scripture usually accommodate. Fackre connects the soteric use of Scripture with the internal witness of the Holy Spirit. Revelation channels not only into prophetic-apostolic inspiration, but into illumination that shapes the Christian community's central message through successive generations and enriches a revered tradition that is revisable but not reversible.[30]This accommodates a role in the Christian community for reliable ecclesiastical tradition in the interpretation of Scripture that most evangelicals resist, especially a consensus of critical scholarship. The Reformers held that medieval Rome had in fact reversed the normative biblical tradition of justification by faith alone and of *sola Scriptura* (scripture alone). Brevard Childs holds that modern historical criticism reversed normative priorities by subordinating the canonical Scriptures to supposedly more reliable prebiblical sources. Fackre challenges the claim of historical criticism to hegemony in its interpretation of the texts. Is his epistemology immune, however, to critical miscarriage and to perversion of tradition?

---

28. Fackre, "The Uses of Scripture", 216.
29. Fackre, "The Uses of Scripture", 216ff.
30. Fackre, "The Uses of Scripture", 223.

For all Fackre's deference to verbal-plenary inspiration, he connects Scripture's reliability only with the biblical report and interpretation of salvific events. Apart from this revelation and inspiration are correlated with fallible human insight. This implies a psychological and cognitive split that is avoided by the doctrine of pervasive inerrancy and by the doctrine of pervasive errancy. The appeal to a "Christological lens" for viewing Scripture did not for the Reformers imply the unreliability of other biblical teaching, whereas the introduction of fallibility in theological and other biblical content connects the affirmational teaching of Scripture with a call to commitment that embraces even error. The notion that the noninerrancy of Scripture protects the identity and centrality of Christ, and the doctrines of biblical authority and inspiration, better than does the full reliability of Scripture, is illogical.

Narrative theology in the broader sense offers us a hermeneutical theory that affirms the comprehensive authority of Scripture yet suspends the question of its ontological truth and historical factuality. It is a theory that affirms that the unity of Scripture has a canon conveyed by the church, yet not necessarily exclusive of pseudepigraphical authorships; a theory that insists on the plenary-verbal integrity of the story form, yet concedes that large portions of the Bible do not fit that form. Although the theory welcomes the whole received tradition as inviolable, it offers no objective criterion for distinguishing truth from error and fact from fiction, as is apparent from rival schools identified with narrative exegesis. While narrative hermeneutics view the Bible as an inspired book, it does not in its popular forms consider divine inspiration the ground of its authority nor as constituting a wholly reliable source of doctrine. It eclipses transcendent divine authority and revelatory truth that initially spurred immense interest in scriptural exegesis.

The narrative approach therefore seems not fully befitting the historic Christian faith, nor fully serviceable to the need for an intellectually compelling argument with modernity. Readers may and often do find in the biblical narrative a means of grace that stirs the spirit. They find claims and evidences which involve a supernatural resolution of the human dilemma and are centered supremely in the resurrection of the crucified Jesus. Neither a transcendent revelatory content nor objective scriptural inspiration lends supernatural sanction to the biblical drama when read on narrative premises. One discerns here an enchantment with the affective, a flight from history to the a "story" that enjoins no universal truth claims, a reflection of the revolt against reason, a reliance on "symbolic truth" and imagination, and an interest in earthly theater more than in revealed theology. In its representations of the Christian faith it too much ignores intellectual analysis to maintain an assured connection of confessional premises with objective reality and valid truth.

Scholars who employ narrative exegesis for theological ends selectively engage its hermeneutical presuppositions. They supplement its use, moreover, by advancing doctrinal considerations initially derived from reading the Bible on traditional orthodox premises, rather than from a consistent application of the narrative approach. The unresolved dilemma facing narrative theology is how the method itself, given its divorce from a truly authoritative text, can escape yielding the divergent and contradictory theological claims that its practitioners advance. Evangelicals dare not ignore the biblical narrative—nor deny its narrative form—but they cannot seek refuge in narrative theology.

# Part V
# Looking Forward, Looking Back

# Coming Home
# and Saying Good-bye

*We know that in His sovereign providence God can enable us to penetrate the world with a living witness to the truth and power of evangelical theism. In that awesome task I wish you Godspeed. May you share as we did in the splendor of a spiritual sunrise, and not only in the sad defection of a secular society.*

I have come home this morning to say good-bye. Since leaving Wheaton and Chicago with college and seminary degrees, I have shared in the beginnings of Fuller Seminary, *Christianity Today* magazine, the Institute for Advanced Christian Studies, and the first great World Congress on Evangelism held in Berlin. Now it is time to come home and say good-bye.

When Christ won my heart in 1933 I was already a Long Island editor and suburban reporter for New York dailies. My immediate superior deleted from all copy any mention of God. The world of religion lay snugly in the lap of modernism. It was not the gospel of a crucified and risen Redeemer but rather the social gospel of a coming Marxist millennium that prevailed in Protestant pulpits and publications. Modernism dominated the denominational colleges and seminaries, and it preempted public service radio time. So evangelical participation was excluded.

You must not, however, misjudge the modernist. They thought they were rescuing Christianity from fundamentalist and evangelical obscurantism. Modernists said many good things about Jesus and the Bible: Jesus towers higher than founders of the other world religions, they said, and the Bible surpasses other books in spiritual wisdom. Yet the essence of modernism was its regard for the scientific method as the one reliable rest of truth. Empirical verification requires that an event occur at least twice before one can be sure it has occurred once. In short, modernism presupposed the absolute uniformity of nature; it ruled out once-for-all miracles in advance.

Whatever tribute modernism paid to the Bible and to Jesus of Nazareth was hedged by a governing conviction that the miracles at the heart of evangelical theism and creedal Christianity are mythical. Evangelical orthodoxy, or biblical theism was deplored as prescientific, unscientific, and antiscientific. In this debate our Christian integrity was at stake, even the legitimacy of attending Wheaton College for liberal arts learning. We evangelicals were a lonely and beleaguered lot and much maligned. Some of that same hostility is emerging again today, despite the claim that 50 million Americans are born again. The present adversarial context is not modernism, but humanism or raw naturalism.

Then as now we were involved in a collision of worldviews. We hungered for truth that exhibited the credibility of Christian belief and that unmasked the weaknesses and even pretensions of competing views. We hated the exams with an unholy disdain, but we wrestled them. Ken Taylor, who would give us *The Living Bible*; Sam and Howard Moffett, who before its evangelistic explosion would return to Korea; Dayton Roberts, who before the charismatic awakening would return with Grace Strachan to Latin America; Harold Lindsell, who with Ken Taylor was on the Illinois state championship debate team; Eleanor Solteau, who became a medical missionary among the Arabs in Palestine, are examples of those who struggled with the Truth. There were others; the roster reads like an evangelical "Who's Who". Some are already with Christ in glory.

When I graduated from Wheaton in 1938, the national radio networks apportioned free public service time only to the mainstream religions. The Federal Council of Churches reserved Protestant programming for ecumenists, and opposed even the sale of network time to religious conservatives. That situation in part stimulated the formation of the National Association of Evangelicals in 1942. It soon had a service constituency of over ten million conservative Protestants. The evangelical resurgence was under way.

Five years later, in 1947, Dr. Wilbur Smith resigned from Moody Bible Institute, Dr. Everett Harrison from Dallas Seminary, and I from Northern Baptist Seminary, were to share in founding Fuller Theological Seminary, the first interdenominational seminary west of the Mississippi. We dedicated it to biblical theology, biblical ethics, biblical apologetics, and biblical evangelism. Had Harold John Ockenga of Park Street Church followed through on his commitment to come as resident president, rather than functioning in absentia, the fortunes not only of Fuller but of all American evangelicalism would have been notably different. Dr. Charles Fuller had promised to sponsor Ockenga on television for a one-year trial run and that, I think, would have changed the course of American televangelism.

Also in 1947 Billy Graham, who had been a Wheaton sophomore during my senior year, became headline news when his Los Angeles crusade attracted Hollywood participants, and the Hearst papers front-paged him coast to coast. Almost from the beginning Graham shocked the independent fundamentalists because he was determined to win converts in modernist churches and included ecumenists on the platform. That same year my *Uneasy Conscience of Modern Fundamentalism* was published. It lamented the withdrawal of fundamentalists from the sociocultural arena and urged them to sound the Christian claims in social affairs as well as in individual life. Soon it was followed by *Remaking the Modern Mind*, which was a declaration that the reigning philosophy had no legitimate claim to finality and a judgment in the context of the Christian world-life view. In 1956 *Christianity Today* was launched. It quickly outstripped the pretentiously named *Christian Century* which for a half century had vocalized the ecumenical left in theology, politics, and economics.

By 1960 those of us specially interested in the scholarly side of evangelical witness were holding serious discussions about a Christian university in a major metropolitan area, notably New York City, where students could get hands-on training in virtually every career choice. Mainly due to the lack of consensus on the part of prospective major donors the effort was abandoned and gave way to the more modest Institute of Advanced Christian Studies promotive of scholarly evangelical books. Others moved into the new evangelical opportunity.

In 1965 a fund-raising telethon by Marion G."Pat" Robertson launched the Christian Broadcasting Network, which gradually linked 190 stations in the U.S. and overseas by satellite. Oral Roberts, who had put healing evangelism on television a year earlier, opened Oral Roberts University in Tulsa in 1965.

In 1966, as a tenth anniversary project, *Christianity Today* sponsored our generation's first global evangelistic conclave, the World Congress on Evangelism in West Berlin; Graham was honorary chairman, and I was chairman. It was the father of Lausanne/74 and the grandfather of Manila/89, and it called for fidelity to the one God of justice and of justification.

Many of you in the last twenty years have shared in the excitement of and even participated in some of the events since then. In 1971 Jerry Falwell formed Liberty Baptist College in Lynchburg, which has become Liberty University with five thousand students. By the late 1970s Pat Robertson had established a full graduate university, now called Regent University, in Virginia Beach. Others of us meanwhile strove for a renewal of evangelical theology, which modernism, neoorthodoxy, and humanism had sidelined, and to that end I wrote my own six-volume work on *God, Revelation and Authority*, to which *Time* magazine in 1976 devoted a full page.

Also in 1976 *Newsweek's* cover story, "The Year of the Evangelical" appeared. It acknowledged that America's fifty million religious conservatives were the nation's fastest-growing spiritual force and noted that three presidential candidates in the 1976 race professed to be born again. This astonishing evangelical initiative surprised Harvey Cox and other gurus of the secular city, who expected a religionless society, and it surprised also the ecumenists whose mainline churches were being sidelined. In that same year Chuck Colson emerged from Watergate notoriety to found Prison Fellowship ministries, the most important humanitarian agency to appear since the founding of World Vision in the 1950s.

On almost every side, American fundamentalism by contrast was thought to be comatose and ready for early burial, despite its many day schools, impressive Sunday Schools, and some notably large churches. It was assumed by the ecumenical movement, by the mainstream evangelicals, and by the charismatics, that fundamentalism was doomed for two reasons: first, its commitment to second-degree separation—that is, separation from both the culture and from ecumenically related churches; and second, its hostility to the Billy Graham crusades because of Graham's inclusive sponsoring committees. Jerry Falwell rallied much of the fundamentalist independency to the importance of political confrontation, and in 1979, he founded the Moral Majority for a national crusade that addressed ethical and social issues and involved a legislative lobby.

All wings of the conservative religious thrust were now aggressively in motion—fundamentalists, evangelicals, charismatics—while ecumenical churches were losing prestige, numbers, and finances as their constituencies increasingly fell away. Then, a decade later, the charismatic evangelism calamities involving Jim Bakker, Oral Roberts, and Jimmy Swaggart, as well as a number of noncharismatic pastors and leaders occurred. In a single decade the secular city refocused its perception of the ecumenical movement and blunted its initiative. The secular media revived the specter of Elmer Gantry along with the old modernist prejudices and viewed evangelical orthodoxy in a context of psychological manipulation and financial exploitation.

You have much to forgive our generation for bequeathing to you this "bag of worms" with your evangelical heritage. You also inherit a worldwide evangelistic initiative, an unprecedented number of theological and commentary literature, improved Bible translations, evangelical colleges and seminaries crowded with students, multitudes of churches where the gospel is now preached, and an enlarging door to the political arena. I dare say also that substantive developments such as the 1989 Evangelical Affirmations conference enabled evangelicals to regain some of their stride, and that the recent pressures for financial integrity and accountability strengthened the movement overall.

In this somewhat murky firmament your own star is now rising. None of us who came before you from the halls of Wheaton was a C. S. Lewis, an Alexander Solzhenitsyn, a Nobel prize winner. Among you this morning may be a future Jonathan Salk, a Supreme Court justice like Sandra Day O'Connor, a president of one of the Big Ten universities, or a future Augustine to do battle with the intellectual Philistines of our time.

I must not mislead you, however, by an in-house perspective. The world spirit outside these walls is deepening its hostility to a supernatural faith. When Protestant modernism dominated into the 1930s, religious humanists who rejected the supernatural were a meager minority. Neoorthodoxy, paced by Karl Barth and Emil Brunner, put both modernism and humanism on the defensive by its summons to hear the transcendent Word of the self-revealing God. It left its mark even upon evangelical seminaries and religious colleges ready to compromise biblical authority. Yet in the great secular universities mediating scholars like Tillich and Barth and Brunner had little more impact than did consistent evangelicals. It was secular humanism that took the initiative in public education, in the mass media, and in the political realm: God was excluded from public significance, religion was assigned only an internal subjective importance, reality was reduced to impersonal processes and quantum events, all philosophical principles and moral imperatives were held to be culture relative, and all life was declared to be temporal, so that the cemetery becomes your final destiny and mine.

In today's cultural setting, therefore, the intellectual initiative is no less hostile to faith than was that which greeted us students of an earlier generation. Secular humanism is in fact moving downward rather than upward; in short, humanism is now losing its humanitarianism and channeling into raw naturalism. Midnight may soon overtake Western culture unless Judeo-Christian theism reverses the present convictional stance. As Chuck Colson warns, many churches already compromised by concessions may not survive the nightfall of the new Dark Ages.

We know that the world lies in the lap of the Evil One and that mere social Band-Aids will neither change it nor long preserve it. We know that our divine mandate is to preach the forgiveness of sins on the ground of Christ's atonement, and to proclaim to the world the standards by which God will finally judge it. We know that the risen Jesus has life-transforming power to make obedient disciples out of a motley company of young converts like ourselves. We know that in His sovereign providence God can enable us to penetrate the world with a living witness to the truth and power of evangelical theism. In that awesome task I wish you Godspeed. May you share as we did in the splendor of a spiritual sunrise, and not only in the sad defection of a secular society. Our turning decade of the century needs a vanguard of future heroes with a special glow, the glow of royal purple. "For Christ and His Kingdom" is still a noble hallmark. Remember who your Ruler is. Don't forget His daily briefing and, above all else, hold His commands in honor.

Almost all my teachers are gone, or I would pay them public tribute. They labored for little of this world's goods, but they knew us by name and they wanted us above all else to serve God well and to honor our Wheaton heritage. You do not know who most of them were, or know many of us who studied hard under them, even as the next generation will remember too few of your present mentors and—amid the onrush of modernity—might all too soon forget some of you. You differ from us in one notable respect: this is your moment. The flaming light, the torch, is being passed to you. Don't let it slip or lose your stride.

So good-bye, until we meet again.

# *Christianity in a Troubled World*

*Not only is the world in dire trouble. It has been ever since humanity's fall into sin, but the West that Christianity long lifted from its pagan mires is today a part of that trouble. Churches—in America and elsewhere in the Anglo-Saxon world—are in real peril of being battered and stunned by the backlash of a secular milieu with which they are too intimately meshed.*

"In the world you will shall have trouble, but take heart, I have overcome the world." (John 16:33). Four words familiar to every beginning student of Greek should frame the way Christians understand their role in a fallen world: *kosmos, thlipsis, Christos,* and *tharsos*—in English: *word, trouble, Christ,* and *courage.* Our mission in the world is global: it is *in the world.* Its context is trouble—tribulation if you will. Its outcome is clear: Christ has overcome, He has overcome the world.

If there were any reason to doubt that world mission ought to be the mind-set of every evangelical Christian, John 16:33 dispels it. The disciples may have been preoccupied with Judea and Galilee, but Jesus speaks of them as *in the world:* "in the world, *you . . .* !" How far do your heart and will stretch beyond the borders of your community and of America, and beyond the Anglo-American West? Does your vision reach to Africa, Asia, and Australia also?

We are motivated in a mission to a world that God the Creator made and sustains. We sing "This is *my* Father's world" and well we may. Day after day it mirrors the Creator's glory, universally so, in general revelation, in nature and history and in the conscience and mind of man. Skewed though God's creation may now be, that deflection is neither the first word nor the last word to be said about history and the cosmos. We glory in God's sovereign rule over the universe, in His redemptive purpose in human affairs, in His covenant with Abraham and Moses and His incarnation in Jesus of Nazareth. We herald the achievements of Christian culture in the Middle Ages, the spiritual renewal wrought through the Protestant Reformers, the great nineteenth-century world missionary expansion, the present resurgence of evangelical orthodoxy in America, and the current awakening of Third World churches to their global missionary imperative. We anticipate further dramatic triumphs of Christian mission. Above all else we are assured that Christ's approaching second coming will decisively subdue evil and will inaugurate the consummatory victory of whatever is good and just. This *is our Father's world*; He had the first word and will have the last word as well. You and I are in it with a global mandate and mission.

The world obtrudes as a ghastly reality. One may even be inclined to shudder at the apostle John's reminder that "the whole world is under the control of the evil one" (1 John 5:19) and that we are not "to love the world or anything in the world" (2:15). Jesus himself cautioned that while "in the world" we are not to be "of it." We may sing that God's "got the whole world in His hands," but we recall also Luther's words about "the prince of darkness grim." We agree with Browning that "God's in his heaven," but we are far less sure that "all's right with the world."

The hideous specter of totalitarian tyranny still scars much of humanity, including mainland China and North Korea, not to mention nearby Cuba? Are we not aware of the tightrope that leaders in Eastern Europe and the former Soviet republics walk between reform and repudiation? Are we unaware of the ongoing tensions in China between the house churches and the Three Self patriotic movement amid the bloody resistance of mainland rulers to democratic change? For all its evident economic failure, socialism continues to snare developing countries.

The so-called Free World is in far deeper trouble than it thinks or admits, despite its positive self-evaluation mainly in economic and political terms. It is no secret that many of our political leaders, emphasizing as they do the superiority of the Free World, bristle at negative moral and spiritual judgments about the Anglo-American West. Of course we rightly extol the prized freedoms we enjoy; I myself serve on the Institute on Religion and Democracy which champions religious liberty and political self-determination in a global context of religious repression and political imposition. Nonetheless, we should also note and concede that the philosophical props for human rights are collapsing all around because humanity is severed from God and from divinely given duties. Human survival becomes trivialized because of confused secular notions of justice and peace and right and wrong. Exalted words like *life* and *love* are in definitional trouble. One vice after another—abortion, alcoholism, drugs, homosexuality—is considered only a matter of one's private business. The deviant behavior of a rebel minority increasingly burdens all of society with costs of many kinds that benefit an aberrant sector of society at the expense of others.

Radical Islam, which relies on violence to extend Koranic power, has struck terror into the heart of the West. Islam perceives itself as the foe both of Israeli claims to Palestinian sovereignty and the West's accommodation to a lascivious life-style. The great conflict of the next century, some social commentators believe, may well rage between Islam and the neopagan West, whose declension to secular humanism and beyond that to naked naturalism is increasingly likely to disown Christianity. Liberal Western intellectual elitism has no serious notion of what blasphemy is, and routinely takes the name of Christ in vain. It allows God no public importance, and tolerates Him only as a private option. It cheapens moral absolutes into pragmatic alternatives. Nobody should be surprised that even world religions long cataloged as pagan by Christian standards sense, in this vacuum of belief, a new missionary opportunity for themselves, and offer something presumably more satisfying to a generation snared by the lust for money, power, and sex.

"If one contemplates the life of the affluent societies of Europe and North America," writes Lesslie Newbigin, "marked as it is by growing violence, drug addiction, and all the signs of the loss of meaning and hope, it is hard to see any future except collapse."[1] Newbigin continues: "Certainly anyone whose beliefs are shaped by the Bible can hardly fail to hear the word of God's dreadful judgment pronounced over that part of our world that calls itself 'developed.' Christians who come from the old 'mission fields' to taste the life of the old 'Christendom' are more and more deeply struck, and wounded, by the contrast between the message they received from the early missionaries and the view of reality they now meet."

---

1. Lesslie Newbigin, "Mission in the 1990a: Two Views", *International Review of Missionary Research*, 13 (July 1983), 101.

Charles Colson writes of "a growing sense of stormclouds gathering on the horizon," of "the crisis . . . in the character of our culture."[2] The current crisis in Western culture, he notes, "presents the greatest threat to civilization since the barbarians invaded Rome." "The times . . . smell of sunset," he says. Colson writes not only of "encroaching darkness (that) casts its long shadows across every institution in our land," but worse yet, warns that "the new barbarians are already all around us, . . . in our families . . . classrooms . . . legislatures . . . courts, film studios and (even) our churches"—"new barbarians who know no higher law than self-interest, who see nothing to champion beyond their individualism, . . . celebrating their own nihilism (and), in effect, torching the very props of virtue."[3] "We live in a new dark age," he writes. "Having elevated the individual as the measure of all things, modern men and women are guided solely by their own dark passions."[4] "Perhaps the great nightfall will soon be upon us." Colson has said, in fact, that the secular tide has now so deeply invaded Christians and their churches that, if Western culture were to sink into oblivion, it is problematical whether the present evangelical churches would rise from the ashes phoenixlike in triumph.

I mention but one more commentator on the urgency of the times, though the list could be extended. In *After Virtue* Alisdair MacIntyre writes of "new dark ages" of moral decay already engulfing us.[5] He reminds us that, despite differences distinguishing the decline and fall of the Roman Empire from circumstances in our own day, there arose nonetheless a time in the context of the Roman imperium when Christians began thinking of alternative types of community. MacIntyre then urges us to consider new forms of society that by sustaining intellectual and moral life will preserve virtue into the future.

In summary, not only is the world in dire trouble, as it has been ever since humanity's fall into sin, but the West that Christianity long lifted from its pagan mires is today a part of that trouble. Churches—in America and elsewhere in the Anglo-Saxon world—are in real peril of being battered and stunned by the backlash of a secular milieu with which they are too intimately meshed.

It would fail the Gospels and the New Testament to equate the tribulation of which they speak simply with the social agonies of countries struggling for world survival, and to concern ourselves primarily with

2. Charles Colson, *Against the Night: Living in the New Dark Ages* (Ann Arbor, MI: Servant Books, 1989), 9.
3. Colson, 33.
4. Colson, 107ff.
5. Alisdair MacIntyre, *After Virtue* (Notre Dame: University of Notre Dame Press, 1981).

cultural perpetuation. In America where believers seldom have had to suffer persecution or torture or adversity for their faith in Christ, it is easy to generalize the notion of trouble and to speak of the mounting ailments of society. Guaranteed freedom of religious expression and subject to little suffering for faith other than the derision of assorted secular media rebels, American churchgoers do not easily grasp the suffering that Jesus and the apostles spoke of and endured. Such tribulation in the modern scene to reports of the harassed underground house churches of China and Russia, or converts from Islam threatened by family rejection, maiming, or even murder, or of courageous frontier missionaries among hidden peoples in remote and erstwhile closed countries, or of believers in communist lands who because of their faith lose access to university studies or forfeit any hope of vocational advancement. It is rather amid a theology of suffering and martyrdom, not where the luxury of a heretical theology of wealth and health often prevails (as in our land), that Christian workers routinely endure the tensions and trials biblically in view. Recent American Christianity, with its liberties and special privileges, has little in common with normative evangelical experience through the centuries; it is very much an historical exception.

Now, however, the situation even in the United States has begun to change. The influx of Two-Third-World refugees and immigrants with their diversity of faiths, and some of whose home countries have denied missionary opportunities to Christians abroad, are now our townspeople and neighbors. The theologically ignorant secular Western media publicize these Oriental faiths as enchanting frontier novelties. Even on government supported public radio and television, evangelical Christianity, the inherited religion of the West, still espoused by fifty-five million Americans, gets less constructive exposure than its due or is even depicted adversely.

The major change in the American condition is not simply a matter of public perception. The major change, rather, is that the present worsening declension of secular humanism to raw naturalism involves a deliberate neopagan repudiation of the Christian heritage. Unless the prevalent stance of the secular universities, the mass media, and the political arena is altered, we will expend our lives and implement our ministries in a cultural context that discounts Christianity as an option unacceptable to the thinking man or woman of the 1990s. It will be perceived as an alternative that has already had its day, one whose erstwhile exclusive claim for faith in Christ as the only way to redemption will be despised as a mark of cultural illiteracy.

Such a development could signal new possibilities of evangelical rejection, even of affliction and imprisonment, in which the threat and power of death may be at work. The New Testament views trials that imperil life as a test of the believer's essential commitment to Christ and the gospel, and of one's readiness to offer one's life to God as the providential Giver and Preserver in the midst of ministry. Here we recall the words of the apostle Paul: "For we would not, brethren, have you ignorant of our trouble which came to us in Asia, that we were pressed out of measure, above strength, insomuch that we despaired even of life; but we had the sentence of death in ourselves that we should not trust in ourselves, but in God which raiseth the dead" (2 Cor. 1:8-9, KJV).

Such tribulation is not merely a byproduct of general social problems; it is an affliction borne by the righteous in the course of their obedient service to God. Israel's election as the chosen people elicited reactionary threats to her historical existence; similarly, under the new covenant, Christ's disciples and apostles and the early church and the people of God throughout the Christian centuries inherit this tribulation. The term *thlipsis* (trouble) occurs forty-five times in the New Testament, more than half of them in Paul's writings. The risen Christ, whose redemptive suffering for sinners was borne and completed on the cross, is seen as entering into the sufferings of His saints; indeed, says Paul, the body is to fill up the sufferings in which the Head of the body continues to share. The martyrs in the Book of Revelation come to God's throne through great tribulation. Suffering for Christ is a normal aspect of Christian living in this world; into that suffering the Risen Lord enters as head of the body. As the eschatological end time approaches suffering, already underway since the resurrection of the crucified Messiah, becomes more intense and will continue until full dawning of the kingdom of God.

"In the world you will have *trouble,*" Christ reminds us. To know Jesus truly and intimately does not render us impervious to trouble. In experiencing suffering as believers we are not to be identified with the world which "lies in the lap of the evil one," but with Christ who has overcome the world. Our message is not primarily the eventual and perhaps imminent collapse of Western culture or a verdict on whether American evangelicalism can escape disaster. It is rather that the world in itself has no future, but that for the people of God the outcome is sure.

Our mission, then, is earth encircling; it is in the world, and it is tinged with *trouble*. The victory is unqualified: Christ has overcome the world! Therefore, as John 16:33 says, be of "good cheer" (KJV); "take heart" (NIV); "take courage" (NASB); "be courageous" (Williams). The Greek term *tharsos* conveys much more than "good morning," "chin up," or a cordial toast, "Cheers!" Jesus used the verb form in exhorting others in their crisis-experiences and often coupled it with the negative

"Stop fearing" or "Stop being afraid." To the disciples terrified by the storm at sea, he says: "Take courage. It is I. Don't be afraid." (Matt. 14:27). And to Paul, imprisoned while foes outside were thirsting for his blood, the risen Lord says "Take courage! . . . you must also testify (about me) in Rome" (Acts 23:11).

Every humanities student knows that courage was among the stellar virtues in Graeco-Roman civilization. Plato lists it after wisdom in his summary of the moral life: wisdom, courage, temperance, and justice. Greek philosophy anchored courage in the supposition that human beings have an intrinsically divine nature, an indestructible spirit, a psychic element that is essentially immortal. The ancient Greeks drew courage from their own inner resources.

Christianity repudiates that speculation. Jesus anchors courage in His victory over the world achieved by His resurrection as the crucified One, a decisive historical event that sets Christian realities uniquely apart from pagan mythology. Not self-reliance but Christ the Overcomer is the hinge of history. Our lives and mission are in the nail-scarred hands of the Victor who vanquished the threatening postures of the world-powers. Jesus says, "Take courage!" Christian courage centers in and around the Messiah who by His sinless life and bodily resurrection won and guarantees victory over all the powers of evil and oppression and even of death. "In the world you shall have tribulation, but," he says, "take courage, *I have overcome* the world" (John 16:33, NASB).

The evangelical movement in America is concluding a spectacular century of faith in which it has sponsored evangelists and missionaries worldwide, built schools, colleges and seminaries, founded major movements, produced books and magazines, trained a vanguard of scholars and workers, and produced important Bible translations. Now the time is at hand for more than faith. The time has come for Christian courage.

The Old Testament prophets defied trouble even when life was at risk; they stood tall for Yahweh in the midst of it. The Christian apostles did not escape trouble; amid the hostility of pagan rulers and of religious bureaucrats they trumpeted Christ's victory. Read all about it in the Book of Acts.

Augustine in his day did not go underground to circumvent pagan philosophers; he confronted them intellectually and exhibited the superior credentials of biblical faith.

Athanasius did not forfeit the case for Christian trinitarianism but by his mastery of the Scriptures and of Greek spared the church from the pit of Arianism.

The Protestant Reformers were not intimidated by Rome's ecclesiastical power but proclaimed *sola fide* (faith alone) and *sola scriptura* (scripture alone) when church leaders on every hand blurred the foundational tenets of Christianity. "Here I stand," said Luther, in his speech at the Diet of Worms; "I can do no other, God help me." William Carey, despite poverty and deprivation, learned Latin, Greek, and Hebrew, and sailed as a pioneer missionary to India. There, alone or with others, he translated the Bible in whole or in part into twenty-six languages.

Third World national Christians in our own day, unintimidated by secular humanism that inundates the West, have sacrificially sent thousands of missionaries to remind us that enduring joy is not dependent on Western affluence.

It is a time for courage, to dare to be a Daniel, to stand alone if need be, to do things in the biblical way and not as the world does them. We have a mission in a world awash in trouble, a mission that calls for courage grounded in Christ who has overcome the world.

It takes courage to be an evangelist when others declare that the age of mass evangelism is over.

It takes courage to expend one's life in missions when others prioritize material goals.

It takes courage to witness to nonchristian immigrants and refugees when sociologists espouse and curry religious pluralism. It takes courage to live virtuously in a licentious age.

It takes courage to serve God when personal adversity challenges trust in God's love.

It takes courage to live in a world that still crucifies Jesus and boldly to declare that "God works for the good of those who love him, who have been called according to his purpose . . ." (Rom. 8:28) and that neither *thlipsis* (trouble) nor hardship nor persecution nor famine nor wickedness nor danger nor sword can separate the believer from Christ's firm love for us. "In all these things" we who know Christ are "more than conquerors." Say it again, even at the heart of a great military power; as Paul did in his day, now we do so in ours. We are "more than conquerors"; we are devoted disciples of the Overcomer, of the risen Lord and coming King.

"In *the world you will have trouble, but take heart* (*tharsos*), *I have overcome the world* (NIV).

# Faith in God
# and Seven Graces

*The self-complete God loved us when we had nothing to offer Him, and when we were due only His wrath for our sins and rebellion. There isn't much you can take into eternity. But you can take agape, self-giving love, for that's what heaven is all about.*

If you profess to be a Christian, and yet are tempted at times as I am to fume over circumstances, or are tempted now and then to blow your top and to tell somebody off, then welcome to the club. Second Peter 1:1-11 has much to say to Christians "on the way to glory"—especially Christians who are more concerned about their own character transformation than public parading to the tune of "When the Saints Go Marching In."

Our passage plunges us at once into some problems of communication. One such problem is anticipated by verse 4, where Peter writes of our being "partakers of the divine nature" (KJV). Understood the wrong way, that notion could be as pagan as one might imagine. Plato taught that our minds are parts of God's mind; the Stoics taught that by nature we in our entirety are parts of the divine; the mystery religions taught that through certain rituals and emotional responses we become partakers of divinity. The whole ancient Hellenic world teemed with the notion that human beings have a divine spark that needs only to be fanned into flame. Pagan theories, not wholly out-of-date, still teach that

**293**

the Deity is a giant self or absolute that absorbs us as parts--so that God is merely *more* than we are and not *other* than we are. Strange modern Buddhist and Hindu cults, New Age teaching, Unity, and Christian Science, all continue to popularize this misconception.

The apostle Peter attributes humanity's corruption to evil desires. We are guilty rebels alienated from God by spiritual sedition. Fallen humankind no longer loves God, no longer wills to do God's will, no longer thinks God's thoughts after Him. We cannot blame our alienation on the stuff of which the cosmos is made, nor could Adam, the head of the race. Greek philosophers taught that matter and the body are evil, and that to nurture a spiritual nature we must escape from the earthly physical world of time and sense. Our problem is not that we have an evil body, for the body is destined for resurrection. Our passions are morally and spiritually rebellious. The world from which the Christian must escape is not the physical universe, but the sphere of voluntary moral rebellion against the Lord of life.

For our rescue and redemption God has taken a self-revealing initiative. We cannot by philosophical reasoning or lofty meditation think our way into the invisible eternal world. God has made Himself known in grace. For the living of a proper life we are given "very great and precious promises" (v.4). The solution of our predicament lies in Jesus Christ alone. Time after time in these few verses, Peter refers to "Jesus Christ," or to "our God and Savior Jesus Christ," or to "Jesus [Christ] our Lord," or "Jesus our Lord." Peter knows that human salvation wholly turns on Jesus Christ whose "servant and apostle" Peter declares himself to be (v.1). It is "through the righteousness of our God and Savior Jesus Christ," writes Peter, that we "have received a faith as precious as ours" (v.2).

To be a partaker of the divine nature involves being "born again" through the mediation of God's only Son, as the apostle John put it (John 3:3),and being "the temple of the living God" (2 Cor. 6:16), as the apostle Paul put it. We are "partakers of the divine nature" (v. 4, KJV), by deliverance from our sins and from allegiance to a spiritually rebellious society. We get a family likeness to God through spiritual regeneration and sanctification. As Michael Green puts it, "participation in the divine nature is the starting-point" (let me emphasize, not the end-all) "of Christian living." Are you sure you are a Christian? The new birth is not all of the new life, but it is the indisputable beginning. "You must be born again" (John 3:7), said Jesus.

Think now about the main thrust of the passage. The apostle Peter is eager that we Christians will find in our lives and experiences a fulfillment of God's "great and precious promises" (v.4). He knew the ups-

and-downs of being a disciple, of coping with emotional immaturity that ranged from a threefold denial of Jesus to that wild swing of a sword by which he tried to decapitate a companion of Judas the betrayer. Peter wants to spare us the plight of fishing all night and catching nothing. He had been a "pebble"; now he had become "a rock." He wants us, aided by God's divine power in Christ, to be delivered from a sense of futility and failure, to escape the devastating consequences of sin, to be linked to the moral excellence of God's Son Jesus, and to rejoice in Christ's conquest of death and to share in His moral victory. Peter puts us on an escalator, as it were, that begins with the faith we have received from Christ (v.2). Faith is the necessary foundation on which the superstructure rests. All that Peter says about the truly moral life presupposes it. You can't stand still long on an escalator. Peter warns us lest we travel downward toward a barren life rather than upward to a fruitful life (vv. 8-9). "Make your calling and election sure," he exhorts, "and you will receive a rich welcome into the kingdom of our Lord and Savior Jesus Christ" (vv. 10-11). The eternal plan of God is on its way to completion, and we are individually involved. To have a barren faith is to come empty-handed.

On the foundation of faith rests the building blocks, and top-most of seven stories is agape. None of the New Testament catalogs of the Christian perfections intends to be complete; each is a sampling of what distinguishes Christian living from the life of the world at large. There is a generous overlapping in the several New Testament lists of moral excellencies and of moral vices. No list of moral qualities downplays love. The journey that begins with faith reaches its climax in *agape*. Just as in the apostle Paul's writings "love" is the climax of the Christian life when he speaks of "faith, hope and agape" (1 Cor.13), so Peter here puts it last for the very same reason that Paul put it first in the fruit-of-the-Spirit passage (Gal. 5:22): Love crowns all the other excellencies.

Any escalator that moves from the foundation floor to the top story usually requires attentive human effort and maneuverability. Peter prefaces the identification of the way stops on this life journey to the summit with the exhortation: "Make every effort" (v:5). Alan K. Chambers says very aptly that we ought to use a bullhorn telling all humanity, "Be ye reconciled to God." But here God is using a bullhorn telling Christians to "make every effort." You can lose your balance on an escalator through inattention or unforeseen hazard. I tumbled down eight or ten icy steps at Union Station in 1989 and two teenagers—God bless them— jumped over me and pulled me to my feet just before my clothes meshed into the steel claws at the bottom of the escalator. I had a month of bruises to remind me of that slip—on ankles, knees, hips, and back.

Peter wants us to be firm-footed, even on the slippery slopes. He wants us to stand tall throughout the trip. He is concerned that our spiritual and moral advance is uninterrupted. It is far easier to fall down than to fall up. Try it sometime. Do you wonder sometimes whether anything can be more important than stopping to talk to people about Jesus Christ? Ask Jim and Tammy Bakker. Ask Jimmy Swaggart. God can put a broken life back together again, but how many others have been hurt in the process. "Make every effort," says Peter. It is as if a train conductor gets off at every way station and calls out: "Next Stop, Self Control; make every effort . . ." or "Next Stop Endurance; make every effort. . . ." We are to "make every effort" to add to our faith these life-transforming graces. Do not frustrate what God can and wants to do in changing our lives; set your heart on the spiritual graces that lie ahead.

There is something surprising, even astonishing, about Peter's list of qualities or perfections. We have already skipped over the apostle's use of *eusebeia* (godliness/goodness) in verse 3; now we take note of it, and also of Peter's use of *arete* (virtue) at the end of that same verse. These Greek terms were in standard use in the pagan world throughout which the Christian Jews to whom Peter writes were scattered, but New Testament writers made little use of them. In the twentieth century the world takes Christian terms and deploys them to a pagan misunderstanding; in the first century Christians ran the risk of encouraging a misunderstanding of the truth of revelation when they used the language of pagan society. Sometimes the apostles avoided the entrenched vocabulary entirely—as with the dominant word for love, *eros*—and sometimes they enlisted it for a different meaning. By *arete* (virtue) the pagans designated what was humanly praiseworthy. Peter was well aware of the tendency of human beings to applaud ourselves, in Paul's words, "to think of ourselves more highly than we ought" (Rom.12:3). Godliness is much easier to come by if one holds that all human beings share a divine spark that needs only to be fanned into flame, and that we are secretly divine, and not sinners under God's wrath. So Peter, notably, has in mind God's "virtue"/"goodness," and not man's when he uses *arete*. By *eusebeia* the pagans means an inherent or latent godliness in human nature; Peter connects the term instead with holiness.

Peter uses the language of the world—which is the only language we have—in a way that prevents a reduction of revealed truth and puts it properly into the service of faith. To use contemporary language to communicate something very different from the sense that the unbelieving world attaches to that language is one of the most demanding tasks of Christian communication. Peter dares to walk into the pagan world of his day and to speak as a moral and spiritual counterforce. Insofar as anything good was to be said for the world's claims to morality, it is but a pale and often distorted shadow of the real thing. Peter channels all the moral qualities into Jesus Christ.

Take the familiar term *gnosis*, by which the pagans meant human knowledge that automatically makes a person moral, assuming that if one knows the truth one will do it. Peter speaks four times instead of *epignosis*—a more complete knowledge, a more perfect knowledge—and he not only stresses "the knowledge of God and of Jesus our Lord" (v. 2:20), but he emphasizes that the graces or moral qualities will "keep you from being ineffective and unproductive in your knowledge of the Lord Jesus Christ" (v. 8). Peter finds all our excellencies in union with Christ; without that union, all else falls apart. The precious promises that lead from faith to *agape* and beyond that to eternity in God's presence are given through Christ's "own glory and goodness" (v. 3).

Peter calls for our eager appropriation of seven supplements to faith. These are, he insists, the work of God in us, yet they do not arise mechanically, for he presupposes a living faith. We live in an computerized age when we expect everything to happen automatically. I am reminded of the Hindu who said he hoped that in his next incarnation he would be a Ford Thunderbird. We are to put into practice what God intends us to be, and what we already are as God sees us positionally in and through Christ. Faith goes stagnant without upward momentum; it needs to be new and fresh every day. Peter exhorts us in verse 5 to "add to our faith" in the Greek, *epichoregesate*, from *epichoregeo*; that is, to supply to, to furnish besides; the *Revised Standard Version* translates the phrase as "to supplement." If the doctor tells you to "supplement" your diet, he does not mean a one-time additive but an ongoing program. Do not just make a momentary effort, but make "every" effort; do it as a decisive life choice. We are in transit to the new era when Jesus Christ will return as part of God's "very great and precious promises." For "the day of the Lord will come like a thief" (3:10). At the end of the Epistle Peter reminds us that the present order of things will be dissolved, and adds: "what kind of people ought you to be? You ought to live lives holy and godly (*eusebeia*) lives, as you look forward to the day of God" (v.11). Meanwhile, we are to claim all the intermediary promises as progressive realities by nurturing the new life to which the Spirit is conforming us. For His "divine power has given us everything we need for life and godliness through our knowledge of Him" (1:3). There are spiritual steroids available to us for progress in Christian living.

Look then at the hurdles that Peter invites us to leap by God's mighty grace: at faith in God and seven graces.

1. "Add to your faith "virtue, [*arete*] goodness" (v.5, KJV).Peter is not commending the pagan delight in human excellence that ignores the fall of humanity and the universal need of redemptive grace. Peter had previously used the term "virtue" in verse 3 specifically of Jesus Christ; faith looks to the sum total of the Savior's perfections. The "virtue" that interests Peter reverses every moral blemish that scars fallen humankind; it holds before us the sinlessness of Christ and the awesome holy image of God. Peter is not skating along the edges of a pagan life-style and applauding human achievement. Believers will ultimately be conformed to the moral image of Jesus; get on with it now, says Peter, and link your life to its ethical goal and final purpose. How much do you yearn to be like Christ, to add to your faith "virtue" as He mirrors it?

2. Add to virtue "knowledge"[*gnosis*] "Knowledge" is one of this epistle's main emphases, not the speculative or conjectural knowledge of the Gnostics but the revelationally based knowledge that involves apostolic eyewitnesses and scripturally inspired prophets and apostles. The moral life requires the guidance of truth and intellect, and an understanding of God's will. Zeal for God without knowledge will lead to doctrinal and moral shipwreck. How much do you read your Bible, study it and reflect on God's will for your life? Are you adding knowledge to virtue?

3. Add to knowledge "self-control [*engkrateia*]" (verse 6). There were long discussions of "self-control" in the philosophical ethics of the ancient Greeks and Romans, among whom the term suggested self-mastery but said very little about God's mastery of us. Many times the turning point comes in a court case when the defendant, broken and in tears, says "I lost control." Our generation has lost control of its sensual desires and sexual impulses. It is steeped in the lust of defiling passion; indeed, the media promote it and we too much accommodate it. In our pagan society sexual appetite overwhelms reason and dominates the whole of the culture. There is nothing wrong with a good sex life, and the relationship of marital partners is not normal without it. The carnal world has left its mark even upon the evangelical community in our time. The pastor of one of America's best-known churches told me years ago that he discontinued interviews with church members because most complaints were husband-wife problems. He turned over to an assistant minister the hearing of all those dissatisfactions voiced by Christians who apparently were looking for a sexual millennium. Behind much of the evangelical forfeiture of the lively life of a Christian mind, of establishment of a Christian mind-set and will-set, lies a chaotic sex life. In the fruit-of-the-Spirit passage in Galatians 5:23, Paul does not hesitate to list self-control as a work of the Holy Spirit.

4. Add to self control "perseverance [hupomone]","patience",(KJV); "steadfastness", (RSV). Perhaps the best translation is "endurance." From the habit of self-control, says Michael Green, "springs 'endurance'. . . , the temper of mind which is unmoved by difficulty and distress, and which can withstand the two Satanic agencies of opposition from the world without and enticement from the flesh within." The Christian who lacks endurance may flash across the sky like a meteor, but the one with endurance will shine like the noon-day sun. Endurance means a dedicated resistance to the solicitations of evil. Behind the exploits of the heroes of the faith in Hebrews 11 was a mindset that had already decided, antecedently to temptation, what to do with temptation if and when it arises. The Christian who perseveres does not wait for temptation to arise to see whether or not he or she will stand fast. Later Jewish writings use this term of a martyr spirit. The martyrs were ready to die for Jesus before they were put to the test. What you do now in the hour of temptation tells much about the bent of your spirit. Will you endure? Are you enduring now?

Peter lists three additional concerns in verse 7, "godliness", "brotherly kindness", and "love" [*agape*].

5. Add to perseverance "godliness"(*eusebeia*). The pagans used this term to describe a religious performance of all one's duties to God and humankind, of an attitude of reverence as one's life outlook--what we might call piety. Paul on Mars Hill noted the piety of the Greeks. In that same context he spoke of the unknown God whom he proclaimed to them. Peter has in mind something more precise than an imitation or perpetuation of pagan piety. It is for real godliness, for holiness, that Peter pleads.

6. Add to godliness/holiness "brotherly kindness" *philadelphia* or brotherly love. In classical Greek *phileo* was a common term for love and was applied to friends, relatives, or to deity. Christians are to treat all fellow believers as the family of God, and are to protect them against gossip, prejudices, and misrepresentation. This grace bears on staff rivalries in Christian organizations, and calls for family unity. The Christian extension of brother love to those beyond the extended family caused pagan contemporaries to exclaim, "See how they love one another." The new family transcends distinctions of nationality, race, and social standing. I can think of no greater brother-love than to share the gospel with unbelievers, and I include Jews no less than Gentiles. I know that some Protestant theologians follow Reinhold Niebuhr's notion that in distinction from the Gentiles, the Jews have another covenant apart from Christ. Even if Jews have no heart to share the Prophets with us, we must love them enough to share the New Testament with them. Many

Christian Jews who have long lived at a distance from both Old Testament and New Testament are today discovering in Christian context what real brother-love is. We are called to live like brothers and sisters to those at our side who are in need.

7. The climax is reached in "add to brotherly-kindness . . . love" (*agape*). There is widespread misunderstanding that the Greek terms *phileo* and *agape* are to be contrasted, and that *phileo* -love is inferior to *agape* love. In John's Gospel Jesus uses the term *phileo* when he tells us that "The Father loves the Son" (John 5:20); the tense is present: "The Father is continually loving (*phileo*) the Son." *Phileo* is used of Jesus' love for Lazarus (11:3) and of the Father's love of the disciples of Jesus (16:27). Paul writes the Corinthians that "if anyone does not love (*phileo*) the Lord, a curse be on him" (1 Cor. 16:22). The real contrast is between the pagan term *eros* and the preferred biblical alternative *agape*, little used in the ancient world. The apostle Paul shunned the term *eros* when he spoke of God's love and of Christian love, not because the term *eros* necessarily connoted carnality, but rather because it designated the only kind of love the nonbiblical world knew—a grasping, self-seeking love. God's love reaches out to others not for the sake of what others can bring to Him, but for the sake of some benefit that the lover bestowed undeservedly on the other. The self-complete God loved us when we had nothing to offer Him, and when we were due only His wrath for our sins and rebellion. There is not much that you can take with you into eternity. You can take *agape*, self-giving love, for that is what heaven is all about.

These then are the marks or qualities of the new nature that the Spirit of God imparts as we walk the path of Christian growth: faith manifests in "goodness", "knowledge", "self-control", "perseverance", "godliness", "brotherly kindness", and "love". Some will excel in more of one excellency than of another, but we are called to nurture them all. For the text ends with a contrast of barren and fruitful lives. It indicates that those who lack these qualities shut their eyes to what Christian living is all about; they have forgotten that they have been purged from their sins and risk a lapse from faith (1:9). Faith centered on Christ is the foundation of our lives. The issue Peter puts is this: how faithfully are you and I attending to a structure of character and service that is to be added to that foundation? Good works are the work of God in and through us, but we bear responsibility if our lives are barren. Faith that is not at work tends to shrivel and wither. Give it a daily workout.

So Peter exhorts us to "make your calling and election sure" (v. 10). We are to manifest God's election of us. If we confirm our calling we shall run the race sure-footed and not be put to shame. We are on the move to the everlasting kingdom and we will be abundantly and richly welcomed if we have allowed God to equip us. We are already participants in the divine nature. God's *agape*, Peter emphasizes, has a moral character. In the perfections of Christian living we anticipate what life will be like in God's eternal presence and with the saints in glory. Keep expanding virtue, knowledge, self-control, perseverance, godliness, brotherly kindness and *agape* in their scriptural intention. "For if you possess these qualities in increasing measure, they will keep you from being ineffective and unproductive in your knowledge of the Lord Jesus Christ. But if anyone does not have them, he is nearsighted and blind, and has forgotten that he has been cleansed from his past sins" (vv. 8-9).

If you are still at the originating station waiting to board a train that has already left, you need to ask yourself whether you have a valid ticket. If you are already aboard and armed with God's knowledge and His dynamic power in your life, then let the "very great and precious promises" be a life-transforming reality. May it be for each of us, that growth in the graces evidences our growth in grace, and confirms our election. "Make every effort," exhorts Peter. To that exhortation I simply add a few lines by the German poet Goethe:

> Are you in earnest? Then seize this very minute.
> What you can do, or think you can, Begin it.
> Courage has genius, power and magic in it.
> Only engage, and then the mind grows heated.
> Begin it, and the task will be completed.

# *God, Man, and the Millennium*

*Modern moral philosophy seems to have tumbled into any abyss of chaos, where exhausted metaphysicians simply cannot come to consensus; the tragic state of things is such that a whirlpool of ideas and ideals increasingly prevails.*

As space time compresses into this century's final decade and trickles into a new succession of centuries, the questions of good and evil, truth and right, meaning and worth, are bantered about in ominous confusion.

Conflicting views of the nature of human life itself divide and perplex learned commentators as much as ever. Are humans merely complex animals whose destiny is the cemetery or crematory? Are we still steeped in sporadic evolutionary development that precludes any pancultural human essence and implies that superman will ultimately supersede us all? Are we moral rebels without historical hope apart from spiritual reconciliation with the Creator and Giver of life; or are we only what we internally and existentially make of ourselves in successive life-or-death decisions? Respected philosophers, moreover, cannot agree on whether human nature—if such there be—is essentially selfish or essentially good, or an elusive and enigmatic mixture of virtue and vice.

On the answers to such questions hang crucial issues, among them, whether Jews, as Hitler held, are but dubious instances of humanity and whether unborn fetuses are human at all (by aborting a million and a half of them a year Americans imply the negative). At no juncture of history has a verdict on whether or not humans find their true selfhood in special relationships to a transcendent God been more important for human destiny. Is Jesus of Nazareth still to be viewed as ideal Man and, if not, who is to replace Him?

Even anthropologists are in disarray over the supposed evolutionary ancestry of human and a precise chronology for the appearance of humanity as we know it. Elwyn L. Simons, director of Duke University's Center for the Study of Primate Biology and History, tells us what will surprise few biblical scholars—that "many attributes or skills by which we define humanity arose much more recently in time than before believed."[1] Indeed, he adds, "Much of what we hold 'near and dear' about ourselves—our very anatomical proportions, our ability to create art and symbols, sophisticated tool manufacture, and construction and use of house and home may have appeared only a few tens of thousands of years ago."[2]

Simons does not even mention the *imago Dei*, or created image of God, which the Judeo-Christian account declares most decisive for human beginnings. He does suggest that just as important as the grave questions raised regarding our species' past development are the "frightening problems of the future arising from our very selves."[3] The matter of human identity is, in fact, no less significant and even more critical than that of human chronology. No cosmic importance whatever attaches itself to humanity's march into a new millennium if, severed from the image of God, the human species can no longer make a persuasive case for its distinctive meaning and worth.

## Areas of Contemporary Concern

Space and communications technology has linked earth's four billion inhabitants intimately, while at the same time shaping dread possibilities of human and planetary destruction through nuclear war. The dawning century inherits a colossal fallout in the form of the present century's unresolved tensions. Among these:

— The technological superiority of the West and Japan, where scientific experiments continue to outrun moral legitimacy, a cultural condition that accommodated the Holocaust.

---

1. "Human Origins", *Science*, vol. 245, 22 September 1989, 1,343.
2. "Human Origins", 1,394.
3. "Human Origins", 1,394.

— The environmental and ecological erosion of the earth as a viable habitat through the rape of nature, inviting cosmic "revenge" in atmospheric and agricultural conditions that endanger human survival.

— The collapse of socialist economies in Eastern Europe and China and the contrasting success of free-market economics in Singapore, Hong Kong, South Korea, and Taiwan, while totalitarian rulers struggle nonetheless to maintain their political and military power.

— The growing difficulty of presenting convincing supports for human equality and dignity on the basis of shaky philosophical theory that reflects Enlightenment views of the world and humankind.

— The affluence of Western society, where daily life has turned sour for the masses despite material abundance, so that ancient religions, modern cults, and physical and chemical perception-altering techniques are welcomed to add new verve to personal survival.

— The capitalist dilemma of coping with large colonies of unemployed and underprivileged persons in a competition-oriented workplace.

The secular humanist outlook of the Anglo-American liberal elite continues to deteriorate. Its unstable humanitarian social ethic ever yields to the pressures of immediate self-interest and accommodates an emerging raw naturalism and neo-paganism that deliberately rejects the Judeo-Christian inheritance.

## The Vacuum of Values

The observation is now commonplace that we live in a time of ethical and intellectual relativism, when truth and the good are often regarded as merely one's subjective preferences. This judgment simply describes a present cultural condition and may characterize only a momentary hiatus in history. It need not define what must necessarily be the case throughout the 1990s or in the twenty-first century.

Philosophers who traffic in technical discussions of the validity of truth claims now disagree over the meaning of truth—and indeed over the meaning of meaning—and many routinely shun discussion of the supernatural and enduring. Even scientific theorists now debate whether their own presumed "objects" of knowledge are merely explanatory myths. They ask whether nature—let alone the supernatural—is an observer-independent reality or primarily an observer-postulated reality. The skeptical judgment passed on the realm of theological entities has come home to face scientific inquiry. Quite apart from theology, does science provide approximately true descriptions of an objectively existing world or is science merely an instrument for revisable prediction? Does scientific progress actually require a real universe? Must the truth

claims of science be grounded upon the notion of an approximate correspondence between scientific theory and an independently real world?

Worse yet, moral relativism has shattered many longstanding ethical
standards. Marriage, long viewed as a divinely established framework
for the procreation of the human race and legitimation of sexual enjoy-
ment, and one of the fundamental struts of a stable society, is under
pressure from no-fault divorce, indiscriminate intercourse, and alternative views of the family. The standards of decency are warped by growing obscenity. The Federal Communications Commission has accepted
midnight-to-dawn radio and television programming—when children
(for the moment) are least likely to be listening—"that depicts or
describes, in terms patently offensive as measured by contemporary
community standards for the broadcast medium, sexual or excretory
activities or organs." At the same time the FCC has abandoned its erstwhile strictures against the "seven dirty words" that it had earlier
banned.

The rise of a pagan youth generation bodes ill for the decades ahead.
It is in part a consequence of educational programs that studiously but
misguidedly avoid significant religious distinctions supposedly in deference to church-state separation. Nor are the evidences limited merely to
occasionally surfacing cults that involve Satan worship and human sacrifice, or even to the large numbers of young people who now indulge in
drugs in quest of consciousness expansion. What has happened, we
must ask, to the spiritual sensitivity of teenagers who give Christmas
cards containing condoms and of rudderless social commentators who
see in this perversity an authentic expression of loving care?

Increasingly, society must cope with behavioral discontrol as the
intellectual schizophrenia of our day collapses the distinction between
good and evil and stigmatizes as dichotomous thinking any call for loyalties both to this world and the next. The rampant rule of excessive
self-interest, under pretenses of self- enrichment, meanwhile takes its
toll on ethical claims, and readies more and more of its victims for psy-
chiatric counseling. The day is gone when one view of life held priority
amid a variety of countergods. Modern moral philosophy seems to have
tumbled into an abyss of chaos, where exhausted metaphysicians simply
cannot come to consensus; the tragic state of things is such that a whirlpool of ideas and ideals increasingly prevails.

## The Shift Toward Neopagan Naturalism

There can be little doubt that since the beginning of this century,
American philosophy has veered away from supernaturalism toward
naturalism. The transition, however, has not been a smooth one. At the

century's outset philosophical idealism, which stressed the supernatural but denied the miraculous, was becoming firmly entrenched and provided a framework that appealed to many Protestant modernists. By the end of the first quarter of the century, humanists were already beginning to make some inroads, denying the supernatural entirely and clinging to notions of transcendence within an ultimate reality depicted in terms of naturalistic evolutionary process. Both humanists and idealists, including a growing personalistic wing, tended to emphasize the inevitability of progress and the essential goodness of humankind. The 1930s saw the rise of theological realism, influenced by the neo-orthodoxy of Karl Barth, with its less optimistic view of human nature and insistence on the distinctiveness of the biblical witness. For all its impact upon modernist seminaries, especially, and a number of theologically mediating seminaries as well, neo-orthodoxy counted for little in the secular academic world. Before mid-century it was increasingly apparent that secular humanism was becoming the covert metaphysics of liberal arts learning.

While radically secular humanism was ontologically reductionistic, and held that the ultimately real world is comprised of impersonal processes and events and that all ideals and ideas are culturally conditioned, it nonetheless insisted on a program of social ethics that it considered universally obligatory. It held, in short, to the dignity and equality of human beings, championed ecological and environmental concerns, voiced compassion for the poor, and opposed racial discrimination. Secular humanism's appeal to university students lay in several factors: its emphasis on empirical science, insistence on social duties (alongside permissiveness in the area of personal ethics), and suspension of commitments required by transcendent theism.

Although these social sensitivities retain the enthusiasm of many humanists, the logical inconsistency of maintaining ethical absolutes in the context of an ultimate reality conceived impersonally in terms of natural processes and events is increasingly apparent to students. More and more, the younger generation finds in naturalism no compelling basis for the absolute obligations that humanism sponsors, tending to view any and all ethical agendas as subjectively grounded. Consequently, the humanitarian aspects of secular humanism are slowly evaporating, and raw naturalism, with its emphasis on unbridled self-interest and survival of the fittest, is gaining power.

Since secular humanism has increasingly become the masked metaphysics of Anglo-Saxon liberal learning and now pervades much of the intellectual outlook of higher education, politics, and the mass media, the West's current drift toward neo-paganism runs counter to every

effort to romance the dawning millennium in terms of whole-world integration of values—at least if by values one means not merely a voluntarily preferred consensus but transcendently grounded absolutes. There
are indeed intellectual forces that would revive one or another metaphysical alternatives from the past that would maintain the objectivity of
moral claims in contrast to subjective, evolutionary, or culture-conditioned alternatives. Among them one may note a renewed emphasis on
natural law (mainly by neo-Thomists), or on the world religions somehow as bearers of a common revelation despite their differences, or on
the one-world potentialities still thought to attach to the United Nations,
as a political framework, or on science and technology. Yet each of
these perspectives is a rerun of sorts of an outlook that has already lost
its hold. Deservedly or not, intellectual and moral relativism has been
the most formative outcome of the controlling thought patterns of the
present century.

## Looking Back to 1900

Any reader of the *Century Dictionary and Encyclopedia*, published in
1906 as "a work of universal reference in all departments of knowledge,
with a new atlas of the world," will be struck immediately both by the
discoveries and inventions that are absent because they belong to later
generations and by the cresting enthusiasm for science as the promising
way into the future.

In 1898 Pierre and Marie Curie discovered radium when extracting
intensely radioactive concentrates from uranium ore. In 1900 Sigmund
Freud's *Interpretation of Dreams* appeared. In 1905 Albert Einstein
unraveled the mystery of atomic energy and contradicted the
entrenched view that matter is indestructible. In his *Relativity: The Special and General Theory* (1918), he published the comprehensive view
that, with the quantum theory, supplies the essential basis of contemporary physics. Sir Oliver Lodge predicted in 1920 that atomic energy
would supplant coal. Nobody dreamed that forty years later the insights
of atomic science might lead to the instant destruction of whole cities.

Not only an intellectual elite but the general public as well was fasci-
nated by the marvels that science was shaping. Henry Ford produced his
first car in 1896, and in 1899 the *Literary Digest* predicted that the horse-
less carriage would never come into as common use as the bicycle. A
U.S. senator, J. W. Bailey of Texas, declared a decade later that automo-
biles should be outlawed on public highways because they endangered
the public.[4]

---

4. Ernest W. Heyn, *A Century of Wonders* (Garden City, NY: 1972), 35.

The younger generation may find it hard to imagine a world without radio, television, airplanes, subway systems, and color photography, much less current medical techniques and cures, but many of us once lived in that world. It was a world that had inherited from nineteenth-century science the conviction that continuous laws govern all physical processes and that any supposed gaps are due to our own blinders. The new century came to acknowledge discontinuities in physics and in other fields and affirmed that atoms are made up of subsidiary particles, some transitory. Something no less significant was under way in the history of thought. Western civilization was in transition from its quite proper admission of the limited validity of science to "the affirmation of its epistemological superiority" and beyond that, finally, to the "exclusivity" of scientism.[5] The new century was on its way to an unprecedented knowledge and communications explosion, one that at the same time nurtured the seeds of its own destruction and was exasperatingly ambiguous about the permanency of Truth and the Good.

No one dreamed that the twentieth century might close with a timorous conviction that its great gods—scientism, education, and politics—had failed the masses and would leave human civilization faced with a possibility of self-destruction. Oswald Spengler, the German philosopher of history, contended in *The Decline of the West* that all civilizations have predictable life cycles and that as the West had already passed through its creative stage, the future could be marked only by irreversible decline. Darwinian theory, which Spengler rejected, undergirded the expectation of historical progress, even if anticipations of a coming utopia were periodically qualified.

One such qualification was evident in Sir William Cecil Dampier's *Short History of Science,* published soon after midcentury as the potential for ever more deadly nuclear war began to shadow the nations. Dampier concluded his work with these words:

> It seems impossible to limit the destructiveness of warfare if indeed, in the last resort, to control its methods. The best safeguard would be to prevent war altogether by the joint action of all nations of good will. That is the tremendous problem which confronts the statesmen of the world. If the horror of the atomic bomb draws them to find a solution, he will have done good and not harm..[6]

Dampier's words in 1957 can only be italicized in view of the subsequent proliferation of nuclear-producing nations, despite the signs of

5. Thomas Molnar, *The Pagan Temptation* (Grand Rapids, Mich.: William B. Eerdmans Publishing Company, 1987), 160.
6. Cecil Dampier, *A Short History of Science* (New York: The World Publishing Company)

glasnost and the relaxing of military tensions in Europe. Even so, his comments were overarched by streaks of optimism that currently formative intellectual forces in the West now question, and the uncertainties of human behavior can only fuel our doubts. Is it within the power and competency of world statesmen, whether through the United Nations or apart from it, "to prevent war altogether"? Do the annals of the United Nations reassure us about the ready assumption of "nations of good will"? No less important, does the once-Christian West—except in broad generalities—still acknowledge a universally fixed and final "Good"?

## The Specter of Relativism

So deeply has intellectual and moral relativism penetrated the arenas of contemporary life that social critics increasingly speak not only of the decline of Western civilization but of its possible end time. Eric Voegelin, Charles Malik, C. S. Lewis, and Alexander Solzhenitsyn all recognized that the loss of transcendent truth sooner or later plunges society into chaotic disorder. A connection prevails between faulty premises and invalid conclusions and the accommodation of Nazi gas chambers and the Maoist Cultural Revolution.

Infatuated with empirical scientific method as the only reliable source of knowledge, Western thought at first looked to science as the guarantor of a bright and better future, one undergirded by evolutionary progress. Most of the East was apt to look upon disconcerting trends in Germany as aberrations, rather than as more consistent expositions of the naturalistic underpinnings that were increasingly shared. "It was in Germany that Darwin's explanation of evolution by the principle of natural selection . . . went," as Dampier wrote, "to build up a thoroughgoing *Darwinismus* and most strongly reinforced the materialist tendencies in both philosophy and political theory, the latter being used by some as a basis for the ideas of communism."[7] Haeckel's *Die Weltratsel* (1899) was less than a great work, but it contained this observation: "One of the most distinctive features of the expiring century is the increasing vehemence of the opposition between science and Christianity. That is both natural and inevitable."[8]

If naturalism is wedded to science, a conflict is inescapable—and not only with supernatural theism but with fixed and enduring distinctions of truth and the good as well. The legitimacy of wedding naturalism to

---

7. Dampier, *A Short History of Science*, 26.
8. Ernst Haeckel, *Die Weltratsel* (*The Riddle of the Universe*), trans. J. McCabe (London: Watts and Co., 1904), 109.

science and science to naturalism is itself in debate, and some contemporary philosophers have given increasing attention to a critical analysis of relativism.[9] Sooner or later the relativism that has smitten Western philosophy will be diagnosed as a fatally self-destructive epistemology, an effort to deflate all traditions while illegitimately exempting itself as normatively confessional. The necessary rethinking of relativism will require the relativist to relativize himself, for only by a self-contradictory stance can he claim to have found "the Truth," when the truth is that the relativist is unaware of what the confession of truth really involves. Not for nothing does Michael Novak write of the "relativity of relativism."[10] The relativist is an intellectual madman in desperate need of a triple pack of logic.

Any deconstruction of relativism will unmask the covert absolute that underlies its pretensions and will call for a return to logocentrism. By affirming its own crown rights, relativism brokenly reflects the ubiquity of truth in asserting its own truth and implies a revelation that in principle it would exclude. Yet relativism cannot really be turned into its opposite, for it is essentially in cognitive rebellion against truth and the good.

The so-called postmodern atheists seek to capitalize on reflexivity not by making relativism the basis of an interpretation of subjectivity that presumably yields knowledge—as do recent critics—but by shifting their focus from selfhood to language and texts that allegedly undermine all certainty. The radical relativism of Nietzsche, extended by Heidegger, is enlarged by Derrida to destroy any metalevel that contradicts relativity. Language loses any and all fixed meaning and becomes a nonrepresentational whirlpool. Here reason and rhetoric empty into themselves and render all meaning indeterminate.

Although relativism fascinates frontier philosophers as a cognitive concern, its significance for the general public consists mainly in moral erosion and doubts about personal meaning and worth. Relativism is perceived as an implicate to scientism and its reductive explanation of human life in terms of ultimately impersonal processes, a thesis that now underlies liberal learning and politics and is more accommodated than questioned by the mass media. As intellectuals discuss the issues in an objective, cognitive way, the masses openly confess that neither technological science, nor university learning, nor political genius has made

---

9. See Michael Krausz and Jack W. Mieland, eds., *Relativism, Cognitive and Moral* (Notre Dame, Ind.: University of Notre Dame Press, 1982).

10. Michael Novak, *The Experience of Nothingness* (New York: Harper & Row, 1970), 52-53.

contemporary society wiser, better, or happier, despite confident humanist assurances that mankind stands at the peak of evolutionary progress.

In view of this disenchantment with liberal reliance on science, education, and politics as catalysts of hopeful change, there increasingly
arises, on the threshold of the twenty-first century, an alternative that for
many becomes a choice between a revitalized rational theism on the
one hand, and a reexamination of the oriental religions and the occult
on the other. In short, the adequacy of empirical naturalism as a worldview is being questioned as essentially reductive rather than explanatory
of the meaning and worth of the human species, and the world of
transendence is being probed anew. Mircea Eliade writes of "the great
variety of worldviews assumed by the religious man"[11] and speculates
that "perhaps for the first time in history we recognize today . . . the
spiritual values and cultural significance" of humanity's religious cre-
ations.[12] The world of religion, devalued by humanism into a merely
psychic source of frameworks of meaning and scorned by scientism as
requiring an inferior theory of knowledge, seems to be bidding again for
centrality.

## Religious Unity and Rivalry

The twenty-first century is likely to probe the unity and conflict of
world religions in new depth. It will focus on what religions have in
common and what distinguishes them. The *Religionsgeschichte* theory,
which regards all religions as having been woven on the same loom and
denies essential differences as well as the biblical insistence on true and
false religions and on its own salvific exclusivity, will likely be debated
anew along with a wide range of mediating projections. There will be
extensive discussion of human relationships to "the sacred"—a highly
nebulous conception that in biblical theology can even be correlated
with the demonic, in contrast to "the holy." Some observers think that
confrontation between Christianity and Islam will be one of the major
events of the new century.

The space and communications era has made near neighbors of devotees of widely divergent faiths. If religion counts for anything transsub-
jective, one can hardly escape a duty to discuss it and to learn from
followers of another way. Scientism itself became the faith of secular
intellectuals even while they repudiated a sovereign living Deity and the

---

11. Preface to *The Encyclopedia of Religion* (New York: Macmilland Publishing Company,
1989), vol. 1, ix.
12. *The Encyclopedia of Religion*, xii.

supernatural. In the sense that it evoked the absolute loyalty of its devotees, scientism was no doubt a modern religion.

The youth counterculture of the sixties moved around the empirical confines of scientism and sought, by resorting to drugs, a consciousness-expanding experience of the transcendent world, one that escaped rational and moral categories and was essentially mystical. The chemical means may have been modern, but as Molnar comments, the pagan quest for mystical union with a divine world through occult physical techniques and drug indulgence has a long history. As he noted, many persons have sought "through integration, often with the help of certain mechanical and chemical aids such as bodily and respiratory exercises or personality-changing drugs," to become "divine."[13]

Judeo-Christian religion insists that God ontologically transcends the universe—that is, humanity and the cosmos. On this affirmation of a divine creation of the world *ex nihilo*, Hebrew-Christian theology comes into sharp conflict with some elements of Asian religion that have been popularized in the West throughout the past several decades. The emphasis that God is ontologically *other* than the cosmos and humankind—and not simply *more* than they are—underlies the whole range of Christian core beliefs, including creation, revelation, incarnation, redemption, and judgment, and distinguishes biblical theism from other worldviews. Christianity rejects theories that the universe is a divine emanate or veiled manifestation of Deity. Human beings are finite not as parts of a divine Self but as created selves fallen into moral revolt; apart from divine salvific rescue, they are spiritually doomed.

If humanism sought to end war by grafting social concern and a comprehensive philosophy of evolutionary development, and if Oriental religion seeks to invigorate humanity by assimilating it to divinity, Christianity, by contrast, insists on a miraculous redemption provided once and for all by Jesus Christ in a substitutionary atonement for sinners. Whereas Dampier concluded his *Short History of Science* with a plea to statesmen to prevent war altogether, another philosopher, Gordon H. Clark, concluded his more extensive work *A Christian View of Man and Things* with the warning that "a continued repudiation of Christian principles promises a future which, even more than the present, will be characterized by social instability, wars and rumors of war, brutality and despair."[14]

---

13. *The Encyclopedia of Religion*, 168.
14. Gordon H. Clark, *A Christian View of Man and Things* (Grand Rapids, Mich.: William B. Eerdmans Publishing Company, 1952), 324.

Oriental religions may have appeal to those who seek a metaphysical escape from Christian principles. For Oriental religion, most notably Hinduism and Buddhism, God is the All, the totality of the universe, of which we are parts; finite existence is not an independent creation but is a veiled and flawed—partial or finite—manifestation of the All. Temporary fusion with and reabsorption into the divine becomes life's spiritual goal. Self-dissolution and self-extinction, Nirvana, are the coveted rewards as reason and personal consciousness are lost in an inexpressible flux of essenceless phenomena.

The return of ordinary experience, as Molnar comments, is not marked by "an increased sense of self-enrichment and worth."[15] Instead there is a denial of the ultimate legitimacy of logic together with an emphasis on feeling, a denial of an absolute beginning in a divine act of creation, a denial of original sin and, indeed, of the objective factuality of sin and evil, and a denial of the need and actuality of divine redemption. The Oriental religions offer, in this life, even more than Christianity reserves for an afterlife; that is, they offer not only total release from all life's temporal burdens but also union with the very substance of divinity and a peace beyond all temporal and logical distinctions.

It is this contrast between pantheistic and theistic worldviews, the role of logic and reason in establishing their validity or invalidity, and the dispute over whether feeling is larger than logic, that promise to be critical concerns in the last decade of our century, as we approach the ominous threshold of a new millennium.

---

15. Clark, *A Christian View of Man and Things.* 158 n. 15

# *Imperatives for the Long Journey*

*The first generation is dramatically converted and is dynamically alive for Christ. The second generation inherits this good fortune but takes it for granted. The third generation lets it slip away. Let us not underestimate the importance for future generations of preserving the biblical heritage in our moment of history.*

The evangelical movement is sometimes better at founding enterprises than preserving them. We lose colleges. We lose seminaries. We lose churches, sometimes even whole denominations. We lose magazines. We lose these enterprises to purposes other than those for which the founders invested their vision, their gifts, and their energies. Credible voices warn that some American evangelical colleges and seminaries may not be effectively transmitting the Christian heritage to the next generation.

The apostle Paul had a similar concern in writing Second Timothy. Here he records numerous imperatives for his beloved Timothy to whom in the course of evangelical succession he is about to pass the torch. The apostle is eager to relay the faith once-for-all delivered without dilution or distortion.

Paul notes that Timothy's family had faithfully communicated the revealed truth of divine redemption across three generations. Paul applauds the "sincere faith which first lived in your grandmother Lois and in your mother Eunice, and . . . now lives in you also" (1:5). Think of it—three generations of faithful spiritual succession. This contrasts sadly with what sometimes happens in our century. The first generation is dramatically converted and is dynamically alive for Christ. The second generation inherits this good fortune but takes it for granted. The third generation lets it slip away. Let us never underestimate the importance for future generations of preserving the biblical heritage in our moment of history.

Paul's concern is that Timothy will be an effective torchbearer. Some whose lives Paul had touched had already been diverted from spiritual truth: "All who are in Asia turned away from me, among whom are Phygelus and Hermogenes" (1:15). Paul's arrest and detention had likely given his opponents an opportunity to attack him and his teaching. In the Gentile churches of Asia, the Judaizers probably stressed a universal need of circumcision. They and others may have pressed legalistic views upon believers and taught other novelties. Some persons had even drifted into a false doctrine that the final resurrection had already taken place (2:18). Some like Demas "loved this world" and had deserted (4:10). Alexander vigorously opposed Paul's teaching (v.15), possibly because it hurt the coppersmith's lucrative business that included the crafting of idols.

In exhorting Timothy, Paul is not calling for sentimental loyalty to a revered tradition or merely offering Timothy a psychological boost. Paul had a God-given mission. This divine mandate enthralled his mind and will and emotions; it enlisted the entire self. Paul had been appointed by God, he says, as "a herald and an apostle and a teacher" (1:11).

The apostle had set "a pattern of sound teaching" (v.13) "which," he told Timothy, "you heard from me." Again and again Paul refers Timothy to "things you have heard me say" (2:2). He reminds Timothy of God's eternal plan to save us through Christ Jesus (1:9), of the gospel of the historical appearance of the Savior (v.10), of the fact that by his resurrection (2:8) Christ Jesus "destroyed death and brought life and immortality to light" (1:10), of the Holy Spirit's role as our indwelling helper (v. 14), of the need that all Gentiles hear the gospel message (4:17), and of the prospect of eternal glory for God's people (2:10). Christ Jesus "will judge the living and the dead" (4:1), Paul states. He is the "Righteous Judge" who at His appearing will reward the faithful (v. 18), and destines us to eternity in God's "heavenly kingdom" (4:18).

Sound doctrine clearly communicated in an orderly way is of vital importance. "The time will come," Paul warns, "when men will not put up with sound doctrine". (4:3). Paul commends trustworthy truths whose repetition in some of the churches may have comprised an early Christian hymn. We can almost hear believers singing the words:

> If we die with him,
> We will also live with him;
> If we endure,
> We will also reign with him;
> If we disown him,
> He will also disown us;
> If we are faithless,
> He will remain faithful,
> For he cannot disown himself (2:11-13).

Scripture is the reliable guidebook for this life's journey. "All Scripture is God-breathed," Paul emphasizes, "and useful for teaching, rebuking, correcting and training in righteousness; that the man of God may be thoroughly equipped for every good work" (3:16-17). He is grateful that from childhood Timothy had been taught "holy Scriptures" (v.15).

Paul speaks of himself as a good soldier of Christ (2:3), who faced hardship gladly, "even to imprisonment as a criminal" (v.9), and endured suffering so others might obtain salvation (v.10). He reminds his young understudy that God gave us not "a spirit of timidity, but a spirit of power, of love, and of self- discipline" (1:7). He has "saved us and" moreover, has "called us to a holy life," the apostle writes (v.9). Paul echoes words from the Septuagint: "The Lord knows those who are His," and "Everyone who confesses the name of the Lord must turn away from wickedness" (2:19). He warns that virtue is not always applauded, far from it. "Everyone who wants to live a godly life in Christ Jesus will be persecuted" (3:12). Lest Timothy doubt that the ugly fury of evil thrusts itself a thwart our mission, Paul warns against "the trap of the devil" who takes the wicked captive to do his will (2:26).

He lists an extended catalog of vices that identifies moral rebels for what they really are (3:1-7). "You followed my teaching, conduct, purpose, faith, patience, love, perseverance, persecutions, sufferings" (n.1, NASB), Paul applauds Timothy. The word "followed" is sometimes translated to "know all about". Timothy, as Paul's companion, knew all about the remarkable life Paul lived and the stellar example he provided. The great apostle writes of himself in 4:7 that he had "finished the course," had "kept the faith," and was now on the very threshold of a consummatory departure to the risen Lord. From the great apostle the baton was about to be passed to Timothy, his intern, and through him to us, along with a series of exhortations for faithfully preserving the Christian heritage.

What imperatives does the great apostle thrust upon us? We can classify them helpfully into three kinds of concerns. Some imperatives deal with control beliefs; some deal with personal behavior; and some bear on our duties as heralds of the gospel.

Concerning distinctive beliefs and mindset Paul exhorts: "Continue in what you have learned and have become convinced of" from the normative apostolic and scriptural source (3:14). We have been given a "God-breathed" word, more "profitable" than anything the world offers: "useful for teaching, for correction, improvement, and training in righteousness." In God-breathed Scripture the truth and salvation we proclaim has its only right to life. A Christian community that has no sure Word of God has no evangelical legitimacy. You can forgive the scientific community for constant revision of its theories, since its empirical way of knowing involves only tentative conclusions. You can forgive the philosophic community for its ever-changing speculations about the real world, since speculative reasoning is vulnerable to shifting winds of doctrines. A Christian community, however, without a sure Word of the living God is not a Christian community at all. "Continue in what you have learned and have become convinced of", the apostle implores. "Present yourself to God as . . . a workman who has no need to be ashamed, rightly handling the word of truth (2:15, RSV). We are to labor in the Word of God with a work-record that befits those entrusted with transcendent truth. God is a worker (what a magnificent worker: "first day"!, "second day"!, and so on); we, his image-bearers, are to be diligent workers. We are to prepare faithfully in order to teach faithfully. We are not to bring shame either upon the word of truth or upon ourselves in heralding that truth to the world. "Present yourself, . . . a workman." Continue in the word of the truth of God.

Paul speaks also of personal demeanor or behavior. He addresses the dynamic and the direction of the Christian torchbearer's life. "Stir up the gift of God that is in you by the laying on of hands", he writes (1:6, NKJV). This special endowment is not merely a natural ability but rather is a "gift of God" for one's task in the world. Paul had personally put his hand on Timothy for his global mission—the hand that once held Stephen's cloak, the hand that wrote the inspired epistles, the hand with which Paul motioned to begin his defense before King Agrippa (Acts 26:1), the hand that execution would soon render limp. That hand he put on Timothy, and now he reminds him to rekindle the divine gift. The fire from above needs attentively to be fanned into flame. "Stir up the gift of God!"

"Do not be ashamed then of testifying to our Lord (1:8, RSV). We must conquer timidity, overcome the sin of silence, and courageously witness to Jesus Christ. What does it matter if the secular mindset regards the preaching of the Cross as foolishness. Paul was doubtless aware of Jesus' statement about our need to confess Him not merely in a private prayer closet but before others as well. Paul's connection of "testifying" with "suffering" gives special focus to courageous witnessing, witnessing in the face of hostility. The Greek term here is *marturion* from which we get our word "martyr." "You shall be my witnesses," said Jesus; "Testify unashamedly," says Paul.

Keep as the pattern of sound teaching with faith and love in Christ Jesus" (1:13). This is one of several exhortations dealing with sound and unsound words. Language is a divine gift so we may speak with God and to others about him. We need not, of course, limit ourselves to Paul's vocabulary, but Paul surely provides a model and standard of verbalization. We are to be unswervingly true to the apostolic message. There is danger today in replacing biblical terminology with contemporary jargon and modern alternatives that carry quite different nuances. There is also danger in trivializing speech.

"Avoid godless chatter (vain babbling)," says Paul, "for it leads to godlessness" (2:16). "Warn them before God against quarreling about words", an unprofitable activity, which is destructive rather than constructive (v.14). All of us know debate-minded persons who, like the ancient Greek Sophists, stand ever ready to take up any side of any argument. Paul sets Christian speech and dialogue in the context of faith and love. Godly conversation seeks to advance the gospel, to honor God, and to glorify Christ in thanksgiving, voicing gratitude for God's great blessings and His many promises. It is a concession to our senseless times when pastors turn the pulpit into a place for laughter and entertainment; congregations unfortunately often remember inane jokes longer than they remember spiritual content. Jesus used humor, but not as an end in itself. Shun godless chatter, says Paul.

"The things that you have heard from me . . . commit these to faithful men who will be able to teach others also" (2:2, NKJV). Timothy is to share the inspired apostolic teaching with the rising generation of promising future leaders. He is to "guard the truth that has been entrusted to you by the Holy Spirit who dwells in us" (1:14, RSV). Paul was concerned that the truth would hold church leaders firmly in its grip. Teaching involves orderly instruction. Paul is unafraid of rational precision and logic. Indeed he insists on these, as does Peter, who urges us to be ready at all times and under all circumstances to give an *apologia*, an apologetic for our faith. God is the source of truth and God-given reason is the divinely provided instrument for recognizing truth. Jesus urged His contemporaries to love God with the whole mind. He addressed them through the intellect. The Holy Spirit uses truth as a means of persuasion. Asian religions often throw logic to the winds, and do so at great cost. Why they do so is clear. If God is misconceived as the **All**, as a pantheistic conglomerate, then anything and everything, however contradictory, belongs to Him as part of a divine mixture.

As you well know, Japan has been adversely conditioned by Shinto pantheism and by numerous branches of Buddhism. The idea of comprehensive harmony has been cherished throughout centuries of Japanese life. This emphasis easily lends itself to blending everything into one harmonious symmetry that can ignore the law of non-contradiction and embrace both good and evil, truth and falsehood. Simply reorganizing the social order then holds promise of a just society in which nihilism, naturalism. and high technology can supposedly coexist. Feeling becomes more important than logic. People will seek fulfillment in life simply by following an ancestral lifestyle and perpetuating traditional ceremony, without raising the question of eternal destiny. Some persons would prefer alienation from Christ—were that the price—to surrendering a sense of the pantheistic interdependency of all things. If God is the **Other**, is the transcendent Creator, as Christians believe, and we humans are not parts of God, then a serious view of sin and of divine judgment confronts us.

People can be spiritually lost and forever separated from God. God alone can cross the otherwise uncrossable bridge to rescue us; we cannot by our own willing or doing save ourselves. Salvation is a transcendent divine gift to be voluntarily received. Jesus was never intended to be just another idol to be added to an expanding Godshelf. Timothy was to guard with his very life this truth of once-for-all revelation and once-for-all redemption, so that the Gospel would resound full and clear.

"Preach the Word . . . in season and out of season; correct, rebuke, and encourage—with great patience and careful instruction" (4:2). Effective pulpit proclamation is not merely an elocutionary demonstration and an explosive haranguing about spiritual things. It comprises a whole range of duties that bear on preparation, delivery, and outreach. As J. N. D. Kelly puts it, Paul's several imperatives involve an appeal to reason, conscience, and the will: "Timothy must *refute* error by reasoned argument, and he must not hesitate to *rebuke* when censure is called for. More positively, he must *exhort* . . . , that is, urge his flock to repentance and perseverance"—all this without losing patience.[1] Paul emphasizes, "Do the work of an evangelist, discharge all the duties of your ministry" (v.5). Paul personified a full-orbed ministry: the apostle was a missionary, writer, church-planter, reformer, martyr. And in each of these aspects, he was a herald of good news, a theologian-evangelist, a doctrinally disciplined preacher of the gospel.

"Share in suffering for the gospel in the power of God" (1:8, RSV). Think of the many Christian leaders as well as their converts who have faithfully endured untold imprisonment and torture throughout the centuries. In Paul's day hostility poured forth from the Roman world empire devoted to polytheism and then to emperor-worship. In more recent times Soviet authorities have condemned to mental institutions those who evangelized aggressively for Jesus Christ. One can only hope that the fall of the Soviet Union will bring that policy to an end. In Romania, a former police state, competent Christian workers were often excluded from promotion simply because they were believers. For all that, God's people throughout the centuries have counted it a privilege to suffer for the One who Himself suffered for us on the cross. "Be a partaker of the afflictions of the Gospel." The Gospel was not the cause of suffering and affliction; it was and is this world's best and everlasting good news. Paul suffered in behalf of the Gospel. Endure hardship with us like a good soldier. Take your share of suffering", he writes (2:3). A good soldier does not get tangled in domestic affairs that keep him from being at the disposal of his commander-in-chief. Don't let Christ's cause and fellow Christians suffer because you are not in the line of duty. "Always be steady; endure suffering" (4:5, RSV).

The remaining imperatives that Paul addressed to this young torchbearer of the Gospel in a wicked pagan society have ethical concerns prominently in view. In his earlier letter to Timothy Paul had already handled such concerns at some length. Now three additional imperatives speak again about morality: "Be strong in the grace that is in Christ Jesus" (2:1). The gospel claims us for a life of ethical integrity. The goal of revealed religion is to restore sinners to fellowship with God and to holiness. Sometimes it is thought that a pursuit of scholarship and a pursuit of holiness and devout faith in Jesus Christ cannot go together. Paul did not see matters in that way. Even in his crowning days, when execution loomed on the horizon, he urges Timothy to bring the books and the parchments he so treasured (4:13). Scripture binds together a devotion to the truth of God and a commitment to moral integrity. God does not want simply to indoctrinate us; He seeks to indwell us by the Holy Spirit in order to etch His law on our hearts. Only the strength of divine

---

1. J. N. D. Kelly, *A Commentary on the Pastoral Epistles* (London: Adam and Charles Black, 1963), 206.

grace that the indwelling Christ imparts can sustain the moral power of a deeply dedicated life.

"Flee the evil desires of youth, and pursue faith, love, and peace" (2:22). God forbids immorality and demands fruit born of the Spirit. Paul is warning Timothy to be specially on guard about his desires. In 1 Timothy (4:12 RSV) he had earlier cautioned youthful leaders in the churches: "Let no one despise your youth, but set the believers an example in speech and conduct, in love, in faith, in purity." Think of it, younger members would provide the example for others! Their purity of speech, conduct, and love and the fervor of their faith would set the pace for everyone's Christian witness. Perhaps in our very midst today some young person by God's grace is earmarked to be a special example to the Church of Christ in this last decade of our century. That one—could it be you?—could, by modeling personal lifestyle and integrity of ministry, quicken the moral and spiritual power of the whole church in our time. Will you help usher in an era of godliness and Christlikeness, of compassionate concern and of devotion to justice, of evangelistic earnestness and social engagement?

Beware of "Alexander the metalworker" who strongly opposed Paul's message and did him a great deal of harm (4:14). In our evangelizing we may need to identify those whose hostility tends to preempt our time and energy. Some may be so hardened against the will of God that our effort may be better concentrated elsewhere. Paul does not say to give up on Alexander, but to beware of him. What a tragedy that a person may here and there stand out as one of whom God's messengers need specially to beware! Paul exhorts Timothy to "avoid" those who have the outward form of religion but deny its inner power. "Avoid such people"—keep your distance—(3:5, RSV), he instructs Timothy. "They include some who will listen to anybody but can never arrive at a knowledge of the truth" (v. 6, RSV) and others "of corrupt mind and counterfeit faith." (v. 8, RSV).

"Understand this, that in the last days will come times of stress" (3:1, RSV). Apostasy lies ahead, says Paul, but Timothy is not to be surprised, confused or overwhelmed by it. Timothy should not think the Gospel has failed, for the apostasy will be a prelude to the Lord's glorious return when the risen Christ "will judge the living and the dead" (4:1). In a long list of vices Paul describes the corruption that will prevail in the last days. He writes of those who are "lovers or self, lovers of money, proud, arrogant, abusive, disobedient to their parents, ungrateful, unholy, inhuman, implacable, slanderers, profligates, fierce, haters of good, treacherous, reckless, swollen with conceit, lovers of pleasure" (3:2-4, RSV). The catalog of evils recalls Romans 1. It is a portrait of humans who do not love the good, but are devoted to pleasure, and who live like self-centered savages. The mind-set and will-set of such barbarians of the end time marks them as determined enemies of God. The list of evils is remarkably contemporary. We are not to be surprised by a spectacular last-days escalation of evil. Nor ought we to be surprised by the inescapable return of the Risen Lord.

In addition to issuing these imperatives to Timothy, Paul assures him of his unceasing prayers. His confidence in the cause of the Gospel rests not simply on Timothy as a promising recruit; it reposes rather in the God who energizes His workers to do His bidding. "I thank God" and "I constantly remember you in my prayers" (1:3), writes Paul. What an imposing list of imperatives he has given to Timothy and to us as well for the long journey! By them the great Apostle to the Gentiles launched the gospel of Christ effectively into a new generation living in a dreadfully pagan society. Those divine imperatives were fully adequate to confront fallen humanity in the ancient Roman Empire with news of impending doom and of bright hope also for a penitent people. These same imperatives are no less adequate for evangelical impact and renewal today.

On Easter morning some years ago I attended a Chicago inner city church; I was seated quite far back. Even before the choir entered, the sanctuary was already crowded with people. I noticed that in the front row at the far right somebody was earnestly sharing some information, and that one by one the people whispered this word row after row in a serpentine chain of succession. I wondered what had gone wrong. Was the speaker incapacitated? Had an unexpected death or tragedy occurred?

The word soon arrived at the end of my aisle and was relayed person-to-person. This is what one after another told to his or her neighbor: "Christ is risen! Pass it on!" So Paul instructs Timothy and through Timothy a succession of Timothy's across twenty centuries: the good news must now be shared with this generation and the next. Imperatives for the long journey! We may summarized them all in this: "Christ is risen!... Pass it on! . . . Pass it on! Pass it on!"

And that is our glorious calling: to pass the gospel of Jesus Christ to our generation, and to all the generations following. With the power of the Holy Spirit and the precious good news of salvation through Jesus Christ, we must call every inhabitant of earth away from the gods of the age, and to the God of the ages.